AF757227

Boardroom Behaviour and the Law

This book examines how various areas of law collectively influence the relationship between a company and its directors, particularly in safeguarding the long-term interests of stakeholders.

Directors' inappropriate actions can expose a company to significant corporate risks, particularly in relation to regulatory violations such as breaches of competition law. When directors engage in such misconduct, company law and corporate governance provide certain control mechanisms that allow the company to manage these risks. Additionally, directors can be discouraged from engaging in such behaviour by the threat of being held accountable for violations of competition law. This book evaluates various tools designed to regulate directors' behaviours and ensure accountability, questioning whether the legal frameworks strike the right balance between corporate liability and personal accountability. It argues that these mechanisms do not sufficiently protect the long-term interests of stakeholders and that shortcomings in the law leave companies vulnerable to directors' misconduct, which cannot be adequately addressed through traditional risk management strategies.

This book will be of interest to researchers in the field of corporate law, competition law, and corporate governance.

Samet Caliskan is a legal and business consultant based in Newcastle, UK. He holds a BA in business from Gazi University, an LLM from Case Western Reserve University, and a PhD from Newcastle University. His publications, in fields such as company law, competition law, and insurance law, appear in renowned journals, including the *Journal of European Competition Law & Practice*, *European Review*, *The Journal of British Insurance Law Association*, and the *Journal of African Law*. In addition to his consultancy practice, Samet lectures at Newcastle Law School, where he teaches LLM students.

Pereowei Subai is a distinguished legal scholar and educator, currently serving as a professor of law at the Faculty of Law, Niger Delta University. He has a robust academic background, including a Bachelor of Laws (LLB) from Rivers State University, a Master of Laws (LLM) from Obafemi Awolowo University and a Doctor of Laws (PhD) from Newcastle University. He has taught not only within Nigeria at institutions such as Niger Delta University and Federal University Otuoke but also internationally at St. Augustine University in Mwanza, Tanzania. Beyond academia, Professor Subai is actively engaged in consulting with local and international organisations.

Routledge Research in Corporate Law

Available titles in this series include:

The Enlightened Shareholder Value and Corporate Social Responsibility
A theoretical and qualitative analysis
Taskin Iqbal

Adjudicating Global Business in and with India
International Commercial and Investment Disputes Settlement
Leïla Choukroune and Rahul Donde

Business, Law and Human Rights in Africa
Oyeniyi Abe

Small and Medium Enterprises, Law and Business
Uncertainty and Justice
Jan Winczorek and Karol Muszyński

Legal and Ethical Standards in Corporate Insolvency
Elizabeth Streten

Corporate Group Legitimacy
Reconceptualising The Corporate Group
Peter Underwood

Corporate Law and Climate Change
Theory, Risk, Governance
Andrew Clarke

The Limits and Logic of Agency Theory in Company Law
Jonathan Hardman

Boardroom Behaviour and the Law
Corporate Governance and Risk Mitigation
Samet Caliskan and Pereowei Subai

Boardroom Behaviour and the Law

Corporate Governance and Risk Mitigation

Samet Caliskan and Pereowei Subai

Routledge
Taylor & Francis Group
LONDON AND NEW YORK

First published 2025
by Routledge
4 Park Square, Milton Park, Abingdon, Oxon OX14 4RN

and by Routledge
605 Third Avenue, New York, NY 10158

Routledge is an imprint of the Taylor & Francis Group, an informa business

© 2025 Samet Caliskan and Pereowei Subai

The right of Samet Caliskan and Pereowei Subai to be identified as authors of this work has been asserted in accordance with sections 77 and 78 of the Copyright, Designs and Patents Act 1988.

All rights reserved. No part of this book may be reprinted or reproduced or utilised in any form or by any electronic, mechanical, or other means, now known or hereafter invented, including photocopying and recording, or in any information storage or retrieval system, without permission in writing from the publishers.

Trademark notice: Product or corporate names may be trademarks or registered trademarks, and are used only for identification and explanation without intent to infringe.

British Library Cataloguing-in-Publication Data
A catalogue record for this book is available from the British Library

ISBN: 978-0-367-44400-6 (hbk)
ISBN: 978-1-032-72805-6 (pbk)
ISBN: 978-1-003-46156-2 (ebk)

DOI: 10.4324/9781003461562

Typeset in Times New Roman
by Apex CoVantage, LLC

To Saliha and Bera and to Tamunodiepiriye, Dotimi, Oyinmiebi, and Oyinkarieibi

Contents

Acknowledgements

This book could not have been written without the help and support of many people. The authors would like to express their greatest appreciation and sincerest gratitude to Prof. TT Arvind and Dr. Jonathan Galloway, who supervised Samet at the Newcastle University Law School, for their patience, valuable guidance, insightful discussions, and continuous support. They are both excellent academics. Their gratitude is also extended to colleagues and friends for their academic support in Newcastle. To Abdullah Yassen; to Zuhal, Leila, Abbas, Mustafa, and Nihan; and to Ekrem. They also express their gratitude to Newcastle Law School staff, especially Catherine, Alison, Gemma, Suzanne, and Richard, for helping them in different ways throughout their studies. And to Sharon Pointer for her excellent proofreading. Special recognition also goes to their parents, brothers, and in-laws for their support. Samet would especially like to thank his beloved mother and father for their endless support, love, trust, prayers, and encouragement.

Cases and Statues

Cases

Statutes

Companies Act 1862

Companies Act 1985

Companies Act 2006

Competition Act 1998

Enterprise Act 2002

Enterprise and Regulatory Reform Act 2013

Companies Directors Disqualification Act 1986

1 Introduction

1.1 Introduction

The central issue that this book seeks to unravel concerns the relationship between a company and its directors. Under company law, directors, as principal officers, are vested with far-reaching powers to manage the affairs of companies. As with all powers, these can be exercised rightly or wrongly. The issue is how should the law respond if directors choose to exercise their powers in a manner that is not in the company's long-term interest? Traditionally, common law jurisdictions deals with this issue by imposing a set of duties on directors to ensure that they managed companies appropriately. These duties applied, and continue to apply *ex ante* and *ex post*. In the former, the duties have some educative elements because they teach directors how they are supposed to behave, and, in the latter, they have some deterrent effect since the negative consequences of breaching their duties can be potentially severe.

A number of recent developments and corporate failures continue to highlight the difficult balance that must be reached between corporate liability and individual accountability, and they have once again raised the question of whether directors' duties are as effective as they should be in deterring wrongdoing and aligning the interests of directors to those of the company.[1] Foremost among these is the problem of corporate wrongdoing, particularly in relation to regulatory wrongs. This book examines the cumulative impact of various areas of law on the relationship between the company and its directors particularly in terms of the former's exposure to the risk of liability and loss that may be caused by the latter's undesirable behaviours, such as the breach of statutory regulations. The questions it seeks to answer concern whether laws have been able to achieve the correct balance between corporate liability and individual accountability, whether the company is able to protect itself against losses that are caused by directors, and whether it can attribute, ascribe or mitigate the risk of liability and loss after they have arisen. Within the context of this book, undesirable behaviour refers to illegal conduct that the directors of a company may engage in that may possibly increase its value in

1 See, for example, Ngozi Okoye, 'The Personality of Company Directors and Behavioural Risks in Corporate Governance: Bridging the Unidentified Gap' (2013) 10(3) IJDG 261, 262; Robert Wearing, *Cases in Corporate Governance* (Sage Publications 2005)

DOI: 10.4324/9781003461562-1

the short term but potentially expose it to serious corporate risks that will cause it to suffer significant losses in the long term. In that regard, this book will examine the impact that a combination of different aspects of the law can have on companies and their overall ability to reduce the risks of undesirable behaviour by directors.

There are different perspectives on the way in which directors may run a company, such as their given level of authority to bind the company by their actions, the extent to which they are accountable for their actions, how they may be deterred from misusing their authority, and how liability and losses are distributed between the actors that converge around the company, such as its directors, shareholders, creditors etc. In protecting the long-term interests of stakeholders, these considerations can be categorised as the company's ability to control its directors, their accountability for regulatory infringements, the attribution and ascription of risks, and the extent to which the company may mitigate risks. This book analyses the aspects of the law that deal with these particular considerations and examines their cumulative impact on the relationship between the company and its directors.

Against this background, the book initially aims to examine the ability of the company to control its directors. Thereafter, it analyses the regulatory infringements and sanctions that may arise when individuals involve the company in anti-competitive behaviour. In addition, it explores the legal mechanisms by which the company can attribute and ascribe risk to its directors and the risk management tools that it can employ to mitigate those risks.

Within this context, there are obstacles that a company must overcome if it must deter its directors from engaging in undesirable behaviour. This is particularly because failure to do so would expose the company to regulatory sanctions. It will also examine the extent to which the company can attribute and ascribe risks to directors by employing legal mechanisms such as insurance. In this regard, there are barriers that the law places on the path of companies in the employment of these strategies as a means of mitigating the risks associated with the potentially undesirable behaviour of directors.

In this context, this chapter will draw on the existing literature on the importance of directorial responsibility. It will also examine relevant case laws that highlight the limitations companies face in taking appropriate actions when they suffer losses as a result of directorial misbehaviour. In order to illustrate this issue, we will use *Safeway Stores Ltd v. Twigger*[2] as a case study to demonstrate how the courts have treated the losses that may arise when directors are involved in undesirable behaviour. Following this, it will present the research questions to illustrate the particular domain that it explores. Then, the methodology behind how the current literature has been reviewed and analysed throughout the book will be presented. This is followed by the conceptual framework, which illustrates how the book approaches the problem and the contribution that the study makes to the existing literature. Finally, the structure of the book and its chapter outlines are presented.

2 [2010] EWHC 11 (Comm), [2010] EWCA Civ 1472

1.2 The Context of the Book

Businesses have been described as 'the cornerstone of prosperity in society', and companies have a significant role in this regard as 'they create the resources that permit social development and welfare'.[3] In this regard, Worthington has noted that:

> [C]ompanies contribute enormously to the economic and social well-being of our society. Their pervasiveness is such that few individuals are left untouched by their activities. The inference is that better-managed companies will produce benefits for all–hence the focus on directors.[4]

In the first half of the statement, Worthington re-emphasised the importance of companies in terms of their roles in society, but she also noted the underlying assumption that companies benefit everyone. She notes that this purpose can be achieved as long as companies are managed in an appropriate way by their directors and suggested that the focus should be on those who are equipped with the power and authority to run such companies by involving them in legally binding transactions.[5]

The logic that underlies this attitude is that even though a company is always regarded as an entity that can intend, decide, or act, it is known that these actions are necessarily conducted by people who act on its behalf.[6] It cannot make its own decisions as 'it is no more than a name for a complex set of contracts among managers, workers, and contributors of capital'.[7] Despite this fact, a company has its own separate and individual personality distinct from members through the doctrine of separate legal personality.[8] In the context of this doctrine, the company has its own rights and obligations and can be liable and accountable for actions conducted by its directors on its behalf. The key rationale for this doctrine is that the company transacts in its own name and not its members.

The personality of the company gives rise to the question of how it can protect itself against actual liability and loss or risk of liability and losses that may arise

3 Svenskt Naringsliv, 'The Role of Business in Society: Questions and Answers on the Role of Business in Society' (2004) 3. <http://www.svensktnaringsliv.se/migration_catalog/the-role-of-business-in-society_532870.html/BINARY/The%20role%20of%20business%20in%20society> accessed 11 May 2024

4 Sarah Worthington, 'Corporate Governance: Remedying and Ratifying Directors' Breaches' (2000) 116 LQR 638, 638

5 The importance of the role of directors has been commonly highlighted by a number of reports and codes published in last three decades. These include the Cadbury report (1992), Greenbury report (1995), Hampel report (1998), and Higgs report (2003); New Combined Code (2003); and the Corporate Governance Codes 2010, 2012, 2014, and 2024, 2018, and 2024, with the last coming into effect in 2025

6 Joshua Knobe, 'Do Corporations Have Minds?' (2015) <https://archive.nytimes.com/opinionator.blogs.nytimes.com/2015/06/15/do-corporations-have-minds/> accessed 11 June 2024

7 Frank H Easterbrook and Daniel R Fischel, 'Limited Liability and the Corporation' (1985) 52 University of Chicago Law Review 89

8 *Salomon v. Salomon* [1897] AC 22

from the actions of its directors. In respect of this, the individual liability of company members is an important matter because 'personal liability promotes responsible conduct', and its imposition 'is an important means of achieving deterrence'.[9] Without this, the individuals who are authorised to act on behalf of the company may misuse their power and cause it to suffer loss. This underlies why this book analyses the extent to which several aspects of law provide for such individuals to bear liability and the extent to which this has been achieved. For example, because shareholders are immune from the company's debt by virtue of liability protection which they 'enjoy', they may be incentivised by that fact to compel or induce directors to take higher risks, which may benefit the company in the short term but expose it to significant risks in the long term. This is particularly where such conduct is inherently illegal or reckless. Similarly, in the absence of personal liability, directors may potentially use their powers to obtain personal benefit at the expense of the company or seek to increase the value of the company at the expense of other stakeholders. To prevent such situations, it is often the case for directors to be held personally liable for their conduct on the company's behalf in some instances. In this sense, 'directorial' liability has become an important and effective compliance and risk-allocation mechanism.[10] However, such liability is limited, as it arises only when the courts pierce the corporate veil. In effect, directors, like shareholders, also 'enjoy' liability protection with the company as a separate entity and ordinarily do not bear liability for the losses that may arise from their conduct on its behalf.

There is no doubt that such limited liability encourages directors to take higher risks in their decision-making with a view to increasing the value of the company. But it may also hinder the law's ability to ensure that companies are managed in an appropriate way. This may consequently expose them to actual liability and loss or the risk of liability and loss. It is trite that in some instances the courts may disregard the separate personality of the company and lift the veil in order to hold directors liable for actions undertaken on the company's behalf. In that regard, it is important to examine how they have done this, as well as the rules that underlie their application. Viel-piercing and the imposition of liability on directors can potentially deter them from misusing their authority and involving the company in transactions that may cause it to suffer loss.

It should be stated, from the onset, that liability protection has been considered an important consequence of the company's separate personality.[11] And perhaps,

9 Noel Wise, 'Personal Liability Promotes Responsible Conduct: Extending the Responsible Corporate Officer Doctrine to Federal Civil Environmental Enforcement Cases' (2002) 21 The Stanford Environmental Law Journal 283, 283 and 288

10 Carsten Gerner-Beuerle, Philipp Paech, and Edmund Philipp Schuster, *Study on Directors' Duties and Liability* (LSE Enterprise Limited 2013) 1. <http://eprints.lse.ac.uk/50438/1/__Libfile_repository_Content_Gerner-Beuerle%2C%20C_Study%20on%20directors%E2%80%99%20duties%20and%20liability%28lsero%29.pdf> accessed 11 June 2024

11 That said, limited liability is not inherently crucial to separate personality. In fact it was only introduced to England in 1855 by the Limited Liability Companies Act of that year, 11 years after the enactment of the Joint Stock Companies Act. Even at that, it is now a crucial aspect of companies,

the starting point for the discussion is the celebrated case of *Saloman v. Saloman and Co.*[12] In that case, Mr. Aron Salomon set up a limited liability company in which he and six members of his family were the only shareholders. The company went bankrupt within a year of its formation, and the liquidator, on behalf of the creditors, claimed that Mr. Salomon should be liable for the debts of the company. The High Court agreed with the creditors on the basis that the company was Mr. Saloman's agent. The Court of Appeal agreed with it but on the grounds that a trust relationship existed between Salomon and the company. However, the House of Lords overruled the decision of the Court of Appeal and held that the company was a separate legal entity. As such, Mr. Saloman could not be held personally liable for its debts. Thus, the court cemented the separate personality doctrine, which, while rooted in Section 18 of the English Companies Act of 1862, required the House of Lords to stamp its approval on the extent to which the doctrine could be applied in practice.

Another consequence of the doctrine of corporate personality is the attribution of directors' acts to the company. What this means is that the court typically does not lift the corporate veil merely on the ground that the company may have suffered losses by virtue of the actions of its directors. But where there is proof that directors use a company to perpetuate fraud, the courts will almost always disregard corporate personality in order to impose liability on the persons behind such fraud. That this is the position adopted in England has now been established by a long line of decided cases, one of which is *Stone and Rolls Ltd v. Moore Stephens*.[13] In that case, Mr. Stojevic, who was the sole shareholder and director of a company, perpetrated serious fraud on the company's creditors by demonstrating from the company's accounts that it was more profitable than it actually was. The creditors suffered losses due to this fraud and instituted an action against the director and the company, following which the latter was found personally liable. It indemnified the claimant creditors and consequently went into liquidation. As neither the director nor the company satisfied their claim, the creditors claimed against the auditors on the ground that they failed to detect the director's fraud. On their part, the auditors argued that, although they were negligent in failing to detect the fraud, it would be contrary to public policy to attribute the liability to them since the company would be relying on its own illegality if it were permitted to bring a claim against them. Consequently, the loss remained with the company.

Although Lady Hale and Lord Walker characterised this case as an example of the operation of piercing the corporate veil doctrine, they considered its application in such a way that the knowledge and actions of the sole director were attributed to the company.[14] The company was thus found directly liable for the fraud of

and the overwhelming majority of companies now 'enjoy' limited liability, despite the unlimited option being available in most Commonwealth countries

12 *Salomon v. Salomon* [1897] AC 22.

13 [2009] UKHL 39, [2009] 1 A.C. 1391

14 Ernest Lim, 'Salomon Reigns' (2013) 129 LQR 480, 484

its director based on its separate personality, and it could be said that such a situation potentially gave rise to the risk of liability and loss on the part of companies.

Allowing for the possibility of piercing the corporate veil can enable individual accountability, which can deter directors from entering into transactions that may harm the company. However, piercing the corporate veil is considered an exception to the principle of Salomon (the principle of separate legal entity) and, for this reason, there may be strong barriers to it. These limitations can be classified into two categories. The first is that when the corporate veil is pierced, the courts need to make an exception to two main rules of company law. These are that (i) the company is separate and independent from its shareholders and directors and that (ii) neither the shareholders nor directors are liable for the debts of the company.[15]

The first category is based on the company's legal separate personality to which certain acts and intentions of directors are attributed. The second category of limitations is based on public policy. In respect of this limitation, Lord Sumption noted that, 'if it is not necessary to pierce the corporate veil, it is not appropriate to do so, because on that footing there is no public policy imperative which justifies that course'.[16] Under the consideration of public policy, the only circumstance in which the corporate veil can be pierced is when directors dishonestly obtain benefit using the company as a vehicle. In such instances, the courts will pierce the corporate veil to prevent them from doing so. Accordingly, directors may not be held personally liable when they cause the company to suffer loss if they never intended to indulge in fraudulent behavior for personal benefit or gain. This was noted by Lord Sumption in *Prest v. Petrodel*,[17] such that,

> [T]he recognition of a limited power to pierce the corporate veil in carefully defined circumstances is necessary if the law is not to be disarmed in the face of abuse. . . . The principle that the court may be justified in piercing the corporate veil if a company's separate legal personality is being abused for the purpose of some relevant wrongdoing is well established in the authorities.[18]

Sealy and Worthington also note that, 'the authorities show that there are limited circumstances in which the law threatens the use of a company as a means of evading the law as dishonest for this purpose'.[19] Therefore, based on these limitations, it can be stated that,

> [T]he corporate veil may be lifted . . . only in accordance with the terms of a specific statutory . . . provision or, in respect of the common law, where the

15 Karen Vandekerckhove, 'Piercing the Corporate Veil' (2007) 4(5) ECL 191
16 *Prest v. Petrodel* [2013] UKSC 34, 35
17 *Prest v. Petrodel* [2013] UKSC
18 *Prest v. Petrodel* [2013] UKSC, 27
19 Sarah Worthington and Sinead Agnew, *Sealy & Worthington's Cases and Materials in Company Law* (12th edn, OUP 2022) XVIII

circumstances of a case fall within so called 'accepted headings', namely instances of either a fraud/sham, agency or national emergency.[20]

However, as Lord Sumption observed in *Prest v Petrodel*, 'the difficulty is to identify what is a relevant wrongdoing' and 'references to a "façade" or "sham" beg too many questions to provide a satisfactory answer'.[21]

Hence, although there are certain circumstances in which it may be possible to pierce the corporate veil by disregarding the separate personality of the company, these circumstances are very limited and rare in the United Kingdom.[22] This casts serious doubt on the approach of holding individuals personally accountable for any misconduct which potentially exposes the company to risk of liability and loss. As such, it can be stated that, 'piercing the corporate veil is an exceptional remedy and is only available where no other relief is appropriate'.[23] Easterbrook and Fischel emphasised that, with this issue, 'piercing seems to happen freakishly. Like lightning, it is rare, severe, and unprincipled'.[24] This point was also highlighted by Ying and Yeo, who stated that, 'there is no common unifying principle . . . in the UK . . . jurisdiction explaining the occasional court decision to pierce the corporate veil'.[25] This gives rise to a discussion put forward by Lord Sumption in *Prest* that, 'the separate personality and property of a company is sometimes described as a fiction, and in a sense it is. But the fiction is the whole foundation of English company and insolvency law'.[26]

The doctrine of a separate legal personality is thus heavily relied on for the prevention of corporate wrongdoing, particularly regulatory wrongs, from happening. If the company is regarded as directly liable for its directors' violations of law, the company, rather than the directors, will typically be sued for the regulatory wrongdoings,[27] and regulatory sanctions will be imposed on it. Consequently, while piercing the corporate veil in order to hold directors individually liable is rarely

20 Stephen Griffin, 'Establishing a Holding Company's Duty of Care to an Employee of a Subsidiary Without the Need to Lift the Corporate Veil' (2011) 300 Co. L.N. 1, 1–2

21 (n 16) 28

22 Griffin (n 20) 1–2. Vandekerchkhove has noted that English Law is the 'most reticent' when it comes to piercing the veil; see Karen Vandekerckhove (n 15) 191

23 Simon Adamyk, 'Piercing the Corporate Veil – Where Are We Now?' (2015) <http://www.newsquarechambers.co.uk/ImageLibrary/pb67_Simon_Adamyk_Article_Dec_2013.pdf> accessed 17 May 2024. See also *Prest* (n 16)

24 Easterbrook and Fischel (n 7) 89

25 Yeo Hwee Ying and Ruth Yeo, 'Revisiting the Alter Ego Exception in Corporate Veil Piercing' (2015) 27 SAcLJ 177, 179

26 *Prest v. Petrodel* [2013] UKSC 34, 35
per Lord Sumption. For this reason, Ying and Yeo defined the separate personality of a company as 'the bedrock of company law'. See Ying and Yeo, 179

27 Exceptionally, under Companies Act 2006, s 30(2), 'every officer is made liable with the company if the company has failed to file certain resolutions with Companies House within a prescribed time period'. In such a case, the officers, in addition with the company, may be held criminally liable. See Karla Dudek, 'United Kingdom' in Alexander Loos (ed.), *Directors' Liability: A Worldwide Review* (2nd edn, Wolters Kluwer 2010) 527, 535

applied, there has been increasing focus on the separate personality of the company, a factor which increases the possibility of holding the company directly liable.

This issue is especially crucial when directors are involved in illegal transactions that benefit the company in the short term but may expose it to legal liability and loss where the behaviour in question is contrary to the law. In such a case, the directors may not have intended to make a personal benefit; rather, they may have sought to increase the value of the company. The issue is that a lack of personal benefit or gain will not change the fact that the company is exposed to the risk of liability and loss due to their conduct. Interestingly, in such cases, the company's separate personality will shield or protect the directors from personal liability, while the risk remains with the company.

The question that arises at this point is whether a company that is found directly liable can pass on liability or loss to its directors. This approach 'constitutes a necessary corollary to control issues within a company', and it is based on the determination of particular duties that restrict directors from exercising their authority.[28] These control issues involve corporate control mechanisms that the company can employ to constrain its directors so that they shirk from misconduct that may cause direct liability to it.[29] If the company is limited to disciplining directors through these mechanisms, there is a possibility that it might be held directly liable for its directors' acts, resulting in the breach of regulatory rules. The risk is that in so doing, the accountability of the company's directors may be disregarded.[30] To prevent the negative consequences of direct liability, the typical argument the company would raise is that the liability belongs to its directors and should be attributed and ascribed to them through invoking legal mechanisms.[31] This claim involves the operation of the doctrine of corporate attribution and the maxim *ex turpi causa non-oritur action* (the 'maxim'), with the second aimed at precluding a claimant from pursuing a legal remedy if it is connected with his/her illegal or immoral act. With limited exceptions, the joint operation of these principles may potentially prevent the company from transferring the risk of liability and loss arising from directors' conduct to them.[32] At this point, however, the only remedy left for the company to mitigate the risk of loss is to institute a claim against its insurer to recover the loss it has suffered. But such actions may still not succeed. This is because considerations of public policy and direct liability on the part of the company may possibly stand as a barrier to it in a claim for recovery.[33]

This situation gives rise to the question of whether the operation of UK law in respect of individual accountability effectively constrains directors *ex ante* and disciplines them *ex post* in respect of their involvement in regulatory wrongs. This

28 Gerner-Beuerle, Paech, and Schuster (n 10) 1
29 This is treated in detail in Chapter 2
30 This is treated in detail in Chapter 3
31 This is treated in detail in Chapter 4
32 This is treated in detail in Chapter 4
33 This is treated in detail in Chapter 5

is because although directors are supposed to exercise their authority in an appropriate way, the crucial issue to consider is the extent to which they are constrained and deterred from such actions. This is an important consideration for companies, as they may still be bound by the behaviour of their directors, despite the fact that they may exercise their authority for improper purposes or in breach of the law. As such, a company can be potentially exposed to a wide range of corporate risks as a consequence of the behaviours or actions of its directors, which may be beneficial to it in the short term, but may have deleterious consequences in the long term. This was the case in *Safeway*.

While subsequent chapters in this book will analyse the specific issues that border around the case as they pertain to the law, it is apposite that we outline the facts of the case, albeit briefly, in order to demonstrate an example of directorial misbehaviour and the consequences that were visited on them for their actions. In the *Safeway* case, eleven former employees of Safeway entered into a price-fixing agreement with rivals, while acting on its behalf. An investigation was initiated by the (then) Office of Fair Trading, following which the company was penalised for engaging in a price-fixing agreement in violation of Section 2 of the Competition Act 1998 (CA98), and a fine of £10.7 million was imposed on it.[34] Safeway sought to recover the loss attributable to the fine from the directors and instituted proceedings against them on the grounds that they were liable for involving the company in the cartel in breach of their fiduciary and contractual duties.

The defendant directors applied for a summary judgement and argued that the fine was the company's own liability which could not be passed to them on the basis of the maxim.[35] After hearing the parties, Flaux J. held that,

> whilst the public policy which lies behind the rule will be engaged where the relevant wrongful act of the claimant on which the claimant relies in bringing the claim is a crime, the rule is not limited to criminal acts.[36]

It was also held that moral turpitude or moral reprehensibility must be involved before the maxim can be applied.[37] Flaux J. concluded that the behaviour of the directors was contrary to the provisions of the CA98 and was sufficiently immoral to invoke the application of the maxim.[38] That said, the learned judge declined to grant a summary judgement on the basis that the claimant company had reasonable prospects of establishing that it was liable by virtue of the general rules of agency

34 Note that this sum was later reduced from £16 million to £10.7 million due to an early resolution agreement. For further reading, see Anna Morfey and Conall Patton, '*Safeway Stores Ltd v. Twigger*: The Buck Stops Here' [2011] Comp Law 57, 58

35 *Safeway* (n 2) [2010] EWHC 11 (Comm). For the cumulative impact of the application of the maxim with corporate attribution doctrine on the issue of risk attribution between the company and directors, see Chapter 4

36 *Safeway* (n 2) [2010] EWHC 11 (Comm) 23

37 *Safeway* (n 2) [2010] EWHC 11 (Comm) 26

38 *Safeway* (n 2) [2010] EWHC 11 (Comm) 28

rather than being directly or primarily culpable. As such, liability for the fine paid in that case was ascribed to the directors.[39]

The defendant directors appealed, and the High Court's decision was reversed by the Court of Appeal. Interpreting Section 2(1) of CA98, which prohibits agreements between undertakings that affect competition in the United Kingdom, the Court of Appeal held that the undertaking/company in this case would bear personal liability on the basis of Section 36 of the CA98.[40] Hence the company was prevented from passing on its liability to the directors even though it stemmed from their undesirable actions.[41] Consequently, the company was held directly liable and suffered significant losses.

The outcome from the case gave rise not only to serious concerns about the effectiveness of the liability-based approach in preventing such behaviour, but also raised the question of whether companies can protect the long-term interests of their stakeholders from the consequences of undesirable behaviour by directors. This is because even though the price-fixing agreement undertaken by directors was for the company's short-term benefit in *Safeway*, it was still undesirable. In essence the behaviour amounted to excessive risk-taking which resulted in regulatory infringement and exposed the company to liability as well as to the possibility that it could be exposed to private enforcement actions. In this sense, *Safeway* is a clear manifestation of the ineffectiveness of the liability-based approach to constraining and deterring directors with respect to their involvement in undesirable behaviours.

1.3 Research Questions

As noted in the preceding section, this book will focus on the relationship between the company and its directors with regard to the distribution of risks that arise from the latter's undesirable behaviour. Its main aim is to analyse the cumulative impact of the operation of the legal rules governing the risk relationship between the company and its directors. It focuses on the ability of companies to protect themselves against the risk of liability and loss that may arise from the undesirable behaviour of their directors for the purpose of protecting the long-term interests of their stakeholders. Based on this aim, the book will examine the nature of the cumulative impact of different aspects of law on the relationship between the company and its directors on the ability of the former to protect the long-term interests of stakeholders against the risk of undesirable behaviour by directors. It will also examine the extent to which companies can control their directors by deploying established internal and external legal mechanisms, the extent to which they can hold their directors accountable for regulatory infringements and sanctions that may be faced

39 *Safeway* (n 2) [2010] EWHC 11 (Comm) 105

40 *Safeway* (n 2) [36]. This is an issue of to what extent competition law holds individuals liable, which will be examined in Chapter 3

41 Company's application for permission to appeal the judgement of the Court of Appeal was rejected

where the latter involve them in anti-competitive behaviour. The book will also interrogate the impact of law on the ability of companies to transfer risks and responsibility for the negative consequences of directorial actions to the directors concerned as well as its ability to mitigate risks of undesirable behaviour by directors through standard commercial risk management tools, such as insurance.

1.4 The Methodology of the Study

This book employs the doctrinal research method, which relies on documentary research alone. It is a mono-jurisdictional study that examines the law in the United Kingdom. For that purpose, it analyses the cumulative impact of different elements of UK law in risk distribution between the company and its directors. Although it primarily focuses on UK law, where necessary, other aspects of EU law and their interactions with UK law are also considered. References are made to articles and cases pertaining to other countries, although their particular legal systems are not the focus of this research. Rather, these are taken into consideration where appropriate because they highlight the general approaches of common law in regard to the research.

The book analyses an issue which has been overlooked from academic and judicial perspectives. And aims to set a doctrine in a new perspective by analysing the issues of directors' undesirable behaviours and the negative consequences that companies may potentially encounter. In this regard, it examines how the current approach adopted in UK law affects the risk relationship between the company and its directors and how important it is to highlight these issues for the protection of the long-term interest of stakeholders. To achieve its aims, five different subjects of law and their approaches to the main issue of risk distribution between the company and directors will be examined. These are company law, corporate governance, competition law, tort law, and insurance law. The choice of these five areas is based on their cumulative impact on the risk relationship between the company and its directors with respect to protecting the long-term interest of stakeholders, which is the primary research question of the book. Each area of law has a particular impact in some form, and the book analyses their cumulative impact on the risk distribution between the company and its directors.

In examining the distribution of risks between the company and its directors, the first consideration that arises is how directors are prevented from engaging in undesirable behaviour that may result in corporate regulatory infringements and expose companies to the risk of liability and loss. For this purpose, the control mechanisms established under company law and corporate governance and their deterrent effectiveness on directors will be initially examined. In addition, the company's possible inability to control directors may subject it to the consequences of their undesirable behaviours, such as the regulatory infringements and sanctions that can arise where directors involve the company in anti-competitive behaviour. In order to analyse these negative consequences on the company, the book examines the approach of competition law based on its interaction with corporate governance and company law. This is because, in terms of measures designed to prevent regulatory wrongs, while competition law concerns the impact of the company's behaviour in the market, corporate governance and company law focus on the behaviour of individuals within the corporate structure. Therefore, the logic that underlies the choice of competition law is based on the question of how competition law sanctions undesirable behaviour, which cannot be prevented internally by companies and upon which the risk of liability and loss is usually left between the company and its directors.

In addition, the fact that companies may be potentially sanctioned for infringing the rules of competition law gives rise to another concern: whether they can attribute and ascribe the risk of liability and loss arising from such punishment to its directors. Thus, the presence of tort law in the book is justified because of its lively interaction with company law in the attribution and ascription of risk between the company and its directors. In this respect, the concept of the maxim in tort law involves a joint operation with the doctrine of corporate attribution in company law, as it prevents a company that is held personally liable through corporate attribution from recovering the losses it has suffered from directors. In this case, the risk of liability and loss will remain with the company.

Lastly, the presence of insurance law in the book can be justified based on the situation of what companies can do if they cannot control their directors who are involved in undesirable behaviour. Consequently, regulatory sanctions may be imposed on them by competition law, and they cannot pass on the same sanctions to their directors. A factor which heightens the risk of liability and loss. In this case, the option that companies typically use is to seek to mitigate the risk through recovering the loss from insurance. Therefore, there will be a discussion of the ability of companies to mitigate the risk of loss that is caused by the undesirable behaviour of its directors through insurance as a risk management mechanism and the restrictions that the law puts in place for this purpose.

But for the limitations of space and to ensure focus, this book would have also considered concepts such as agency law, equity, and fiduciary law in some depth. These foregoing are largely concerned with the unique nature of the relationship between the company and its directors. In contrast, this book is more focused on the negative consequences of particular undesirable behaviours of directors and how the law not only provides an inadequate control mechanism for companies, but also how it prevents them from employing the risk management mechanisms that they usually invoke.

1.5 Conceptual Framework

This book addresses the problem of the undesirable behaviour of directors in the way in which it involves companies in regulatory wrongdoings and exposes them to the risk of liability and loss. Based on the nature of undesirable behaviour, it adopts a taxonomy of exhaustive risks, which is divided into four. These are insolvency risks, the risk of liability for regulatory penalties, the risk of third-party litigation, and the risk of reputational loss. The research analyses the different ways in which these risks affect the company in terms of protecting the long-term interests of stakeholders.

After identifying the problem and its potential negative consequences on companies, the book explores the different ways that companies can protect themselves from risks. Firstly, it analyses the inadequacies of the existing control mechanisms for protecting companies from directorial misbehaviours. Following this, the book analyses public enforcement mechanisms, private law, and insurance law. In respect of public enforcement mechanisms, it examines the particular approach adopted by competition law to prevent infringements and its effect on companies in terms of exploring the risk of liability and loss for regulatory sanctions as a result of directors' illegal actions. The idea of passing the risk of liability and loss to directors requires an examination of private law, as the ability of companies to attribute and ascribe the risk to directors is determined based on the doctrine of corporate attribution and the illegality defence maxim, which are concepts of company and tort law, respectively. Recovering losses through insurance is the last option that the company can apply to mitigate the risk; however, there are potential limitations that debar it from this. This examination illustrates the cumulative impact of the five subjects of law on the distribution of the risk of liability and loss between a company and its directors.

From the onset of this book, it is crucial that we explain some recurring concepts that will undergird our research. Some of these concepts include the *ex turpi causa* maxim, long-term interests of corporate stakeholders, corporate attribution, and corporate governance.

1.5.1 Long-Term Interests of Corporate Stakeholders

One recurring theme that cuts across this book is how to ensure that directors consider and cater to the long-term interests of corporate stakeholders. In corporate governance, a distinction is often made between the short-term interests and long-term interests of corporate stakeholders. A person may invest in a company in order to make profits in the short term and perhaps exit from it by disposing of his shares. Some others, such as institutional investors, may, however, invest in a company for the long-term, with a view to profiting over time. The issue is that long-term investors are often exposed to greater risks if the company is poorly governed or embarks on an illegal course of action, which, over time, will impact its profitability and outlook. One of the challenges of corporate governance has been how to ensure that company directors pursue the company's long-term goals. Another challenge is how to tie directors' remuneration to the company's long-term performance. In this regard, it is important to note that directors may seek to shore up the company's short-term profitability in order to benefit from bonuses and perks arising from its short-term profitability. This motivation to make short-term benefits may thus spur directors to engage in actions that may increase the company's profitability in the short term while harming its future prospects.[42] Sadly,

42 See Lynn A Stout, *The Shareholder Value Myth: How Putting Shareholders First Harms Investors, Corporations and the Public* (Barett-Kohler 2012) 67; R Anderson, 'The Long and Short of Corporate Governance' (2015) 23 Geo Mason Law Review

as previously shown, some of these courses of action may be illegal or immoral. For example, the directors of a company may engage it in a cartel with a view to manipulating prices. But engagement in a cartel violates competition law, which, while having the potential to shore up the company's profits in the short run, may expose it to significant fines and sanctions, in addition to reputational damage, all of which would affect the company's long-run prospects. And because markets tend to respond to events and occurrences in the short term, company directors may also manipulate markets and engage in insider trading or market abuse in order to make short-term profits. To curtail this tendency, some companies issue share options to their directors, which can only be cashed in the long term. This is done with a view to ensuring that directors pursue the company's long-term interests. This book will explore how corporate governance rules can be deployed to foster the long-term benefits of companies.

1.6 Contribution to Knowledge

The book fills a significant gap in the existing literature, which does not pay adequate attention to assessing how the cumulative impact of several areas of law has serious and undesirable consequences for the operation of the practical relationship between the directors and the company. It adds value to the literature by appraising the cumulative impact of different areas of law on the relationship, over and above the existing literature's tendency to focus on particular areas of law. Issues that arise from directorial management of companies are narrowly examined and are limited in the context of a wider range of issues concerning the undesirable behaviour of directors and the potential risks to which companies can be exposed. The book thus raises new points that implicitly challenge inherent assumptions in the literature, and it also makes a number of timely contributions to the current literature, given increasing corporate crises around the world.

This research aims to address the issue of a company's exposure to a number of corporate risks due to undesirable behaviour and how the company is unable to mitigate these risks for the sake of protecting the long-term interests of stakeholders. It notes that the law is deficient to the extent that it permits directors to engage in such behaviour without adequately providing tools by which companies may control their directors and mitigate the risks of undesirable behaviour. In consideration of the importance of individual liability for achieving greater deterrence, the book illustrates how the law impedes access to directors and how its entire premise does not work on matters of individual liability. Therefore, the book not only contributes to the understanding of the concept of directors' behaviour and the potential risks to which the company is subjected, but it also raises concerns in respect to the inability of the company to mitigate these risks and the nature of these issues, as well as why they exist.

The book consists of evaluative and critical analyses. It initially argues that there are barriers that impede companies from controlling their directors through available control mechanisms. Then it evaluates the framework for directorial accountability for undesirable behaviour such as competition law breaches and acts which expose companies to risks and to potential liability for regulatory wrongdoings. Thereafter it analyses the inadequacy of the legal mechanisms that are employed to apportion the risk of liability and loss between the company and directors. Then it considers the hurdles that the law has placed before companies in their employment of standard commercial risk management tools, such as insurance, to mitigate risks by recovering from insurers the losses which they suffer. Based on these arguments, the study demonstrates that, instead of alleviating the problem of undesirable behaviour of directors, the law severely hampers companies' ability to mitigate the risks they face. It concludes that the law does not adequately deal with the issue of undesirable behaviour by directors.

The book also shows that there have been positive developments in identifying the inadequateness of the way in which the law operates, but these developments are still not good enough to recognise the issues of the company's exposure to the risk of directors' undesirable behaviours and the negative consequences of such behaviours upon the long-term interests of stakeholders. Despite this, the book considers these developments a promising foundation for future developments in law.

1.7 Structure of the Book and Chapter Outlines

The book comprises six chapters. Chapter One (the present chapter) provides a brief explanation of the main considerations the book takes into account. Chapter Two introduces the concept of 'undesirable behaviour' as potentially conducted by directors, as well as the taxonomy of risks to which the company can be exposed. It explains in detail why this taxonomy is appropriate and why it covers the main types of harm which are likely to strike the company as a result of the actions of directors. It also examines the negative consequences of the occurrence of these risks on the present and future status of the company. Following this, the types of control mechanisms that are operated by the company to keep directors under control will be theoretically explored, alongside how effective these are at preventing directors from engaging in undesirable behaviour. These mechanisms can constrain directors *ex ante* and discipline them *ex post* in respect of misusing their authority, but the crucial question is how they fulfil this purpose as, in case of the presence of any limitation prior to these mechanisms, the company is likely to be exposed to significant corporate risk of liability and loss.

Chapter Three aims to illustrate the consequences of the inability of the company to control its directors. Public enforcement mechanisms adopted by UK competition law and the impact of their implications on the risk relationship between the company and its directors are taken into consideration. In this chapter, the approach adopted by the legal authorities to prevent regulatory infringements and deter potential wrongdoers from engaging with such misconduct is examined. For this purpose, the chapter initially examines the UK competition law regime, its interaction with EU competition law, their policy objectives, the primary public enforcement mechanism to promote and protect these objectives, and the impact of this approach on the distribution of risk of liability and loss between the company and directors. In addition, the chapter will assess compliance and deterrence theories, how they approach the prevention of corporate regulatory wrongdoings, and whether they influence the regulatory sanction of administrative fining adopted by competition law. Moreover, individual sanctions as part of a public enforcement strategy, their deterrent effectiveness on directors, and whether they help the company mitigate the risks of undesirable behaviour will be discussed. After this, it focuses on the question of whether the current approach of competition law corrects the wrongdoer or exposes the victim of the wrongdoer to risk of liability and loss.

Chapter Four analyses the ability of the company to attribute and ascribe the risk of liability and loss to its directors by examining the legal mechanisms of the doctrine of corporate attribution and the maxim under company and tort laws. In terms of the distribution of the risk of undesirable behaviour between the company and directors, the chapter will illustrate the joint operation of these mechanisms. The chapter will also take into account whether the company is able to push the risk of liability and loss onto directors though invoking their fiduciary duties. It will be demonstrated that while the doctrine of corporate attribution aims to determine the attribution of directors' acts to the company, who can be consequently held personally liable for particular misconduct, the maxim prevents the personally liable company from recovering the loss through not allowing it to benefit from its wrongdoing and deters it and others from engaging in similar conduct in order to maintain consistency in law. Promising developments in respect of the way in which the doctrine of corporate attribution and the maxim operates will also be discussed.

Chapter Five considers insurance as a risk management method and investigates whether the company is able to mitigate risk through loss recovery via this method. For this purpose, the chapter elaborates on the operation of general liability insurance, particularly Directors and Officers Liability Insurance (D&O Insurance), and it initially answers the question of whether liability insurance aims to protect the victim third party or the insured. Following this, the chapter illustrates the recoverability of the potential loss that the company may suffer as a result of the occurrences of the risks examined in Chapter Two. Also, the discussion will assess the role of the maxim principle and the doctrine of corporate attribution in limiting the risk management role of insurance. In addition, the chapter will demonstrate the positive developments that have been happening and provide a suggestion for further development for the issue raised in the chapter based on these developments.

Lastly, Chapter Six concludes the book by summarising the key outcomes reached in the study. This chapter also revisits the primary and secondary research questions to ensure that they are addressed throughout the book. In addition, the contribution of the research on a wide range of aspects and suggestions for further development in the particular subjects of law will be presented.

Bibliography

Adamyk S, 'Piercing the Corporate Veil –Where Are We Now?' (2015) <http://www.newsquarechambers.co.uk/ImageLibrary/pb67_Simon_Adamyk_Article_Dec_2013.pdf> accessed 17 May 2024

Dudek K, 'United Kingdom' in Alexander Loos (ed.), *Directors' Liability: A Worldwide Review* (2nd edn, Wolters Kluwer 2010) 527, 535

Easterbrook FH and Fischel DR, 'Limited Liability and the Corporation' (1985) 52 University of Chicago Law Review 89

Gerner-Beuerle C, Paech P, and Schuster EP, *Study on Directors' Duties and Liability* (LSE Enterprise Limited 2013) 1

Griffin S, 'Establishing a Holding Company's Duty of Care to an Employee of a Subsidiary Without the Need to Lift the Corporate Veil' (2011) 300 Co LN 1, 1–2

Knobe J, 'Do Corporations Have Minds?' (2015) <https://archive.nytimes.com/opinionator.blogs.nytimes.com/2015/06/15/do-corporations-have-minds/> accessed 11 June 2024

Morfey A and Patton C, 'Safeway Stores Ltd v. Twigger: The Buck Stops Here' [2011] Comp Law 57, 58

Naringsliv S, 'The Role of Business in Society: Questions and Answers on the Role of Business in Society' (2004) 3 <http://www.svensktnaringsliv.se/migration_catalog/the-role-of-business-in-society_532870.html/BINARY/The%20role%20of%20business%20in%20society> accessed 11 May 2024

Okoye N, 'The Personality of Company Directors and Behavioural Risks in Corporate Governance: Bridging the Unidentified Gap' (2013) 10(3) IJDG 261, 262; Wearing R, *Cases in Corporate Governance* (Sage Publications 2005)

Vandekerckhove K, 'Piercing the Corporate Veil' (2007) 4(5) ECL 191

Wise N, 'Personal Liability Promotes Responsible Conduct: Extending the Responsible Corporate Officer Doctrine to Federal Civil Environmental Enforcement Cases' (2002) 21 Stanford Environmental Law Journal 283, 288

Worthington S, 'Corporate Governance: Remedying and Ratifying Directors' Breaches' (2000) 116 LQR 638

Worthington S and Agnew S, *Sealy & Worthington's Cases and Materials in Company Law* (12th edn, Oxford University Press 2022) XVIII

Ying YW and Yeo R, 'Revisiting the Alter Ego Exception in Corporate Veil Piercing' (2015) 27 SAcLJ 177, 179

2 Individual Behaviour, Company Liability, and Risk

Traditional Corporate Control Mechanisms as a Constraint

2.1 Introduction

Considering the fact that directors are conferred with extensive powers to run companies, the question is how can a company restrain its directors from abusing their powers and from acting contrary to its best interests? It is trite that companies are artificial bodies which have no soul, no body, no beliefs, and no thoughts.[1] In this regard, Hudson once noted that a company is a 'fiction' whose arms and brains are the directors and employees who perform actions on its behalf.[2] Therefore, issues regarding the behaviour of company directors have a potential impact on the general effectiveness of a corporate governance regime. Hence, there is a need for an evaluation of the consequences of their wrongdoing on the company's performance.[3]

In this respect, this chapter focuses on directorial actions that expose companies to high degrees of risk over and above 'ordinary' commercial risks. There is the general misbehaviour of directors, which arises when directors engage in self-enrichment to the detriment of the company. The literature abounds with scholarly works that attempt to explain and understand the issue of directorial self-enrichment. As such, this chapter will not focus on it but on directorial misbehaviours that arise when directors engage the company in regulatory wrongdoings which expose it to risks that would harm the long-term interests of its stakeholders.

Various established control mechanisms can be employed to address such behavioural issues. These mechanisms are not designed to directly control directors, but rather to compel them to act in the company's best interest. This chapter will primarily strive to assess the adequacy and effectiveness of these measures

1 John C. Coffee, '"No Soul to Damn: No Body to Kick": An Unscandalized Inquiry into the Problem of Corporate Punishment' (1981) 79 Michigan Law Review 386. See also Eilis Ferran, 'Corporate Attribution and the Directing Mind and Will' (2011) 127 LQR 239, 239

2 Alastair Hudson, *Understanding Company Law* (1st edn, Routledge 2012) 93. See also Anjali Anchayli, 'The "Directing Mind and Will" Test in Corporate Attribution: Iridium and Meridian – A Comparison' (2012) 33(8) Comp Law 252

3 See, Ngozi Okoye, *The Personality of Company Directors as a Behavioural Risk Contributor in the Corporate Governance Process Regulatory Intervention as a Risk Management Mechanism* (PhD Thesis, University of Dundee 2012) 89

DOI: 10.4324/9781003461562-2

in deterring directors from engaging in undesirable behaviour. It will also explore potential limitations that could undermine the effectiveness of these measures, underscoring the urgency of this research.

Following the introduction, Section 2.2 of the chapter will attempt to define 'undesirable behaviour of directors'. It will also attempt to define a criterion for determining when a behaviour is undesirable and differentiate them from 'common' directorial behaviours. Thereafter, Section 2.3 will explore the types of risks to which companies can be exposed due to the occurrence of such behaviours and will analyse their negative impacts on companies. Section 2.4 introduces a wide range of control mechanisms that may be applied to constrain directors, following which it will examine whether companies are able to employ them in controlling their directors. The chapter concludes by exploring measures that can be deployed in order to overcome limitations that companies may face as they attempt to deter their directors from engaging in undesirable behaviour.

2.2 The Problem of the Undesirable Behaviour of Directors

This chapter focuses on regulatory breaches and actions that directors indulge in for the short-term benefits of the company, which can potentially expose it to significant corporate risks that may jeopardise its present and future status in the market. Such actions are undesirable due to the negative consequences that they may cause to companies in the long term. The question that arises at this point is from whose perspective is a behaviour undesirable? Hodges and Wilson have employed the terminology of desirable behaviour[4] in different contexts. Desirability in behaviour was previously linked to ethics and morality and to the vital elements of social well-being. In light of these approaches, the desirability of a behaviour can be measured based on its impact on society, and such behaviour can be considered as contrary to the objectives of society. However, in company law, the nature of the desirability or undesirability of directorial behaviour must be determined from the objective of running the company, and this can typically be identified based on legislative statements.

Up until the enactment of the Companies Act 2006 (CA06), statute law did not outline the main objective of the company.[5] In the build-up to the passage of the 2006 Act, the Company Law Review Steering Group (CLRSG) published a number of reports between 1998 and 2001, which, among other things, sought to resolve the issue of 'in whose interest company law should be formulated'.[6] The CLRSG accepted that the shareholder value theory prevailed and that increasing the value of the company for the benefit of shareholders was a commonly agreed corporate

4 Gary Wilson, 'Business, State, and Community: "Responsible Risk Takers," New Labour, and the Governance of Corporate Business' (2000) 27 Journal of Law & Society 151, 154

5 Andrew Keay, 'Tackling the Issue of the Corporate Objective: An Analysis of the United Kingdom's 'Enlightened Shareholder Value Approach' (2007) 29 Sydney Law Review 577

6 Andrew Keay, 'Enlightened Shareholder Value, the Reform of the Duties of Company Directors and the Corporate Objective' [2006] Lloyd's Maritime and Commercial Law Quarterly 335, 346

objective. However, it suggested the adoption of an enlightened shareholder value approach in the future.[7] A suggestion that the government accepted and included in the Company Law Reform Bill.

The CLRSG also suggested that listed companies should provide Operating and Financial Reviews (OFR), which are 'to disclose a range of "qualitative" and "forward-looking" information of a kind that is not normally found in traditional financial statements'.[8] The government agreed on the need for OFRs, and this requirement was included in a draft of the Companies Bill that was attached to Section II of the White Paper on Modernising Company Law in July 2002.[9] Based on these OFR clauses, companies were to provide information regarding 'future plans, opportunities, risks and strategies'.[10] These clauses also recognised that,

> [I]n deciding in good faith what would be most likely to promote the success of the company, directors need to take account . . . of a wide range of factors within and outside the company which are relevant to achieving its objectives. These include relationships with employees, customers and suppliers and the company's impact on the wider community.[11]

In this regard, the government considered the OFR as a provider of a major benefit for a wider cross-section of a company's stakeholders.[12] Despite the fact that OFRs have never been implemented, these suggestions, which embody the enlightened shareholder value theory, came to shape the approach adopted in the CA06.[13] Thus, while the Act still obliges directors to run the company's business in consideration of shareholder value, they must do so in an 'enlightened' manner.[14] This requires that a director must act 'in the way he considers, in good faith, would be most likely to promote the success of the company for the benefit of its members as a whole, and in doing so have regard (amongst other matters) to' the interests of several

7 Andrew Keay, 'Enlightened Shareholder Value, the Reform of the Duties of Company Directors and the Corporate Objective' [2006] Lloyd's Maritime and Commercial Law Quarterly 337

8 Andrew Johnston, 'After the OFR: Can UK Shareholder Value Still Be Enlightened?' (2006) 7 EBOR 817, 818

9 Department of Trade and Industry, 'Modernising Company Law' (Cm 5553, 2002) paras [4.28]–[4.41]. Two more papers were also published in March and October 2005, but the proposals of White Paper were accepted

10 Department of Trade and Industry, 'Modernising Company Law' (Cm 5553, 2002) para [4.30]

11 Department of Trade and Industry, 'Modernising Company Law' (Cm 5553, 2002) para [4.31]

12 Department of Trade and Industry, 'Modernising Company Law' (Cm 5553, 2002) para [4.33]

13 Andrew Keay, *Moving Towards Stakeholderism? Constituency Statutes, Enlightened Shareholder Value, and All That: Much Ado About Little?* (University of Leeds School of Law, Centre for Business Law and Practice Working Paper 2010) 19 <http://papers.ssrn.com/sol3/papers.cfm?abstract_id=1530990> accessed 21 May 2024. See also Andrew Keay, *The Enlightened Shareholder Value Principle and Corporate Governance* (1st edn, Routledge 2013). For the review of this book, see also Gary Wilson, 'Corporate Law Theory' (2013) 22 Nottingham Law Journal 155, 158

14 Peter N Taylor, *Enlightened Shareholder Value and the Companies Act 2006* (PhD Thesis, Birkbeck College 2010) 5

relevant stakeholders.[15] Directors are thus required to consider 'the impact of their decisions in the light of a non-exhaustive list of factors which went beyond the direct shareholder interest'.[16] It should be noted that before the passage of the Act, directors had been required to consider the interest of stakeholders when they acted in the interest of the company, most primarily, the shareholders.[17] However, 'what the Act adds to the common law is a duty . . . to take account of stakeholder interests when it is in the interests of the members to do so'.[18] In this sense, Margaret Hodge MP (as she then was), in referring particularly to Section 172 of the Act, observed that 'it marks a radical departure in articulating the connection between what is good for a company and what is good for the society at large'.[19] Lady Justice Arden supported this view when she noted that the Act 'has struck a new balance between companies and society, and it is hoped that by that new balance companies and society may reconnect'.[20] It is now clear that legislation encourages companies to consider the interests of society in their decisions, and, in this sense, undesirable behaviour can be understood from the perspective of Hodges and Wilson.

The first consequence of adopting such an approach is that this objective is extended to recognise the importance of looking towards the long-term interests of the company.[21] Even at that, the Companies Act of 2006 requires directors to increase shareholder value. But this approach is usually perceived as causing 'sub-optimal consequences in encouraging short-termism and failing to develop the cooperation and trust required of other stakeholders in the company'. On the other hand, the requirement of taking the interests of non-shareholder stakeholders into account ensures that decision-making is done in consideration of long-term consequences.[22] The approach thus promotes 'an "inclusive" approach towards all stakeholders and the adoption of a "long-term" view towards achieving economic

15 S 172(1) Companies Act 2006; RT Hon Lady Justice Arden, 'Regulating the Conduct of Directors' (2010) 10(1) JCLS 1, 7

16 Wilson, Corporate Law Theory (n 13) 156

17 Paul Davies and Jonathan Rickford, 'An Introduction to the New UK Companies Act' (2008) 5 ECFR 48, 66

18 Paul Davies and Jonathan Rickford, 'An Introduction to the New UK Companies Act' (2008) 5 ECFR 66. See also Andrew Keay, *The Duty to Promote the Success of the Company: Is It Fit for Purpose?* (University of Leeds School of Law, Centre for Business Law and Practice Working Paper 2010) 4. <http://papers.ssrn.com/sol3/papers.cfm?abstract_id=1662411> accessed 20 May 2024

19 Department of Trade and Industry, *Companies Act 2006: Duties of Company Directors, Ministerial Statements* (DTI London 2007) 1

20 Arden (n 15) 1

21 Keay, *The Enlightened Shareholder Value Principle and Corporate Governance* (n 13) 593; David Millon, *Enlightened Shareholder Value, Social Responsibility, and the Redefinition of Corporate Purpose without Law* (Washington & Lee Public Legal Studies Research Paper Series, Working Paper 2010) 19. <http://papers.ssrn.com/sol3/papers.cfm?abstract_id=1625750> accessed 25 August 2024; Gary Wilson, 'From Black Box to Glocalised Player? Corporate Personality in the Twenty-First Century and the Scope of Law's Regulatory Reach' (2011) 62 Northern Ireland Legal Quarterly 433, 446

22 Gary Wilson, 'From Black Box to Glocalised Player? Corporate Personality in the Twenty-First Century and the Scope of Law's Regulatory Reach' (2011) 62 Northern Ireland Legal Quarterly 446; Keay, *The Duty to Promote* (n 18) 22

performance'.[23] This is because a company's stakeholders comprise its employees, suppliers, investors, creditors, customers, and the community, who are typically concerned about the issues of safety, stability, timely payments, risk-free ventures, a continuing long-term relationship, high-quality goods and services with fair prices, and protecting the environment. These considerations obviously require directors to consider the long-term impact of their decisions, which captures the importance of sustainability.[24]

The concept of sustainability was described by Elkington as covering three aspects: society (people), environment (planet), and economy (profit).[25] While people and the planet are the social and environmental aspects of sustainability, profit is its financial aspect, which is necessary for the company to survive and grow in the market. These facets constitute the mutual point where the interests of shareholders and stakeholders collide.[26] Based on this approach, long-term sustainability can be maintained by considering the interests of stakeholders. Keay stated that the purpose of requiring directors to have regard to the interests of stakeholders in the CA06

> was primarily to emphasise the fact that directors should not run a company for short-term gains alone, but [must also] take into account long-term consequences. The policy intention is to encourage decision-making based upon a longer-term perspective and not just immediate returns.[27]

Making profits in the short term without the consideration of people and the planet cannot thus be sustainably maintained in the long term.

Previous reforms had also advocated for the adoption of a long-term perspective. Section 309(1) of the Companies Act 1985 (CA85), for example, emphasised that 'the matters to which the directors of a company are to have regard in the performance of their functions include the interests of the company's employees in general, as well as the interests of its members'. In addition to this, the Hampel report drew attention to the need to consider stakeholders by noting that directors 'can pursue the objective of long-term shareholder value successfully, only by developing and sustaining these stakeholder relationships'.[28] The report also encouraged directors to consider the impact of their decisions in the long term by suggesting that long-term incentive plans should be one of the considerations determining directors' remuneration.[29]

23 Taylor (n 14) 5 and 16
24 Taylor (n 14) 204
25 John Elkington, *Cannibals with Forks: The Triple Bottom Line of 21st Century Business* (Capstone Publishing 1999) 70, 73
26 Özlem Alikılıç, 'Broadening the Concept of Green Marketing: Strategic Corporate Social Responsibility' in Ulas Akkucuk (ed.), *Handbook of Research on Developing Sustainable Value in Economics, Finance, and Marketing* (Business Science Reference 2015) 86, 95
27 Keay, *The Duty to Promote* (n 18) 10–11 (emphasis added)
28 Hampel Committee, 'Final Report' (1998) para [1.18]
29 Hampel Committee, 'Final Report' (1998) para [4.6]

Post CA06, some other reforms have also advocated for the consideration of the interests of several stakeholders. For example, the Financial Report Council stated in the Review of the Combined Code that 'the purpose of the Code is to promote high standards of corporate governance in the belief that good governance should contribute to better long-term performance'.[30] For this purpose, it suggested that, 'performance-related remuneration [should] be aligned to the long-term success of the company'.[31] The Code of Corporate Governance 2016 also suggests that

> the purpose of corporate governance is to facilitate effective, entrepreneurial and prudent management that can deliver the long-term success of the company', and each company must be controlled by an effective board of directors, which is jointly accountable to achieve this purpose.[32]

The idea of requiring companies to consider the long-term consequences of their decisions has also been substantially engaged by several corporate governance scholars, and the literature abounds with it. As such, there is little controversy regarding this matter.[33] For example, the issue was highlighted in the 'Innovation and Short-termism' Conference, which was jointly organised by the *Financial Times* (FT) and the Department of Trade and Industry (DTI) in 1990, regarding the fact that short-termism is an existing problem in British companies.[34] Grinyer, Russell, and Collison considered this problem as accounting for a reduction of the long-term success of companies.[35] And Mullins also remarked that 'seeking short-term gain [causes] the exclusion of long-term achievement'.[36] In addition, the importance of this consideration was emphasised by the CFA Institute, which confirmed academic research which suggests that,

> [T]he obsession with short-term results by investors, asset management firms, and corporate managers collectively leads to the unintended consequences of destroying long-term value, decreasing market efficiency, reducing investment returns, and impeding efforts to strengthen corporate governance.[37]

30 Financial Reporting Council, '2009 Review of the Combined Code: Final Report' (2009) para [2.3]

31 Financial Reporting Council, '2009 Review of the Combined Code: Final Report' (2009) para [2.3] (emphasis added)

32 Financial Reporting Council, '2009 Review of the Combined Code: Final Report' (2009) para [A.1]

33 Keay, *The Enlightened Shareholder Value Principle and Corporate Governance* (n 13) 593

34 John Grinyer, Alex Russell, and David Collison, 'Evidence of Managerial Short-Termism in the UK' (1998) 9 British Journal of Management 13

35 John Grinyer, Alex Russell, and David Collison, 'Evidence of Managerial Short-Termism in the UK' (1998) 9 British Journal of Management 13

36 D Mullins, 'Foreword' in M. Jacobs (ed.), *Short-Term America* (Harvard Business School Press 1991) (emphasis added). Quoted in Keay, *The Duty to Promote* (n 18) 10–11

37 Dean Krehmeyer, *Breaking the Short-Term Cycle: Discussion and Recommendations on How Corporate Leaders, Asset Managers, Investors, and Analysts Can Refocus on Long-Term Value* (CFA Centre for Financial Market Integrity and the Business Roundtable Institute for Corporate Ethics 2006) 1 <http://www.npr.org/documents/2006/jul/shortterm2006.pdf> accessed 27 August 2024

Keay also highlighted the importance of long-term sustainability by formulating a theory that he called the entity maximisation and sustainability model (MSM). The theory argues that 'a company should be managed in such a way as to maximise the wealth of the company and ensure that it is sustained financially over the long term'.[38] Hess also suggested that 'corporations [should be] focused on long-term value creation through sustainable economic development'.[39] Millon, in advocating for the adoption of the enlightened shareholder value, suggested that 'US corporations also need to discard their preoccupation with short-term, quarter-to-quarter financial results in favour of long-term, sustainable growth and profits'.[40] In the same vein, Lydenberg was of the view that 'companies that look to the long term can create value that would persist even if they went out of business tomorrow'.[41]

The foregoing demonstrates that the idea of setting long-term sustainability goals for companies is not new in itself but has been aptly captured in reform and corporate governance literature. It is our view, that requiring directors to consider the long-term interests of companies by taking the interests of stakeholders into account through the CA06 may 'have a major influence in changing behaviours and the climate of decision-making'.[42] However, this may give rise to the fact that achieving this aim is 'really a matter of a commercial judgment on the director's part'.[43]

There are two main types of commercial judgements that directors may take that may imperil the long-term sustainability of companies. The first occurs when they enrich themselves at the company's expense. Here, directors typically commit wrongdoing by using the company as a vehicle for personal aggrandisement or by plundering its assets for personal benefit. Such behaviour is clearly undesirable and would adversely impact the short- and long-term interests of the company. A director's desire to enrich himself typically arises when there is a conflict between his interest and that of the company.[44] It is equally worth noting that deterring directors from pursuing their self-interest is a fundamental aim of corporate governance.[45] In this regard, the duty of loyalty and the traditional duties imposed by company

38 Andrew Keay, 'The Ultimate Objective of the Company and the Enforcement of the Entity Maximisation and Sustainability Model' (2010) 10(1) JCLS 35, 71. See also Andrew Keay, *The Corporate Objective* (1st edn, Edward Elgar 2011). For the review of this book, see also Wilson, Corporate Law Theory (n 13)

39 David Hess, 'Public Pensions and the Promise of Shareholder Activism for the Next Frontier of Corporate Governance: Sustainable Economic Development' (2007) 2 Virginia Law and Business Review 221, 228 (emphasis added)

40 Millon (n 21) 4

41 Steven Lydenberg, *Corporations and the Public Interest: Guiding the Invisible Hand* (1st edn, Berrett-Koehler 2005) 31

42 Taylor (n 14) 90

43 Keay, Tackling the Issue of the Corporate Objective (n 5) 581

44 Andrew Griffiths, 'Interlocking Directorships and the Danger of Self-Dealing: The Duties of Directors with a Conflict of Interest' (1999) 10(9) ICCLR 280

45 Kose John, Lubomir Litov, and Bernard Yeung, 'Corporate Governance and Risk-Taking' (2008) 63(4) The Journal of Finance 1679

law require directors not to exercise their powers in this way. For example, under Section 171 of CA06, directors are required to 'exercise powers for the purposes for which they are conferred'. This requires them to use their discretion for proper purposes.[46] Also, under Sections 175, 177, and 182 of the CA06, directors are required to avoid conflicts and are required to disclose their personal interests in any transaction in which they are involved. This prevents them from exploiting the company's opportunities. These duties can respectively be defined 'as the no conflicts rule, no profits rule, and the self-dealing rule'.[47]

Besides these company law duties, the duty of loyalty, which is an equity obligation, also prohibits directors from using the company's opportunities for their own personal benefit. This is also referred to as the corporate opportunity doctrine, which, as Prentice points out, is defined as that which 'makes it a breach of fiduciary duty by a director to appropriate for his own benefit an economic opportunity which is considered to belong rightly to the company which he serves'.[48] Directors who breach this duty would be subjected to a wide range of liabilities, such as disgorging the profit, returning the subject property, and indemnifying the company for the loss it suffered. The decision of the court in *Jetivia SA and Another v. Bilta (UK) Limited (in liquidation) and others* is quite illustrative of this point.[49] In that case, the respondent company was forced into insolvent liquidation as a result of fraud perpetrated on it by its directors. The liquidators, acting on behalf of the respondent, brought a claim to recover the loss on the assertion that two of the directors had breached their duties by perpetrating a fraud on the company, with the assistance of the appellant. In that case, Bilta was considered a victim,[50] while its directors and the appellant were found liable to compensate for the loss. The imposition of liability in this case can potentially deter directors from engaging in conduct that benefits them personally to the detriment of the company.

With respect to the second type of directors' behaviour, the concept of undesirable behaviour can be widened beyond the traditional focus on making a profit at the company's expense to encompass a broader range of actions that put the company at risk. In essence, while a director may not seek to enrich himself at the company's expense, he may still put the company at risk if, in seeking to advance its short-term interests, he engages in undesirable behaviour.

Concerns over excessive risk-taking have arisen as a result of the financial crises of the last two decades. It has been commonly argued that managerial incentives to take excessive risk are the fundamental cause of these unfortunate consequences,[51] and 'in a number of cases boards were not aware of such strategic decisions and

46 S 171, Companies Act 2006

47 Alan Dignam and John Lowry, *Company Law* (8th edn, OUP 2014) 363

48 Dan Prentice, 'The Corporate Opportunity Doctrine' (1974) 37(4) MLR 464

49 [2015] UKSC 23

50 [2015] UKSC 23 [7] per Lord Neuberger

51 Christine Hurt, 'The Duty to Manage Risk' (2014) 39 The Journal of Corporation Law 253, 254–257; Steven L. Schwarcz, 'Excessive Corporate Risk-Taking and the Decline of Personal Blame' (2015) 65 Emory Law Journal 533, 541

had not put control mechanisms in place to oversee their risk appetite'.[52] There is no doubt that companies are required to take risks to increase their value in achieving a competitive advantage, but 'unsophisticated attempts to curtail risk-taking could inadvertently destroy that value'.[53] This is because such behaviour is likely to expose the company to serious corporate risks that may have various negative consequences. Although excessive risk-taking 'is not and should not necessarily be illegal',[54] this does not mean that it is desirable for companies.

Directors may take excessive risks in two ways. The first may occur from the exercise of commercial business judgement. Regardless of whether the impact of a business decision is minor or major, directors have a duty to ensure that all potential issues and negative consequences are considered before they decide in respect of the company's business. That notwithstanding, there is always the risk of loss in respect of expected returns. Excessive risk-taking typically results from poor decisions and bad judgement, particularly when directors overlook some potential negative consequences. It is arguable that excessive risk-taking contributed immensely to the Enron scandal.[55] Thus, while Enron has remained a classic case of corporate failure that arose as a result of poor monitoring and weak internal controls, the main issue in the wider context is that the board failed to understand 'the risks which were inherent in the company's business plan and failing to implement an effective system of internal control'.[56] This is because, while the business of Enron was both legitimate and useful, the firm's directors and managers also engaged in risky behaviour which ultimately resulted in the company's failure.[57]

The shareholders of companies that engage in excessive risk-taking may question the commercial judgement of their directors through derivative actions. In such actions, they may argue that the directors have breached their duty to the company by taking excessive risks. The matter for the court to consider in such situations would be whether the directors acted in 'good faith'. This poses the question as to 'how far the courts will interfere in the "good faith" judgments of directors'.[58] This question has been addressed in a long line of decided cases. In *Re*

52 Grant Kirkpatrick, 'The Corporate Governance Lessons from the Financial Crisis' (2009) Financial Market Trends 8 <http://www.oecd.org/dataoecd/32/1/42229620.pdf> accessed 13 May 2024. See also Anu Arora, 'The Corporate Governance Failings in Financial Institutions and Directors' Legal Liability' (2011) 32(1) Comp Law 3, 4

53 Schwarcz (n 51) 541

54 Schwarcz (n 51) 554

55 Simon Deakin and Suzanne J Konzelmann, 'Learning From Enron' (2004) 12(2) Corporate Governance 134

56 Simon Deakin and Suzanne J Konzelmann, 'Learning From Enron' (2004) 12(2) Corporate Governance 134

57 Simon Deakin and Suzanne J Konzelmann, 'Learning From Enron' (2004) 12(2) Corporate Governance 136

58 David Cabrelli, *The Reform of the Law of Directors' Duties in UK Company Law* (Bocconi University Milan 2008) 16 <https://www.research.ed.ac.uk/files/13215836/CABRELLI_D_PRESENTATION_FOR_UNIVERSITA_BOCCONI_ON_THE_REFORM_OF_THE_LAW_OF_THE_DIRECTORS_DUTIES_IN_UK_COMPANY_LAW.pdf> accessed 13 May 2024

Smith & Fawcett Ltd,[59] for instance, Lord Greene M.R. stated that directors 'must exercise their discretion bona fide in what they consider – not what a court may consider – is in the interests of the company, and not for any collateral purpose'.[60] In *Howard Smith Ltd v. Ampol Petroleum Ltd*,[61] Lord Wilberforce opined that 'it would be wrong for the court to substitute its opinion for that of the management, or indeed to question the correctness of the management's decision . . . if bona fide arrived at'.[62] In addition, Dillon J in *Devlin v. Slough Estates Ltd and Others*[63] remarked that 'the court does not interfere with the business judgment of directors in the absence of allegations of mala fides'.[64] Cabrelli expressed that on the face of these words, 'as long as the director acts in good faith, what matters is the director's view, not that of the courts – and the courts will be unable to substitute their own judgment for that of the director'.[65] The foregoing demonstrates a historical reluctance on the part of the courts to challenge the commercial judgement of directors that are made in good faith.[66] The issue is that such judgements, where poorly made, may expose companies to the risk of liability and losses.

The reluctance of the courts to interfere in the judgement of directors also exists in the second type of directors' excessive risk-taking that puts the company at risk of regulatory action either through the violation of binding legal rules or by engaging the company in an illegal grey area. Undesirable behaviour covers both commercial risk-taking and illegal excessive risk-taking, which may potentially attract regulatory sanctions. Commercial excessive risk-taking concerns what is reasonable risk and what is unreasonable risk and entails discussion far broader than what this book sets out to address. On the other hand, this book will concentrate on the circumstances which may result in regulatory infringements. In this regard, there are several regulatory laws that companies are required to comply with, and they are captured in environmental law, health and safety law, financial regulations etc. We have noted that, this book uses competition law as its main case study, given the significant level of sanctions that can be imposed on firms. The second reason competition law is chosen is due to the high-profile competition law cases that deal with these issues, one of which is *Safeway Stores Ltd v. Twigger*.[67]

A company that infringes its regulatory obligations as a result of directorial misbehaviour or engagement in undesirable may be exposed to losses that are no less significant than what it would suffer when its directors involve themselves in

59 [1942] Ch. 304
60 [1942] Ch. 304 [306] per Lord Greene M.R.
61 [1974] AC 821
62 [1974] AC 821 [832]
63 [1983] BCLC 497
64 [1983] BCLC 497 [504]
65 Cabrelli (n 58) 16. Cabrelli also discussed that Section 171(1) of the Companies Act 2006 preserves this common law tradition
66 Charles Wander, 'Directors' Duties' (2007) <http://www.fladgate.com/2007/09/directors-duties/> accessed 13 May 2024
67 [2009] UKHL 39, [2009] 1 A.C. 1391

excessively risky commercial ventures. That said, the former has its distinctive characteristic in that such behaviour may result in the imposition of legal liability on the company since the conduct in question may entail a breach of the law. Such a consequence is potentially serious as it may result in liability for financial penalties and the loss suffered by third parties, reputational damage, and eventual bankruptcy. Breaching regulatory rules may benefit the company in the short term by increasing its profit, but because such conduct is inherently illegal, it is likely to expose it to significant corporate risks in the long term. It gives rise to the problem of short-termism, which has been condemned by the legal literature and legal system in the United Kingdom. Despite the fact that directors do not typically aim to gain direct personal benefit by being involved in such behaviour, executive compensation and private benefits may incentivise them as these would be for their indirect benefit.[68]

Undesirable behaviour was demonstrated in *Safeway Stores Ltd v. Twigger*.[69] In that case, Safeway, having been fined for participating in a cartel, sought compensation against its former directors and employees for the recovery of losses it suffered due to the sanction imposed on it as a result of the cartel involvement. Not surprisingly, it argued that the directors and employees had breached their contractual and fiduciary duties by engaging the company in a cartel. While successful at the trial court, its claim was dismissed at the Court of Appeal. In effect, while the company benefitted from the price-fixing deals its directors and employees had entered into on its behalf, it was not allowed to recover the fine paid for them on the ground of *ex turpi causa*. The issue is that behaviour which is undesirable may have adverse long-term effects which may affect the fortunes and interests of the company's stakeholders. And directors are required to consider these interests when they make decisions on the company's behalf.

In *Safeway*, the company suffered some losses, which it could not recover from its erring directors. The issue was that another supermarket chain had already acquired the company,[70] and the burden was thus transferred to the shareholders of the acquirer. Interestingly, the consequences of engaging the company in a cartel could have been harsher if it had not been acquired. This is because, in *Safeway*, the company was only exposed to regulatory risks whose occurrence caused shareholders to suffer loss, but if the company had not been acquired, it could possibly have been exposed to other risks which would have threatened its long-term sustainability. First, there is the risk that a third party may institute a claim for losses suffered. There is also the risk of reputational damage, as the company would be perceived as a wrongdoer by society. Lastly, there is the risk of insolvency, as it may not be able to fulfil its financial obligations as a result of the loss it suffers.

68 As Ginsburg and Wright discussed the personal interest of directors in respect to company's involvement in cartel that, '[t]hey may capture some of the gains in the form of increased compensation and perquisites, and the increased value of shares in the corporation enhances their reputations and career opportunities'. See Douglas Ginsburg and Joshua Wright, 'Antitrust Sanctions' (2010) 6(2) Competition Policy International 3, 17

69 (n 67)

70 After the takeover, most of the stores of the company were rebranded as Morrisons

The involvement of directors in excessive risk-taking is commonly considered the main cause of the financial crises in the last two decades.[71] This chapter has examined the risks to which a company can be exposed and their adverse consequences.[72] It has been shown that corporate failures resulting from these actions can be wholly or in part attributed to company officers' behaviours, particularly those of directors.[73] It thus follows that it is the responsibility of directors to perform their managerial functions effectively so as to prevent such actions from occurring.

Among other things, the CA06 was enacted to further good corporate governance. Additionally, several codes and guidance have been introduced in the United Kingdom.[74] Despite these efforts, corporate failures are still occurring as a result of directorial misbehaviour.[75] This has raised serious concerns as to whether these publications are actually considered by directors in order to achieve better corporate management. There are also concerns about whether the potential liabilities directors may face under the CA06 are enough to deter them from being involved in behaviour that impairs good corporate governance practices. These concerns can be consequently extended to the company's ability to manage the risks to which it is exposed due to directors' excessive risk taking.

2.3 The Risks of Directors' Undesirable Behaviours

Finch once stated that corporate 'activities give rise to risks'.[76] The majority of these risks arise from doing business in a particular market and thus can be identified as business risks. The amount that the company bears may vary depending on the nature of the business that it carries out. Behavioural risk[77] is one type of business risk that companies have to deal with, and majorly, it borders on issues with directors' behaviours. The extent of behavioural risks is determined by the personality and the attitude of the decision-makers of the company.

Using the financial crises that have occurred in the last two decades as an example, it is clear that behavioural risks can subject companies to serious risks,[78] which may result in serious negative consequences such as job losses for employees, impaired trust by the public in the company, and huge financial losses. These adverse effects

71 See I Ferrero-Ferrero, MA Fernández-Izquierdo, and MJ Muñoz-Torres, 'The Impact of the Board of Directors Characteristics on Corporate Performance and Risk-Taking Before and During the Global Financial Crisis' (2012) 6 Review of Managerial Science 207–226; VF Mollah and K Keasey, 'Does the Impact of Board Independence on Large Bank Risks Change After the Global Financial Crisis?' (2017) 44 Journal of Corporate Finance 149–166

72 See Ngozi V Okoye, 'The Personality of Company Directors and Behavioural Risks in Corporate Governance: Bridging the Unidentified Gap' (2013) 10(3) IJDG 261; Schwarcz (n 51) 541

73 Okoye (n 72) 262

74 See Section 2.4.7

75 Okoye (n 72) 262

76 Vanessa Finch, 'Personal Accountability and Corporate Control: The Role of Directors' and Officers' Liability Insurance' (1994) 57 Modern Law Review 863, 889

77 See Okoye (n 72)

78 For the analysis of the examples, See Okoye (n 72)

are clearly not in the best interests of stakeholders, who, as noted earlier, directors are bound to have regard for when making decisions for companies.

For each type of director's behaviour, as identified earlier, there are risks that the company would have to contend with. In this respect, when directors engage in self-enrichment behaviour, the company becomes exposed to the risks of suffering losses as well as being exposed to the risk of insolvency. In effect, companies face the risk of suffering huge losses as an inevitable consequence when their directors engage in direct self-enrichment behaviour at the expense of the company. Companies may also suffer loss of opportunities as well as the risk of insolvency, where they are unable to fulfil their obligations to their creditors.

There is also the risk that directors' poor business judgement can expose a company to losses and subject it to contractual obligations in relation to third parties. In the worst-case scenario, these actions can result in corporate insolvency. What this means is that when directors exercise poor judgement in decision-making, the company may not only initially suffer loss, as the expected return would not be gained from the transaction, but it might also be held liable to third parties if, as a result, it is unable to fulfil its financial and contractual obligations. These would ultimately expose it to the risk of insolvency.

Regarding directors' undesirable behaviour, which benefits companies in the short term but impairs their long-term interests, we identify four broad categories of risks in this regard: (i) regulatory risk,[79] (ii) litigation risk,[80] (iii) reputational risk,[81] and (iv) the risk of insolvency.[82] In the next four sub-sections, the impacts of the occurrences of these risks on the company will be individually examined.

2.3.1 Regulatory Risk

Ramakrishna has defined regulatory risk as the risk 'of not complying with regulatory guidelines, requirements, and expectations'.[83] Company directors may sometimes engage in excessive risk-taking that can potentially result in companies breaching their regulatory obligations or engaging in activities that are illegal in

79 See Simon Goldring, 'Insurers' Liability for Civil Fines and Penalties' (2011) <http://www.lexology.com/library/detail.aspx?g=762e2955-82dd-45f0-86f6-6a6dc1d57cbe> accessed 6 April 2015. See also Saloni Ramakrishna, *Enterprise Compliance Risk Management: An Essential Toolkit for Banks and Financial Services* (1st edn, Wiley 2015) 232

80 Such risk was examined by Ramakrishna in respect to banks' exposure. See Saloni Ramakrishna, *Enterprise Compliance Risk Management: An Essential Toolkit for Banks and Financial Services* (1st edn, Wiley 2015) 227, 230

81 Robert G Eccles, Scott C Newquist, and Roland Schatz, 'Reputation and Its Risks' (2007) 85(2) Harvard Business Review 104; John Armour, Colin Mayer, and Andrea Polo, *Regulatory Sanctions and Reputational Damage in Financial Markets* (Oxford Legal Studies Research Paper No. 62/2010 2010) <http://papers.ssrn.com/sol3/papers.cfm?abstract_id=1678028&download=yes> accessed 21 April 2024

82 Andrew Keay, *Company Directors' Responsibilities to Creditors* (1st edn, Routledge-Cavendish 2007) 205–208

83 Ramakrishna (n 79) 232

nature. Where this occurs, they face the risk of punishment through regulatory sanctions such as monetary fines. While regulatory breaches may increase the value of companies in the short term, they can potentially cause them to be subject to significant risks as the potential loss may have a significant implication for their current and future life in the market.

A classic example of the occurrence of regulatory risk was seen in the *Safeway* case, where, as a result of directors' infringement of UK competition law by engaging in price-fixing activities, an investigation was initiated by the OFT, which resulted in the imposition of stiff fines on the participant companies. In that regard, the OFT proposed a fine of £16.5 million for Safeway, which was eventually reduced by 35% to £10.7 million following an early resolution agreement between the OFT and Safeway. The *Safeway* case demonstrated that in spite of the fact that the directors' conduct was aimed at benefitting the company in the short term, it entailed excessive risk-taking, which resulted in the company suffering a significant loss. This example illustrates that a company may be exposed to regulatory risks if its directors engage in undesirable behaviour.

2.3.2 Litigation Risk

Secondly, directors' undesirable behaviours may result in huge losses for companies when third parties institute claims for compensatory or punitive damages against the company to recover the loss they have suffered. For this reason, this risk is called 'litigation risk'.[84] Typically, the company would be the defendant in this context since the directors are regarded as its agents.[85] Litigation risk may have different implications because its occurrence may have a significant impact on the present and future life of the company in the market.

The high significance of this risk is based on the fact that the company can be punished not only through the imposition of compensatory damages, which are based on the actual loss suffered by a third party but also by the imposition of punitive damages, which are usually awarded to third parties to deter companies from further misconduct. The amount of potential punitive damages can be underestimated, but it is surely more than compensatory damages.[86]

A typical example of litigation risk can be seen in *2 Travel Group PLC (in liquidation) v. Cardiff City Transport Services Limited*.[87] In that case, 2 Travel brought a claim for compensatory and punitive damages against Cardiff Bus to recover the loss it had suffered due to Cardiff Bus's abuse of its dominant position,

84 John E Core, 'On the Corporate Demand for Directors' and Officer Insurance' (1997) 64(1) The Journal of Risk and Insurance 63, 64

85 Roberta Romano, 'What Went Wrong with Directors' and Officers' Liability Insurance' (1989) 14(1) The Delaware Journal of Corporate Law 1, 3

86 *2 Travel Group PLC (in liquidation) v. Cardiff City Transport Services Limited* [2012] CAT 19; [2012] Comp. A.R. 211

87 *2 Travel Group PLC (in liquidation) v. Cardiff City Transport Services Limited* [2012] CAT 19; [2012] Comp. A.R. 211

which 'drove' 2 Travel out of the market.[88] Cardiff Bus was punished for compensatory damages of £33,819 for loss of profits (plus interest) and punitive damages of £60,000.[89] In the case at hand, what the directors of Cardiff Bus did was use the dominant position of the company for the company's benefit in the short term, as it would have made more profit in a less competitive market. But to achieve this aim, the directors took an excessive risk in consideration of the potential liability that the company might incur against 2 Travel. This risk caused the company to suffer a considerable loss. As such, while the excessive risk of the directors was beneficial to the company in the short term, it was obviously undesirable because of its extensive impact on the company when the conduct was exposed.

2.3.3 Reputational Risk

This refers to the risk of having a bad reputation due to public perception that a company has, or continues to engage in, misconduct. Reputational risk has been defined by Vaughan and Vaughan as 'the potential that negative publicity will cause a loss'.[90] It is one of the negative consequences that a company may suffer when the engagement of its directors in undesirable behaviour is made public.

Companies, as entities, are only able to create their own reputation within society. They are enabled to build their brand values within the market and become well-known. The issue is that there is also a downside—the fact that the reputation of a company greatly depends on how well and appropriately its decision-makers behave.

The subject of reputation is too fragile and, as Benjamin Franklin stated, 'it takes many good deeds to build a good reputation, and only one bad one to lose it'.[91] This statement is very much valid for public companies which are usually well-known. As such, members of the public may reconsider their expectations and opinions about a particular company if they hear adverse events about its business. Such negative situations can affect public confidence and result in negative perceptions. Hence, the risk of reputational damage, which can cause the company to indirectly lose funds gradually as a result of the loss of confidence of its customers, suppliers, and investors.[92] For this reason, as Power explained, 'today, most business people, when asked about the risk which worries them most, will often mention reputation'.[93]

88 The claim brought against Cardiff Bus was based on the investigation conducted by the OFT on it because the OFT did not impose fine as it considered the act of Cardiff Bus as "conduct of minor significance"

89 Kim Dietzel, Stephen Wisking, and Molly Herron, 'Nearing the End of the Line in Cardiff Bus' [2012] Comp Law 289

90 Emmett J Vaughan and Therese M Vaughan, *Fundamentals of Risk and Insurance* (10th edn, John Wiley 2008) 15

91 Quoted in Eccles, Newquist, and Schatz (n 81) 106

92 Armour, Mayer, and Polo (n 81) 1

93 Michael Power, 'The Risk Management of Everything' (2004) 5(3) The Journal of Risk Finance 58, 61

The issue is that as the company may not directly suffer losses as a result of reputational issues, it may have a false sense of security that it has not suffered much as a result of reputational damage; however, such a risk is likely to be significant for the future of the company and can even lead to bankruptcy since very few companies can survive with a bad reputation in the market.[94] This is because the company will be named as a wrongdoer, and it will suffer shame by the loss of its reputation.[95]

The recent Volkswagen (VW) scandal is an example of reputational risk. In that case, it was alleged that VW was involved in cheating on diesel car emission tests, and it admitted that it had installed software to manipulate the tests.[96] As a result of this, the company faces various risks. Financially, it is exposed to significant risks of liability for not only the damage claims that may be brought by customers but also fines that are likely to be imposed by legal authorities. For example, VW suffered significant reputational damage as the incident has now spread globally, and the faith that customers had in the company became greatly shaken. One of the company's directors, Olaf Lies, said that 'huge damage has been done because millions of people have lost their faith in VW'.[97] The extent of the reputational damage can also be seen from the statement given by Ferdinand Dudenhoeffer that 'made in Germany is quality and trust: 'now that trust is lost'.[98] Also, the managing director of Volkswagen, Martin Winterkorn, expressed his sadness by stating that

> millions of people across the world trust our brands, our cars and our technologies . . . and I am endlessly sorry that we have disappointed this trust. I apologize in every way to our customers, to authorities and the whole public for the wrongdoing.[99]

In this case, although the wrongdoing was for the benefit of the company in the short term, as it would have saved it a considerable amount of money by installing

94 As an example, Arthur Andersen, which was formerly considered one of the five biggest accounting firms, collapsed in 2002 due to its criminal handling of Enron. See 'The Fallout of Arthur Anderson and Enron on the Legal Landscape of American Accounting' <https://www.hg.org/article.asp?id=31277> accessed 23 May 2024

95 John Armour, 'Regulatory Sanctions and Reputational Damage in Financial Markets' (2010) <https://corpgov.law.harvard.edu/2010/10/27/regulatory-sanctions-and-reputational-damage-in-financial-markets/> accessed 21 April 2024

96 Chris Bryant, 'Directors Meet to Decide Volkswagen Chief's Fate' (2015) <http://www.ft.com/cms/s/0/decc3722-6112-11e5-a28b-50226830d644.html#axzz3tfIjevVo> accessed 7 May 2024

97 Sean Farrell, 'Volkswagen Director Says Staff Acted Criminally Over Emissions Tests' (2015) <http://www.theguardian.com/business/2015/sep/30/volkswagen-vw-director-staff-acted-criminally-over-emissions-tests> accessed 30 May 2024

98 Sarah Knapton, 'Volkswagen Scandal: How Two Campaigners Exposed the World's Biggest Car Company' (2015) <http://www.telegraph.co.uk/news/uknews/road-and-rail-transport/11883343/volkswagen-scandal-campaigners-expose-world-biggest-car-company.html> accessed 30 May 2024

99 Geir Moulson and Pan Pylas, 'VW CEO Says He's 'Endlessly Sorry' for Tarnishing Brand' (2015) <http://phys.org/news/2015-09-vw-ceo-endlessly-tarnishing-brand.html> accessed 23 May 2024

the 'deceptive' software, the amount of risk taken to do this was excessively high, and it not only threatened the financial status of the company but also, more importantly, its reputational status. Volkswagen is now regarded as dishonest by regulators and the public.[100]

As can be seen, reputational risk is a much more fragile matter than other financial risks to which the company is subjected because, although it can be estimated when the loss arising from the occurrence of financial risks can be replaced, there is no guarantee that the negative consequences of reputational loss will be completely eliminated.

2.3.4 Insolvency Risk

Lastly, there is insolvency risk, which is the inability of a company to fulfil its contractual or financial obligations. To become officially insolvent, the value of the assets the company holds would have to be less than its debts. In this regard, the role of directors, as decision-makers of the company, is important because their considerations and decisions are important in the present and future life of the company in the market. In the case of *Stone & Rolls Ltd v. Moore Stephens*,[101] the sole director and shareholder of a company perpetrated various frauds on some banks in order to benefit the company.[102] The banks brought a claim against the company and the director for the losses they had suffered, and the company was found liable based on the rules of corporate attribution. It indemnified the claimant banks for their losses and, consequently, went into liquidation.

In that case, the company not only suffered significant losses but also its presence in the market went into jeopardy as a result of excessive risk-taking by its director. Although the fraud conducted by the director was for the short-term benefit of the company, it was exposed to serious risks as a result of the director's behaviour. It can be seen that the risk of insolvency is one of the major corporate risks that companies face due to the undesirable behaviours of their directors. The first three risks may have different implications for the financial and reputational position of the company; however, this risk is arguably the most serious as it has definite implications for the future of the company in the market. Since the occurrences of these risks cause companies to face significant unfortunate consequences, without a doubt, they should seek to control their directors so that they do not engage in such behaviour. In the next section, the control mechanisms that companies can employ to prevent and deter directors from becoming involved in such behaviour and their shortcomings will be examined.

100 Graham Ruddick, 'Volkswagen Scandal: US Chief Says Carmaker "Totally Screwed Up"' (2015) <http://www.theguardian.com/business/2015/sep/22/volkswagen-scandal-us-chief-carmaker-totally-screwed-up-michael-horn> accessed 30 May 2024

101 [2009] UKHL 39, [2009] 1 A.C. 1391

102 As the director was sole shareholder of the company, it can be stated that he used the company as a vehicle to gain personal benefit, but the benefit was initially for the company

2.4 Control Mechanisms

There are a number of control mechanisms that companies can employ to control their directors. They include defining the level of their authority to bind the company, the duties that they owe to the company, and the remedies available to the company where these duties are breached. Others include the appointment of independent non-executive directors (NEDs), external auditors, and internal audit committees by the board of directors; market controls through takeovers; and disclosure requirements through reporting.

2.4.1 Defining the Authority of Directors

The first control mechanism is to define the authority of the company's directors. Limitations placed on the authority of directors to enter into a binding transaction can constrain them regarding their involvement in undesirable behaviour. In order to determine the level of authority with which individual directors are typically equipped, it is imperative that we examine the structure of the board of directors and how the company is typically run.

A public limited company's 'decision-making structure is principally an authority-based one'.[103] This leads to a 'board-centric form of corporate governance' that Bainbridge identified as 'director primacy'.[104] The board of directors in modern companies is an organ invested with great power to make decisions to run the company. However, the board does not normally make all the day-to-day decisions by itself. Its power is allocated to a particular director who automatically becomes responsible for a specific task. This allocation of power is clearly recognised by statute and common law.[105]

The authority of directors to bind the company and authorise others is also conferred by Table A and by the Model Articles.[106] Regulations 70, 71, and 72 of Table A confer authority on directors to delegate their powers and allocate their responsibilities. Regulation 70 states that,

> Subject to the provisions of the Act, the memorandum and the articles, and to any directions given by special resolution, the business of the company shall be managed by the directors who may exercise all the powers of the company. . . . The powers given by this regulation shall not be limited by any special power given to the directors by the articles, and a meeting of directors at which a quorum is present may exercise all powers exercisable by the directors.

103 Stephen Bainbridge, *Director Primacy* (UCLA School of Law, Law-Econ Research Paper No 10-06, 2010) 7 <http://papers.ssrn.com/sol3/papers.cfm?abstract_id=1615838> accessed 15 May 2024

104 Stephen Bainbridge, *Director Primacy* (UCLA School of Law, Law-Econ Research Paper No 10-06, 2010) 3 <http://papers.ssrn.com/sol3/papers.cfm?abstract_id=1615838> accessed 15 May 2024

105 See Section 2.4.1.1

106 Companies registered after 1 May 2009 can design their articles of association based on the Model Articles, and Table A for companies registered before this date

Also, under Regulation 71, directors can appoint any person to act as an agent of the company, and he may be thus authorised to allocate such powers to others. Furthermore, under Regulation 72, directors can also delegate their powers to other directors designated to manage specific tasks. Although the Model Articles modified Table A, the wording is still similar. While Article 5 of the Model Articles empowers the board of directors to delegate its powers to any director and to other individuals,[107] Article 3 also confers the responsibility on directors to manage the company. It also determines the breadth of their powers.[108]

In this regard, the problem of excessive risk-taking for the short-term benefit of the company may arise where the power delegated to a particular director is exercised without adequate limitation. Providing authority to directors is required since they run the company's business on behalf of the shareholders; however, far-reaching authority may lead to undesirable behaviour, which causes the company to be subjected to risks.

2.4.1.1 Statutes and Common Law Approach

The authority of directors is regulated under statutes and common law. The common law approach to the authority of directors is established from a long line of decided cases culminating in *Royal British Bank v. Turquand*.[109] In that case, a company had alleged that the conduct of its manager was invalid as he did not have the authority to be involved in the transaction under the company's deed of settlement. This is because the ordinary resolution required to authorise a director's action was not obtained by him. Despite this, the company was held to be bound by its manager's conduct based on the reasoning that the claimant believed that the manager had complied with the required resolution at the time of the transaction.

This reasoning was also supported by Lord Hatherly in the House of Lords in *Mahony v. East Holyford Mining Co*[110] that,

> [W]hen there are persons conducting the affairs of the company in a manner which appears to be perfectly consonant with the articles of association, then those so dealing with them, externally, are not to be affected by any irregularities which may take place in the internal management of the company.[111]

This common law attitude was adopted by statutory law, and the authority of directors was regulated under Section 35A of the CA85, and codified under Section 40 of the CA06. Despite the codification, the wording of Section 40 remains similar to Section 35A of the CA85. This provision generally recognises that statutory

107 Companies (Model Articles) Regulations 2008 (plc) [5]
108 Companies (Model Articles) Regulations 2008 (plc) [3]
109 *Royal British Bank v. Turquand* [1856] 6 E&B 327
110 (1874–75) LR 7 HL 869
111 (1874–75) LR 7 HL [894]

authority to manage companies belongs to directors, and the option of setting up certain restrictions on them is left to the discretion of the company through its articles of association.

Section 40(1) states that 'in favour of a person dealing with a company in good faith, the power of the directors to bind the company, or authorise others to do so, is deemed to be free of any limitation under the company's constitution'.[112] In addition, Section 40(2) explicates this issue further, in that a third party dealing with the company is not responsible for inquiring into the limitations on the authority of directors to bind the company or to delegate such powers to others.[113]

In a broad interpretation, these provisions may arguably override the limitations placed by the articles of association on the power of directors in favour of third parties.[114] While they enhance the authority of directors to bind the company, they may decrease the ability of the company to avoid being bound by the transaction made by the directors. Even if the company seeks to avoid a contract by alleging that its directors were not authorised to act at the time in question, such an argument is, as Dignam considered, 'unmeritorious'.[115] This is because the courts have developed the attitude that the company is ordinarily bound by the conduct of its directors, who are presumed to be authorised by the company to embark on that particular task.[116]

In addition, the statement that 'a person dealing with a company is not bound to enquire as to any limitation on the powers of the directors to bind the company or authorise others to do so' under Section 40(2)(b)(i) illustrates that directors can delegate their powers to employees and agents to act on behalf of the company, and a third party dealing in good faith may assume that such a delegation is valid.[117] In respect of the wording under Section 40(1), despite the fact that companies are deemed to be free to limit the power of directors to enter into a binding transaction, there is no statement that empowers companies to limit the power of any individual to act on their behalf.[118] Thus, the statute's purpose is to enhance the discretion of the directors to bind the company and also to authorise others to act on its behalf.

Another issue with Section 40 is that the power is conferred on directors instead of the board of directors.[119] The unanimity of the directors as a board is arguably not required in the statute, and the intention of lawmakers behind this is probably to ensure that the third party dealing with the company can still rely on the decision even if the decision is taken by the improperly constituted board or by *de*

112 S 40(1), Companies Act 2006
113 S 40(2), Companies Act 2006
114 Susan Mclaughlin, *Unlocking Company Law* (3rd edn, Routledge 2015) 303, 305
115 Alan Dignam, *Hicks & Goo's Cases and Materials on Company Law* (7th edn, OUP 2011) 245
116 Alan Dignam, *Hicks & Goo's Cases and Materials on Company Law* (7th edn, OUP 2011) 245
117 Adam Goodison, 'Directors' Powers and Responsibilities' in QC Simon Mortimore (ed.), *Company Directors Duties, Liabilities, and Remedies* (2nd edn, OUP 2013) 76, 87
118 Mclaughlin (n 114) 305
119 Paul Davies and Jonathan Rickford, 'An Introduction to the New UK Companies Act' (2008) 5 ECFR 66 59

facto directors.[120] Protecting the third party dealing with the company is actually 'the obvious intention of the legislation', and despite the fact that the legislation is 'ill-conceived and not well drafted', the courts will 'make the best of it . . . to diminish the circumstances in which the third party is adversely affected by limitations contained in the constitution' when it has to make a decision on the meaning of the statute.[121] Accordingly, protecting the interests of the third party rather than that of the company is likely to be the priority consideration of the courts. This may impair the control power of the company on directors as it would not be able to avoid the negative consequences of a binding transaction in which they are involved.

2.4.1.2 The Requirement of Good Faith

The only restriction that the company can invoke to avoid the consequences of directors' misbehaviours is to establish bad faith on the part of the third party. This is because, in order for the action of a director to bind a company, Section 40(2) of the CA06 requires third parties to be in good faith when involved in a transaction. Therefore, the company can still avoid being bound by the consequences of directors' undesirable behaviours if the third party entered the transaction in bad faith. However, there are some difficulties that statute law has put in place that the company must overcome in order to escape liability in this regard. Firstly, the statutory law presumes that 'a person dealing with a company . . . [has] acted in good faith unless the contrary is proved'.[122] Nevertheless, based on the wording in Section 40(2)(b), the third party dealing with the company is almost always presumed to be acting in good faith for the purposes of Section 40.[123] This leaves the burden of proving the third party's bad faith on the company.[124] In addition, Section 40(2)(b)(iii) states that the third party 'is not to be regarded as acting in bad faith by reason only of his knowing that an act is beyond the powers of the directors under the company's constitution'. Based on this provision, the third party would not be regarded as acting in bad faith even if he entered into the transaction knowing that limitations had been placed on the authority of the director in the company's constitution. These issues potentially decrease the ability of the company to avoid being bound by the transactions in which its directors are involved, and it may consequently be exposed to the risk of liability and loss caused by directors' undesirable behaviours.

Besides this issue, with respect to the company's ability to prevent directors' undesirable behaviours, the control mechanism over directors' authority may not be adequate in all circumstances that expose the company to risk. This is because

120 Paul Davies and Jonathan Rickford, 'An Introduction to the New UK Companies Act' (2008) 5 ECFR 66 59
121 John P Lowry and Arad Reisberg, *Pettet's Company Law: Company Law & Corporate Finance* (4th edn, Pearson 2012) 137
122 S 40(2)(b)(ii), Companies Act 2006
123 Mclaughlin (n 114) 303
124 Goodison (n 117) 88

this mechanism can only assist the company when its directors are involved in a contractual relationship with a third party. The concept of directors' undesirable behaviours, however, is not limited to third-party transactions, and it mainly involves regulatory wrongdoings that do not require contractual relationships with third parties. Therefore, even assuming that limiting the authority of directors was a control mechanism that effectively deterred directorial misbehaviour, this mechanism would only be invoked by the company to avoid being bound by the contract entered by its directors with third parties. This is based on the reason that either the commercial business judgement that was made by the directors was not for the company's benefit or that they transacted to enrich themselves at the company's expense. This behaviour can still be considered undesirable and excessive risk-taking by directors, but this is not taken into account for the purposes of this book.

To summarise this section, the undesirable behaviour of directors will bind the company to a large extent. And limitations, even where imposed on directors' authority in the company's constitution, are largely overridden by statutory law in a bid to protect third parties. Another limitation of this approach is that it does not capture instances where directors expose the company to serious risk. In effect, it neglects the fact that

> although the directors may have had authority to enter into the agreement or do the act in question, it must be a rare case in which the company could be said to have authorised its directors to undertake an illegal agreement.[125]

Therefore, it can be safely concluded that limiting the authority of directors as a way of preventing undesirable behaviour is hardly effective in the current dispensation.

2.4.2 Duties of Directors and Remedies to the Company

The second mechanism that may be used to control directors is through their duties and the enforcement of the remedies available to the company where they breach them. The logic behind developing different types of directors' duties with various remedies is to enable the company to institute actions against directors in order to 'deliver the social and economic motivations, incentive and consequences intended'.[126] Accordingly, they may be vital for the company to protect the long-term interests of its stakeholders. In this sense, the question that this section examines is whether the duties and remedies are effective in deterring directors from engaging in undesirable behaviour.

Directors' duties can be classified into two categories: fiduciary duties and common law duties. Fiduciary duties are the responsibilities that directors, as

125 Ross Grantham, 'Illegal Transactions and the Powers of Company Directors' (1999) 115 LQR 296
126 Sarah Worthington, 'Corporate Governance: Remedying and Ratifying Directors' Breaches' (2000) 116 LQR 638, 640

fiduciaries, owe to the company. These duties are 'characterised by spelling out what a fiduciary cannot do'.[127] And they consist of two main responsibilities. These are (i) the duty to use discretionary powers in good faith and for proper purposes and (ii) the duty of loyalty. In addition, the general duties of directors under common law are codified based on 'certain common law rules and equitable principles' for the first time under the CA06, and their interpretations and applications are to be performed 'in the same way as common law rules or equitable principles'.[128]

These common law duties can be outlined as follows: to exercise powers according to the company's constitution and for the purposes for which they are conferred,[129] to promote the company's success, to exercise independent judgement, and to exercise reasonable care, skill, and diligence.[130] Other duties include the duty to avoid conflict of interest with the company,[131] not to accept benefits from third parties while a person is acting as director,[132] and to declare interest in proposed transactions or arrangements.[133]

These duties oblige directors to run the company's business appropriately, and they carry a clear deterrent value. However, they are 'useful only if they can be enforced effectively'.[134] This is because when they are not effectively enforced, their deterrence value tends to be lower, and the perceived consequences that breach of these duties may cause on directors' personal and professional lives become less likely and less visible. For example, under Section 171 of the CA06, directors are obliged to act according to the company's constitution and to exercise their powers for appropriate purposes. The important question that arises, however, is whether companies can enforce this duty effectively against directors who breach it. This question is important since duties can only be effective as long as directors who breach their duties are meant to bear responsibility as a result of claims brought against them by the company. Despite the remedies associated with the duties of directors taking effect only after a breach of duties has occurred, they still play an important role in constraining directors since a potential liability against the company for breach of duties is likely to deter them from breaching these duties. This depends, however, on the availability and effectiveness of the remedies. For this reason, the availability of the remedies that enable the company to sue its directors directly or indirectly in the event of a breach of these duties should be examined.

127 Vicki Vann, 'Causation and Breach of Fiduciary Duty' [2006] Singapore Journal of Legal Studies 86, 88
128 Companies Act 2006, ss 170, 170(3), and 170(4)
129 S 171, Companies Act 2006
130 S 174 Companies Act 2006
131 S 175 Companies Act 2006
132 S 176 Companies Act 2006
133 S 177 Companies Act 2006
134 Janet Dine and Marios Koutsias, *Company Law* (8th edn, Palgrave Macmillan 2014) 190. This is the main reason as to why the section heavily concentrates on the consequences of breach of these duties by directors rather than their nature

The remedies available to the company can be separated into three categories. These are fiduciary duties and equitable remedies, common law duties and remedy of damages, and directors' disqualification.

2.4.2.1 Fiduciary Duties and Equitable Remedies

Section 178 of the CA06 outlines the remedies available to companies where directors breach their duties under Sections 171–177.[135] According to the section, these fiduciary duties are enforceable in the same way as any other fiduciary duty owed to a company by its directors.[136] Hence, if directors breach these duties, a claim for equitable remedies can be brought by the company against them to disgorge the gains they have obtained or to recover the loss suffered as a result of the breach. From this aspect, remedies can be defined as 'duty based preventative measures' that can be brought against directors who 'have either made [personal] profits or caused loss' to their companies through breaching their duties.[137] In this sense, the remedies 'maintain the strength of this rule'.[138]

2.4.2.1.1 RESCISSION AND GAIN-BASED REMEDIES

The first type of remedy available to the company is rescission, and this gives an opportunity to void a transaction carried out by directors in breach of their duties. This remedy is usually applied by companies 'in the context of the improper issue or forfeiture of shares, unlawful dividends, unlawful distributions of assets, resolutions approving remuneration, or pension payments for directors'.[139]

A common example may arise where a director sells his property to the company. The company may typically seek to rescind the transaction if the director did not disclose that the property was personally owned by him and the price he/she paid for it in the first place. In such a case, the company can void the transaction and have the money restored. In another scenario, the company can also rescind the transaction if the director has purchased property from the company and failed to disclose his/her own personal interest in the transaction.[140] Through this remedy,

135 S 178 Companies Act 2006, with the exception of s 177, however, which deals with breach of the duty of reasonable care and skill

136 S 178(2) Companies Act 2006

137 Denis Ong, 'Breach of Fiduciary Duty: The Alternative Remedies' (1999) 11(2) Bond Law Review 336

138 Mihir Naniwadekar, 'Remedies against Directors' Undue Gains: Personal or Proprietary?' (2013) <http://indiacorplaw.blogspot.co.uk/2013/09/remedies-against-directors-undue-gains.html> accessed 30 May 2024

139 QC Antony Zarcaroli, 'The Company's Remedies for Breach of Directors' General Duties' in QC Simon Mortimore (ed.), *Company Directors Duties, Liabilities, and Remedies* (2nd edn, Oxford University Press 2013) 419, 424–425

140 Matthew Conaglen, 'Equitable Compensation for Breach of Fiduciary Dealing Rules' (2003) 119 LQR 246, 248

the director can be prevented from using his/her fiduciary position within the company for personal benefit.

The consequence of awarding the remedy of rescission gives rise to two other gain-based remedies[141] that obligate a director who has made a personal profit or obtained property by breaching their duties to reimburse the company for the amount they gained or restore the subject property. The first type of gain-based remedy is constructive trust. This remedy is proprietary in nature and based on ordinary trust principles. Therefore, it is 'not only to describe the trust itself but also to describe a particular proprietary remedy, and even as shorthand for saying that proprietary relief is available in equity'.[142] In respect of the breach of fiduciary duties, the company can bring a claim against directors to restore the subject property obtained by depriving the company of its entitlements. To claim this remedy, there must be a pre-existing fiduciary relationship between a director and the company, and this relationship has to be breached.

The second type of gain-based remedy is to require directors to account for profits made. In this regard, a company can bring a claim against its directors to confiscate profits they have gained by breaching their fiduciary duties. This is a personal remedy which covers various issues including secret commissions and bribes, and it is appropriate and applicable when the personal gain made by directors is not a property which is subject to the remedy of constructive trust. For example, when a director sells his/her property to the company without disclosing his/her own interest, the company can obtain an account of the profit for the money that the director made. The remedy is, however, commonly regarded as being unavailable if the director was not in a fiduciary relationship with the company when he/she purchased the subject property.[143]

The issue is that these remedies are aimed at restitution rather than compensation. And this decreases their deterrent effect on directors, despite the fact that these remedies aim at placing companies back into the position in which they would have been if such breaches had not occurred. As such, they are unlikely to deter directors from breaching their fiduciary duties, as they only risk losing the 'fruits of the wrongful venture'.[144] This is because, even if the breach of fiduciary duty is detected and the company brings a claim against directors, they will not lose more than what they gained.[145]

With regard to accounts of profit, it is 'confined to profits actually made, its purpose being not to punish the defendant but to prevent its unjust enrichment'.[146] This issue was also discussed in *My Kinda Town Ltd v. Soll and Another*.[147] The remedy

141 Matthew Conaglen, 'Equitable Compensation for Breach of Fiduciary Dealing Rules' (2003) 119 LQR 248–251
142 Peter J Millett, 'Restitution and Constructive Trusts' (1998) 114 LQR 399, 400
143 Conaglen (n 140) 249
144 Worthington (n 126) 639
145 Worthington (n 126) 639
146 *Dart Industries Inc. v. Decor Corp. Pty Ltd and Another* (1993) 179 CLR 101 [111]
147 *My Kinda Town Ltd v. Soll and Another* [1982] FSR 147

of requiring directors to account for profits made is aimed at preventing 'an unjust enrichment of the defendant by compelling him to surrender those profits, or those parts of the profits, actually made by him which were improperly made and nothing beyond this'.[148] Worthington highlighted this issue by noting that although the director who is in default may be forced to disgorge 'all the profits of the breach', it is still difficult to predict its deterrent effect on directors.[149] It should be noted that the remedy of constructive trust has a similar issue in that it 'does not . . . arise because of a manifestation of an intention to create it, but is imposed as a remedy to prevent unjust enrichment'.[150]

In consideration of the drawbacks of these remedies and the nature of the particular undesirable behaviours of directors examined in this chapter, it is arguable that these remedies are insufficient tools through which companies can control, deter, and constrain their directors from engaging in undesirable behaviour. This is because undesirable behaviour is typically conducted by directors to increase the short-term value of the company rather than obtaining direct personal benefit. These remedies are silent when directors breach their fiduciary duties for purposes which do not involve making personal gain since there would not be any profit or property gained by directors to be counted.[151] In respect of the remedy of accounts of profit, Worthington argued that,

> The flip side is that profit disgorgement is the limit of the remedy for breach of fiduciary duties [because] if the director's disloyal behaviour is not profitable to the director, then the company cannot obtain a remedy for breach of the duty of loyalty [and] there is a modern tendency to ignore this.[152]

It should be noted that the fact that directors did not obtain personal gain from their actions does not make their behaviour desirable for the company, which stands exposed to the risk of liability and loss as a result of the directors' breach of fiduciary duties.

2.4.2.1.2 EQUITABLE COMPENSATION

An aggrieved company may also seek the remedy of equitable compensation. This essentially entails it recovering the losses that it suffers when its directors breach their fiduciary duties. This remedy had 'languished, apparently unnoticed and unwanted'[153] in the past, but it is now commonly recognised as a viable avenue for

148 *My Kinda Town Ltd v. Soll and Another* [1982] FSR 147 [156]
149 Worthington (n 126) 639
150 Quoted in Millett (n 142) 403
151 Aiman Sulaiman, 'Directors' Fiduciary Duty to Disclose Wrongdoing and Appropriate Remedy – Case Commentary' (2012) 38(1) CLB 91, 100
152 Worthington (n 126) 664
153 Paul D Finn, 'Fiduciary Law and the Modern Commercial World' in Ewan McKendrick (ed.), *Commercial Aspects of Trusts and Fiduciary Obligations* (1st edn, Clarendon 1992) 7, 40

obtaining reliefs where a director breaches their fiduciary duty.[154] Its main objective is to compensate the company by putting it in the position that it was in before the breach. In this sense, equitable compensation can potentially serve as an effective deterrent mechanism on directors since even a 'minor breach' of their duties may expose them to significant losses.[155] That said, there has been a lack of clarity in the implementation of this remedy, which has cast doubts on its preventative effect.

Sealy noted that the remedy of equitable compensation was surely better known by the Chancery judges who determined the case of *Re Cape Breton Co* in 1855,[156] than it is currently known.[157] He noted that since then the legal system has yet to take a definite stance on the remedy by either overruling it or reversing it by statute.[158] The primary issue which may decrease the deterrent effect of the remedy is its availability, which has attracted very little attention in England.[159] Meagher *et al* argue that rescission is the only remedy available to the company where a fiduciary had purchased the property before he/she became a fiduciary of the company.[160] Sealy also supported this view and argued that rescission is the only remedy that can be justified based on the wrongdoing of the fiduciary, but that beyond that, there are no other remedies available[161] as the rules are disabilities rather than duties.[162]

This view primarily relies on two main cases.[163] In *Re Cape Breton Co*, a company brought a claim to disgorge the profit gained by its director from selling his property, which he acquired before he became a fiduciary to the company. Despite the fact that the director breached his fiduciary duties by not disclosing his personal interest in the transaction, the Court of Appeal rejected the suggestion that the profit made from the price difference could be recovered by the company. The outcome of this case was also supported by the House of Lords in *Jacobus Marler Estates Ltd v. Marler*.[164] In that case, Lord Moulton stated that a director could be held accountable for the profit he made from selling a property that he did not

154 Matthew Conaglen, *Fiduciary Loyalty: Protecting the Due Performance of Non-Fiduciary Duties* (1st edn, Hart 2010) 87
155 Worthington (n 126) 639
156 (1885) 29 Ch.D. 795, CA; the case is one of the well-known cases that dealt with equitable compensation
157 Len Sealy, 'Directors' Duties Revisited' (2001) 22(3) Comp Law 79, 81
158 Len Sealy, 'Directors' Duties Revisited' (2001) 22(3) Comp Law 81
159 John D Heydon, 'Causal Relationships Between a Fiduciary's Default and the Principal's Loss' (1994) 110 LQR 328, 335
160 Roderick P Meagher, John D Heydon, and Mark J Leeming, *Meagher, Gummow and Lehane's Equity: Doctrines and Remedies* (4th edn, Butterworths LexisNexis 2002) para [2.155]–[2-320]
161 Len Sealy, 'Some Principles of Fiduciary Obligations' [1963] CLJ 119, 124, 135–137. See also Sealy (n 157) 81
162 Len Sealy, 'Some Principles of Fiduciary Obligations' [1963] CLJ 119, 124, 135–137. See also Sealy (n 157) 80–81. He stated that, 'the self-dealing rule imposes a *disability* on a director who has a conflicting interest, or other counterparty connected with him, but no *duty* carrying any sanction *vis-à-vis* the director personally'. See Sealy (n 157) 80
163 See Conaglen (n 154) 252
164 (1916) 114 L.T. 640n

acquire as a fiduciary of the company. Lord Parker stated that 'the appellant company is asking for the court to fix a proper price between vendor and purchaser, and estimate the damage with reference to such price. This the court cannot do'.[165]

Based on the approaches of the courts in these cases, Meager, Gummow, and Lehane argued that the remedy of equitable compensation may not be available due to inadequate application of the 'fusion fallacy' theory.[166] The fusion fallacy is a view adopted by scholars who desire to merge the common law and equity.[167] The main logic of this view is to remove the inconsistencies between common law and equity in terms of restitution of loss. But Meager, Gummow, and Lehane have rejected this view on the basis of the unavailability of equitable remedies other than rescission.[168] Ordinarily, 'the remedy is based on the jurisdiction of the court of equity to compel the defaulting fiduciary to make good any loss suffered by the beneficiary'.[169] And it is awarded in the 'exclusive jurisdiction of equity for the breach of a purely equitable obligation'.[170] However, Meager, Gummow, and Lehane suggested that there is a tendency to fuse and mingle the common law and equity, so that the availability of the remedy would be determined under a 'new body of principle, neither common law nor equity, but partaking of some of each'.[171]

Conaglen observed that it is difficult to see the relevance between mingling the common law and equity and the availability of equitable remedies.[172] However, this issue might be relevant because while damages under the common are awarded for the misconduct of an agent, equitable remedies are awarded for the breach of fiduciary duties. Mingling them under a new body of principles may undermine the underlying foundations of equity, and such a situation may have an impact on the availability of equitable compensation.

In order to investigate whether such fusion is present in law, the application of the causation test in common law and equity needs to be examined. This is because, whereas causation is the main issue that is considered in the award of damages, 'the considerations of causation, foreseeability, and remoteness do not readily enter into the matter' in cases of equitable remedy'.[173] This issue was discussed by Judge Tipping, who noted that,

> a breach of trust followed by a loss to the trust estate to which the breach was material, was enough to establish the liability of the trustees for that loss,

165 (1916) 114 L.T. 640n [641]

166 Meagher, Heydon, and Leeming (n 160) para [2.155]–[2-320]

167 See Samantha Hepburn, *Principles of Equity & Trusts* (2nd edn, Cavendish 2001) 29–31

168 Meagher, Heydon, and Leeming (n 160) para [2.155]–[2-320]

169 Lee Aitken, 'Developments in Equitable Compensation: Opportunity or Danger?' (1993) 67 ALJ 596, 597. Quoted in Charles Rickett and Tim Gardner, 'Compensating for Loss in Equity: The Evolution of a Remedy' (1994) 24 Victoria University of Wellington Law Review 19, 25

170 Rickett and Gardner (n 169) 26

171 Meagher, Heydon, and Leeming (n 160) para [2.275]

172 Conaglen (n 154) 252

173 *Re Dawson* [1966] 2 NSWR 211 [214] per Street J

> without regard to questions of foreseeability, remoteness or common law concepts of causation.[174]

This view was also supported by the Privy Council in *Brickenden v. London Loan & Savings Co.*[175] In that case, the Privy Council held that a fiduciary who breached his duty by failing to disclose his interests or the facts regarding the transaction could not plead that his disclosure would not have changed the decision of his principal. Thus, the fiduciary was held liable regardless of whether the disclosure would have changed the decision.

This was the general approach adopted for the application of the causation doctrine under equity; however, this attitude has been modified in *Target Holdings Ltd v. Redferns*,[176] where two common law principles were employed in the award of equitable compensation. These principles were (i) that the damage must have been caused by the wrongful action of the defendant, which is the 'but for test', and (ii) the claimant should be put in the same position in which he would have been if the breach had not been committed through compensation and reparation.[177] Hence, *Target* has 'materially modified the strictness of the Brickenden approach'.[178] The logic behind adopting these common law principles for awarding the remedy of equitable compensation is that 'foreseeability is not a concern in assessing compensation, but it is essential that the losses made good are only those which, on a common sense view of causation, were caused by the breach'.[179]

This approach increases the involvement of the causation test in equitable compensation cases, which may illustrate the fusion between common law and equity because the claimant company will be required to prove the causal link between the loss it has suffered and the breach that its directors have committed. However, as Lord Millet opined,

> it is misleading to speak of breach of trust as if it were the equitable counterpart of breach of contract at common law; or to speak of equitable compensation for breach of fiduciary duty as if it were common law damages masquerading under a fancy name.[180]

The problem in this regard is that the differences that exist between the duties owed by fiduciaries to the beneficiary under equity and regular duties owned by agents to the principal under common law might have disappeared.

174 RT Hon Justice Tipping, 'Causation at Law and in Equity: Do We Have Fusion?' (2000) 7 Canterbury Law Review 443, 446
175 [1934] 3 DLR 465
176 *Target Holdings Ltd v. Redferns* [1996] 1 AC 421
177 *Target Holdings Ltd v. Redferns* [1996] 1 AC paras [432]–[434]
178 Tipping (n 174) 447
179 *Canson Enterprise Ltd v. Boughton & Co* [1991] 85 DLR (4th) 129 [163] *per* McLachlin J
180 Peter J Millett, 'Equity's Place in the Law of Commerce' (1998) 114 LQR 214, 225

In addition, the application of the causation test may potentially make the availability of equitable compensation less likely since the court needs to consider tests such as causation, remoteness, or foreseeability. This is because, as Conaglen observed, 'proving a causal link between non-disclosure and loss can be somewhat speculative, given that the court must consider what would have happened had the relevant facts been properly disclosed'.[181] If directors make a counterargument that the loss would have been suffered by the company regardless of whether they breached their duties,[182] the application of this principle would require the company to prove the contrary and 'the supposed difficulties in proving this "negative", are more apparent than real'.[183]

In short, the approach of mingling the common law and equity may limit the availability of equitable compensation to the company for the loss arising from the directors' breach of fiduciary duty. This approach, however, can be criticised in terms of its pessimistic attitude[184] because there are some types of loss for which recovery can still be available, such as a loss arising from directors' fraud perpetrated on the company for their personal interests. Such a situation was seen in *Bilta*.[185] In that case, directors were found personally liable for the fraud they perpetrated on their company and the recovery for the loss the company suffered was awarded. On the other hand, there are still some other types of losses that the company may not recover from its directors. The outcomes of the *Stone*[186] and *Safeway*[187] cases demonstrate this. Although common law considerations such as causation were not involved in the cases, the companies' claims against their directors for involvement in directors' undesirable behaviours failed.[188] The difference between these groups of cases was illustrated by Rickett and Gardner, in that equitable compensation is available in equity when there is fraud, whereas it 'now seems to be unavailable for loss caused by misrepresentations'.[189] The outcomes of *Stone* and *Safeway* cast serious doubts on whether remedies founded on equity when directors breach their fiduciary duties actually have any deterrent effect. They also cast down on whether such remedies are sufficient to enable companies to control directors in order to ensure that they do not engage in undesirable behaviour. These cases will be extensively examined throughout this book.

181 Conaglen (n 154) 268
182 Worthington (n 126) 656
183 Conaglen (n 154) 266. See also Kewin W Saunders, 'The Mythic Difficulty in Proving a Negative' (1985) 15 Seton Hall Law Review 276
184 Roderick P Meagher, John D Heydon, and Mark J Leeming, *Meagher, Gummow and Lehane's Equity: Doctrines and Remedies* (5th edn, Butterworths LexisNexis 2015) para [2.330]
185 [2015] UKSC 23
186 [2009] UKHL 39, [2009] 1 A.C. 1391.d
187 [2010] EWHC 11 (Comm), [2010] EWCA Civ 1472.
188 In order to see the tension between fiduciary duties, availability of equitable remedies, and attribution of liability in the relationship between the company and directors in the concept of undesirable behaviour, see Chapter 4, Section 4.2.3
189 Rickett and Gardner (n 169) 26

2.4.2.2 Duty of Care and the Remedy of Common Law Damages

Based on the fact that the duty to exercise reasonable care, skill, and diligence under Section 174 of the CA06 is not considered as a fiduciary duty, the remedy available to the company where this duty is breached is to claim for damages by way of compensation. The remedy is available where the conduct of the directors has harmed the company in some way. In effect, where, as a result of the incompetence of the directors, a company suffers losses and financial crisis,[190] the company would be entitled to sue the directors on the basis of breach of duty of care.[191] It must be emphasised that the duty to operate with skill and care is not fiduciary in obligation. It is a duty imposed to ensure that directors act competently and with care. Where enforced diligently, the duty of care and the attendant remedy of damages where it is breached can be one of the mechanisms through which a company can control its directors. This is because the potential liability and loss that the directors may suffer is likely to deter them from becoming involved in behaviour that would result in a breach of duty. However, there are two important issues that may impair the deterrent effect of the doctrine.

The first issue is the lack of clarity in determining when a director has acted unreasonably in order to decide whether he has breached his duty of care. In this test, the question of '[w]hat would a reasonable director or board regard as the interests of the company?' is to be asked.[192] This test embraces two different limbs. The first, which is objective refers to what a reasonable person would do in that position. The second is subjective, and it entails determining what a reasonable person with the level of skills, knowledge, salary and social responsibility as the director in question would do.[193] For this reason, determining whether directors have breached their duty of care is usually based on the facts and circumstances of the particular case.[194] And in this regard, several factors are considered, such as the director's experience, their functions within the company, particular skills that they have, the degree of the director's skills, and their relation to the discharge of his functions. The issue is that these considerations can easily differ depending on the particular circumstances, and conduct that may constitute a breach of duty in one case may not give rise to a breach of

190 Demetra Arsalidou, 'The Banking Crisis: Rethinking and Refining the Accountability of Bank Directors' [2010] JBL 284, 285

191 Joan Loughrey, 'The Director's Duty of Care and Skill and the Financial Crisis' in Joan Loughrey (ed.), *Directors' Duties and Shareholder Litigation in the Wake of the Financial Crisis* (Cheltenham 2013) 12, 13

192 Rosemary Teele Langford and Ian M. Ramsay, 'Directors' Duty to Act in the Interests of the Company – Subjective or Objective?' [2015] JBL 173, 175

193 Adolfo Paolini, 'Lending Sub-Prime and Advising on Financial Investments From a D&O Insurance Perspective' [2012] JBL 432, 435

194 Mark Arnold, 'Duty to Exercise Reasonable Care, Skill, and Diligence' in Simon Mortimore QC (ed.), *Company Directors Duties, Liabilities, and Remedies* (2nd edn, Oxford University Press 2013) 296, 297

duty in another case. And interestingly, the guidance that we can derive from the authorities appears to be limited[195]—a factor that may impair the extent to which the duty of care and the attendant remedy of damages can deter directors from engaging in undesirable behaviour that may arise as a result of a breach of their duty of care. This is because even the directors themselves, lacking sufficient guidance from the courts, may not know what type of conduct will constitute breach of duty of care.

In respect to the second issue, even if assuming that breach of duty of care on the part of directors can easily be determined, the company would still have limited ability to recover the loss from directors. This is not to suggest that the remedy of damages is not available, as was the case in the remedy of equitable compensation. But it suggests that even if the company is able to bring a claim against directors and the remedy is awarded by the court, it is unlikely that directors would be able to compensate for the amount of loss that the company would have suffered since the losses are likely to be very significant. For example, in *Safeway*, the company was fined more than £10 million for its directors' breaches, an amount that its directors were unlikely to be able to compensate for. This fact accounted for why the company indirectly sought compensation through directors' insurance. The fact that directors are often unable to compensate their companies fully would also reduce the deterrent value of the remedy of damages where they breach their duty of care to the company.

2.4.2.3 Sanction of Directors' Disqualification

Besides the remedies that may arise where directors breach their fiduciary and common law duties, there is also the possibility of disqualification. This is in addition to the fact that disqualified directors may be held liable to the creditors of an insolvent company. Directors' disqualification is governed by the Company Directors Disqualification Act 1986 (CDDA86), and it is a civil proceeding that involves punitive elements even though punishment is not the primary objective underlying the law.[196] Under the CDDA85, a director can be disqualified for up to 15 years for the following reasons: if he is convicted for an indictable offence in relation to the promotion, formation, or management of a company;[197] is managing a company that is persistently in breach of company legislation;[198] is involved in fraudulent trading or other fraud;[199] or is found to be unfit on the basis of corporate insolvency.[200] Other grounds include when an investigation finds a person

195 Mark Arnold, 'Duty to Exercise Reasonable Care, Skill, and Diligence' in Simon Mortimore QC (ed.), *Company Directors Duties, Liabilities, and Remedies* (2nd edn, Oxford University Press 2013) 298

196 Brenda Hannigan, *Company Law* (4th edn, Oxford University Press 2015) 374

197 S 2, Company Directors Disqualification Act (CDDA) 186

198 S 3, CDDA

199 S 4, CDDA

200 S 6, CDDA

to be unfit to direct a company,[201] infringement of competition law,[202] and civil liability for fraudulent trading or wrongful trading under Sections 213 and 214 of the Insolvency Act 1986 (IA86) respectively.[203] In addition, disqualified directors may also be required to compensate the creditors of insolvent companies. Until 2015, when the Small Business, Enterprise and Employment Act 2015 (SBEEA15) was enacted, directors did not bear personal liability for the debts or wrongs of the company. But that Act introduced new rules that oblige disqualified directors of insolvent companies to disgorge any gains they may have obtained in order to compensate the creditors of such companies for losses they suffered when directors breached their duties to the company.[204]

As can be seen, there are a number of grounds on which disqualification can be imposed on directors, and directors can not only be disqualified but also be held personally liable for the breach of their duties. To the extent that directors may be disqualified and held liable to the creditors of companies, disqualification can be regarded as a mechanism that 'provide[s] a measure of indirect enforcement' on directors' duties to the company.[205] Despite its positive elements, the imposition of disqualification in practice can still be problematic. This is because the number of directors who are disqualified per year tends to be between 1200 and 1400. On the face of it, these numbers can be perceived as large; however, when it is considered that there are approximately 2.4 million registered companies in the United Kingdom, with each having at least one director, these numbers can be said to be very small.[206] The sparse implementation of the provisions on directors' disqualification may impair its deterrence effect and the extent to which it can be used to regulate the behaviour of directors.

Additionally, it is worrisome that nearly all disqualifications appear to be founded under Section 6 of the CDDA86, which imposes a duty on the courts to disqualify unfit directors of insolvent companies in certain cases.[207] This may imply that the disqualification mechanism is sparsely invoked for directors of companies who do not become insolvent, even where they indulge themselves in wrongdoing. This factor will further impinge on the deterrent effect of disqualification on directors of companies in general. Besides these, some other factors may impact the extent to which companies may control their directors through disqualification, and they will be examined in detail in Chapter 3.[208]

To conclude this section, directors' duties and the remedies made available to companies when they breach them are limited in the extent to which they can deter directors from undesirable behaviour. The actual objective of gain-based remedies

201 S 8, CDDA
202 Ss 9A–9E CDDA
203 S 10, CDDA
204 S 110, Small Business, Enterprise and Employment Act 2015
205 Hannigan (n 196) 375
206 Hannigan (n 196) 374
207 Hannigan (n 196) 375
208 Which considers competition law enforcement mechanisms. See Chapter 3, Section 3.5.1

is to restore the company to the position that it was in before the directors' breach of duties. However, when the behaviour of excessive risk-taking for the short-term benefits of the company is considered, these remedies are unlikely to deter directors. This, as was shown earlier, is because they are limited primarily to the rescission of contracts and curtailing the personal enrichment of directors. Even at that, other issues serve to further whittle the extent to which companies can control their directors. As noted, they include the limited extent and effect of equitable compensation, a lack of clarity in determining where a director breaches his duty of care, coupled with the limited extent to which companies may recover losses caused by such breaches. Others include a general absence of the imposition of liability on disqualified directors. The effect of the aforementioned is that the negative consequences caused to companies when directors engage in undesirable behaviour will arguably remain with companies.

2.4.3 Non-Executive Directors

The third mechanism that companies can employ to control their directors is by harnessing the strengths of their non-executive directors (NEDs). NEDs are members of the board who are not part of the company's executive management team.[209] While executive directors manage the affairs of the company as decision-makers, NEDs, as outsiders, are expected to monitor the way the executives manage the company. They also have strategic policy roles within the corporate structure. Byrd and Hickman explained that the

> inside directors provide valuable information about the firm's activities, while outside directors may contribute both expertise and objectivity in evaluating the managers' decisions. The corporate board, with its mix of expertise, independence, and legal power, is a potentially powerful governance mechanism.[210]

The role of NEDs, however, has not been that straightforward in the United Kingdom. In order to clarify this, a number of committee reports have been published which made recommendations on their roles. They include the Cadbury report (1992),[211] the Greenbury report (1995),[212] the Hampel report (1998),[213] and the Higgs report (2003).[214] The first three reports were collapsed into the Old Combined Code in 1998. The subsequent versions of the Code as amended by the Financial Reporting Council in 2003, 2006, and 2008 incorporated the suggestions of the

209 Ade Asefeso, *Non Executive Directors: Best Kept Secret Revealed* (Global Sourcing 2013) 3
210 John W Byrd and Kent A Hickman, 'Do Outside Directors Monitor Managers' (1992) 32 Journal of Financial Economics 195, 196
211 Cadbury Committee, 'Report on the Financial Aspects of Corporate Governance' (1992)
212 Greenbury Committee, 'Directors' Remuneration: Report of a Study Group' (1995)
213 Hampel Committee, 'Final Report' (1998) para [1.18]
214 Higgs Committee, 'Review of the Role and Effectiveness of Non-Executive Directors' (2003)

Higgs report. Later on, the suggestions provided in these reports were combined in the UK Corporate Governance Code 2010.[215] They were revised in 2012;[216] 2014;[217] 2016, 2018, and in 2024.[218] One of the purposes of the reports and codes was to review and clarify the functions of NEDs within a company and increase their effectiveness at controlling executives and maintaining good corporate governance. The debate on the roles of NEDs was launched in the early 1990s by a business initiative with governmental support.[219] The government considered the issue as being 'too much of a hot potato for legislation'.[220] The outcome of such an approach was to have business sponsored committees which were serviced by civil servants.[221]

2.4.3.1 Roles and Independence of NEDs

In order to determine the extent to which companies can control their directors through NEDs, it is imperative that we study their suggested roles within the company as well as their independence from executives. This is because the effectiveness of NEDs in controlling executives greatly depends on how independent they are from the latter. For this purpose, the suggested roles of NEDs by committees and reports, and their independence, will be examined.

The role of NEDs in the UK corporate governance system was initially mentioned in the report by the Cadbury Committee in 1992. The report provided clear recommendations in terms of the requirement of NEDs on boards and their potential assistance for operating the company efficiently.[222] The '"Code of best practice" was suggested in respect of the issues of the independence of NEDs, internal monitoring, and appointments'.[223] The report stated that,

> [NEDs] should bring an independent judgement to bear on issues of strategy, performance, resources, including key appointments, and standards of conduct. We recommend that the calibre and number of [NEDs] on a board should be such that their views will carry significant weight in the board's decisions.[224]

215 Financial Reporting Council, 'The UK Corporate Governance Code' (2010)
216 Financial Reporting Council, 'The UK Corporate Governance Code' (2012)
217 Financial Reporting Council, 'The UK Corporate Governance Code' (2014)
218 Financial Reporting Council, 'The UK Corporate Governance Code' (2024) <https://www.frc.org.uk/library/standards-codes-policy/corporate-governance/uk-corporate-governance-code/> accessed 5 July 2024
219 The Cadbury, Greenbury, and Hampel reports were issued by the private sector, while the Higgs Report was issued under the auspices of the UK Government
220 Paul Davies, *Introduction to Company Law* (2nd edn, Oxford University Press 2010) 195
221 Paul Davies, *Introduction to Company Law* (2nd edn, Oxford University Press 2010) 195–196
222 Helen Short, 'Non-Executive Directors, Corporate Governance and the Cadbury Report: A Review of the Issues and Evidence' (1996) 4 C.G. 123
223 Cadbury Committee, 'Report on the Financial Aspects of Corporate Governance' (1992) 211
224 Cadbury Committee (n 211) para [4.11]

The Committee considered the role of NEDs as similar to that of executives because they expect NEDs to have an important influence on board decisions. It was also suggested that the nomination and appointment committees to the board should be mainly composed of NEDs, while audit committees should be composed of only NEDs, the majority of whom should be independent.[225] The report also suggested that

> the emphasis . . . on the control function of [NEDs] is a consequence of our remit and should not in any way detract from the primary and positive contribution which they are expected to make, as equal board members, to the leadership of the company.[226]

NEDs were thus considered not only as monitors of executive activities but also as participants in management by giving direction to corporate strategies. Despite their monitoring roles, NEDs were considered to have the same responsibilities as executives in terms of company management. Based on these suggestions, NEDs should be able to control the appointment of executives and monitor their activities. They would also be expected to be involved in managerial activities since their roles are not restricted to monitoring. This issue was discussed by Ezzamel and Watson, who stated that 'unfortunately, the Cadbury recommendation with respect to [NEDs] virtually fails at the first hurdle, for it does nothing to resolve the problem in UK law regarding the conflicting roles expected of them'.[227] Due to this suggested dual function of NEDs, they considered them to be 'wear[ing] two hats'.[228]

The issue with the suggested dual functions of NEDs is the potential impairment of their independence from executives. While the report emphasised the importance of their independence, the meaning referred to their not having any pre-existing business relationship with the company. Therefore, the suggestion proposed by the report was very likely to draw NEDs into the management of companies and potentially impair their independence from executives.

Following the Cadbury report, in order to clarify the role of NEDs, the Greenbury Committee also published a report in 1995. The committee suggested that corporate boards should establish remuneration committees to determine the remuneration packages of executives and that such committees should be solely

225 Cadbury Committee (n 2113) paras [4.11], [4.30], and [4.35]

226 Cadbury Committee (n 211) para [4.10]

227 Mahmoud Ezzamel and Robert Watson, 'Wearing Two Hats: The Conflicting Control and Management Roles of Non-Executive Directors' in Kevin Keasey, Steve Thompson, and Mike Wright (eds), *Corporate Governance: Economic, Management, and Financial Issues* (Oxford University Press 1997) 54, 68

228 Mahmoud Ezzamel and Robert Watson, 'Wearing Two Hats: The Conflicting Control and Management Roles of Non-Executive Directors' in Kevin Keasey, Steve Thompson, and Mike Wright (eds), *Corporate Governance: Economic, Management, and Financial Issues* (Oxford University Press 1997) 68

composed of independent NEDs.[229] Through this strategy, it was intended that the monitoring function of NEDs on executives could be enhanced; however, the issue of the independence of NEDs was overly neglected.

The Hampel Committee published another report in 1998. The report emphasised the importance of 'good governance' so as to ensure that the interests of stakeholders were taken into account by outlining the same issues considered by the Cadbury and Greenbury committees.[230] It stated that '[NEDs] are normally appointed to the board primarily for their contribution to the development of the company's strategy. This is clearly right. We have found general acceptance that [NEDs] should have both a strategic and a monitoring function'.[231] The report reaffirmed the dual roles of NEDs suggested in the previous reports but went further by emphasising that the strategic development of the company should be regarded as the primary role of NEDs. That said, the report neglected that where NEDs get involved in management, it may impair their independence because it will bring them closer to the company's executives.

In 1998, these three reports were collapsed into the Old Combined Code, which still shapes an appendix to the United Kingdom Listing Rules. The Code broadly mentioned the monitoring role of NEDs on executives and adopted the approach of 'comply or explain'.[232] In addition, the Code suggested that one-third of a company's board should be composed of NEDs.[233] Despite this development, 'the role of the NEDs was still apparently extended into managing a company's business', and the issue of the independence of NEDs was still left without adequate consideration.[234]

Following the major global financial crisis at the beginning of the millennium, the monitoring role of NEDs gained more attention, and the UK government appointed the Higgs Committee to illuminate the role of NEDs in corporate governance. The committee adopted a similar attitude to that of previous committees in respect of the dual role of NEDs. It noted that

> in the UK, the general legal duties owed to the company by executives and [NEDs] are the same. . . . Each has a role in ensuring the probity of the business and contributing to sustainable wealth creation by the company as a whole.[235]

The basis of this attitude was that 'there was no essential contradiction between the monitoring and strategic aspects of the role of the [NEDs]'.[236] However, in

229 Greenbury Committee (n 219) para [A1]
230 Hampel Committee (n 213)
231 Hampel Committee (n 213) para [3.8]
232 Financial Reporting Council, 'Old Combined Code on Corporate Governance' (2000)
233 Financial Reporting Council, 'Old Combined Code on Corporate Governance' (2000) para [A.3.1]
234 Richard C Nolan 'The Legal Control of Directors' Conflicts of Interests in the United Kingdom: Non-Executive Directors Following the Higgs Report' (2005) 6(2) Theoretical Inquiries in Law 413, 438
235 Higgs Committee (n 214) para [4.4]
236 Higgs Committee (n 214) para [6.2]

respect of the independence of NEDs from executives, this approach may fail. This is because while executives are responsible for formatting the strategy of companies, the duty of NEDs should be to monitor how they fulfil this responsibility. In general, 'the role of independent NEDs should be the audit of management',[237] and combining the monitoring and managing functions substantially inhibits the effective performance of NEDs in monitoring.

Based on the suggestions of the Higgs report, the New Combined Code was published in 2003. In order to emphasise the monitoring role of NEDs on executives, it was suggested that at least half of the members of boards should be composed of NEDs.[238] It was also recommended that the majority of the nomination committee,[239] the remuneration committee,[240] and the audit committee be composed of independent NEDs.[241] The Code re-emphasised the view adopted in the Old Combined Code, which was that 'all directors should bring an independent judgement to bear on issues of strategy, performance, resources, including key appointments, and standards of conduct'.[242]

Following this development, the suggestions put forward in the committees were adopted by the UK Combined Codes on Corporate Governance published in 2003, 2006, and 2008. Following these, Corporate Governance Codes were published in 2010,[243] 2012,[244] 2014,[245] and 2016, 2018, and in 2024.[246] The attitude adopted in the previous reports is still in place as it was stated that 'as part of their role as members of a unitary board, NEDs should constructively challenge and help develop proposals on strategy'.[247]

Despite the reports and codes consistently supporting the independence of the NEDs, understanding the concept of 'independence' in the context of their functions may be problematic. This issue was also raised by the Corporate Affairs Minister in 1990, and 'truly independent' NEDs were recommended.[248] However, it is difficult to state that this concept has been fully clarified. It can be seen from the statement of the Cadbury Committee that,

> We recommend that the majority of non-executives on a board should be independent of the company. This means that apart from their directors' fees

237 Nolan (n 234) 440
238 Financial Reporting Council, 'New Combined Code on Corporate Governance' (2003) para [A.3.2]
239 Financial Reporting Council, 'New Combined Code on Corporate Governance' (2003) para [A.5.1]
240 Financial Reporting Council, 'New Combined Code on Corporate Governance' (2003) para [B.2.1]
241 Financial Reporting Council, 'New Combined Code on Corporate Governance' (2003) para [C.3.1]
242 Financial Reporting Council, 'Old Combined Code on Corporate Governance' (2000)
243 The UK Corporate Governance Code (2010) (n 259)
244 The UK Corporate Governance Code (2012) (n 260)
245 The UK Corporate Governance Code (2014) (n 261)
246 Financial Reporting Council <https://www.frc.org.uk/library/standards-codes-policy/corporate-governance/uk-corporate-governance-code/> accessed 5 July 2024
247 The UK Corporate Governance Code (2024), Section 2 <https://www.frc.org.uk/library/standards-codes-policy/corporate-governance/uk-corporate-governance-code/> accessed 5 July 2024
248 Vanessa Finch, 'Company Directors: Who Cares About Skill and Care?' (1992) 55 MLR 179, 207

> and shareholdings, they should be independent of management and free from any business or other relationship which could materially interfere with the exercise of their independent judgement.[249]

The term independence in the context of the role of NEDs is considered as not having any previous business relation with the company. Based on this suggestion, for example, a former retired executive director or one who works for another organisation which supplies goods or services to the company is considered less independent.[250] Such an approach can be problematic as it only covers the narrow scope of the concept of independence because the dual role of NEDs is another issue that may cause them to be closer to executives and impair their independence.

Besides the tendency of the reports and codes to suggest that NEDs function in a dual role, there is another issue that may impair their independence from executives, which arises when NEDs are newly appointed. A NED's lack of knowledge of the company's business when reviewing the decisions of the management may cause them to have a close relationship with executives because while they familiarise themselves with the company's business, their relationship with the executives is likely to become closer, and this may arguably cause them to be less independent.[251] This contradiction is also argued by Demb and Neubauer in that,

> The dilemma is that in the process of obtaining the knowledge and understanding necessary from critical judgement, outside board members must become closer to the company, and may find themselves losing the detachment that permits an independent view.[252]

Another crucial issue that may impair the independence of NEDs is that in practice, they are appointed by the executives. In this situation, there may be a possibility that executives will appoint 'friendly "rubber stamping" [NEDs] in order to appear accountable to external parties'.[253] This issue was discussed by Stanley, who suggested that directors consider [NEDs], as '"one of us" . . . rather than independent watchdogs'.[254] Accordingly, 'there is a serious and possibly insurmountable difficulty over the need for [NEDs] to be independent'.[255]

Even assuming that there were no issues that may impair the independence of NEDs from executives and they completely fulfilled their monitoring roles,

249 Cadbury Committee (n 2113) para [4.12]

250 Charlie Weir and David Laing, 'Governance Structures, Director Independence and Corporate Performance in the UK' (2001) 13(2) European Business Review 86, 87

251 Short (n 222) 126

252 Ada Demb and Friendrich Neubauer, *The Corporate Board: Confronting the Paradox* (1st edn, Oxford University Press 1992) 100

253 Short (n 222) 125

254 Christopher Stanley, 'An Approach to the Internal Regulation of the Corporation: A Critical Analysis of the Recommendations of the Cadbury Committee' (1993) 2(1) JFR&C 48, 53

255 Short (n 222) 126

companies would still struggle to prevent executives from being involved in undesirable behaviour. This is particularly true with regard to undesirable behaviour that may increase the company's value in the short term. Where this is so, NEDs may arguably not be concerned about the potential long-term consequences of executives' behaviour as long as it increases the value of the company. This argument can be endorsed by the generally accepted tendency of shareholders to appoint NEDs when the company is not performing well financially.[256]

In short, although NEDs could potentially be a significant tool for the company to control executive directors, the ambiguity in their function and potential lack of independence from executives means that the company is unlikely to achieve this aim. Despite all the efforts of the last two decades, it is difficult to state that these proposals have provided clear guidance on the roles of NEDs within the company. Their involvement in management has always been supported, but the issue of their independence from executives has been overly neglected. Thus, it is difficult to expect NEDs to monitor executives and prevent undesirable behaviour, and, as Nolan expressed, 'as long as the role of [NEDs] remains mixed and unfocused, there is no reason to believe this will change'.[257]

2.4.4 Auditors

The fourth mechanism companies can employ to control their directors is auditors. Auditing is an examination of the financial statements of the company in an objective and fair way to ensure that they provide accurate information about the company's transactions. With respect to the issue of controlling the directors, auditing plays a crucial role as the auditory control and review of the company's accounts can provide suggestions to the board of directors.[258] Auditing is one tool that informs stakeholders about the financial status of the company so that they can effectively manage potential financial risks. Its importance was emphasised in the Cadbury report as follows:

> The annual audit is one of the cornerstones of corporate governance. The audit provides an external and objective check on the way in which the financial statements have been prepared and presented, and it is an essential part of the checks and balances required.[259]

However, what may be even more important than auditing is the accuracy of the reports because 'the question is not whether there should be an audit, but how to ensure its objectivity and effectiveness'.[260] These issues have drawn much more

256 See Section 2.4.7.4
257 Nolan (n 234) 461
258 See Stanley (n 254) 54–55
259 Cadbury Committee (n 211) para [5.1]
260 Cadbury Committee (n 211) para [5.1]

attention following major corporate failures such as Enron and WorldCom, and the rules that govern auditing under the CA06 'have been significantly tightened' in the United Kingdom to ensure that auditors act independently from the company.[261]

The first recommendations regarding auditing were put forward by the Cadbury Committee.[262] These recommendations were revised by the Smith Review in 2003.[263] Following the financial crisis in 2008, the Financial Reporting Council (FRC) appointed the working party that formed the Revised Guidance in Audit Committees by updating the Smith Report in 2008.[264] This guidance considered the concerns of companies regarding external auditors and provided guidance to audit committees. The UK Code of Corporate Governance was issued in 2010. It has since been updated in 2012, 2014, 2016, 2018, and recently in 2024, with the latest version coming into force in 2025.

Based on the suggestions of these reports and codes, there are now two organs responsible for the auditing of companies. The first group is the internal audit committee of the company. According to Code 2024, the committee is to be composed of at least three independent NEDs, with at least one member of the committee having experience in auditing and finance.[265] In addition, the Code also governs the roles and responsibilities of the audit committee, which are mainly to control the integrity of financial statements and the review of internal financial controls and their effectiveness.[266] In addition, the primary responsibilities of the committee are providing suggestions to the board regarding the appointment, reappointment, removal, and remuneration of external auditors; reviewing their performance, independence, and effectiveness; and determining the degree of non-audit services performed by external auditors.[267] Thus, the audit committee can be considered a 'bridge' between the board and the external auditors.[268]

The second group is the external auditors appointed by the board according to the provisions of the CA06.[269] The main responsibility of external auditors is to prepare a report for the company's members on the annual accounts of the company.[270] They investigate whether the records that have been kept by the company are adequate, whether the individual accounts are consistent with the accounting records, and whether the financial information provided by directors is consistent

261 Mclaughlin (n 114) 486
262 Cadbury Committee (n 211) para [4.33]–[4.38]
263 Financial Reporting Council, 'Audit Committees Combined Code Guidance' (2003)
264 Financial Reporting Council, 'Consultation on Proposed Changes to Guidance on Audit Committees (The Smith Guidance)' (2008)
265 The UK Corporate Governance Code (2024), Section 4
266 The UK Corporate Governance Code (2024), Section 4
267 The UK Corporate Governance Code (2024), Section 4
268 Bob Tricker, *Corporate Governance: Principles, Policies, and Practices* (2nd edn, Oxford University Press 2012) 187
269 S 475 obliges companies to employee auditors to control the account of companies. The rules under chapter 2, 3, and 4 of Part 16 of the Companies Act 2006 govern the appointment (ss 485–494), functions and duties (ss 495–509), removal (ss 510–526) and liability (ss 532–538) of auditors
270 S 495(1) Companies Act 2006

with these records.[271] They also provide suggestions to the audit committee on audit-related matters and control whether there is compliance with the Code. External auditors, who can be individuals or firms, are also entitled to attend the meetings of audit committees, and their performance and independence are to be reviewed by the internal audit committee. That said, the extent to which auditors are independent of the control of executives will determine whether auditors will be able to control directorial involvement in undesirable behaviour.

2.4.4.1 Independence of Auditors

The independence of an auditor can be defined whether he/she is impartial and objective when evaluating and investigating the company's financial documents. Although the performance of auditors as controllers is based on their level of independence, 'throughout the history of auditing, independence has proved to be the requirement that the auditing profession had the most difficulty in satisfying'.[272] However, recent corporate scandals and the financial crisis have again illustrated that auditors' lack of independence is a major issue that may cause significant unfortunate consequences.[273]

In this respect, there are two issues to examine. The first is whether the auditors can be completely independent while the decisions regarding their payment, remuneration, and appointments are made by directors based on the suggestion of the audit committee.[274] The issue here is whether the clients of the auditors are the directors or shareholders. The legal response to this question is that although auditors are employed to report on the company's financial situation to its shareholders, their client is the company, which is managed by the board of directors.[275] By extension, the directors can be considered as the clients of the auditors because decisions on the auditors' appointment and pay are typically made by them. This gives rise to doubts regarding how auditors can achieve effective monitoring and auditing of financial documents that are prepared by directors when they are paid and hired by the latter. In this situation, the independence of auditors may be impaired in consideration of the proverb that 'whose bread I eat, his song I sing'.[276]

The second issue is the extent to which the legal system enhances the independence of auditors. Typically, internal audit committees should monitor whether external auditors are independent. The issue is that members of the internal audit committees are also paid and employed by directors, and they may be dependent

271 Ss 496 and 498(1) Companies Act 2006

272 Joshua Ronen, 'Corporate Audits and How to Fix Them' (2010) 24(2) Journal of Economic Perspectives 189, 192

273 For example, concerns about Arthur Anderson's independence following Enron. See Ronen (n 272) 192

274 These are the decision rights provided to directors under the Companies Act 2006

275 Tricker (n 312) 480

276 Quoted in Ronen (n 272) 189

on them for several benefits.[277] In this context, it is very difficult to expect internal audit committees to be independent.[278] To maintain a great level of independence, a certain distance must be maintained between auditors and directors. Otherwise, auditors may arguably shade all grey area judgements taken by directors.

Besides the fact that auditors are hired and paid by directors, there are also two other important issues that may impair the independence of auditors. These are (i) the involvement of auditors in non-audit services and (ii) competition among them.

2.4.4.2 Non-Audit Services

In addition to providing audit services, auditors may also provide some non-audit services to companies.[279] These services may be in respect of information technology, taxation, litigation, recruitment, remuneration, valuation, actuarial services etc.[280] These functions may be beneficial for the company. The drawback is that it may lead to a closer relationship with directors, as follows:

> consulting and other services may shorten the distance between the auditor and management. Independence . . . becomes a more elusive proposition. When an audit firm performs valuations of numbers that appear in its client's financials, the mandate for independence is threatened.[281]

The involvement of auditors in such services may potentially cause them to avoid drawing directors' attention to detected problems if doing so would adversely affect their consulting fees.[282] This is because the fees for independent audit committees that meet four times a year and do not involve non-audit services may be

277 Ronen (n 272) 198

278 Especially when it is considered that the committees are comprised of NEDs whose independence is still with serious drawbacks. See Section 2.4.3

279 See Vivien Beattie and Stella Fearnley, 'Auditor Independence and Non-Audit Services: A Literature Review' (2002) <http://www.icjce.es/images/pdfs/TECNICA/C06%20-%20Normativa%20UK/C.06.040%20-%20Estudios%20y%20otros/Auditor%20Independence%20and%20Non-audit%20Services%20-%20A%20Literature%20Review.pdf> accessed 10 June 2024

280 Vivien Beattie and Stella Fearnley, 'Auditor Independence and Non-Audit Services: A Literature Review' (2002) 19 <http://www.icjce.es/images/pdfs/TECNICA/C06%20-%20Normativa%20UK/C.06.040%20-%20Estudios%20y%20otros/Auditor%20Independence%20and%20Non-audit%20Services%20-%20A%20Literature%20Review.pdf> accessed 10 June 2024

281 Arthur Levitt, 'Renewing the Covenant with Investors' (Speech by Chairman of US Securities and Exchange Commission, 10 May 2010) <https://www.sec.gov/news/speech/spch370.htm> accessed 1 May 2024

282 For example, in the Enron scandal, Arthur Anderson was management consultant of the company besides its auditing role. See James A Hall, *Accounting Information Systems* (6th edn, Cengage Learning 2008) 126. See also Chaudhry Ghafran and Noel O'Sullivan, 'The Governance Role of Audit Committees: Reviewing a Decade of Evidence' (2013) 15 International Journal of Management Reviews 381, 389

low[283] when compared to what they may earn from non-audit services. A major risk arises when the possible amount of non-audit fees is more than the audit fee because, in this scenario, auditors are likely to neglect their main responsibility of auditing and concentrate on non-audit services. Consequently, the increased involvement of auditors in management would provide them with higher fees, but their level of independence would be considerably less.

2.4.4.3 Competition Among Auditors

The final issue is the competition among auditors to obtain employment from companies.[284] Since directors are empowered by the legal system to hire or dismiss them, auditors may neglect to disclose any omissions in the financial documents that are prepared by directors. This is because the opposite scenario may potentially cause tension between auditors and directors and decrease the possibility that the latter would rehire the former for the next financial year. According to Section 489(2) of the CA06, the decision to appoint auditors must occur annually. Thus, there is a risk that auditors may not be employed by the same company the following year if the directors are unhappy with their performance. This makes auditors dependent on the directors and 'may create a tension between good auditing practice and satisfying the requirements of the company'.[285]

These issues cast serious doubts with respect to the independence of auditors from directors and the quality of auditing they provide for the company. For this reason, it can be argued that although 'auditors are supposed to be watchdogs, but in the last decade or so, they sometimes looked like lapdogs'.[286] Besides these issues that impair the independence of auditors, another matter that may limit the ability of the company to control directors through this mechanism is the tension between the role of auditors and the nature of the particular undesirable behaviour. Since undesirable behaviour is obviously beneficial to the company in the short term, auditors may not pay adequate attention to the potential negative consequences of such behaviour in the long term as long as the financial documents illustrate no unusual fall.

2.4.5 Market Control

The market is one external control mechanism which fills the control gap that arises from the separation of control and ownership. Shareholders who are unhappy with the performance of directors can accept a takeover bid from an external company to discipline or remove them from management. The theory of market control has

283 Lawrence J Abbott, Susan Parker, Gary F Peters, and K Raghunandan, 'An Empirical Investigation of Audit Fees, Nonaudit Fees and Audit Committees' (2003) 20 Contemporary Accounting 215, 226

284 Stanley (n 254) 55

285 Stanley (n 254) 55

286 Ronen (n 272) 189

been identified and articulated by Manne, and it is recognised as a tool for dispersed shareholders to ensure the accountability of management through the threat of a possible takeover.[287] Besides this function, market control can also make a significant constraining impact on directors since the possibility of removal from the management of the company by a potential bidder can be a strong disciplinary threat.

The operation of market control, its regulatory basis, and its disciplining effect on directors have been analysed in the literature.[288] And there are different thoughts about its effect on disciplining directors. Bradley opined that 'the idea that the market for corporate control functions as a threat to the management of companies and therefore benefits shareholders, and society, by ensuring that management acts efficiently and maximises profits is attractive'.[289] In line with Bradley, Rappaport also noted that 'it is impossible to overstate how deeply the market for corporate control has changed the attitudes and practices of U.S. managers'.[290] But contrary to these views, Stokes argued that the perception that the market would act to constrain company managers from misusing their power is flawed.[291]

In order for a potential takeover to achieve the aim of constraining the directors of companies, 'existing managers must be spurred by fear to behave themselves'.[292] To determine whether the law achieves this purpose, this section will examine the rules which regulate takeover bids for market control mechanisms under common law and statute, and their effectiveness in constraining directors in respect of their involvement in undesirable behaviour.

2.4.5.1 The Common Law Approach to Market Control

Despite the fact that shareholders are empowered by the legal system to discipline directors through takeover bids, there may be some limitations prior to this strategy in achieving the desired disciplining impact on directors. The first and main limitation arises when the power of directors to resist such bids is unrestricted. To prevent directors from using resistance tactics, the only device provided to the target company in common law is to bring litigation against them for breaching fiduciary

287 Henry G Manne, 'Mergers and the Market for Corporate Control' (1965) 73(2) The Journal of Political Economy 110

288 For example, Manne (n 287); Mary Stokes, 'Company Law and Legal Theory' in William Twining (ed.), *Legal Theory and Common Law* (Blackwell 1986) 155, 174–175; Alfred Rappaport, 'The Staying Power of the Public Corporation' (1990) 68(1) Harvard Business Review 96, 100; Caroline Bradley, 'Corporate Control: Markets and Rules' (1990) 53(2) MLR 170

289 Bradley (n 288) 172

290 Rappaport (n 288) 100

291 Stokes discussed that this idea is flawed in two ways. The first is that it is not empirically demonstrated. The second is that it 'overlooks the fact that the very notion that the market is capable of legitimating power is widely acknowledged as being open to serious doubt today'. See Stokes (n 288) 174–175

292 Gerald E Frug, 'The Ideology of Bureaucracy in American Law' (1984) 97 Harvard Law Review 1276, 1362

duties. This involves a concern as to how the courts apply the duty owed by directors under Section 171(b) of CA06, as this duty obliges directors to 'only exercise powers for the purpose for which they are conferred'.[293] However, despite this method being completely compatible with the current managerial system of company law, it is unlikely to satisfy investors since it would cause some 'considerable uncertainty and delay', which would make the success of the takeover less likely.[294]

This limitation can be seen in the cases of *Hogg* v. *Cramphorn Ltd*[295] and *Howard Smith Ltd v. Ampol Petroleum Ltd.*[296] In *Hogg*, Cramphorn received a takeover bid from Baxter. In order to defeat the bid, the directors issued shares to the employees, giving them the right to vote as trustees who were chosen by the directors. The trustees voted in favour of the directors who were thus enabled to retain control of the company. Despite the fact that forming a trust with the employees was considered by the parties as not using their powers for improper purposes, the trust would not have been established with the employees if Baxter had not placed an offer. It was clear that the directors' main purpose in establishing the trust was to remain in control of the company by defeating Baxter and preventing the takeover.[297] However, Buckley J. held that the directors acted in good faith and stated,

> I am also satisfied that the directors and the trustees of the trust deed genuinely considered that to give the staff through the trustees a sizeable, though indirect, voice in the affairs of the company would benefit both the staff and the company.[298]

Despite the fact that the court considered the subjective and objective tests in determining whether the directors acted in good faith for proper purposes, the outcome of the case casts some doubts about the disciplining power of market control. This is because the directors apparently used their position to manipulate the voting, the takeover failed, and they remained in the company. This approach is likely to still be in place because, as Johnston stated, 'since Hogg, the common law has had little opportunity to refine its treatment of takeover defences'.[299]

In addition, in *Howard Smith Ltd*, two different takeover bids were made on the company by two different companies. The board was in favour of one of them, and they issued shares to it to reduce the control of the controlling shareholders. The board argued that the aim of this action was to run the company properly by raising capital, but this argument was rejected, and the directors were found liable

293 S 171(b) Companies Act 2006

294 Andrew Johnston, 'Takeover Regulation: Historical and Theoretical Perspectives on the City Code' (2007) 66(2) CLJ 422, 436

295 [1967] Ch. 254, [1966] 3 All E.R. 420

296 [1974] A.C. 821, P.C., [1974] 1 All E.R. 1126

297 *Hogg v. Cramphorn Ltd* [266]–[267]

298 *Hogg v. Cramphorn Ltd* [265]

299 Johnston (n 294) 441. Except the case of *Howard Smith*, which arose from an appeal to the Privy Council from the Supreme Court of New South Wales

for using their fiduciary authority for improper purposes.[300] The Privy Council held that 'it must be unconstitutional for directors to use their fiduciary powers over the shares in the company purely for the purpose of destroying an existing majority, or creating a new majority which did not previously exist'.[301]

In this case, based on the substantial purpose test that was introduced by Lord Wilberforce,[302] the court more heavily relied on the objective test of good faith and considered the directors' duty of exercising power for proper purposes. That said, it is still significant that the word 'purely' was used in the dictum of the court.[303] A fact that clearly illustrates that directors will not be considered to be in breach of fiduciary duty if they 'incidentally affect the balance of voting power in the general meeting'.[304] The answer to the question of whether directors have used their power for a proper purpose will be different depending on how the courts interpret the facts of a particular case. This demonstrates 'factual complexity', which means it is not possible to 'define in advance exact limits beyond which directors must not pass'.[305] Such uncertainty casts some doubt on whether shareholders will be able to fully discipline company directors through market control.

2.4.5.2 The Approach of the Takeover Code

The inability of common law to establish a system that ensures managerial accountability in the takeover process and the lack of clarity persisting in instituting litigation against directors led to the emergence of the City Code on Takeovers and Mergers. This consists of rules to regulate the takeover process for market control. The Code established the Takeover Panel, which is a self-regulatory organisation without a formal legal basis, but its function and the rules of the Code have been given a statutory footing in the CA06 following the implementation of the Takeovers Directive (2004/25/EC). The Panel is equipped with significant powers and responsibilities under Sections 942–946 of the CA06 to curtail directors' defensive measures. Despite the fact that the Code has brought a new approach to market control, it appears to 'suffer' from some limitations that may reduce its disciplinary impact on directors.

300 *Howard Smith Ltd v. Ampol Petroleum Ltd* (n 340) [821]–[822]
301 *Howard Smith Ltd v. Ampol Petroleum Ltd* (n 340) [837]
302 Lord Wilberforce stated that; 'it is necessary to start with a consideration of the power whose exercise is in question. . . . Having ascertained, on a fair view, the nature of this power, and having defined as can best be done in the light of modern conditions the, or some, limits within which it may be exercised, it is then necessary for the court, if a particular exercise of it is challenged, to examine the substantial purpose for which it was exercised, and to reach a conclusion whether that purpose was proper or not. In doing so it will necessarily give credit to the bona fide opinion of the directors, if such is found to exist, and will respect their judgment as to matters of management; having done this, the ultimate conclusion has to be as to the side of a fairly broad line on which the case falls'. See *Howard Smith Ltd v. Ampol Petroleum Ltd* (n 340) [835]
303 Johnston (n 294) 439
304 Johnston (n 294) 440
305 Johnston (n 294) 439

2.4.5.2.1 DIRECTORS' DEFENSIVE TACTICS

As it is a major issue in common law, the first issue with the Code concerns directors' 'defensive tactics'.[306] Bradley classified these tactics into 'general defensive tactics and specific defensive tactics'.[307] The former are strategies that directors employ before specific bidders are identified, while the latter are implemented against specific bidders. Rule 21.1(b) of the Code prevents directors from employing such tactics[308] before, during, and after a takeover bid; however, the level of compliance with these provisions is still unclear. This is because although many of the provisions of the Code that regulate the process of takeover are uncontroversial, the provisions that regulate defensive tactics of management are 'far more controversial'.[309] They are 'so riddled with occasions' when the outcome of the takeover bid can be influenced by directors if they are aware that the aim of the takeover is to discipline them or remove them from the company's management.[310] Therefore, the issue with the approach of common law that impairs the ability of shareholders to prevent directors from employing defensive tactics is also a problem with the Takeover Code.

2.4.5.2.2 THE MATTER OF COST

The second issue is the matter of cost that a bidding company may bear. A market control mechanism can be considered as a cost-effective mechanism by shareholders for disciplining directors. However, the cost is an important issue which may discourage the bidding company from entering into the transaction, as the takeover will be less attractive where the transaction cost is high.

The first issue that may increase the cost of a takeover is the defensive tactics of directors in the target company. Overcoming the barriers that the directors may put in place will potentially consume more time and cost. The requirement of a 'mandatory offer' is another issue that may increase the cost to the bidder as the Code requires general offers to be made by bidding companies to shareholders of the target company.[311] The precise policy behind this rule is to require the company to announce the offer immediately, and there is no doubt that the rule aims to protect the interest of shareholders by giving them an opportunity to consider competitive offers. The issue is that this strategy may, in turn, discourage potential bidders

306 Caroline Bradley, 'Corporate Control: Markets and Rules' (1990) 53(2) MLR 170, 173
307 Caroline Bradley, 'Corporate Control: Markets and Rules' (1990) 53(2) MLR 173
308 The behaviour that can be considered under these tactics are listed under the Code as '(i) issue any shares or transfer or sell, or agree to transfer or sell, any shares out of treasury; (ii) issue or grant options in respect of any unissued shares; (iii) create or issue, or permit the creation or issue of, any securities carrying rights of conversion into or subscription for shares; (iv) sell, dispose of or acquire, or agree to sell, dispose of or acquire, assets of a material amount; or (v) enter into contracts otherwise than in the ordinary course of business'
309 Johnston (n 294) 422
310 Stokes (n 288) 175
311 Rule 9, City Code on Take-over and Mergers

from entering into the takeover because competition among the bidders potentially increases the cost of the takeover and may cause its success to be less likely.

2.4.5.2.3 TAKEOVERS FOR PURPOSES REMOVED FROM THE NEED TO DISCIPLINE DIRECTORS

The third issue is based on third parties disciplining directors. In this regard, Smith observed that,

> [I]n the context of controlling the conduct of directors, the market is a means of control external to the company, and unlike, for example, shareholder regulation of corporate activity is beyond the influence of the company or its shareholders. The fact that the control exercised by the free market is external to the company is one of its principal attractions.[312]

The issue here is that a takeover company may have different purposes that have no bearing on disciplining directors or dismissing the management. For instance, it may be informed by the need to increase the size of the company, improve its growth in the short term, or lower its tax duty by benefitting from the target company's unused investment tax credits.[313] Where this is so, the disciplining function of market control on directors is unlikely to occur since the bidding company, in this case, is not motivated to enter into a takeover 'arena' for such a purpose.[314]

2.4.5.2.4 PROTECTING THE INTERESTS OF SHAREHOLDERS

Rule 21.1.(a) of the Code states that

> the board must not, without the approval of the shareholders in general meeting, take any action which may result in any offer or bona fide possible offer being frustrated or in shareholders being denied the opportunity to decide on its merits.

Since target shareholders are authorised to approve the takeover,[315] protecting their interests can be considered as its primary purpose. This objective can be seen from the requirement of 'mandatory offers' under Rule 9 of the Code, which obliges takeover companies to offer a bid to target shareholders so that they

312 Clare M Smith, *Controlling the Conduct of Company Directors* (Master Thesis, Durham University 1996) 3
313 Frug (n 292) 1362
314 See the study undertaken by Fransk and Mayer on lack of disciplining role of hostile takeovers. Julian Fransk and Colin Mayer, 'Hostile Takeovers and the Correction of Managerial Failure' (1996) 40 JFE 163
315 See Louise Gullifer and Jennifer Payne, *Corporate Finance Law: Principles and Policy* (2nd edn, Hart Publishing 2015) 696

determine the best offer to protect their interests. According to empirical studies, shareholders in target companies make significant gains from takeovers, although it remains unclear whether takeovers result in broad wealth maximisation for shareholders.[316] This again casts serious doubt on whether takeovers actually protect the interests of other non-shareholder stakeholders.

These considerations are exacerbated when it is considered that the mechanism of market control is usually implemented by shareholders who are dissatisfied with the financial performance of the company. In effect, the strategy is used to 'frighten' directors so that they work harder to increase the profit for their interests.[317] Therefore, to ward off any possible threat of takeovers, directors may seek to increase the short-term profits at the expense of the long term.[318] This causes the 'danger of short-terminism', which is one of the main characteristics of directors' undesirable behaviours and exposes the company to serious corporate risks in the long term.

To conclude this section, despite the fact that market mechanisms can be used to discipline or remove non-performing directors, the truth remains that they are not without serious drawbacks if it is to be used to protect the long-term interests of the company's stakeholders. They may even spur directors to make decisions that are geared towards promoting the short-term interests of shareholders at the expense of other non-shareholder stakeholders.

2.4.6 Disclosure Requirements

Another control mechanism that may deter directors from undesirable behaviour is disclosure requirements. Directors are required to prepare financial and narrative reports to disclose certain information regarding the financial status of the company and the transactions they are involved in on behalf of the company. While financial reporting is for disclosing the financial activities carried out within the company and the financial status of the company through producing financial statements, narrative reporting provides non-financial information about the overall business of the company, its performance and position in the market, and the transactions involved. Since the latter type of report is considered the directors' commentary on the position of the company, they are defined as narrative reports.

There are two types of narrative reports that directors are required to produce, and these are the directors' report and the business review regulated by the CA06 and the directors' report and the strategic report regulated by the CA06 (Strategic Report and Directors' Report) Regulations 2013. Despite the fact that the business review has been replaced by the strategic report, it may still be relevant. Therefore, reporting requirements under these reports, the rigidity of the requirements of

316 Louise Gullifer and Jennifer Payne, *Corporate Finance Law: Principles and Policy* (2nd edn, Hart Publishing 2015) 678

317 Frug (n 292) 1361

318 Pieter W Moerland, 'Alternative Disciplinary Mechanisms in Different Corporate Systems' (1995) 26 Journal of Economic Behavior and Organization 17, 29

disclosure, and whether the directors can be deterred from undesirable behaviour through this mechanism will be examined.

2.4.6.1 The Directors' Report and the Business Review

Before the introduction of the CA06, companies[319] were required to prepare irectors' reports and business reviews under Section 234 of the CA85; however, the format and content of the reports were not specified. In 2000, the CLRSG suggested that listed companies should prepare a voluntary OFR according to the Reporting Statement of best practice principles published by the Accounting Standards Board (ASB). In March 2005, based on this recommendation, OFR and Directors' Report Regulations were created, and the provisions under the CA85 were updated but never enacted.[320]

As a part of the implementation of the Modernisation Directive,[321] this regulation[322] was abolished by the then Chancellor Gordon Brown,[323] and the requirements of the report and disclosure were regulated under Sections 415–419 of Chapter 5 of the CA06. According to these provisions, companies were required to prepare a directors' report to review their activities during the financial year.[324] Particularly, the report must include the names of the directors in management at any time during the financial year, the company's principal activities,[325] a business review[326] which provides a fair review of the company's business, a statement of the principal risks, and any uncertainties facing the company.[327]

The business review disclosed a comprehensive analysis of the performance and development of the company during the financial year and its position in the market at the end of the year.[328] Companies were also required to include an analysis of key performance indicators (KPIs), which are the main factors that affect the performance, development, and position of the company and enhance members' understanding of the performance and development of the company.[329]

In addition, Section 417(5) required quoted companies to provide a more detailed business review. This review should include the main factors that are likely to affect the future development, performance, and position of the company's business as well as information about the company's employees, social and community

319 Except small companies
320 See Section 2.2
321 Directive (2003/51/EC)
322 The Companies Act 1985 (Operating and Financial Review and Directors' Report etc.) Regulations 2005
323 Olaojo Aiyegbayo and Charlotte Villiers, 'The Enhanced Business Review: Has It Made Corporate Governance More Effective?' (2011) 7 Journal of Business Review 699, 699–700
324 S 415 Companies Act 2006
325 S 416(1), Companies Act 2006
326 S 417 Companies Act 2006
327 S 417(3) Companies Act 2006
328 S 417(4) Companies Act 2006
329 S 417(6) Companies Act 2006

issues, persons with whom the company has contractual relationships, and policies adopted by the company.[330]

Section 417(2) stated that the purpose of the business review was to inform the company's members to help them evaluate the directors' performances in fulfilling their duty of promoting the success of the company under Section 172.[331] The role of the business review assigned by the CA06 was that '[Section] 417 reflect[ed] the government's intention that the restated duty in Section 172 should bring about a cultural change in how companies perceive their responsibilities rather than generate pointless bureaucratic procedures restricting decision-making'.[332] Therefore, the directors' duty to have regard for the long-term consequences of their decisions was emphasised.[333]

As a result of the high demand from regulatory bodies and the introduction of the directors' report and business review, voluntary disclosure of non-financial information by companies increased. Aiyegbayo and Villiers observed that '[S]ection 417, led to longer annual reports',[334] which on average comprise 149 pages with '60% of these documents dedicated to narrative, contextual and nonfinancial information'.[335] This fitted the purpose of enacting the section, but according to the report published by Yeldar, companies were still tending to adopt a tick box approach to narrative reporting.[336] Phillips agreed with Yeldar that 'a box-ticking culture . . . degraded some annual reports to the point where they are legally compliant, but, as a communication document, dreadful'.[337] Moreover, according to a study undertaken by the Virtuous Circle, despite business reviews requiring companies to make more detailed disclosures, only one of the companies did so.[338] This may be because companies were required to report detailed information to 'the extent that they consider [was] necessary for an understanding of the development, performance or position of the company's business'.[339] The link between the information identified for the report and the duty to promote the success of the company under Section 172 was to be considered by directors

330 S 417(5) Companies Act 2006
331 S 417(2) Companies Act 2006
332 Brenda Hannigan, *Company Law* (3rd edn, Oxford University Press 2012) 197–198
333 Virtuous Circle, 'Preparedness for New Corporate Reporting Requirements' (2006) 12 <http://www.thevirtuouscircle.co.uk/NEWS_27TH-NOV.html> accessed 25 May 2024
334 Aiyegbayo and Villiers (n 323) 708
335 See Price Water House Coopers (PwC), 'Corporate Reporting – A Time for Reflection: A Survey of the Fortune Global 500 Companies' Narrative Reporting' (April 2007) 7 <https://www.pwc.com/gx/en/corporate-reporting-services/pdf/reflection.pdf> accessed 28 March 2024
336 Radley Yeldar, 'Narrative Reporting Content in the FTSE 100 – How Does It Stack Up?' (September 2006). Refer to Aiyegbayo and Villiers (n 323) 708
337 David Phillips, 'PwC Partner Speaks Out Over 'Dreadful' Annual Reports' (2009) <http://www.accountancyage.com/aa/news/1745982/pwc-partner-speaks-dreadful-annual-reports> accessed 25 May 2024
338 Virtuous Circle (n 334)
339 Charlotte Villiers, 'Directors' Duties and the Company's Internal Structures Under the UK Companies Act 2006: Obstacles for Sustainable Development' (2011) 8 ICCLJ 47, 59

who determined whether the information needed to be disclosed. None of the particular matters stated under Section 417(5) must be covered in the review, and the section did not oblige directors to explain as to why these matters were not included.[340] This approach was also supported by the Minister in Parliament regarding the requirement of providing information about the suppliers, and it was stated that information about 'major suppliers and key customers', who might significantly affect the performance and development of the company's business, should be included in the review and this judgement was left to the directors' discretion.[341] This could be considered as protection for those who are linked to the company[342] and for the benefit of the company itself; however, it also gave considerable flexibility to directors about what information to disclose. Thus, Section 417(5) was 'vague on the points it identifies for coverage and what is to be included [was] left very open'.[343]

In addition, according to the review published by the FRC to determine how well companies disclosed the required information regarding their relationships, 12% of companies clearly did not address these requirements and it was not clear that 52% of them did so specifically. Clear explanations were provided by only 8% of the companies.[344] This might be because 'the [CA06] specifically mention[ed] employee and environmental non-financial KPIs, [and] many companies [were] choosing peripheral disclosures of KPIs in these areas over the more important key drivers of their business'.[345] For example, although using refillable glass bottles in meetings is good practice, this is not such an important detail that it can be considered a 'decision changing piece of information'.[346] Accordingly, despite the belief that information that may affect the interests of stakeholders would be automatically reported, 'the business review [did] not appear to be serving' this intended purpose.[347] In short, although reporting requirements increased the amount of information provided by directors, the lack

340 Charlotte Villiers, 'Directors' Duties and the Company's Internal Structures Under the UK Companies Act 2006: Obstacles for Sustainable Development' (2011) 8 ICCLJ 59

341 Simon Howley and Peter Bateman, 'Companies Act 2006: An Overview: Part 2' (2007) 11 Co. L.N. 1, 2

342 Simon Howley and Peter Bateman, 'Companies Act 2006: An Overview: Part 2' (2007) 11 Co. L.N. 2

343 Aiyegbayo and Villiers (n 323) 707

344 Financial Reporting Council, 'Rising to the Challenge' (2009) 8 <https://www.frc.org.uk/Our-Work/Publications/ASB/Rising-to-the-Challenge/Rising-to-the-challenge.aspx> accessed 30 May 2024

345 Financial Reporting Council, 'Rising to the Challenge' (2009) 8 <https://www.frc.org.uk/Our-Work/Publications/ASB/Rising-to-the-Challenge/Rising-to-the-challenge.aspx> accessed 30 May 2024

346 Financial Reporting Council, 'Rising to the Challenge' (2009) 11 <https://www.frc.org.uk/Our-Work/Publications/ASB/Rising-to-the-Challenge/Rising-to-the-challenge.aspx> accessed 30 May 2024

347 Adrian Henriques, 'The Reporting of Non-Financial Information in Annual Reports by the FTSE100' (2010) 9 <http://www.henriques.info/downloads/Reporting%20of%20Non-Financial%20Information%20FINAL.pdf> accessed 29 May 2024

of quality was still an issue[348] because of the fact that 'longer reports do not guarantee better quality'.[349]

According to reports on the state of UK narrative reporting from a number of agencies, firms, and regulators, 'the drive by most . . . companies to comply with existing regulations [was] producing stale and incoherent reports which [were] frustrating both regulators and stakeholders and possibly also leading to new forms of creative compliance'.[350] Aiyegbayo and Villiers concluded that 'business review legislation [was not] as effective as the regulators had hoped' since reporting requirements did not provide any significant improvement in practice.[351] Therefore, in 2009, the discussion paper published by the FRC suggested that the reporting requirements were more complex and less relevant in the United Kingdom, and this led to the introduction of the Strategic Report.

2.4.6.2 The Directors' Report and the Strategic Report

In 2013, the CA06 (Strategic Report and Directors' Report) Regulations 2013, as secondary legislation, was enacted and a number of amendments were proposed in respect of the requirements of corporate reporting. The main aim of these regulations is to 'simplify and strengthen companies' non-financial reports'[352] by requiring directors to prepare a 'strategic report' which replaces the business review. Regulation 3 inserted the rules regulating the preparation of the strategic report in a new chapter, Chapter 4A, into Part 15 of the CA06.[353] Distinct from the business review, the strategic report must be prepared separately from the directors' report, with the aim of reducing the 'red tape' on corporate governance.

Despite this development, the content has remained broadly similar.[354] As with the business review, Section 414C(1) clearly illustrates the intention of the government in introducing the strategic report, initiating a radical departure from the previous law to change the culture of how responsibilities are perceived by companies.[355] However, additional reporting requirements have been added.[356] The key

348 See Aiyegbayo and Villiers (n 323) 708–709

349 Charlotte Villiers, 'A Global Framework for Management Commentary Disclosure?' (2009) 60 Northern Ireland Legal Quarterly 63, 83

350 See Aiyegbayo and Villiers (n 323) 708–709

351 Aiyegbayo and Villiers (n 323) 723

352 Sweet & Maxwell and Its Contributors, 'Key Company Reporting Reforms Come into Force' (2013) 34(9) Comp Law 281

353 Under this chapter, directors' duty to prepare strategic report (414A), small companies' exemption (414B), contents (414C), and approval and signing of strategic report (414D) have been regulated

354 The main aim of assessing as to how directors have performed their duty to promote the success of company under the Companies Act 2006, s 172 and the contents of report have remained same. See Glynis D Morris, 'Good Corporate Reporting' (2014) 25(4) Tolley's Practical Audit & Accounting 45

355 Hannigan (n 332) 226–227

356 PwC, *PwC Manual of Accounting Narrative Reporting 2014* (1st edn, Bloomsbury 2013). See also Glynis D Morris, 'Good Corporate Reporting' (2014) 25(4) Tolley's Practical Audit & Accounting 45

changes are that the quoted companies are now required to report their policies on issues of human rights,[357] include the description of the company's strategy[358] and business model[359] (already suggested under the Corporate Governance Code), and include a gender breakdown of the board.[360] Directors are also required to prepare a full strategic report with supplementary material for shareholders.[361]

On the other hand, some of the reporting requirements under the CA06 have been removed.[362] For example, the requirements of disclosure of information in the strategic reports to auditors have been abolished from the regulations;[363] however, this requirement under the directors' report is still in place under Section 418 of the CA06. In addition, two provisions have been removed: the provision of 417(5)(c), which requires the company to include information about the persons with whom the company is in a relationship, and the provision of 417(11), which is an exception to the disclosure of information about the persons.[364] Whereas the requirement to disclose the principal actions of the company in the directors' reports under Sections 416(1)(b) and 416(2) has been removed, the requirement to obtain the board's approval of the directors' report and strategic report, and the signature of a director or secretary, has not been amended.[365] In short, 'the purpose and required content of the strategic report does not differ significantly from that of the business review which it replaces'.[366] This casts some doubts about the difference that the strategic report would make on effective disclosure practices.

2.4.6.3 Deterrent Effect of Disclosure Requirements

Following the explanation of disclosure requirements, this section examines to what extent the reports and reviews that directors are required to produce can serve to deter them from undesirable behaviour. Certain limitations of disclosure requirements may make this less likely. The first and main problematic issue is that directors review their own performance, determine what type of information they should report, and decide how to present this information to shareholders and investors. In this light, the disclosure requirements can be considered flexible and voluntary, and the regulations lack guidance regarding the extent of information

357 The Companies Act 2006 (Strategic Report and Directors' Report) Regulations 2013, s 414C 7(b)
358 The Companies Act 2006 (Strategic Report and Directors' Report) Regulations 2013, S 414C 8(a)
359 The Companies Act 2006 (Strategic Report and Directors' Report) Regulations 2013, S 414C 8(b)
360 The Companies Act 2006 (Strategic Report and Directors' Report) Regulations 2013, S 414C 8(c)
361 Rosie Graham, 'Revised Narrative Reporting Regs' (2013) 37(7) CSR 49
362 Ben Macdonald, 'Changes to Narrative Reporting' (2012) 36(15) CSR 118
363 Graham (n 361) 50
364 The reason behind this is that the respondents to consultations thought that consideration of principal risks covers this area. See Macdonald (n 408) 118–119
365 Companies Act 2006 (Strategic Report and Directors' Report) Regulations 2013 (n 403), ss 414D(1) and 419(1)
366 Sarah Hawes, 'Guidance on the Strategic Report' (2013) 37(12) CSR 89, 90

that directors are required to provide.[367] Broad and vague provisions have led to the absence of specific practice and a lack of comparability between reports.[368]

This issue arises due to the principle-based approach adopted in the United Kingdom,[369] which may be problematic in terms of controlling the directors' behaviour. Because the 'principle-based approach requires effective disclosure practices',[370] it 'relies on and reinforces the image of the self-observing, responsible organization'.[371] This provides a good amount of flexibility to companies and, consequently, directors in respect of what to disclose. Despite certain guidance being provided, the observation and interpretation of the affairs of the company and determining what type of information must be disclosed is left to the directors' discretion.

Besides the issue of flexibility, another drawback of the disclosure requirements in terms of protecting the long-term interests of the stakeholders is that the reports typically provide information regarding the performance of the company and the potential risks to investors and shareholders. This consideration has been emphasised in different platforms. For example, Aiyegbayo and Villiers considered it a tool that shareholders require to evaluate the performance of companies.[372] Villiers additionally argued that Sections 172 and 417 of the CA06 both 'highlight the continued predominance of company shareholders as the main interest group to be considered by directors'.[373] In addition, in respect of Regulations 2013, Melanie McLaren, Executive Director of Codes & Standards in the FRC, stated that 'the proposed guidance will act as a catalyst for companies to publish more relevant narrative reports, facilitating communication and engagement with investors'.[374]

Accordingly, the approach adopted by reporting requirements places shareholders and investors in a position to challenge the actions of directors. This can be a tool for the company to control its directors in respect of their possible involvement in undesirable behaviour; however, this depends on the attitude of shareholders and investors because they may be interested in short-term gains, which causes them to disregard the risks to which the company can be exposed in the long term. Thus, placing the interests of investors and shareholders as a priority aim of the reporting requirements does not guarantee the protection of the interests of all other non-shareholder stakeholders.

The last concern about the preventative measure of disclosure requirements on directors is that disclosure through directors' reports is generally made *ex post.*

367 Villiers (n 349) 80
368 Villiers (n 349) 80
369 Villiers (n 349) 72
370 Villiers (n 349) 75
371 Julia Black, 'Forms and Paradoxes of Principles Based Regulation' (2008) 9 <http://eprints.lse.ac.uk/23103/1/WPS2008-13.pdf> accessed 10 May 2024
372 Aiyegbayo and Villiers (n 323) 723
373 Villiers (n 349) 62
374 Financial Reporting Council, 'FRC Consults on Strategic Report Guidance' (2013) <https://www.frc.org.uk/News-and-Events/FRC-Press/Press/2013/August/FRC-consults-on-strategic-report-guidance.aspx> accessed 3 May 2024

Therefore, even assuming that disclosure requirements were strictly implemented, there would still be the possibility that directors would be involved in undesirable behaviour because shareholders or investors would still be unable to control directors' behaviour at the time that they are involved in the conduct, as the reports are presented to them at the end of the financial year.

2.4.7 The Code of Corporate Governance

Another mechanism that companies can employ to control directors is to hold them accountable under the rules that were first introduced by the UK Corporate Governance Code in April 2016. The main purpose of enacting the Code was to maintain 'good corporate governance' by placing certain restrictions on directors' decision-making powers. In this section, the effectiveness of the Code in deterring them from engaging in undesirable behaviour will be examined.

2.4.7.1 The Comply or Explain Approach

The most important feature of the Code is its 'comply or explain' approach. Introduced into the UK corporate system more than 20 years ago, it requires companies to either comply with the Code or to justify why they do not.[375] As Keay explained, 'compliance with [the Code] is not mandatory, but what is compulsory is disclosing non-compliance'.[376] Nolan also described the Code as it 'does not lock practice into a particular path in anything like the same firm way as mandatory statute law'.[377]

Legislative restructuring was not considered while the Code was being prepared; rather, it was introduced as a main supplementary mechanism.[378] The main logic behind this approach is to reject the attitude of 'one size fits all' as the different listed companies have different structures. As stated by the FRC, 'the provisions describe one route by which the principles might be met, but not the only route'.[379] Comply and explain requirements can arguably lead to more transparent corporate governance practices as companies need to publicly justify why they depart from the Code.[380] However, because the Code gives excessive flexibility to directors to comply with its provisions, this factor may hinder its provisions from preventing bad corporate governance practices. In order to determine the Code's effect on preventing directors from engaging in undesirable behaviour, the degree of compliance with its provisions, the nature of explanations that companies give for non-compliance, and the assessment of compliance and non-compliance will be examined.

375 Davies (n 221) 197

376 Andrew Keay, 'Comply or Explain in Corporate Governance Codes: In Need of Greater Regulatory Oversight?' (2014) 34(2) LS 279, 281

377 Nolan (n 234) 454

378 See Section 2.4.3. The issue was considered as too much of a 'hot potato'

379 2009 Review of the Combined Code: Final Report (n 30) para [2.8]

380 Paul Coombes and Simon Chiu-Yin Wong, 'Why Codes of Corporate Governance Work' [2004] The McKinsey Quarterly 48, 51

2.4.7.2 Degree of Compliance With the Code

Evaluating whether the approach of the Code works effectively is a difficult task. There is little public information on whether companies actually comply with its provisions.[381] According to Thornton, 50% of companies have complied with the Code.[382] On their part, Seidl, Sanderson, and Roberts examined 129 listed companies and endorsed this outcome.[383] These studies, however, were based on the assessment of companies, and there is a substantial difference between the percentage of the companies that consider themselves as complying with the Code (47%) and the percentage of companies that actually complied (34%) based on the findings of the Pensions Investment Research Consultants Ltd (PIRC).[384] This is because compliance is a subjective test that is assessed by directors. In addition, Arcot, Bruno, and Grimaud note that almost one in five examples of non-compliance (17%) during the period of 1998–2004 were not explained.[385] The effect is that compliance with the provisions of the Code is arguably low.

2.4.7.3 Nature of Explanations of Non-Compliance

The assessment of the adequacy of the explanations provided by companies is also a crucial point to examine, and the question that arises is 'how non-compliance is monitored and excused'.[386] According to a study undertaken by Arcot and Bruno, an important number of companies who believe that they comply with the Code provide poor explanations with customary and uninformative statements.[387] In addition, MacNeil and Li found that the explanations provided by companies are generally brief, poor, and sub-standard.[388] Seidl, Sanderson, and Roberts also demonstrated that a substantial number of companies are not presenting 'full and proper justifications' for departure from the Code.[389] This illustrates the increased number

381 Keay, Comply or Explain in Corporate Governance Codes (n 376) 284

382 Grant Thornton, 'A Challenging Climate; Fresh Challenges Ahead' 6 <http://www.grant-thornton.co.uk/pdf/corporate_governance.pdf> accessed 25 May 2024

383 David Seidl, Paul Sanderson, and John Roberts, 'Applying "Comply-or-Explain": Compliance with Codes of Corporate Governance of the UK and Germany' (2009) 12 <http://www.cbr.cam.ac.uk/fileadmin/user_upload/centre-for-business-research/downloads/working-papers/wp389.pdf> accessed 25 May 2024. (51.94% of the companies are compliant with the Code)

384 Pension Investment Research Consultants, *Corporate Governance Annual Review 2004* (PIRC 2004) 9. Refer to Iain MacNeil and Xiao Li, 'Comply or Explain: Market Discipline and Non-Compliance with the Combined Code' (2006) 14(5) Corporate Governance 486, 488

385 Sridhar Arcot, Valentina Bruno, and Antoine Faure-Grimaud, 'Corporate Governance in the UK: Is the Comply or Explain Approach Working?' (2010) 30 International Review of Law and Economics 193, 196

386 MacNeil and Li (n 384) 494

387 Sridhar Arcot and Valentina Bruno, 'In Letter But Not in Spirit: An Analysis of Corporate Governance in the UK' (2006) 3–4 <http://ssrn.com/abstract=819784> accessed 25 March 2024

388 MacNeil and Li (n 384). See also Arcot, Bruno, and Faure-Grimaud (n 385); Keay, Comply or Explain in Corporate Governance Codes (n 376)

389 Seidl, Sanderson, and Roberts (n 383) 27

of 'boilerplate' disclosures generated by companies.[390] The FRC also accepted that some of the companies 'continue to give only perfunctory explanations or occasionally no explanation at all'.[391]

The problem that leads to perfunctory explanations is the flexibility and lack of guidance of the Code provided to companies regarding what constitutes good explanations and what type of explanation is proper.[392] This issue has drawn the attention of the FRC, and it held two meetings to shed some light on this issue with senior investors and companies in December 2011. The suggestions were published in February 2012[393] that the companies should provide full explanations, including context and historical background, a convincing rationale of the action, and a description of mitigating action to refer to possible additional risks and to preserve conformity with the relevant principle. Also, it was proposed that companies should indicate whether deviations from the Code are temporary and when they will start complying with the provisions of the Code.[394] However, 'whether this is done and how it is done is, again, a matter for directors'.[395]

2.4.7.4 Enforcement of the Code

The last but not least issue with the Code is its monitoring and enforcement. Shareholders are primarily entrusted to control whether the company complies with the Code and assess whether the provisions have been implemented or whether the response of the directors for departure from the Code is adequate. The codes have always promoted the comply or explain approach but have typically had no provision that empowers regulatory bodies to evaluate the explanations that companies provide.[396] The 2024 Code states that what is appropriate is, 'a statement of how the listed company has applied the Main Principles set out in the Code, in a manner that would enable shareholders to evaluate how the principles have been applied'.[397] Shareholders can also collaborate with other investors, who are one of the monitoring constituencies of the company, to assess whether the company complies with the Code and evaluate the explanations for departure from its provisions.

390 Financial Reporting Council, '2007 Review of the Combined Code: Summary of Responses to Consultation' (November 2007) para [42]

391 Financial Reporting Council, 'Developments in Corporate Governance 2011' (2011) 3 <https://frc.org.uk/FRC-Documents/FRC/Developments-in-Corporate-Governance-2011-The-impa.aspx> accessed 26 May 2024

392 Keay, Comply or Explain in Corporate Governance Codes (n 376) 291

393 Financial Reporting Council, 'What Constitutes an Explanation Under Comply or Explain?' (February 2012) <https://www.frc.org.uk/Our-Work/Publications/Corporate-Governance/What-constitutes-an-explanation-under-comply-or-ex.pdf> accessed 26 May 2024

394 Financial Reporting Council, 'What Constitutes an Explanation Under Comply or Explain?' (February 2012) <https://www.frc.org.uk/Our-Work/Publications/Corporate-Governance/What-constitutes-an-explanation-under-comply-or-ex.pdf> accessed 26 May 2024 6

395 Keay, Comply or Explain in Corporate Governance Codes (n 376) 292

396 Keay, Comply or Explain in Corporate Governance Codes (n 376) 282

397 Financial Reporting Council, 'The UK Corporate Governance Code' (2024), Introduction, at 3

However, according to a study that was undertaken by Arcot, Bruno, and Faure-Grimaud on 245 non-financial companies, shareholders have limited monitoring abilities, which may discourage them from exercising pressure on directors to provide better explanations.[398] Nolan also argued that 'there is still the risk that investors will not read and give due consideration to the explanations of those who do not comply and that this will therefore encourage a 'box-ticking' mechanistic approach to compliance'.[399] Hopper also discussed that 'explanations of non-compliance by companies are at best ignored by some shareholders organisations or at worst the company is criticised for not achieving a full set of ticked boxes'.[400]

The issue that underlies such a lack of monitoring incentives on the part of shareholders and investors is that they usually raise issues of non-compliance and poor explanations when companies are not financially performing well.[401] This may be because such shareholders are typically dispersed.[402] As such, even if they must intervene, it would come at a considerable cost in terms of time and finances.[403] The example of the Morrison case can be used to demonstrate this tendency. Morrison did not comply with most provisions of the Code and provided no or a poor explanation for departure. Its shareholders did not take any action as they were satisfied with the performance of the company.[404] In 2004, the first profit warning in 106 years of history was announced, and three more warnings followed. There was no unusual movement in the stock price before 2004; however, after July 2004, the performance of Morrison was notably under the FTSE100. Consequently, the shareholders took action by pressuring the board to appoint the first NED. Four more NEDs were also appointed subsequently.[405]

This example clearly illustrates that the tendency for shareholders to intervene in the management of companies is stronger only when they struggle financially. They are less likely to do so if the company is operating profitably, albeit in the short term. The issue, however, is that the fact that the company performs well does not imply that its directors have operated properly for the long-term interests of stakeholders. As shown repeatedly in this chapter, directors' undesirable behaviours are likely to expose companies to risks that would harm the interest of stakeholders in the long term even though they may be beneficial to shareholders and investors in the short term.

To summarise this section, the 'comply or explain' approach that was adopted by the Code has been in place in the United Kingdom for more than 20 years, and

398 Arcot, Bruno, and Faure-Grimaud (n 385) 193

399 Nolan (n 234) 453

400 Richard Hooper, 'No More Discussion and Debate-It is Time to Cry: 'Higgs, Enough!' (2005) <http://www.ft.com/cms/s/0/bbfff43e-4b44-11da-aadc-0000779e2340.html> accessed 10 July 2024

401 MacNeil and Li (n 384) 487. See also Arcot, Bruno, and Faure-Grimaud (n 386) 199

402 John Armour, *Enforcement Strategies in UK Corporate Governance: A Roadmap and Empirical Assessment* (ECGI-Law Working Paper 2008) 1 <http://papers.ssrn.com/sol3/papers.cfm?abstract_id=1133542> accessed 25 May 2024

403 Keay, Comply or Explain in Corporate Governance Codes (n 376) 286

404 Arcot, Bruno, and Faure-Grimaud (n 385) 199

405 Arcot, Bruno, and Faure-Grimaud (n 385) 199

it was introduced in order to foster good corporate governance from a flexible and adaptable perspective. The issue, however, is that its flexibility, the lack of compliance on most parties by companies, as well as poor explanations and the absence of appropriate enforcement mechanisms, have tended to reduce its constraining effect on directors.

2.4.8 Shareholders

Lastly, the exercise of the rights of shareholders can be used to discipline and control directors. While this chapter has examined several control mechanisms that may entail shareholder involvement, this section will further analyse other rights and powers of shareholders which inhere in them as residual controllers and 'residual risk bearers' of the company.[406] Shareholders are equipped with certain tools under the articles of association, statute law, and common law, which they can employ to constrain and prevent directors from pursuing improper purposes. They include approval or disapproval of directors' decisions,[407] the power to remove directors,[408] and the power to institute legal action against them.[409]

2.4.8.1 Approving or Disapproving of the Decisions of Directors

The primary power which shareholders have over their directors is the power to approve or disapprove of their decisions. In theory, this power appears substantial and sufficient to keep directors under control and to prevent them from being involved in undesirable behaviour. The issue is that, in practice, it is limited to a few acts of the board, such as director's service contracts, substantial property transactions, and loan transactions between the company and its directors.[410] What this means is that these rights can only be rarely used in situations that do not usually occur on a daily basis in the management of company business. Dooley defines these situations as 'extraordinary transactions'.[411] In effect, shareholders cannot employ these rights to curtail involvement in undesirable transactions that may occur in the usual course of the company's business.

2.4.8.2 Removing or Opposing the Re-Election of Directors

Shareholders also have the power to remove directors and to oppose their re-election. This right, which is provided under Section 168 of the CA06, enables

406 Gary Wilson, 'The Significance of Corporate Collective Power to New Labour's Project: Market Values, Corporate Regulation and the Possibilities for a Progressive Politics' (2005) 56 Northern Ireland Legal Quarterly 492, 518
407 Ch. 4, Companies Act 2006
408 Ch. 4, Companies Act 2006, s 168
409 Ss 260-269 of the CA 2006
410 Ss 260-269 of the CA 2006, Ch 4
411 Michael Dooley, 'Two Models of Corporate Governance' (1992) 47(2) Business Law 461, 468

them to remove directors by the passage of an ordinary resolution at a general meeting.[412] Additionally, shareholders who are dissatisfied with the performance of directors and wish to avoid the burden of their removal before the expiration of their tenure can vote against their re-election when the election is due. This power of removal, if judiciously exercised, can potentially constrain directors. However, there are serious limitations that may possibly discourage them from implementing it.[413] First there is the issue of 'shareholder apathy'.[414] Then there is the issue of potential cost, time consumption, and the difficulties involved in forming a coalition of shareholders.[415] Minority shareholders particularly lack the tendency for such a coalition as they have 'minimal or seemingly insignificant interests in a business'.[416] Despite the fact that majority shareholders have a key interest, the cost that they may bear is potentially huge not only in terms of paying compensation to the director but also in lobbying the dispersed shareholders and receiving legal advice. For this reason, voting against the directors' re-election rarely occurs, and the majority of shareholders usually vote to elect persons who have been chosen by the nominating committees of companies.[417] Wheeler noted that,

> The reality is that the appointment of directors, both executive and non-executive, is approved by the shareholders without, in the overwhelming majority of cases, any discussion. The board, in many ways, is a self-perpetuating oligarchy. Its existing members put up new members for election and re-election.[418]

This argument was also supported by the findings of the Manifest Voting Agency about proxy votes in 2001, which observed that 92.54% of the votes were in favour of management, and only a mere 4.04% of votes were in opposition.[419] This outcome illustrates two potential issues, which are, namely, the presence of noteworthy passive shareholders and the existence of limitations in 'attempting to foster reliance on shareholder input in the operation of efficient corporate governance'.[420] In brief, as Keay discussed, 'it is difficult for the shareholders to orchestrate the removal of a director, and it might well be regarded as not viable, too costly or too risky or all

412 S 168, Companies Act 2006

413 See generally Andrew Keay, 'Company Directors Behaving Poorly: Disciplinary Options for Shareholders' [2007] JBL 656. See also Pontian Okoli, 'Controlling Directors in a Troubled Economy: A UK Perspective' (2012) 23(7) ICCLR 234

414 Keay, Company Directors Behaving Poorly (n 413) 663

415 Keay, Company Directors Behaving Poorly (n 413) 663

416 Okoli (n 413) 237

417 Robert Webb, Matthias Beck, and Roddy McKinnon, 'Problems and Limitations of Institutional Investor Participation in Corporate Governance' (2003) 11 *Corporate Governance* 65, 68

418 Sally Wheeler, 'Non-Executive Directors and Corporate Governance' (2009) 60 Northern Ireland Legal Quarterly 51, 52

419 Webb, Beck, and McKinnon (n 417) 68

420 Webb, Beck, and McKinnon (n 417) 68

of these'.[421] These issues typically give rise to the attitude that 'removing a director was more of a problem than retaining one who is not performing'.[422]

2.4.8.3 Derivative Actions

The last shareholders' right to examine in this regard is derivative actions. These are actions which allow minority shareholders to institute legal proceedings against directors of companies. Derivative actions can be instituted against directors 'in respect of a cause of action arising from an actual or proposed act or omission involving negligence, default, breach of duty or breach of trust by a director of the company'.[423] Shareholders who desire to institute a derivation action must establish that the directors have committed wrongdoing. In essence the action can only arise from an actual or proposed act or omission involving negligence, default, breach of duty, or breach of trust by a director of the company.[424] Also, before shareholders can commence the action, they must obtain the leave of the court, which can only grant leave if persuaded that the preconditions have been satisfied.[425]

The logic behind requiring court approval is based on the rule established by *Foss v. Harbottle*.[426] According to this rule, where a wrong is done to a company or an irregularity is done in the course of its business, it is only the company, being a separate legal entity, that has the right to sue to remedy that wrong or to regularise the irregularity.[427] As such, where directors commit a wrong, it is the company that ordinarily has the right to bring a claim against them to recover its losses.[428] The issue here is that circumstances may arise where the majority shareholders acting in a general meeting may ratify a transaction which benefits them, even if it would be detrimental to the company's long-term interests. And while the minority shareholders will consequently be bound by such transactions, they would not be entitled to bring an action to protect their long-term interests unless they can prove that it was an outright illegality. For this reason, *Foss* is the starting point of the evolution of this rule 'whose principal effect is to bar minority shareholders' actions'.[429]

Besides this obstacle, shareholders also encounter other limitations that cast some doubt about their ability to exercise governance control mechanisms through litigation. These limitations can be mainly listed under three categories: the hardship of forming a coalition of dispersed shareholders, the potential cost that they

421 Keay, Comply or Explain in Corporate Governance Codes (n 376) 675
422 Keay, Company Directors Behaving Poorly (n 413) 675
423 S 260(3) CA06
424 S 260(3) CA06
425 Companies Act 2006, s 261(1)
426 (1843) 2 Hare 461
427 Hudson (n 2) 150. See also Anthony J Boyle, *Minority Shareholders' Remedies* (2nd edn, Cambridge University Press 2004) 1
428 A commonly accepted exception to this rule is fraud perpetrated on a minority. See Keay, Company Directors Behaving Poorly (n 413) 677
429 Boyle (n 427) 1

may personally suffer, and the length of the process.[430] The first limitation is forming a coalition amongst shareholders. It was emphasised in *Bamford v. Bamford*[431] that,

> [I]t would be for the company to decide whether to institute proceedings to avoid the voidable allotment: and again this decision would be one for the company in general meeting to decide by ordinary resolution. To litigate or not to litigate, apart from very special circumstances, is for decisions by such a resolution.[432]

This rule consequently requires shareholders to gain support from other shareholders in order to form a coalition. The hardship of forming a coalition is a major obstacle since shareholders are very dispersed in UK companies,[433] and they typically lack incentives to 'gather the information necessary to actively participate in decision making'.[434] Consequently, they may either easily sell their shares to avoid more risks or regard the invitation to a shareholder meeting as not 'unlike a junk mail'.[435]

Also, coalitions can sometimes be fragile.[436] The burden to keep coalitions together is typically left on the leading shareholders. Utset identified such shareholders as,

> [P]olitical entrepreneurs [who] will usually emerge only if the expected return from acting as an entrepreneur, that is, the sum of the entrepreneur's share of the collective good and any private benefits received by the entrepreneur, exceeds the costs to the entrepreneur of organizing the group.[437]

Thus, the possibility of bearing the burden as a result of a failed coalition is likely to discourage such shareholders from initiating derivative action. This issue is strongly linked with the cost of collective actions, which involves three factors. The first is the cost of forming and maintaining the coalition.[438] The second factor is based on the 'loser pays' principle.[439] According to this principle, where litigation is successful, the expenses of the litigation and the profit that the directors

430 Helen Short and Kevin Keasey, 'Institutional Shareholders and Corporate Governance in the United Kingdom' in Kevin Keasey, Steve Thompson, and Mike Wright (eds), *Corporate Governance: Economic, Management and Financial Issues* (Oxford University Press 1997) 18. See also Keay, Company Directors Behaving Poorly (n 413)

431 [1970] Ch 212

432 [1970] Ch 212 [242]

433 Alessio M Pacces, 'Controlling the Corporate Controller's Misbehaviour' (2011) 11(1) JCLS 177, 180

434 Robert Clark, *Corporate Law* (1st edn, Brown 1986) 68

435 Mclaughlin (n 114) 253

436 Keay, Company Directors Behaving Poorly (n 413) 660

437 Manuel A Utset, 'Disciplining Managers: Shareholder Co-Operation in the Shadow of Shareholder Competition' (1995) 44 Emory Law Journal 71, 106

438 See Section 2.4.8.2

439 Armour (n 402) 11

might have made are to be reimbursed to the company, but where the action is unsuccessful, the claimant shareholders bear the cost of the litigation. This potential serious risk of loss decreases the likelihood of initiating the process, as shareholders will be reluctant to join the coalition. Such a risk may also discourage those who are approached by leading shareholders because they may believe that it is better to wait and let the leading shareholders 'make the running and bear the costs'.[440] Thirdly, sharing the coalition cost among shareholders is another uncertainty for which there is no mechanism of resolution.[441] This exposes the leading shareholders to the risk of suffering a significant loss.

In addition to the issue of cost, the length of the process is another factor taken into account by shareholders before initiating or joining the coalition. For example, up to one year to form an institutional coalition in the companies of Brown and Jackson and Great Western Resources, and this resulted in a consistent decline in their share prices.[442] This is in respect of the time that may be spent on persuading shareholders to join the collision and preventing any exits, and it is linked to the issue of cost as 'the time element raises the cost of building and maintaining a coalition'.[443]

These issues not only discourage leading shareholders from initiating collective actions against directors, but they also dissuade other shareholders from joining such coalitions. Paolini and Nambisan discussed this:

> Given the widespread distribution of the share capital of a listed plc, it would be an extremely rare case indeed where a shareholder could derive any appreciable benefit from initiating a derivative action on behalf of the company. Thus, there is virtually no prospect of the directors of a listed plc facing personal liability to the company, as derivative actions simply do not exist in practice.[444]

To summarise, there are key obstacles to implementing the powers of shareholders to discipline and control directors. Due to the issues of cost and the hardship of forming a coalition, minority shareholders may decide to sell their shares and exit so that they are not exposed to the risk of suffering further loss; however, this strategy would not assist the company in protecting the long-term interests of its stakeholders. In short, 'shareholders are effectively impaired in disciplining directors because of both practical and legal reasons, and those reasons explain why it appears little disciplining by shareholders actually occurs'.[445]

440 Keay, Company Directors Behaving Poorly (n 413) 662
441 Keay, Company Directors Behaving Poorly (n 413) 661
442 Bernard S Black and John J Coffee, 'Hail Brittania? Institutional Investor Behavior Under Limited Regulation' (1994) 92 Michigan Law Review 1999, 2046–47
443 Bernard S Black and John J Coffee, 'Hail Brittania? Institutional Investor Behavior Under Limited Regulation' (1994) 92 Michigan Law Review 1999, 2047
444 Adolfo Paolini and Deepak Nambisan, *Directors' and Officer's Liability Insurance* (1st edn, Informa 2008) 58
445 Keay, Company Directors Behaving Poorly (n 41) 657

2.5 Conclusion

This chapter examined the problem of directors' undesirable behaviours, the importance of the protection of the long-term interests of stakeholders, the corporate risks of undesirable behaviours to which the company is subjected, and the corporate control mechanisms that are typically exercised by the company to control its directors. It demonstrated that directors' undesirable behaviours are a major threat to the protection of the long-term interests of stakeholders as they expose the company to a number of corporate risks, and the control mechanisms available have serious limitations which decrease the disciplining effect on directors.

Directors' undesirable behaviours have a distinct nature from other types of behaviours, and even though they may benefit the company in the short term, they exposes the company to serious corporate risks whose occurrences will harm the interests of stakeholders, which are supposed to be taken into account by directors. For this reason, the control mechanisms were examined in such a way as to determine the extent to which they can stop directors' undesirable behaviours. These mechanisms are typically exercised by internal and external constituencies to maintain good corporate governance, but they have limitations.

For example, the board of directors is the company's primary organ, which is equipped with the power to manage the company's business, but individual directors are typically assigned to undertake particular transactions on behalf of the company. The approach adopted by statute and common law is limited to restricting directors from employing their authority in an appropriate way, as the interest of third parties tends to be protected when conflicts arise. In respect of duties and remedies, duties can be a great deterrent mechanism, as long as they are enforced effectively. In this connection, gains-based remedies are unlikely to have the desired deterrent effect on directors as what they possibly lose is not more than what they have gained, whereas there are serious questions about the availability of equitable compensation when the company suffers a loss due to directors' undesirable behaviours. Also, lack of clarity on when the duty of care is breached by directors and directors' personal inability to compensate the company for the possible loss arising from such a breach causes serious concerns about the deterrent effectiveness of duty of care on directors. There are also serious issues with the remedy directors' disqualification, which impair its deterrence on directors. In addition, the factors that cause NEDs and auditors to be involved in the management of the company with executive directors may impair their independence, which may weaken their objective monitoring on directors.

Moreover, the fact that directors may employ defensive tactics against a potential takeover bid is a primary shortcoming of the market control mechanism, and interestingly, common law and the Takeover Code remain limited in respect of preventing such tactics. Furthermore, the issue of flexibility and lack of clarity in the requirements to disclose the strategy that directors adopt to run the company and guidance for maintaining good corporate governance put forward by the legal system for directors to follow are the key limitations to consider them as generating a strong deterrent effect on directors. Shareholders and investors are empowered to control how directors fulfil these requirements or to the extent which they follow the guidance. However, the provisions give far-reaching flexibility to directors regarding the type of information they disclose and their compliance with the provisions of the guidance. Lastly, the rights of shareholders to approve directors' decisions, remove those who are not performing well, and institute legal proceedings against them are very rarely implemented due to serious considerations that shareholders need to take into account before they employ these rights.

Accordingly, there are serious obstacles that companies have to overcome to control, discipline, and prevent directors' undesirable behaviours. This lack of control over directors raises concerns about the way in which they employ their authority and the negative consequences of their behaviour on the long-term interests of stakeholders.

The next chapter will examine the consequences of not being able to control directors by reference to a company's exposure to the risk of liability and loss caused by regulatory sanctions for regulatory infringements when directors are involved in anti-competitive behaviour.

Bibliography

Abbott LJ, Parker S, Peters GF, and Raghunandan K, 'An Empirical Investigation of Audit Fees, Nonaudit Fees and Audit Committees' (2003) 20 Contemporary Accounting 215

Aitken L, 'Developments in Equitable Compensation: Opportunity or Danger?' (1993) 67 ALJ 596

Aiyegbayo O and Villiers C, 'The Enhanced Business Review: Has It Made Corporate Governance More Effective?' (2011) 7 Journal of Business Review 699

Alikılıç Ö, 'Broadening the Concept of Green Marketing: Strategic Corporate Social Responsibility' in Ulas Akkucuk (ed.), *Handbook of Research on Developing Sustainable Value in Economics, Finance, and Marketing* (Business Science Reference 2015) 86

Antony Zarcaroli QC, 'The Company's Remedies for Breach of Directors' General Duties' in KC Simon Mortimore (ed.), *Company Directors Duties, Liabilities, and Remedies* (2nd edn, Oxford University Press 2013) 419

Arcot S and Bruno V, 'In Letter But Not in Spirit: An Analysis of Corporate Governance in the UK' (2006) 3–4 <http://ssrn.com/abstract=819784> accessed 25 March 2024

Arcot S, Bruno V, and Faure-Grimaud A, 'Corporate Governance in the UK: Is the Comply or Explain Approach Working?' (2010) 30 International Review of Law and Economics 193

Armour J, *Enforcement Strategies in UK Corporate Governance: A Roadmap and Empirical Assessment* (ECGI-Law Working Paper 2008) 1

Armour J, 'Regulatory Sanctions and Reputational Damage in Financial Markets' (2010)

Armour J, Mayer C, and Polo A, *Regulatory Sanctions and Reputational Damage in Financial Markets* (Oxford Legal Studies Research Paper No. 62/2010 2010)

Arnold M, 'Duty to Exercise Reasonable Care, Skill, and Diligence' in KC Simon Mortimore (ed.), *Company Directors Duties, Liabilities, and Remedies* (2nd edn, Oxford University Press 2013) 296

Arora A, 'The Corporate Governance Failings in Financial Institutions and Directors' Legal Liability' (2011) 32(1) Comp Law 3

Arsalidou D, 'The Banking Crisis: Rethinking and Refining the Accountability of Bank Directors' [2010] JBL 284

Asefeso A, *Non Executive Directors: Best Kept Secret Revealed* (Global Sourcing 2013) 3

Bainbridge S, *Director Primacy* (UCLA School of Law, Law-Econ Research Paper No 10–06 2010) 7
Beattie V and Fearnley S, 'Auditor Independence and Non-Audit Services: A Literature Review' (2002)
Black BS and Coffee JJ, 'Hail Brittania? Institutional Investor Behavior Under Limited Regulation' (1994) 92 Michigan Law Review 1999
Black J, 'Forms and Paradoxes of Principles Based Regulation' (2008) 9
Bryant C, 'Directors Meet to Decide Volkswagen Chief's Fate' (2015)
Byrd JW and Hickman KA, 'Do Outside Directors Monitor Managers' (1992) 32 Journal of Financial Economics 195
Clark R, *Corporate Law* (1st edn, Brown 1986) 68
Coffee JC, '"No Soul to Damn: No Body to Kick": An Unscandalized Inquiry into the Problem of Corporate Punishment' (1981) 79 Michigan Law Review 386. See also Eilis Ferran, 'Corporate Attribution and the Directing Mind and Will' (2011) 127 LQR 239
Conaglen M, 'Equitable Compensation for Breach of Fiduciary Dealing Rules' (2003) 119 LQR 246
Conaglen M and Loyalty F, *Protecting the Due Performance of Non-Fiduciary Duties* (1st edn, Hart 2010) 87
Coombes P and Wong SC-Y, 'Why Codes of Corporate Governance Work' [2004] The McKinsey Quarterly 48
Core JE, 'On the Corporate Demand for Directors' and Officer Insurance' (1997) 64(1) The Journal of Risk and Insurance 63
Davies P, *Introduction to Company Law* (2nd edn, Oxford University Press 2010) 195
Davies P and Rickford J, 'An Introduction to the New UK Companies Act' (2008) 5 ECFR 48
Deakin S and Konzelmann SJ, 'Learning From Enron' (2004) 12(2) Corporate Governance 134
Demb A and Neubauer F, *The Corporate Board: Confronting the Paradox* (1st edn, Oxford University Press 1992) 100
Dietzel K, Wisking S, and Herron M, 'Nearing the End of the Line in Cardiff Bus' [2012] Comp Law 289
Dignam A, *Hicks & Goo's Cases and Materials on Company Law* (7th edn, Oxford University Press 2011) 245
Dignam A and Lowry J, *Company Law* (8th edn, Oxford University Press 2014) 363
Dine J and Koutsias M, *Company Law* (8th edn, Palgrave Macmillan 2014) 190
Eccles RG, Newquist SC, and Schatz R, 'Reputation and Its Risks' (2007) 85(2) Harvard Business Review 104
Elkington J, *Cannibals with Forks: The Triple Bottom Line of 21st Century Business* (Capstone Publishing 1999) 70
Ezzamel M and Watson R, 'Wearing Two Hats: The Conflicting Control and Management Roles of Non-Executive Directors' in Kevin Keasey, Steve Thompson, and Mike Wright (eds), *Corporate Governance: Economic, Management, and Financial Issues* (Oxford University Press 1997) 54
Farrell S, 'Volkswagen Director Says Staff Acted Criminally Over Emissions Tests' (2015)
Finch V, 'Company Directors: Who Cares About Skill and Care?' (1992) 55 MLR 179
Finn PD, 'Fiduciary Law and the Modern Commercial World' in Ewan McKendrick (ed.), *Commercial Aspects of Trusts and Fiduciary Obligations* (1st edn, Clarendon 1992) 7
Fransk J and Mayer C, 'Hostile Takeovers and the Correction of Managerial Failure' (1996) 40 JFE 163
Frug GE, 'The Ideology of Bureaucracy in American Law' (1984) 97 Harvard Law Review 1276
Ghafran C and O'Sullivan N, 'The Governance Role of Audit Committees: Reviewing a Decade of Evidence' (2013) 15 International Journal of Management Reviews 381

Ginsburg D and Wright J, 'Antitrust Sanctions' (2010) 6(2) Competition Policy International 3
Goodison A, 'Directors' Powers and Responsibilities' in Simon Mortimore KC (ed.), *Company Directors Duties, Liabilities, and Remedies* (2nd edn, Oxford University Press 2013) 76
Graham R, 'Revised Narrative Reporting Regs' (2013) 37(7) CSR 49
Grantham R, 'Illegal Transactions and the Powers of Company Directors' (1999) 115 LQR 296
Griffiths A, 'Interlocking Directorships and the Danger of Self-Dealing: The Duties of Directors with a Conflict of Interest' (1999) 10(9) ICCLR 280
Grinyer J, Russell A, and Collison D, 'Evidence of Managerial Short-Termism in the UK' (1998) 9 British Journal of Management 13
Gullifer L and Payne J, *Corporate Finance Law: Principles and Policy* (2nd edn, Hart Publishing 2015) 696
Hannigan B, *Company Law* (3rd edn, Oxford University Press 2012) 197
Hannigan B, *Company Law* (4th edn, Oxford University Press 2015) 374
Hawes S, 'Guidance on the Strategic Report' (2013) 37(12) CSR 89
Hepburn S, *Principles of Equity & Trusts* (2nd edn, Cavendish 2001) 29
Hess D, 'Public Pensions and the Promise of Shareholder Activism for the Next Frontier of Corporate Governance: Sustainable Economic Development' (2007) 2 Virginia Law and Business Review 221
Heydon JD, 'Causal Relationships between a Fiduciary's Default and the Principal's Loss' (1994) 110 LQR 328
Hooper R, 'No More Discussion and Debate-It is Time to Cry: 'Higgs, Enough!' (2005)
Howley S and Bateman P, 'Companies Act 2006: An Overview: Part 2' (2007) 11 Co LN 1
Hudson A, *Understanding Company Law* (1st edn, Routledge 2012) 93. See also Anchayli A, 'The "Directing Mind and Will" Test in Corporate Attribution: Iridium and Meridian – A Comparison' (2012) 33(8) Comp Law 252
Hurt C, 'The Duty to Manage Risk' (2014) 39 The Journal of Corporation Law 253, 254–257; Schwarcz SL, 'Excessive Corporate Risk-Taking and the Decline of Personal Blame' (2015) 65 Emory Law Journal 533
John K, Litov L, and Yeung B, 'Corporate Governance and Risk-Taking' (2008) 63(4) The Journal of Finance 1679
Johnston A, 'After the OFR: Can UK Shareholder Value Still Be Enlightened?' (2006) 7 EBOR 817
Johnston A, 'Takeover Regulation: Historical and Theoretical Perspectives on the City Code' (2007) 66(2) CLJ 422
Keay A, 'Enlightened Shareholder Value, the Reform of the Duties of Company Directors and the Corporate Objective' [2006] Lloyd's Maritime and Commercial Law Quarterly 335
Keay A, *Company Directors' Responsibilities to Creditors* (1st edn, Routledge-Cavendish 2007) 205
Keay A, 'Tackling the Issue of the Corporate Objective: An Analysis of the United Kingdom's 'Enlightened Shareholder Value Approach' (2007) 29 Sydney Law Review 577
Keay A, *Moving Towards Stakeholderism? Constituency Statutes, Enlightened Shareholder Value, and All That: Much Ado About Little?* (University of Leeds School of Law, Centre for Business Law and Practice Working Paper 2010)
Keay A, 'The Ultimate Objective of the Company and the Enforcement of the Entity Maximisation and Sustainability Model' (2010) 10(1) JCLS 35
Keay A, *The Corporate Objective* (1st edn, Edward Elgar 2011)
Keay A, 'Company Directors Behaving Poorly: Disciplinary Options for Shareholders' [2007] JBL 656. See also Okoli P, 'Controlling Directors in a Troubled Economy-A UK Perspective' (2012) 23(7) ICCLR 234

Keay A, *The Enlightened Shareholder Value Principle and Corporate Governance* (1st edn, Routledge 2013)
Kirkpatrick G, 'The Corporate Governance Lessons from the Financial Crisis' (2009) Financial Market Trends 8 <https://www.oecd.org/finance/financial-markets/42229620.pdf> accessed 13 May 2024
Knapton S, 'Volkswagen scandal: how two campaigners exposed the world's biggest car company' (2015) https://www.telegraph.co.uk/news/uknews/road-and-rail-transport/11883343/volkswagen-scandal-campaigners-expose-world-biggest-car-company.html
Krehmeyer D, *Breaking the Short-Term Cycle: Discussion and Recommendations on How Corporate Leaders, Asset Managers, Investors, and Analysts Can Refocus on Long-Term Value* (CFA Centre for Financial Market Integrity and the Business Roundtable Institute for Corporate Ethics 2006)
Langford RT and Ramsay IM, 'Directors' Duty to Act in the Interests of the Company – Subjective or Objective?' [2015] JBL 173
Levitt A, 'Renewing the Covenant with Investors' (*Speech by Chairman of US Securities and Exchange Commission* 10 May 2010)
Loughrey J, 'The Director's Duty of Care and Skill and the Financial Crisis' in Joan Loughrey (ed.), *Directors' Duties and Shareholder Litigation in the Wake of the Financial Crisis* (Edward Elgar Publishing 2012)
Lowry JP and Reisberg A, *Pettet's Company Law: Company Law & Corporate Finance* (4th edn, Pearson 2012) 137
Macdonald B, 'Changes to Narrative Reporting' (2012) 36(15) CSR 118
MacNeil I and Li X, 'Comply or Explain: Market Discipline and Non-Compliance with the Combined Code' (2006) 14(5) Corporate Governance 486, 488
Manne HG, 'Mergers and the Market for Corporate Control' (1965) 73(2) The Journal of Political Economy 110
Mclaughlin S, *Unlocking Company Law* (3rd edn, Routledge 2015) 303, 305
Meagher RP, Heydon JD, and Leeming MJ, *Meagher, Gummow and Lehane's Equity: Doctrines and Remedies* (4th edn, Butterworths LexisNexis 2002) para [2.155]–[2.320]
Meagher RP, Heydon JD, and Leeming MJ, *Meagher, Gummow and Lehane's Equity: Doctrines and Remedies* (5th edn, Butterworths LexisNexis 2015)
Millett PJ, 'Restitution and Constructive Trusts' (1998) 114 LQR 399
Moerland PW, 'Alternative Disciplinary Mechanisms in Different Corporate Systems' (1995) 26 Journal of Economic Behavior and Organization 17
Morris GD, 'Good Corporate Reporting' (2014) 25(4) Tolley's Practical Audit & Accounting 45
Moulson G and Pylas P, 'VW CEO Says He's 'Endlessly Sorry' for Tarnishing Brand' (2015)
Mullins D, 'Foreword' in M. Jacobs (ed.), *Short-Term America* (Harvard Business School Press 1991)
Naniwadekar M, 'Remedies Against Directors' Undue Gains: Personal or Proprietary?' (2013)
Nolan RC, 'The Legal Control of Directors' Conflicts of Interests in the United Kingdom: Non-Executive Directors Following the Higgs Report' (2005) 6(2) Theoretical Inquiries in Law 413
Okoye N, *The Personality of Company Directors as a Behavioural Risk Contributor in the Corporate Governance Process Regulatory Intervention as a Risk Management Mechanism* (PhD Thesis, University of Dundee 2012) 89
Ong D, 'Breach of Fiduciary Duty: The Alternative Remedies' (1999) 11(2) Bond Law Review 336
Pacces AM, 'Controlling the Corporate Controller's Misbehaviour' (2011) 11(1) JCLS 177
Paolini A, 'Lending Sub-Prime and Advising on Financial Investments from a D&O Insurance Perspective' [2012] JBL 432

Paolini A and Nambisan D, *Directors' and Officer's Liability Insurance* (1st edn, Informa 2008) 58
Phillips D, 'PwC Partner Speaks Out Over 'Dreadful' Annual Reports' (2009)
Power M, 'The Risk Management of Everything' (2004) 5(3) The Journal of Risk Finance 58
Prentice D, 'The Corporate Opportunity Doctrine' (1974) 37(4) MLR 464
Rappaport A, 'The Staying Power of the Public Corporation' (1990) 68(1) Harvard Business Review 96, 100; Bradley C, 'Corporate Control: Markets and Rules' (1990) 53(2) MLR 170
Rickett C and Gardner T, 'Compensating for Loss in Equity: The Evolution of a Remedy' (1994) 24 Victoria University of Wellington Law Review 19
Romano R, 'What Went Wrong with Directors' and Officers' Liability Insurance' (1989) 14(1) The Delaware Journal of Corporate Law 1
Ronen J, 'Corporate Audits and How to Fix Them' (2010) 24(2) Journal of Economic Perspectives 189
RT Hon Justice Tipping, 'Causation at Law and in Equity: Do We Have Fusion?' (2000) 7 Canterbury Law Review 443
Ruddick G, 'Volkswagen Scandal: US Chief Says Carmaker "Totally Screwed Up"' (2015)
Sealy L, 'Some Principles of Fiduciary Obligations' [1963] CLJ 119
Sealy L, 'Directors' Duties Revisited' (2001) 22(3) Comp Law 79
Seidl D, Sanderson P, and Roberts J, 'Applying "Comply-or-Explain": Conformance with Codes of Corporate Governance of the UK and Germany' (2009) Centre for Business Research, University of Cambridge Working Paper No. 389
Short H, 'Non-Executive Directors, Corporate Governance and the Cadbury Report: A Review of the Issues and Evidence' (1996) 4 CG 123
Short H and Keasey K, 'Institutional Shareholders and Corporate Governance in the United Kingdom' in Kevin Keasey, Steve Thompson, and Mike Wright (eds.), *Corporate Governance: Economic, Management and Financial Issues* (Oxford University Press 1997) 18
Smith CM, *Controlling the Conduct of Company Directors* (Master Thesis, Durham University, 1996) 3
Stanley C, 'An Approach to the Internal Regulation of the Corporation: A Critical Analysis of the Recommendations of the Cadbury Committee' (1993) 2(1) JFR&C 48
Stokes M, 'Company Law and Legal Theory' in William Twining (ed.), *Legal Theory and Common Law* (Blackwell 1986) 155, 174
Sulaiman A, 'Directors' Fiduciary Duty to Disclose Wrongdoing and Appropriate Remedy – Case Commentary' (2012) 38(1) CLB 91
Taylor PN, *Enlightened Shareholder Value and the Companies Act 2006* (PhD Thesis, Birkbeck College 2010) 5
Thornton G, 'A Challenging Climate; Fresh Challenges Ahead' 6
Tricker B, *Corporate Governance: Principles, Policies, and Practices* (2nd edn, Oxford University Press 2012) 187
Utset MA, 'Disciplining Managers: Shareholder Co-Operation in the Shadow of Shareholder Competition' (1995) 44 Emory Law Journal 71
Vann V, 'Causation and Breach of Fiduciary Duty' [2006] Singapore Journal of Legal Studies 86
Vaughan EJ and Vaughan TM, *Fundamentals of Risk and Insurance* (10th edn, John Wiley 2008) 15
Villiers C, 'A Global Framework for Management Commentary Disclosure?' (2009) 60 The Northern Ireland Legal Quarterly 63
Villiers C, 'Directors' Duties and the Company's Internal Structures Under the UK Companies Act 2006: Obstacles for Sustainable Development' (2011) 8 ICCLJ 47
Webb R, Beck M, and McKinnon R, 'Problems and Limitations of Institutional Investor Participation in Corporate Governance' (2003) 11 Corporate Governance 65

Weir C and Laing D, 'Governance Structures, Director Independence and Corporate Performance in the UK' (2001) 13(2) European Business Review 86, 87
Wheeler S, 'Non-Executive Directors and Corporate Governance' (2009) 60 The Northern Ireland Legal Quarterly 51
Wilson G, 'Business, State, and Community: "Responsible Risk Takers," New Labour, and the Governance of Corporate Business' (2000) 27 Journal of Law & Social Policy 154
Wilson G, 'Corporate Law Theory' (2013) 22 Nottingham Law Journal 155, 158
Yeldar R, 'Narrative Reporting Content in The FTSE 100 – How Does It Stack Up?' (September 2006).

3 Individual Behaviour, Company Liability, and Risk

Competition Law and Regulatory Liability*

3.1 Introduction

In the previous chapter, we examined the types of undesirable behaviours that directors may involve themselves in and the risks that the company may face as a result of such behaviours. It was shown that several hurdles stand in the way of a company that attempts to control directors—hurdles which would decrease its ability to prevent directors from engaging in undesirable behaviour.

This chapter will examine the adverse effects that a company may suffer if its directors infringe on competition law. To that end, it will seek to ascertain the extent to which companies can hold their directors accountable for infringing competition law as well as the sanctions that companies may be liable to in that regard. For this purpose, the interaction between corporate governance concerning the internal relationships within the company and competition law, which focuses on the behaviour of the company in the market, will be taken into consideration.[1] The common point that unites these different areas of law is the fact that the behaviour of the company in the market is typically determined and conducted by its directors, and competition law seeks to prevent anti-competitive conduct that would potentially harm the objectives of competition policy. Therefore, the enforcement mechanisms adopted by competition law and the actors against whom they are implemented are crucial issues in terms of the particular relationship between the company and its directors. This may give rise to tension between company law and competition law, as the former concerns the internal structures of the company, while the latter focuses on the possible effects of a company's behaviour and the extent to which competition in the market could be adversely affected.

In this tension, the questions that arise are whether competition law considers the different internal structures and divisions within the corporate structure when determining the enforcement mechanisms that are designed to achieve its objectives and whether it seeks to localise the source of the conduct by taking into account the legally established partitions that exist within the company taking

1 Florence Thepot, *The Interaction Between Competition Law and Corporate Governance: Opening the 'Black Box'* (PhD Thesis, University College London 2014) 3

DOI: 10.4324/9781003461562-3

its distinct nature into cognisance. In essence, it is crucial to determine whether the role of corporate decision-makers in anti-competitive behaviour is taken into account by competition law.

Further to this, the chapter examines the tension between the objectives of the UK competition policy and the ability of companies to convince their directors to comply with the rules of competition law. The impact of the operation of UK competition law on the relationship between the company and directors, and, in particular, whether it protects the company against or exposes it to undesirable behaviour on the part of its directors will also be examined. For this purpose, UK competition law and its policy objectives will be taken into consideration in this chapter.

In order to address the main question, general information about the operations of UK and EU competition laws will be provided in Section 3.2. Secondly, Section 3.3.1 will discuss the respective objectives of UK competition policies. Section 3.3.2 will define the concept of an undertaking in competition law, while Section 3.3.3 will examine the role of policy objectives in forming the enforcement mechanisms of competition law and the impact of these enforcement strategies on the relationship between the company and its directors. Following this, Section 3.4 will analyse the theoretical bases that underlie the approach adopted by UK competition law to shape the current competition enforcement strategies. In that regard, it will examine whether the approach adopted by these theories exposes the company to the risk of liability and loss arising from the undesirable behaviour of its directors. Fourthly, the deterrent effect of individual sanctions and whether they may reduce the risk of liability and loss on the company by deterring directors from engaging in undesirable behaviour will be examined in Section 3.5. Lastly, conclusions will be drawn on the ability of the company to avoid being exposed to the risks of undesirable behaviour as a result of UK competition law and policy.

3.2 UK Competition Law Regime

Companies in the United Kingdom operate within the limits of UK law. Understanding the impact that UK competition law has on the relationship between the company and directors is important. Competition law, as defined by Dabbah, 'applies a body of legal rules and standards to deal with market imperfections and restore desirable competitive conditions in the market'.[2] UK competition laws consist of strict rules that the firms, known as undertakings, are obliged to act upon, and any infringements cause heavy fines.[3]

Competition law has certain policy goals and in order to achieve them, enforcement is primarily based upon the concept of deterrence. As such, it seeks to impose severe sanctions as a means of achieving its objectives. UK competition law also

2 Maher M Dabbah, 'Measuring the Success of a System of Competition Law: A Preliminary View' (2000) 21(8) ECLR 369, 371

3 Susan Singleton, *Competition Law Compliance 2008* (Thorogood 2008) 2. UK competition law also imposes individual sanctions. See Section 3.5

targets individuals through criminal cartel offences and directors' disqualification orders in order to deter them from behaviour that may undermine the policy goals underlying the competition law regime.

The statutory basis for UK competition law is the Competition Act 1998 (CA98) and the Enterprise Act 2002 (EA02). The UK competition law as embodied in CA98, is largely modelled on EU competition law. This step was taken by the UK government to complete the Europeanisation of its domestic competition law.[4] In fact, before introducing the CA98, UK competition law had no sense of semblance to EU competition law.[5] In this sense, the Chapter 1 and 2 prohibitions of the CA98 can be considered as domestic versions of Articles 101 and 102 of the Treaty on the Functioning of the European Union (TFEU).[6]

A primary objective of the CA98 is to detect hidden cartels or any agreements that may potentially restrict competition and to enhance the deterrent effect of UK competition law by empowering regulators to investigate and impose fines, where necessary.[7] The aim of these prohibitions is to promote economic efficiency[8] by providing greater incentives to undertakings to obey competition law and prevent them from exploiting others for their own benefit.[9]

This chapter focuses on the UK competition regime as distinct from EU competition law, with a primary focus on EA02, which was enacted with the objective of enhancing the deterrent effect of UK competition law by introducing individual sanctions in the form of a criminal cartel offence and competition disqualification orders.[10] The driver of these sanctions was the 'disjunction between the incentives of the company and the incentives of the company executives'.[11] In this sense, the UK competition regime can be considered Europeanised (civil) and Americanised (criminal). In 2013, the EA02 was significantly amended by the Enterprise and Regulatory Reform Act 2013 (ERRA13), which was put in force once again to increase the deterrent effect of the individual sanctions.

4 Barry J Rodger, 'The Competition Act and the Enterprise Act Reforms: Sanctions and Deterrence in UK Competition Law' in Gerhard Dannecker and Oswald Jansen (eds), *Competition Law Sanctioning in the European Union: The EU-Law Influence on the National Law System of Sanctions in the European Area* (Kluwer 2004) 101

5 Stephen Weatherill, 'Country Analysis-United Kingdom' in Gerhard Dannecker and Oswald Jansen (eds), *Competition Law Sanctioning in the European Union: The EU-Law Influence on the National Law System of Sanctions in the European Area* (Kluwer 2004) 859

6 Cosmo Graham, *EU and UK Competition Law* (2nd edn, Pearson 2013) 19

7 See Jonathan DC Turner, 'The U.K. Competition Act 1998 and Private Rights' 1999 20(2) ECLR 62; George Peretz, 'Detection and Deterrence of Secret Cartels Under the UK Competition Bill' (1998) 19(3) ECLR 145, 147; David Cowan and Julie S Nazerali, 'Importing the E.U. Model into U.K. Competition Law: A Blueprint for Reform or a Step into "Euroblivion"?' (1999) 20(2) ECLR 55

8 Jonathan DC Turner, 'The U.K. Competition Act 1998 and Private Rights' 1999 20(2) ECLR 72

9 David Parker, 'The Competition Act 1998: Change and Continuity in U.K. Competition Policy' [2000] JBL 283, 300–301

10 Jonathan Galloway, 'Chapter 2A: Competition Disqualification Orders' in His Honour Judge Abbas Mithani (ed.), *Mithani: Directors' Disqualification* (Butterworths 2009) III-351

11 Andrew Scott, *The Evolution of Competition Law and Policy in the United Kingdom* (LSE Working Papers 2009) 17 <http://ssrn.com/abstract=1344807> accessed 15 April 2024

The question is whether corporate and individual sanctions for competition law breaches are adequately implemented and whether they are adequate to make companies accountable for involvement in anti-competition activities. This chapter will examine whether the sanctions that may be imposed where directors violate competition law are adequate to deter wrongdoing. It will, in that regard, examine whether the objective behind the sanctions under the Act is being achieved, as well as their impact on the relationship between the company and directors.

3.3 The Policy Objectives of Competition Law and the Company's Exposure to Risk

The objectives of competition policy are the foundations of competition law rules, and they give guidance as to how the rules are to be applied and upon whom. The issue is that tension may arise between these policy objectives and the relationship that exists between companies and their directors. The question is whether, in seeking to promote or to what extent, competition law actually takes into account the way in which companies are run internally. For this purpose, this section examines the policy objectives of UK competition law and whether in promoting these objectives, regulators consider companies' exposures to the risk of liability and loss by their directors.

3.3.1 The Primary Aim of Policy Objectives of UK Competition Law

The policy objectives of competition law play an important role in the enforcement of competition law sanctions, and they illustrate whose interest competition law protects.[12] For this purpose, we will examine what competition policy is and what its objectives are. Motta defined competition policy as 'the set of policies and laws which ensure that competition in the marketplace is not restricted in a way as to reduce economic welfare'.[13] Aaronson described it as aiming 'to secure the optimal allocation of resources in the economy, through the interplay of independent decisions by producers and consumers, in the interest of providing, at minimum cost, the goods and services which consumers value most highly'.[14] On the other hand, Dabbah adopts a different perspective by defining it as 'an element of politics, which deals with public authorities' intervention beyond certain market imperfections, such as in the case of market failure'.[15] In this connection, Sir Leon Brittan asserts that 'a positive competition policy should not be determined in isolation'.

12 Laura Parret, 'Shouldn't We Know What We Are Protecting? Yes We Should! A Plea for a Solid and Comprehensive Debate about the Objectives of EU Competition Law and Policy' (2010) 6(2) ECJ 339

13 Massimo Motta, *Competition Policy – Theory and Practice* (2nd edn, Cambridge University Press 2004) 30

14 Robin Aaronson, *The Future of UK Competition Policy* (Commission on Public Policy and British Business 1996) 1

15 Dabbah (n 2) 371

Rather, it should be related to and integrated with economic, industrial, and also social policy.[16]

Based on these definitions, there are currently two main schools of thought on what the actual objectives of competition policy are. The first approach is that of the Chicago school. The primary goal of this approach is to ensure that a competitive economy is maintained in society. For this purpose, competition policy ought to maximise economic efficiency, protect 'consumer welfare',[17] and prevent 'inefficient allocation of resources'.[18] In doing so, this approach excludes the socio-political concerns. On the other hand, the Brussels school adopts a more balanced attitude to competition. According to this view, considerations in respect of competition, economy, and socio-politics are taken into account. For example, in contrast to the Chicago school, this school of thought is more heavily concerned with the protection of small and medium-sized firms.[19]

From a broad perspective, there are many purposes that can be identified as the objectives of competition policy. They include economic and consumer welfare, the defence of smaller firms, the promotion of market integration, economic freedom, fighting inflation, and fairness and equity.[20] All these considerations individually can be regarded as the objectives of competition policy. However, as Willimsky discussed, particular 'objectives and policies ought to be borne in mind when looking at particular legislative enactments'.[21] This is because there are two categories into which these objectives can be classified: ultimate and intermediate.[22] For example, while some consider that promoting consumer welfare is an ultimate objective, an effective competition process is an intermediate objective. On the other hand, some others consider consumer welfare as a step to promoting effective competition in the market.[23]

The 'core competition objectives based on consumer welfare'[24] are the main drivers of competition law. The objective of consumer welfare was also emphasised in a speech by former Competition Commissioner Kroes, who stated that

> Consumer welfare is now well established as the standard the Commission applies when assessing mergers and infringements of the Treaty rules on cartels and monopolies. Our aim is simple: to protect competition in the market as a means of enhancing consumer welfare and ensuring an efficient allocation of resources.[25]

16 Quoted in Sonya M Willimsky, 'The Concept(s) of Competition' (1997) 18(1) ECLR 54
17 Okeoghene Odudu, 'The Wider Concerns of Competition Law' 30(3) (2010) OJLS 599
18 Willimsky (n 16) 55
19 Willimsky (n 16) 55
20 Motta (n 13) 17–26
21 Willimsky (n 16) 57
22 Parret (n 12) 340
23 Parret (n 12) 340
24 Parret (n 12) 359
25 Neelie Kroes, 'European Competition Policy: Delivering Better Markets and Better Choices' (SPEECH/05/512, 15 September 2005) 2 <europa.eu/rapid/press-release_SPEECH-05-512_en.pdf> accessed 15 April 2024

Hence, from the view of the Commission, promoting consumer welfare should be the ultimate objective of intervening in the area of competition law.[26] It should be noted that while EU competition law is heavily concerned about the impact of anti-competitive behaviour on the ultimate objective of consumer welfare and other intermediate objectives, it may be unconcerned with or disconnected from the internal issues within the company. In respect of the objectives of UK competition policy, there have been 'multiple goals and objectives' which have changed from time to time.[27] Before the introduction of the CA98, the public interest and the promotion of full employment were the objectives of competition policy.[28] This view was criticised on the ground that it left the matter of preserving 'free and fair competition' without consideration while protecting the public interest.[29] As Rodger stated, 'the utilitarian model of public interest assessment [was] central to a system which concentrated on market failure and not necessarily some form of reproachable behaviour'.[30] Therefore, the policy objectives of UK competition law have been changed radically through the CA98. As Walker demonstrated, 'the Act substitutes the old "form" based competition law with an "effects" based regime prohibiting not particular types of restrictions per se, but restrictions which are perceived to have anticompetitive effects'.[31] Adopting a more effect-based approach has increased consideration of the economic issues regarding the competition policy.[32]

The objectives of the UK competition policy, however, have never been clearly defined because the governments have always referred to 'strong' competition policy without defining what such a policy means precisely and highlighted the place of competition policy in economic growth without illustrating how the particular relationship between these concepts is considered.[33] This is because a programmatic statement has always been rejected by UK governments.[34] Despite the fact that mission statements were adopted by the OFT and the Competition Commission, no statutory objective was given to them.[35] Whereas the Commission's stated goal was to 'help to ensure healthy competition between companies in the UK for the ultimate benefits of consumers and economy', the OFT

26 Philip Lowe, 'The Design of Competition Policy Institutions for the 21st Century: The Experience of the European Commission and DG Competition' (2008) 3 Competition Policy Newsletter 1, 6
27 Cosmo Graham, 'The Reform of UK Competition Policy' (2012) ECJ 539, 556
28 Scott (n 11) 6
29 Michael B Hutchings, 'The Need for Reform of UK Competition Policy' (1995) 16(4) ECLR 211, 212
30 Barry J Rodger, 'Competition Policy, Liberalism and Globalization: A European Perspective' (2000) 6 The Columbia Journal of European Law 289, 310
31 Julian Maitland-Walker, 'The New U.K. Competition Law Regime' (1999) 20(2) ECLR 51
32 Simon Pilsbury and Helen Jenkins, 'The Evolution of Effects-Based Analysis Under the Competition Act 1998' [2010] Comp Law 216
33 Graham (n 26) 555
34 Graham (n 26) 555
35 Graham (n 26) 555. Note that the OFC and the CC have now been merged into the Competition and Markets Authority (CMA)

suggested that its objective was to 'make markets work well for consumers', which 'seems to be a populist version of consumer welfare'.[36] This approach has been formalised by the ERRA 2013 by creating the Competition and Markets Authority (CMA—formerly the OFT), which seeks to encourage competition for the benefit of consumers.[37] In the process of the ERRA 2013 being formed, 'throughout the government documents and statements, there [was] no discussion of what the objectives of competition law are and how this might affect enforcement policy'.[38] However, the ERRA 2013, for the first time, required the CMA to 'seek to promote competition, both within and outside the United Kingdom, for the benefits of consumers'.[39] This illustrates that other non-economic objectives are no longer under consideration within the frame of enforcement of competition law.[40] The influence of the objective of consumer welfare on enforcement strategies can be seen from the past educational materials published by government authorities. The defunct OFT stated that,

> We prioritised the work we did around five key themes: vulnerable consumers and those challenged by the adverse economic climate; pricing used as a barrier to fair choice; improving trust in online markets; intellectual property and high innovation markets; and public markets.[41]

The CMA also indicated that, 'the likely direct effect of enforcement on consumer welfare in the market or sector where the intervention takes place' needs to be carefully taken under consideration.[42] This is to ensure that the intervention of the CMA is proportionate in terms of promoting consumer welfare. Accordingly, UK competition law is heavily concerned with the impact of anti-competitive behaviour on consumers, and internal issues would be clearly regarded as irrelevant for the sake of promoting its policy objective. This gives rise to concerns about the extent of accountability on the parts of the company and directors for competition law infringements. In order to analyse this issue, in the next two sections, the primary enforcement mechanism of competition law, which is being targeted by this enforcement strategy, and its impact on risk distribution between the company and directors will be examined.

36 See OFT and CC web archives <http://webarchive.nationalarchives.gov.uk/20140525130048/http://www.oft.gov.uk/about-the-oft/;jsessionid=9EEEE525FE054F2C06E2DE92082E562D> and <http://webarchive.nationalarchives.gov.uk/20140402141250/http://www.competition-commission.org.uk/about-us> accessed 23 August 2024. See also Graham (n 26) 20

37 Graham (n 26) 20

38 Graham (n 26) 561

39 Enterprise and Regulatory Reform Act 2013, s 25(3)

40 Graham (n 26) 20

41 Office of Fair Trading, 'Annual Report and Accounts 2012–13' (2013) 6 <https://www.gov.uk/government/uploads/system/uploads/attachment_data/file/246793/0023.pdf> accessed 16 April 2024

42 Competition and Markets Authority, 'Consumer Protection: Guidance on the CMA's Approach to Use of Its Consumer Power' (March 2014) para [5.14]

3.3.2 The Concept of Undertaking

The first and primary enforcement strategy adopted by UK competition law is the imposition of fine undertakings. In order to achieve the policy objective of maximisation of consumer welfare, the provisions of Chapter 1 and Chapter 2 of the CA98 essentially prohibit 'undertakings' from engaging in anti-competitive behaviour. Curiously, despite the extensive usage of the term, the CA98 does not define 'undertaking'.[43] In that respect, two groups of questions need to be considered.[44] The first relies on the factor of 'economic activity' in explaining the operation of competition law. In this respect, the term undertaking is defined in *Höfner and Elser v. Macrotron*[45] as follows:

> It must be observed, in the context of competition law, first that the concept of an undertaking encompasses every entity engaged in an economic activity, regardless of the legal status of the entity and the way in which it is financed and, secondly, that employment procurement is an economic activity.[46]

The second group of questions, which focus on the 'boundaries of undertaking', are based on the scope of the term undertaking. This set of questions is complex because various forms differ, from single actors to corporate structures. In this regard, a definition of undertaking has been given in two cases. In *Hydrotherm v. Compact*,[47] an undertaking was defined as 'designating an economic unit for the purpose of the subject matter of the agreement in question, even if in the law that economic unit consists of several persons, natural or legal'.[48] In that case, two companies, and the natural person who managed them, were considered as a single undertaking.[49] In addition, in *Mannesmann v. High Authority*,[50] undertaking was defined as 'a single organisation of personal, tangible, and intangible elements, attached to an autonomous legal entity and pursuing a given long-term economic aim'.[51]

Even though the concept of undertaking, on its face, may cover individuals, the term is usually interpreted to refer to companies as far as competition law is concerned. This is because, as argued by Thepot, 'internal relations or mechanisms, including that of corporate governance, are outside of competition law scrutiny'.[52] In a broader sense, competition law considers an undertaking as the firm, and

43 Galloway (n 9) III-381
44 Wouter PJ Wils, 'The Undertaking as Subject of E.C. Competition Law and the Imputation of Infringements to Natural or Legal Persons' (2000) 25(2) European Law Review 99, 100
45 Case C-41/90 *Höfner and Elser v. Macrotron* [1991] ECR I-1979, [1993] 4 CMLR 306
46 Case C-41/90 *Höfner and Elser v. Macrotron* [1991] ECR I-1979, [1993] 4 CMLR 306 [21]
47 Case 170/83 *Hydrotherm v. Compact* [1985] ECR 3016
48 Case 170/83 *Hydrotherm v. Compact* [1985] ECR 3016 [11]
49 Case 170/83 *Hydrotherm v. Compact* [1985] ECR 3016 [10]–[11]
50 Case 19/61 *Mannesmann v. High Authority* [1962] ECR 357
51 Case 19/61 *Mannesmann v. High Authority* [1962] ECR 357 [371]
52 Thepot (n 1) 3

established corporate structures tend to be disregarded. In this sense, competition law challenges long-established principles of company law, including the separate and distinct corporate legal personality, in that it does not consider these issues as relevant. This is suggestive of the fact that it does not place weight on the individuals who run the company's business.

Through prioritising competition policy, which focuses on consumer welfare, competition law considers the effect on the market of the conduct and focuses far less on the cause of that conduct or the identification of the source from particular parts of a corporate structure.[53] Competition law does not pay adequate attention to where responsibility should be attributed or where liability should remain and whether it is more suitable to attribute these to the company as a whole or to particular individuals. Consequently, it highlights the economic entity and the conduct of the company in the market as its concern. For this reason, the internal dimension of the company is barely concerned with enforcement strategies, as they usually target the company.[54]

This casts serious doubts as to how competition law leaves liability and whether it imposes sanctions in the right place due to the fact that it focuses on *ex-post* objectives by its willingness to disregard the long-established norms and principles of company law. Moreover, there is a real question as to whether it attributes the liability to the more appropriate individual. In the next section, how the primary enforcement instrument is implemented and its impact on the risk relationship between the company and its directors will be examined.

3.3.3 Public Enforcement and the Company's Exposure to Risk

Based on the discussions put forward in the previous sections, UK competition law aims to advance the policy objective of consumer welfare. And for this purpose, it primarily targets undertakings by imposing fines.[55] These issues have been examined because there is a strong connection 'between the objectives of competition policy and the way in which the policy is enforced and ultimately infringements are sanctioned'.[56] In order to achieve the objective of competition policy, UK competition law adopts different enforcement strategies. These mechanisms have been put in force in the light of three significant dynamics which presumably would deter anti-competitive conduct.[57] They are 'the risk of reputational damage for the company, criminal sanctions for individuals, and financial penalties for the company'.[58]

53 Thepot (n 1) 77

54 Thepot (n 1) 3

55 Arguably the behavioural remedy is just as important, and often used, sanction in the competition authority toolkit as the fine

56 Parret (n 11) 365

57 Office of Fair Trading, 'The Impact of Competition Interventions on Compliance and Deterrence Final Report (OFT1391, December 2011) para [6.5.]

58 Office of Fair Trading, 'The Impact of Competition Interventions on Compliance and Deterrence Final Report (OFT1391, December 2011) para [6.5.]

Based on the first and third factors, in order to prevent competition law infringements and in order to ensure consumer welfare, regulatory authorities tend to impose monetary sanctions on companies. The next two sections will consider how this mechanism is implemented and its impact on the particular relationship between the company and its directors. As such it will examine corporate exposure to the risk of regulatory sanctions for regulatory infringements where individuals are involved in anti-competitive behaviour.

3.3.3.1 Public Enforcement: The Administrative Enforcement Strategy

The public enforcement strategy is typically implemented by public authorities that are empowered to enforce the rules of competition law. The main purpose of implementing such an enforcement mechanism is to deter anti-competitive behaviour so that wrongdoers would be aware that the potential punishment is greater than the expected gains.[59] The effectiveness of this enforcement mechanism requires that the authorities take two steps, namely, the detection of infringement and intervention against the wrongdoer. In a general sense, the state has many forms of sanctions that can be imposed on defaulters, which depend largely on the nature of a particular infringement. These can include 'pecuniary fines or incarceration'.[60] In furtherance of the public enforcement strategy, the UK Competition Act provides for the imposition of fines on companies and undertakings, which can be up to 10% of their turnover for the previous year. [61] By any means, this sanction is considerably large. It is hoped that this power to impose fines, coupled with the fear of reputational damage, would spur companies to shirk from breaching competition law.[62] The foundation of this enforcement strategy can be, as Wils suggested, that the imposition of fines contributes to competition law in three ways: 'through deterrent effects, through moral effects, and by raising the cost of setting up and running cartels'.[63]

A survey that was undertaken by Frazer on the tendency of companies to comply with the law also supports this attitude that companies tend to comply with the law where there is a likelihood that penalties would be imposed on them if they fail to comply.[64] According to the survey, 43.6% of companies agreed strongly, and 28.7% agreed with this finding. This outcome may support the view that financial

59 Kai Hüschelrath, 'Public Enforcement of Anti-Cartel Laws – Theory and Empirical Evidence' in Kai Hüschelrath and Heike Schweitzer (eds), *Public and Private Enforcement of Competition Law in Europe Legal and Economic Perspectives* (Springer 2014) 9, 10

60 Kai Hüschelrath, 'Public Enforcement of Anti-Cartel Laws – Theory and Empirical Evidence' in Kai Hüschelrath and Heike Schweitzer (eds), *Public and Private Enforcement of Competition Law in Europe Legal and Economic Perspectives* (Springer 2014) 9–10

61 Competition Act 1998, s 36. Imprisonment and directors' disqualification are also public enforcement mechanisms, but they are going to be examined in Section 3.5

62 Office of Fair Trading, 'Drivers of Compliance and Non-Compliance with Competition Law' (OFT 1227, May 2010) para [1.10]

63 Wouter PJ Wils, 'Optimal Antitrust Fines: Theory and Practice' (2006) 29(2) World Competition 183

64 Tim Frazer, 'Monopoly, Prohibition and Deterrence' (1995) 58(6) MLR 846, 853

penalties can sufficiently incentivise companies to comply with the rules of law—a factor that may explain the imposition of monetary sanctions in the first place. But imposing fines is not enough. The amount of the fine must also be taken into account. In essence, a company would probably not enter into wrongdoing if the possible fine exceeds the gains it expects from the wrong. If that is so, the desired deterrent aim of the fine would have been achieved. In consideration of the high level of harm that anti-competitive behaviour causes and the low possibility of detection, the main theoretical basis of UK competition law regimes is to ensure that fines as set as high as possible. However, Combe and Monnier argue that 'fines imposed against cartels by the Commission are still far from optimal, even if we consider a 100% probability of detection'.[65] This attitude was supported by Ginsburg and Wright, who noted that 'corporate fines seem not to take the profit out of price-fixing'.[66]

Indeed, although average corporate fines have dramatically increased in UK competition regimes since 1990, the question still remains as to whether this has succeeded in generating greater deterrence.[67] This is because, besides the considerations of the enforcement strategy of fining and the amount of the fines, there is another factor that may have been neglected for the purpose of achieving greater deterrence. This dynamic can be defined as targeting the correct wrongdoer. Attention also needs to be given to the matter of who is targeted by the imposition of a fine since the desired deterrence may not be achieved unless enforcement is accurately targeted. Concerns about the effectiveness of the deterrent fining strategy may potentially lie on this ground, as Stephan discussed how 'corporate fines (however high they may be) largely punish the wrong people'.[68] He went on to argue that these fines 'tend to be imposed many years after an infringement was instigated, with little or no direct effect on the individual decision makers responsible'.[69] Accordingly, 'monetary penalties directed at the corporation will often prove inadequate to deter illegal behaviour'.[70]

The best evidence for the lack of deterrent effect with the fine strategy is the current practice adopted by EU competition law, which consists of almost entirely of corporate fines. The issue is that this strategy may provide very little enforcement to prevent anti-competitive offences.[71] This was also illustrated by research

65 Emmanuel Combe and Constance Monnier, 'Fines Against Hard Core Cartels in Europe: The Myth of Over Enforcement' (2011) 56 Antitrust Bull 235, 260
66 Douglas Ginsburg and Joshua Wright, 'Antitrust Sanctions' (2010) 6(2) Competition Policy International 3, 18
67 Douglas Ginsburg and Joshua Wright, 'Antitrust Sanctions' (2010) 6(2) Competition Policy International 11, 16
68 Andreas Stephan, 'Disqualification Orders for Directors Involved in Cartels' (2011) 2(6) Journal of European Competition Law 529, 535
69 Andreas Stephan, 'Disqualification Orders for Directors Involved in Cartels' (2011) 2(6) Journal of European Competition Law 529
70 See Coffee (n 42) 389
71 Aaron Khan, 'Rethinking Sanctions for Breaching EU Competition Law: Is Director Disqualification the Answer?' (2012) 35 World Competition 77, 78

undertaken by the OFT (currently CMA) on businesses. In fact, fines were found to be the fourth most effective sanction, following criminal penalties, disqualification of directors, publicity, and private actions.[72] Criminal penalties and disqualification were ranked as the most important sanctions in deterring competition law infringements. The potential reason that underlies this finding is that the decisions of companies are typically taken by directors, and considering their potential roles in competition law infringements, they may require the authorities to try a new approach to deterrence.

The problem with solely relying on corporate fines is that the sanctions that are imposed on companies do not always achieve a deterrent effect on individuals because, in many cases, the company may not be in a position to control its directors effectively. Consequently, the desired deterrent effect of sanctions is unlikely to be achieved. This is because when the fines are imposed on the company, the ones who bear the burden are the consumers and potentially shareholders, who are almost definitely limited in their ability to affect the company's conduct, rather than the individuals, who are unlikely to be deterred through this strategy as no preventative sanction is taken against them.[73] This enforcement strategy illustrates that competition law does not tend to localise the source of conduct or particular decisions.[74] Rather, it attributes liability to the larger corporate holding. Thus, it would seem that what the regulator is more interested in is being able to attribute liability in a way that can attract and highlight sanctions. In this sense, competition law is unconcerned with the legally respected and established corporate structures, and the next section will examine the negative consequences that ignoring these nuances may potentially have for the company.

3.3.3.2 A Company's Exposure to the Risk of Liability and Loss

As has been seen, public enforcement through administrative fines aims to deter companies from breaching competition law as a means of advancing consumer welfare. The issue is that while competition law targets companies as a means of promoting its policy objectives, the public enforcement strategy does not seek to deter the individuals 'behind' the company from engaging in anti-competitive conduct. It is at this point that the tension between the purposes and objectives of corporate governance and competition law arises because, as Rock states, antitrust 'is about markets; corporate law is about firms. Antitrust is about competition; corporate law is about cooperation. Antitrust regulates relations among firms; corporate law governs relations within firms'.[75] The tension is more about how these subjects operate because corporate governance deals with the 'internal dimension' of the

72 Office of Fair Trading, 'Drivers of Compliance and Non-Compliance with Competition Law' (OFT 1227 May 2010) para [1.10]
73 Ginsburg and Wright (n 65) 22
74 Except the individual sanctions, which will be examined later on in the chapter
75 Edward B Rock, 'Corporate Law through an Antitrust Lens' (1992) 92 Columbia Law Review 497, 498

company, while competition law is concerned with its 'external dimension'.[76] From the perspective of competition law, the company is a 'black box'. In this regard, competition law is generally indifferent to the internal dimensions of companies.[77] As such it is enforced without considering how the company form operates as well as the internal structures that underpin its workings.

Public enforcement through corporate fines illustrates this lack of tendency of competition law to intervene in the particular relationships that exist within the company, such as those of the company and its directors. That said, whether the approach exposes the company to the risk of liability and loss when competition law is breached by its directors is often overlooked. This is because, from the perspective of competition law, anti-competitive conduct would inevitably occur as a result of the actions of a handful of employees who either engage in it personally or permit others to do so.[78] Thus, they are presumably aware that what they are conducting is illegal and may harm the company in some way.[79] In this sense, competition law misunderstands or oversimplifies the particular relationship between the actors of corporate governance, and it is not connected to and concerned with the company's exposure to risk of liability and loss as a result of the illegal conduct of its directors.

In respect to the undesirable behaviour of directors examined in this book, there is no doubt that while directors' involvement in anti-competitive behaviour may benefit the company in the short term, it may potentially expose it to significant risks of liability and loss in the long term. The way in which breaches of competition law are sanctioned illustrates such exposure because, for example, while the formation of a cartel would likely increase the short-term value of the company, the adverse implication is that it may suffer financial and reputational damage. Again, fines that are imposed on companies are not 'paid by the individuals who are responsible for the infringements but by companies and, ultimately, by their shareholders and consumers'.[80] For this reason, 'firm-level liability is generally regarded as inefficient because it imposes significant externalities' since the punishment imposed usually goes beyond those who are responsible and impacts third parties as well.[81] The long-term interests of other non-shareholder stakeholders will also be impaired since the value of the company would be decreased as a result of the imposition of fines. Of all we have been saying, this is the sum: imposing fines on companies for competition infringements without more is not effective enough

76 Thepot (n 1) 14–15

77 Thepot (n 1) 17

78 Andreas Stephan, 'See No Evil: Cartels and the Limits of Antitrust Compliance Programs (2010) 31(8) Comp Law 231, 236–239. See also Florence Thepot, 'Antitrust v. Anti-Corruption Policy Approaches to Compliance: Why Such a Gap?' (2015) 2 CPI Antitrust Chronicle 1, 4

79 Andreas Stephan, 'See No Evil: Cartels and the Limits of Antitrust Compliance Programs (2010) 31(8) Comp Law 231, 236–239. See also Florence Thepot, 'Antitrust v. Anti-Corruption Policy Approaches to Compliance: Why Such a Gap?' (2015) 2 CPI Antitrust Chronicle 239

80 Andreas Weitbrecht, 'From Freiburg to Chicago and Beyond: The First 50 Years of European Competition Law' 29(2) (2008) ECLR 81, 88

81 SL Schwarcz, 'Excessive Corporate Risk-Taking and the Decline of Personal Blame' (2015) 65 Emory Law Journal 533

in deterring directors from engaging in such conduct. It also leaves companies with the responsibility to take action against defaulting directors, but again, this is often difficult since directors tend to control companies. The next section will examine some theories that underlie this approach in UK competition law.

3.4 Regulatory Compliance and Deterrence Theories

The main logic behind the approach adopted by competition law may be that the company is in such a position that it can sufficiently motivate its individuals to avoid any competition law infringement, which may potentially result in fines. The foundation of this approach is based on the cumulative impact of regulatory compliance and deterrence theories that aim to persuade potential wrongdoers not to be involved in misconduct or to impose punishment where there is a default in complying with the law. Thus, despite the fact that their strategies are different, with the compliance theory employing persuasion as a tool and the deterrence theory relying on the threat of punishment, their objectives are arguably similar. This section will examine whether these theories are based on an effective foundation that persuades or prevents potential wrongdoers from becoming involved in misconduct. It will, in that vein, examine their connection to the approach adopted by UK competition law.

3.4.1 The Regulatory Compliance Theory Approach

The first theory that may underlie the approach embodied in the current competition policy is the regulatory compliance theory. Here, the company is considered an entity that provides guidance to its members on how to behave. In order to avoid any adverse consequences that may arise from public enforcement of laws, the company is required to set up insider norms and regulatory compliance programmes designed to train its employees so as to ensure that they do not infringe competition law what acting on its. These 'compliance strategies' are typically implemented through internal compliance programmes, which can be defined as tools 'which will enable companies to detect, deter and prevent any non-compliance with the applicable laws'.[82] The reason for relying on these internal strategies is based on the widely accepted statement that 'corporate culture is an important factor in explaining the engagement of companies in competition law infringements'.[83]

Such programmes have two important functions in increasing social welfare.[84] Firstly, they increase the level of corporate compliance as each member within the

82 Gönenç Gürkaynak, Ç Olgu Kama and Burcu Ergün, 'How to Establish and Operate an Anti-Corruption Compliance Program in Emerging Markets: The Turkish Example' (2015) 1(2) Turkish Commercial Law Review 145

83 Florence Thepot, 'Corporate Compliance with Competition Law' (Ascola Annual Conference, Meiji University 2015) 1

84 Sharon Oded, 'Enforcement Strategies, Compliance Programs, and the Intermediary Gatekeepers' (2010) 22–23 <https://editorialexpress.com/cgi-bin/conference/download.cgi?db_name=ALEA2010&paper_id=197> accessed 1 March 2024

company would be aware of the required regulatory standards. Secondly, the cost of investigation by public regulators would be reduced since these programmes presumably monitor the behaviour of employees to ensure that they do not infringe on competition law.

Insider programmes and norms typically include the issuance of ethics codes, training, guidelines, manuals, close monitoring, and the provision of comprehensive working procedures.[85] Through these mechanisms, corporate agents can be guided and trained so as to be aware of what is considered lawful and what is not. Where such awareness is sufficient, it is presumed that it would result in good corporate governance by ensuring in the attainment of an acceptable compliance level by company directors and other relevant agents.

In this view, the compliance theory may underlie the approach that is adopted by UK competition law, which always encourages companies to incentivise their employees with a view to attaining significantly high compliance with the rules of competition law. This can be seen from the considerable efforts shown by the OFT (currently CMA), which provides some guidance to companies[86] and organises compliance and awareness workshops across the United Kingdom in respect of how they should maintain compliance with competition law.[87] In respect of guidance, it was recognised that a one-size-fits-all approach is not suitable for ensuring compliance with competition law and that a principle-based approach should rather be supported.[88] In this respect, it has been stated that

> [T]he key point is that businesses should find an effective means of identifying, assessing, mitigating and reviewing their competition law risks in order to create and maintain a culture of compliance with competition law that works for their organisations.[89]

Despite the fact that the importance of these compliance programmes has been acknowledged by UK competition law authorities,[90] their effectiveness in incentivising employees to comply with the law requires further consideration. Even at that,

85 Sharon Oded, 'Enforcement Strategies, Compliance Programs, and the Intermediary Gatekeepers' (2010) 22 <https://editorialexpress.com/cgi-bin/conference/download.cgi?db_name=ALEA2010&paper_id=197> accessed 1 March 2024

86 Office of Fair Trading (n 71); Office of Fair Trading, 'How Your Business Can Achieve Compliance with Competition Law' (OFT1341 2011) <https://assets.publishing.service.gov.uk/media/5a7c2572e5274a1f5cc7613f/oft1341.pdf> accessed 6 July 2024

87 Competition and Markets Authority, 'Motivating Businesses to Comply with Competition Law' (2024) <https://events.lawsociety.org.uk/uploads/files/43a2c764-5209-4c5f-bb07-fba051e77f95.pdf> accessed 1 June 2024

88 Office of Fair Trading (n 71) para [1.5]

89 Office of Fair Trading, 'How Your Business Can Achieve Compliance with Competition Law' (OFT1341 2011) para [1.2] <https://www.gov.uk/government/uploads/system/uploads/attachment_data/file/284402/oft1341.pdf> accessed 1 June 2024

90 The company, which has established a strong compliance programme, would be granted up to 10% reduction in fines

the extent of their impact is doubtful. In this regard it is strange that '[t]here have been no attempts in the literature to estimate empirically the general effects, positive or negative, of antitrust compliance programmes'.[91] Admittedly, some empirical studies have been undertaken in the United States to determine whether these programmes are effective in deterring infringements of some other areas of law. Even at that, the outcomes have been hardly positive.[92] In this connection, Krawiec argued that 'the data regarding the effectiveness of internal compliance-based organisational liability regimes is both preliminary and disturbing'.[93] She argued further that although empirical studies illustrate that diversity training programmes increase the awareness and knowledge of employees, they provide little information on the extent to which they contribute to behavioural change.[94]

It thus remains unclear whether these programmes positively influence employee behaviour. One reason for this is that they are largely voluntary. In fact, they can only incentivise effective compliance if employees are 'forced' to consider ethical codes and are adequately motivated to remember what they learn from training programmes before they act. The effectiveness of an ethics code is based on the determination of the individual as to whether they have been involved in any conduct contrary to the ethics code and whether they tend to report it.[95] In respect of the involvement of executives and controllers in fraudulent financial reporting, Brief, Dukerich, Brown, and Brett also demonstrated that, 'neither personal values, codes of conduct, nor the interaction of the two factors played a significant role'.[96] The findings of interviews undertaken by Schwartz also support this argument that some individuals do not even remember the provisions of the codes and, consequently, they hardly influence behaviour.[97]

The problematic issue in this sense is that even though companies establish several training programmes and comprehensive ethics codes, they may not ensure that they translate into good directorial behaviour since their application is largely left to the discretion of these directors in practice. In essence, while internal structures may improve the knowledge of employees on the different issues that may

91 Wouter PJ Wils, 'Antitrust Compliance Programmes & Optimal Antitrust Enforcement' (2013) 1(1) JAE 52, 63

92 Marie McKendall, Beverly DeMarr, and Catherine Jones-Rikkers, 'Ethical Compliance Programs and Corporate Illegality: Testing the Assumptions of the Corporate Sentencing Guidelines' (2002) 37 Journal of Business Ethics 367; Kimberly D Krawiec, 'Cosmetic Compliance and the Failure of Negotiated Governance' (2003) 81 Washington University Law Quarterly 487, 510–515

93 Kimberly D Krawiec, 'Organizational Misconduct: Beyond the Principal: Agent Model' (2005) 32 Florida State University Law Review 571, 596

94 Krawiec (n 93) 514–515

95 Alan Kitson, 'Taking the Pulse: Ethics and the British Cooperative Bank' (1996) 15 Journal of Business Ethics 1021

96 Arthur P Brief, Janet M Dukerich, Paul R Brown, and Joan F Brett, 'What's Wrong With the Treadway Commission Report? Experimental Analyses of the Effects of Personal Values and Codes of Conduct on Fraudulent Financial Reporting' (1996) 15 Journal of Business Ethics 183

97 M Schwartz, 'The Nature of the Relationship Between Corporate Codes of Ethics and Behaviour' (2001) 32 Journal of Business Ethics 247, 253

arise in the company, existing research is limited on whether they actually translate into positive behavioural changes.

At this point, the issue of companies' exposure to the risk of regulatory punishment arises, as its efforts to set up compliance programmes cannot be effective unless their directors act on them. This is because, based on a survey undertaken by McKenzie, '[a]nti-trust/competition was most frequently identified as the number one legal risk (18.1% of respondents) and was the most likely to be identified in the top three legal risks (38.6% of respondents)'.[98] These results demonstrate how the potential risk of competition law infringement is likely to incentivise companies to set up strong compliance programmes. In addition, the survey also showed that the legal risks which may be potentially faced by executive directors underlie the reason to implement compliance programmes. The logic behind this issue is that the implementation of compliance programmes in practice is in the hands of directors, and they are typically incentivised to do so through the personal liability that they may face. In essence, compliance programmes hardly serve to mitigate the risk that a company would be visited with financial sanctions for competition breaches. This is because they are unlikely to incentivise directors to implement them in practice in the first place.

Another issue regarding the tension between compliance theory and the company/directors relationship is that where the company fails to control its directors, and any infringement arises, it might be punished for non-compliance with the law.[99] The company is typically regarded as a better monitor and investigator of its employees' behaviour than the authorities, and for this reason, corporate sanctions can encourage it to seek ways to improve its monitoring and compliance mechanisms so as to induce its employees to comply with the law.[100] Krawiec defined such internal compliance programmes as a 'negotiated governance mechanism'[101] and considered this attitude as a 'disturbing fact'.[102] She continued to discuss that,

> Even more disturbing, however, is the fact that the evidence that does exist is decidedly mixed, with many of the most recent and methodologically sound studies finding no significant correlation between the most widely-used internal compliance structures and reduced organizational misconduct.[103]

98 Baker McKenzie, 'Legal Risk and Compliance: Special Report' (2008) 12 <http://www.bakermckenzie.com/files/Publication/cfd093ec-a4d7-4009-9d6c-46dfafafd935/Presentation/PublicationAttachment/7020eac4-e025-4ca6-8fb3-484e82407e5f/london_rmc_importance_rms_survey_2008.pdf> accessed 5 April 2024

99 It can be understandable that if the company is punished for non-existence of compliance programme it would be considered as its ignorance of law

100 Jennifer Arlen and Refier Kraakman, 'Controlling Corporate Misconduct: An Analysis of Corporate Liability Regimes' (1997) 72(4) *New York University of Law & Review* 687, 693

101 Krawiec (n 93) 541

102 Krawiec (n 94) 591

103 Krawiec (n 94) 591

The logic that may underlie this approach is that 'mild law does not induce widespread law-abiding behaviour if it is imposed by an exogenous authority'.[104] The concept of mild law can be defined as a 'soft law'[105] that relies on compliance through persuasion, and the role of the company for this purpose is regarded as greater and more influential than the outside enforcers.

Hence, although there is little existing evidence in the literature on the effectiveness of these internal compliance programmes on individuals, their perceived role as a 'liability determinant' of the company has been commonly relied on.[106] Having an established corporate compliance programme could be a consideration point when a company's liability is determined, and the amount of punishment imposed on the company can be reduced if it has established a strong compliance structure. For this reason, this method can be called 'duty-based liability'.[107]

In respect of this issue, two opposite approaches have been adopted by different competition law regimes. While the EU competition law authorities do not, and the US authorities almost never take compliance programmes into account as a reason to mitigate the punishment for competition law infringements, UK competition law authorities may reduce fines for up to 10% if they are satisfied with the company's compliance efforts.[108] It was illustrated in a 2011 policy document that a reduction of a penalty imposed for anti-competitive behaviour might be provided if adequate efforts were made for the purpose of ensuring compliance.[109] An example of such a reduction was seen in the case of the market-sharing agreement undertaken between Arriva Plc and First Group plc.[110] In this case, there was proof that the company had provided training manuals and had conducted training. There was also proof that genuine compliance systems were put in place and were generally followed and adhered to. As a result, the penalties imposed on the company were reduced by 10%.[111]

The possibility of obtaining a reduction in fines should incentivise the company to establish an effective compliance programme.[112] The question that arises, however, is whether the strengthening of a compliance programme can be determined by the number of times a breach occurs. In other words, does a single breach imply

104 Jean-Robert Tyran and Lars P Feld, 'Achieving Compliance When Legal Sanctions Are Non-Deterrent' (2006) 108(1) The Scandinavian Journal of Economics 135, 153

105 Thepot (n 82) 2

106 Krawiec (n 94) 591

107 Oded (n 83) 23

108 Florence Thepot, 'Antitrust v. Anti-Corruption Policy Approaches to Compliance: Why Such a Gap?' (2015) 2 CPI Antitrust Chronicle 1, 4. See also Office of Fair Trading, 'OFT's Guidance as to the Appropriate Amount of a Penalty' (OFT423 2012) para [2.15] <https://www.gov.uk/government/uploads/system/uploads/attachment_data/file/284393/oft423.pdf> accessed 14 March 2024

109 See also Office of Fair Trading, 'OFT's Guidance as to the Appropriate Amount of a Penalty' (OFT423 2012) para [2.15] <https://www.gov.uk/government/uploads/system/uploads/attachment_data/file/284393/oft423.pdf> accessed 14 March 2024

110 Decision of the Directors General of Fair Trading, No. CA98/9/2002

111 Decision of the Directors General of Fair Trading, No. CA98/9/2002 [66]

112 Singleton (n 3) 102

that there is a complete failure of the entire corporate compliance structure? This question is important since the fact remains that even when a company may have established a strong compliance programme, it is the directors who implement these programmes in practice. This issue has also been noticed by UK competition law authorities, who noted that

> [D]irectors play a key role in establishing and maintaining an effective competition law compliance culture within their company. Without the full commitment of individual directors to compliance with competition law, any compliance activities undertaken by the company are unlikely to be effective.[113]

Based on this consideration, we submit that in the United Kingdom, companies should be 'entitled' to reductions for their compliance efforts, even where their directors are involved in competition law breaches. In this regard, we can draw lessons from the price-fixing agreement between Hasbro UK Ltd, Argos Ltd, and Littlewoods Ltd.[114] In that case, Hasbro demonstrated that it established compliance programmes which its senior management ignored. But despite arguing that the actions of its directors should not be an aggravating element, the OFT (now CMA) found that the company had entered into a price-fixing agreement in breach of a section of the Competition Act.[115] Normally, although the existence of compliance programmes may be regarded as a mitigating factor in many cases, the OFT (now CMA) determined that this factor may be 'offset by the fact that it was blatantly ignored at a very senior level within Hasbro and no adjustment is appropriate'.[116] Even at that, the disciplinary actions taken later on by the company against guilty employees were taken under consideration, and accordingly, Hasbro was granted a 10% fine reduction.[117]

Hence, whether the particular compliance programme established in the company is sufficient to prevent employees from becoming involved in anti-competitive behaviour is not the sole focus of the UK competition law authorities. They also consider the efforts put in place by the company to achieve greater compliance. The possibility of fine reductions may encourage companies to make more effort to take greater compliance measures without considering whether their directors would comply with them. It is thus submitted that companies should be entitled to reductions regardless of whether their directors ignore or comply with the compliance programme. The possibility of fine reduction, however, does not eliminate the primary responsibility of the company for the sanctions that may be imposed on it.

113 Office of Fair Trading, 'Company Directors and Competition Law' (OFT1340 2011) para [1.2] <https://www.gov.uk/government/uploads/system/uploads/attachment_data/file/284410/oft1340.pdf> accessed 15 May 2024

114 Decision of Director General of Fair-Trading No. CA98/2/2003

115 Decision of Director General of Fair-Trading No. CA98/2/2003 [404]

116 Decision of Director General of Fair-Trading No. CA98/2/2003 [404]

117 Decision of Director General of Fair-Trading No. CA98/2/2003 [405]

This is because even though it may have made a great effort to set up compliance programmes, it would still be liable to pay at least 90% of the amount of the fine. One reason for this is that even when a company has adequate internal compliance structures, the role of implementing them is left to the directors.

The main problem, thus, lies in the fact that the company is regarded as the controller of its directors through compliance programmes. This attitude to corporate internal compliance structures and sanctions is not holistic enough as it tends to measure the company's liability by looking at the actual infringements while ignoring the fact that its employees may have failed to implement the compliance programmes that it may have put in place.[118] Accordingly, 'if a company has made a reasonable effort to comply with the antitrust law, and an employee nevertheless engages in price-fixing, then it makes no sense to fine the corporation'.[119]

What this means is that, despite the fact that competition law authorities have made some efforts by publishing guidance, organising compliance workshops, and providing a fine reduction for companies which have compliance instruments, companies' exposure to the risk of liability and loss due to the anti-competitive behaviour of its directors is still likely to be in place. This is because although these efforts are erected for the benefit of the company, they are still subjected to administrative enforcement strategies in the event of non-compliance.

3.4.2 The Deterrence Theory Approach

The second philosophy that may underlie the current UK approach to competition law enforcement is the deterrence theory, which aims to deter wrongdoing by punishing the particular wrongdoer who engages in misconduct by the imposition of monetary and criminal sanctions. The modern deterrence theory is largely based on the thoughts of classical philosophers such as Thomas Hobbes, Cesare Beccaria, and Jeremy Bentham.[120] The common point that unites these early approaches is that, in order to maintain the desired deterrence, the potential benefit from a crime should be less than the punishment imposed on the defaulter.[121] In other words, the cost of the punishment to the wrongdoer should be greater than the potential benefit he/she would gain. According to this, the pain and pleasure, as potential consequences of the misconduct, are tools that disincentivise or incentivise individuals, and when the pain outweighs the pleasure, the deterrent effect is achieved. Reiss described this as being how 'the presumption in deterrence . . . is that [the] behaviour is rational to the degree that it responds to incentives and disincentives,

118 *Hasbro*, analysed earlier, can be an example of such situation as it illustrates the difference between the motivation of the company and its senior management employees
119 Ginsburg and Wright (n 65) 18
120 Ihekwoaba Onwudiwe, Jonathan Odo, and Emmanuel C Onyeozili, 'Deterrence Theory' in Mary Bosworth (ed.), *Encyclopedia of Prisons & Correctional Facilities* (Sage 2005) 234
121 Ihekwoaba Onwudiwe, Jonathan Odo, and Emmanuel C Onyeozili, 'Deterrence Theory' in Mary Bosworth (ed.), *Encyclopedia of Prisons & Correctional Facilities* (Sage 2005) 234–235

particularly to the disincentives of negative sanctions'.[122] Thus, the degree of compliance with the relevant law is based on the level of pain of possible detection. This approach was also supported in the economic models of Becker and Stigler. It can also be found in Posner's context of microeconomic theory.[123]

Regarding the concern of enforcement to prevent corporate misconduct, four assumptions underlie these early deterrence theories. They are that

(i) corporations are fully-informed utility maximisers
(ii) legal statutes unambiguously define misbehaviour
(iii) legal punishment provides the primary incentive for corporate compliance
(iv) enforcement agencies optimally detect and punish misbehaviour, given available resources.[124]

According to these assumptions, the company is regarded as an entity that is aware of how its employees behave and knows how to incentivise them to prevent wrongful behaviour through compliance strategies. The main logic behind this attitude is that 'many corporate crimes . . . cannot be readily detected by the government', and the company is usually in a better position to discover crimes and identify particular individuals who are engaged in them.[125] According to this approach, the fact that misbehaviour arises within a company is proof that the company has failed to apply its power to prevent its employees from breaking the law.

Onwudiwe, Odo, and Onyeozili observe that these early deterrence theories were framed according to the three elements of 'severity, certainty, and celerity'.[126] The roles of these elements in deterrence theory are significant because, under the consideration of severity, the effectiveness of the punishment is measured based on whether the pain outweighs the pleasure, while the element of certainty ensures that the misconduct has occurred and the punishment is imposed. In addition, the element of celerity ensures that the investigation is finalised and the required punishment is imposed as quickly as possible.

To achieve the desired deterrence, these three elements are crucial. That said, to focus solely on these is to overlook another important element, which is to target the correct wrongdoer. Identifying this person is vital since, if the target is wrongly determined, these three underlying elements would be meaningless as far as achieving deterrence is concerned. This is due to the attitude which asserts that the harm must have arisen because of corporate error. Scholz described how the

122 Albert J Reiss, 'Consequences of Compliance and Deterrence Models of Law Enforcement for the Exercise of Police Discretion' (1984) 47(4) LCP 83, 94
123 John T Scholz, 'Enforcement Policy and Corporate Misconduct: The Changing Perspective of Deterrence Theory' 60(3) LCP 253, 254
124 John T Scholz, 'Enforcement Policy and Corporate Misconduct: The Changing Perspective of Deterrence Theory' 60(3) LCP 254
125 Jennifer Arlen, 'The Potentially Perverse Effects of Corporate Criminal Liability' (1994) 23 Journal of Legal Studies 833, 835
126 Onwudiwe *et al* (n 121) 235

'deterrence model reflects a common assumption that rules are imposed on corporations against their wishes, and, therefore, that legal penalties provide the primary motivation to counterbalance the profitability of misconduct'.[127] The underlying assumption of this approach is that targeting companies is always considered less costly and time consuming. This ensures that state agents are able to deploy their resources and time to address a greater number of violations.

The approach of the deterrence theory has been adopted in a number of areas of law,[128] but

> it is particularly suited to cartel regulation as it might be expected that business people, whose main aim is profit maximisation, can be expected to act as 'amoral calculators' in that they will calculate the expected costs and benefits of any behaviour before acting.[129]

Undoubtedly, the UK approach of imposing administrative sanctions that target companies in order to achieve deterrence has influenced UK competition law. This was illustrated in guidance published by the OFT, and followed by the CMA, as two purposes of imposing financial penalties were explained:

> (i) to impose penalties on infringing undertakings which reflect the seriousness of the infringement, and (ii) to ensure that the threat of penalties will deter both the infringing undertakings and other undertakings that may be considering anticompetitive activities from engaging in them.[130]

Another common factor in the deterrence theory and UK competition law regime is the severity of the punishment. This is because the deterrent effect of administrative fines has always been considered in competition law at various levels.[131] In this regard, a six-step approach adopted by the CMA also illustrates this common ground. This approach was adopted to calculate the appropriate fine to impose on a particular company. The aim is to ensure that the sanction imposed achieves the greatest deterrence possible in the circumstance. These steps consider (i) the seriousness of the infringement and turnover of the undertaking, (ii) the duration of the infringement, (iii) mitigating factors, (iv) deterrence and proportionality, (v) a maximum penalty of 10% of worldwide turnover, and (vi) how leniency and settlement discounts are taken under consideration.[132] The purpose of such determination is to deter the company from infringing competition law by making

127 Scholz (n 124) 261

128 Such as criminal law, consumer law, and environmental law. See Barry J Rodger and Angus MacCulloch, *Competition Law and Policy in the EC and UK* (5th edn, Routledge 2015) 25

129 Barry J Rodger and Angus MacCulloch, *Competition Law and Policy in the EC and UK* (5th edn, Routledge 2015) 218

130 Office of Fair Trading (n 622) para [1.4]

131 Rodger and MacCulloch (n 129) 221–222

132 Office of Fair Trading (n 622) para [2.1]

it aware that the potential punishment is severe and outweighs the gains of misbehaviour.

Based on the administrative enforcement strategy and attitudes of competition law authorities in the United Kingdom, the deterrence theory may potentially underlie its approach, and solely targeting the company as a means of deterring potential infringements exposes it to the risk of liability and loss due to directors' breach of law. In consideration of the last stage of the six-step approach shown earlier, it is arguable that the company can still protect itself from potential punishment since it can obtain immunity from liability through leniency and settlement discounts. This argument is supportable in the sense of receiving a certain amount of fine reduction; however, this does not change the fact that the company is still primarily targeted, and the risk of liability and loss for competition law infringements remains with it. Therefore, although some remedies are provided to the company, this strategy does not completely eliminate the fact that it is primarily responsible for infringements.

In respect of the risk distribution between the company and directors, the issue with this approach, as it was in compliance theory, is that whereas the company is targeted to maintain the desired deterrence, the role of employees, particularly directors, in the potential infringement is overly disregarded. Individual accountability is not considered as a matter of maintaining the desired deterrence and, consequently, the deterrence theory is unlikely to be tailored to be able to recognise the distinctive incentives for the company and directors.

3.4.3 The Mixed Approach

Although the deterrence and compliance theories are both established for the purpose of maintaining compliance with the law, they are distinctively different approaches to achieving this aim. Whereas compliance is encouraged by the punishment of misconduct through imposing sanctions on the company under the deterrence theory, the company is in turn encouraged to obey the rules of law under the compliance theory. While 'repair' is the main objective in compliance theory, 'retribution' is that of deterrence theory.[133] From this point of view, competition law might have adopted both theories to form the foundations of its enforcement strategies.

With the natures of these theories under consideration, it can be seen that they are in conflict as 'following one approach means abandoning the other'; however, it has been seen in the literature that the approaches may not be mutually exclusive[134] because enforcement strategies should be flexible given that there is more than one way to incentivise entities to comply with the law. Braithwaite and Ayres remarked that 'to reject punitive regulation is naive; to be totally committed to it is

133 Keith Hawkins, 'Bargain and Bluff: Compliance Strategy and Deterrence in the Enforcement of Regulation' (1983) 5(1) Law and Policy Quarterly 35, 36

134 Oded (n 83) 3

to lead a charge of the light brigade. The trick of successful regulation is to establish a synergy between punishment and persuasion'.[135] A number of 'imperfections' have been identified in the deterrence and compliance theories. As such it has been suggested that there should be a synergy of both strategies in order to combat their individual imperfections.[136] For example, in order to achieve balance, the potential wrongdoer should be persuaded to comply *ex ante* and punished with sanctions in the event of default *ex post*.

In respect of the application of the mixed approach in the context of corporate governance, the foundation for the reconciliation of the compliance and deterrence philosophies was established by Scholz based on the game theory.[137] Under this approach, the company is perceived to be in a position to determine whether to comply with the rules of law and, based on the level of its compliance, either the cooperative or deterrence enforcement method should be employed by the enforcement authorities.[138] For example, a certain lower limit of compliance is determined by the state, and if the level of the company's compliance goes below this limit, the deterrence strategy should be applied on the company through punishment. If the degree of compliance by the company remains above this limit, the cooperative response will be made by the authorities.[139]

The second strategy in this approach is known as 'responsive regulation'. It was postulated by Braithwaite and Ayres.[140] The main objective of this strategy is to view the company as being law-abiding in nature, and from this point of view, the theory can be perceived as closer to the compliance strategy due to it being more persuasive than punitive. The enforcement strategies are classified into the levels of an 'enforcement pyramid' based on the degree of punishment.[141] The pyramid illustrates when either the strategy of punishment or persuasion is appropriate to employ. The bottom of the pyramid consists of persuasion and guidance, which are the least strict methods. In between are harsher methods, such as warnings and civil sanctions. On the top level, the strictest methods, such as criminal sanctions, are employed.[142] The aim of creating this type of pyramid is to guide the agents to

135 John Braithwaite and Ian Ayres, *Responsive Regulation: Transcending the Deregulation Debate* (Oxford University Press 1992) 25. See also John Braithwaite, *To Punish or Persuade- Enforcement of Coal Mine Safety* (State University of New York 1985) 182

136 Oded (n 83) 1

137 See generally John T Scholz, 'Cooperation, Deterrence, and the Ecology of Regulatory Enforcement' (1984) 18 Law and Society Review 179

138 Oded (n 83) 23

139 John T Scholz, 'Voluntary Compliance and Regulatory Enforcement' (1984) 6(4) Law & Policy 385, 393

140 John Braithwaite and Ian Ayres, *Responsive Regulation: Transcending the Deregulation Debate* (Oxford University Press 1992) 25

141 John Braithwaite and Ian Ayres, *Responsive Regulation: Transcending the Deregulation Debate* (Oxford University Press 1992) 141

142 John Braithwaite and Ian Ayres, *Responsive Regulation: Transcending the Deregulation Debate* (Oxford University Press 1992) 141

start with the compliance strategy.[143] If the company fails to comply with the law by improving its behaviour, the authorities can employ harsher sanctions.

These different approaches are examples of the mixed method, which combines the compliance and deterrence theories. The logic behind this approach is that the persuasion to comply with the law is employed *ex ante* and, should it be found inadequate in incentivising the wrongdoer, punishment should be applied *ex post*. In this sense, it can be discussed that the mixed approach may be identical with the administrative fine strategy adopted by UK competition law regime. This is because it is based on the belief that 'expressly including competition compliance in the business's code of conduct and making it clear that activity that risks causing an infringement of competition law attracts disciplinary sanctions'.[144] This can also be seen from the three key pillars of compliance identified by the OFT to encourage competition compliance and improve deterrence. These are

> (i) [K]nowledge and awareness of competition law: providing guidance and information on compliance measures and risks, (ii) sanctions and enforcement: ensuring the penalties regime is designed to achieve optimal deterrence, and (iii) voluntary compliance measures: facilitating a culture of compliance within firms through efficient and effective provision of the first two pillars.[145]

Rodger also suggested that, before the enactment of the CA98,

> the OFT had adopted a three-pronged strategy, or an 'enhanced carrot and stick' approach, incorporating a deterrent strategy; an educative strategy; and a third, 'legitimising' strategy involving OFT officials touring the country to explain the nature and rationale of the new legislation.[146]

This enforcement strategy has also been promoted by the CMA (formerly the OFT) to encourage companies to set up their own compliance programmes to educate their employees, and it seeks to deter infringements through administrative fining. Support for this approach was also given by the CMA's erstwhile chief executive, Alex Chisholm, who observed that,

> the more we can promote awareness of competition and consumer law and a culture of compliance amongst firms, the more we will be able to demonstrate

143 John Braithwaite, *Restorative Justice & Responsive Regulation* (Oxford University Press 2002) 29–43

144 International Chamber of Commerce, 'Promoting Antitrust Compliance: The Various Approaches of National Antitrust Authorities' (April 2011) 31 <http://ec.europa.eu/competition/antitrust/compliance/icc_comparative_study_en.pdf> accessed 6 April 2024

145 Office of Fair Trading, 'The Impact of Competition Interventions on Compliance and Deterrence Final Report' (OFT1391 December 2011) para [6.5.]

146 Barry J Rodger, 'A Study of Compliance Post-OFT Infringement Action' [2009] ECJ 65, 95

> that those firms who do not comply merit the serious punishments that we are empowered to impose.[147]

Consequently, targeting companies is primarily in place in the mixed approach, and this has influenced UK competition law in respect of the enforcement strategy of administrative fining. However, this gives rise to the issue that the 'root causes'[148] of competition law infringements may be heavily disregarded. The UK competition law authorities have always sought to motivate companies and employees to comply with competition law through education, guidance, compliance seminars, leniency, and settlement discounts; however, enforcement strategies primarily target companies through administrative fines, and what is overlooked is the role of the individual in any wrongdoing.[149]

3.4.4 The Mixed Approach and the Company's Exposure to the Risk of Liability and Loss

The approach adopted by UK competition law based on the mixed approach relies on the view that corporate culture fosters compliance. As such the company's ability to prevent its directors from being involved in anti-competitive behaviour depends on how it incentivises them to comply with the law through internal compliance programmes. The company is considered as an entity that is above its directors, and 'monitoring, investigating, [and] reporting their misconducts' are its responsibilities.[150] If misconduct arises, it is likely to be due to the company's failure to set up effective compliance programmes, and it is considered to be ignorant of competition law. In such a case, targeting the company through an administrative enforcement strategy, which is the classic economic approach and is currently being employed by the competition authorities in the United Kingdom, should not be surprising.[151]

In respect of the risk distribution between the company and its directors, the issue with this approach is that companies, regardless of whether they have made a great effort to establish strong compliance programmes, would still be punished for the infringements done by their employees while acting on their behalf.[152] In a nutshell, the company is subjected to the risk of liability and the cost of such preventative measurement. This was discussed by Gray, who stated that,

> Companies are not protected from legal responsibility for the acts of their employees by the existence of quality-control and preventative compliance

147 Alex Chisholm, 'Achieving a Culture of Compliance' (Law Society Competition Section Annual Conference London 16 May 2014) <https://www.gov.uk/government/speeches/achieving-a-culture-of-compliance> accessed 6 April 2024

148 Krawiec (n 94) 615

149 Individuals are additionally punished through individual sanctions. See Section 3.5

150 Ginsburg and Wright (n 65) 16

151 Ginsburg and Wright (n 65) 16

152 Such effort provides only 10% fine reduction to the company. See Section 3.4.1

> systems designed to ensure that all employees act in such a way that legislation and regulations are never infringed. No matter how seemingly watertight and superior those controls are, if someone within the company subverts them and takes the company outside the law, the company cannot escape ultimate responsibility by pleading that it tried its best and its preventative systems ought to have worked. The simple fact is they did not and the task of the law here is to punish effective non-compliance no matter from where it was generated within the company.[153]

This approach is likely to disregard the distinctive incentives to the company and its directors to obey the rules of competition law because even though the company seeks to keep directors away from anti-competitive behaviour through compliance strategies, it cannot escape the responsibility for the infringement that may have arisen from ignorance of the rules of law by its directors. Such a situation is likely to expose the company to risk of liability and loss due to the punishment imposed on it for infringement.

This is not to suggest that the company should be completely immune from any sort of responsibility arising from an infringement by its directors, because it has some power[154] to incentivise them to act according to ethics and restrictions through insider tools. For this reason, it can still be held responsible for any infringement that arises because infringements may arise as a result of the company's failure to set up a strong compliance programme. However, the extent to which directors implement what the company teaches and reminds them of is a crucial question which should be considered in deciding whether to discipline them for their involvement in competition law infringements. This is based on the matter that, as Whelan suggested, the capability of the company to discipline its directors is not 'without serious drawbacks'.[155] This is because setting up a strong compliance programme to educate and train directors does not guarantee that the desired disciplinary effect and compliance with the relevant law would be achieved. For this reason, it can be suggested that the efforts the company puts in place to educate its directors, and how they implement what they learn from compliance programmes in practice, need to be investigated to find the root cause of a particular anti-competitive behaviour. This is because punishing the company for an infringement without investigating the source of the wrongdoing is likely to neglect the fact that the company and its directors are distinctively incentivised to obey the rules of law. In this scenario, directors' ignorance of the law and the compliance programme set up by the company would be left without punishment.

153 Joanna Gray, 'Company Directors and Ignorance of the Law' (1996) 17(10) Comp Law 296, 299–300

154 Stephen Calkins, 'Corporate Compliance and the Antitrust Agencies' Bi-Modal Penalties' (1997) 60 LCP 127, 147

155 Peter Whelan, 'A Principled Argument for Personal Criminal Sanctions as Punishment Under EC Cartel Law' (2007) 4(1) Comp Law Review 7, 27

There are two reasons underlying this view. The first reason is the existing understanding in respect of the relationship between the company and its directors. The company is regarded as an entity that has strong tools to monitor the activities of individuals to check whether they have fulfilled their duties. This is because the company is perceived as being in the 'best position' to identify and discipline particular individuals.[156] Full protection and freedom are provided to the company, and if any wrongdoing emanates from its affairs, it would be responsible. The company's compliance with the relevant law is the main focal point because it is assumed that if the company desires to comply with the law, it will seek and find a way to encourage its directors to comply with it. Its liability is determined based on its perceived ability to monitor its directors, based on the assumption that 'the true fault lay with the company'.[157]

The second reason is that the authorities tend to be reluctant to find the particular wrongdoer among other individuals within the company because there are a number of individuals but only one principal, which is the company. Each company has its own complicated structure, and it is very difficult for outside authorities to investigate and determine which individual within the company is the actual wrongdoer.[158] This difficulty is very much linked to the issues of potential costs and length of the process. This is because identifying the actual responsible individual among the numbers of individuals within the company requires a comprehensive investigation which can be costly and time consuming.[159]

In short, competition law heavily adopts the mixed approach of compliance and deterrence theories, which leaves the responsibility of establishing certain compliance programmes to the company to encourage directors to comply with the relevant law and punishes it for any non-compliance that arises. However, it may not be appropriate to employ enforcement strategies that solely and primarily target the company because this attitude disregards the potential role of directors in regulatory infringements. Any failure to take preventative measures by the company to educate and train its directors should be its own failure, and for that it should be rightly punished. But the existence and scope of the company's compliance programmes that are designed to encourage its directors to comply with the law and the role of individuals in infringement should also be seriously considered before determining punishment. Consequently, the mixed approach does not tend to recognise the distinctive incentives for the company and its directors, and it is likely to cause the company to be exposed to the risk of liability and loss as a result of regulatory punishment caused by directors' infringement of law.

156 Chris Clarkson, 'Kicking Corporate Bodies and Damning Their Souls' (1996) 59(4) MLR 557, 563
157 Chris Clarkson, 'Kicking Corporate Bodies and Damning Their Souls' (1996) 59(4) MLR 563
158 Chris Clarkson, 'Kicking Corporate Bodies and Damning Their Souls' (1996) 59(4) MLR 563
159 To do this effectively, the authorities would mostly likely appoint qualified agents to investigate the managerial relationships between individuals and documents so that they can find the right wrongdoing individual

3.5 The Deterrent Effect of Individual Sanctions

In addition to the enforcement mechanism of corporate fining that is embodied in the UK competition regime, directors may also be subjected to individual sanctions. There is no doubt that while the company, as principal, should bear some responsibility for competition law infringements, the truth remains that the decisions that lead to such misbehaviours are made by its agents, of whom directors are prime. In this sense, it would be 'unpalatable' if such individuals were not sanctioned for such infringements.[160] Stephan noted that 'without a sanction against individuals, corporate fines . . . will become subject to increasing criticism and diminishing legitimacy'.[161] For this reason, it was suggested that,

> [T]hese problems could be solved by combining corporate sanctions with individual penalties imposed on the responsible decision-makers or actors within the firm [and] [a]dding individual penalties could solve . . . the problems of firms being unable to control their agents.[162]

Khan also pointed out that 'through an analysis of corporate governance theory, it will be established that there is a real need for individualized sanctions to target those who are truly responsible for the implementation of anticompetitive conduct'.[163] In addition, Kriesberg discussed how 'effective legal policy concerning corporate crime must be founded on an understanding of the decision-making process underlying corporate action'.[164] Moreover, Polinsky and Shavell suggested that 'publicly imposed sanctions' on individuals can be helpful for maintaining a certain level of deterrence.[165] They went on to note that by imposing severe sanctions, regulatory authorities can provide a higher level of incentive to individuals. As such, leaving the responsibility of incentivising or punishing individuals to the company may fail to maintain deterrence.[166] Furthermore, Hammond asserted that,

> All else being equal, a jurisdiction without individual liability and criminal sanctions will never be *as effective* at inducing amnesty applications as a

160 Mark Furse, *The Criminal Law of Competition in the UK and in the US-Failure and Success* (1st edn, Cheltenham 2012) 43

161 Stephan (n 77) 536

162 Wouter PJ Wils, *The Optimal Enforcement of EC Antitrust Law, Essays in Law & Economics* (Kluwer, 2002) 253

163 Khan (n 70) 77

164 SM Kriesberg, 'Decision-Making Models and the Control of Corporate Crime' (1976) 85 Yale Law Journal 1091, 1092

165 Mitchell A Polinsky and Steven Shavell, 'Should Employees Be Subject to Fines and Imprisonment Given the Existence of Corporate Liability?' (1993) 13 International Review of Law and Economics 239, 240

166 Mitchell A Polinsky and Steven Shavell, 'Should Employees Be Subject to Fines and Imprisonment Given the Existence of Corporate Liability?' (1993) 13 International Review of Law and Economics 240

> programme that does. Individuals stand the most to lose and so avoiding jail sentences is the greatest incentive for seeking amnesty.[167]

The truth is that directors are unlikely to be motivated to obey the rules of law by reason of the possibility of sanctions that may be imposed on the company.[168] To persuade them to comply with the law, a 'high powered incentive'[169] is needed, one which, if applied, would impact their future career prospects. To some extent, this strategy, which has been applied in UK competition law in the last two decades, can be considered a positive development to the extent that it entails the distribution of the risk of liability and loss for infringements between the company and its directors. Melanie Johnson, Parliamentary Under Secretary of State for Trade and Industry (as she then was), stated in her speech during the process of introduction of the EA02 that,

> There is an important relationship between an offence on the statute book and a deterrent. The current measures do not have that deterrent effect, as they do not deal with individuals, but allow them to hide behind companies. There are commercial trade-offs for companies between fines that they may receive for entering into such arrangements and any commercial gain that, as we all accept, they may receive from cartels.[170]

This statement referred to the CA98 because there was no individual sanction in the UK competition law regime before the enactment of the EA02. Although the European Commission rejected the idea of introducing individual sanctions and preferred to increase the level of fines to which companies would be subjected, UK competition law authorities adopted a different strategy by introducing individual sanctions through the EA02 as a means of increasing the level of deterrence on individuals. These reforms have brought UK competition law regime closer to US antitrust law.[171] This section examines whether these individual sanctions effectively deter directors from engaging with competition law infringements and whether the risk of loss and liability for an infringement on the company could be mitigated through these mechanisms.

3.5.1 Competition Disqualification

The disqualification of directors is an individual sanction that prohibits or bars company directors from being involved in the management of companies for a

167 Scott D Hammond, 'Cornerstones of An Effective Leniency Program' (November 2004) <http://www.justice.gov/atr/public/speeches/206611.htm> accessed 23 June 2024

168 Polinsky and Shavell (n 166) 240

169 Oliver Hart, 'Corporate Governance: Some Theory and Implications' (1995) 105 The Economic Journal 678, 679

170 House of Commons, 'Enterprise Bill in Standing Committee B' (Fifth Standing, 23 April 2002) column 169 <http://www.publications.parliament.uk/pa/cm200102/cmstand/b/st020423/am/20423s07.htm> accessed 5 July 2024

171 Graham (n 26) 241

specified period of time. While this sanction has existed in companies for some time, it has now been extended to directors of companies who engage in anti-competitive conduct. The implementation of strategy can complement the efforts of the company in reining its directors, and it can be an effective tool to incentivise directors of companies to ensure compliance with competition law. In the United Kingdom, directors' disqualification was first introduced by the Companies Act 1928 (CA28). Currently, it is embodied in the CDDA86, which in turn was amended by Section 204 of the EA02 in order to extend its application to UK competition law.

Additionally, the EA02 introduced competition disqualification orders (CDOs), under which a director may be disqualified for up to 15 years, and competition disqualification undertakings (CDU). In essence, the disqualification sanction can be applied to any person who occupies the position of director, regardless of 'whatever name called'.[172] CDOs are provided for in Section 9A of the CDDA86. Under it, the CMA (previously OFT) may apply to the UK High Court for a CDO to be imposed on a director.[173] To impose a CDO on a director, two conditions must be satisfied. First, the director of an undertaking or company must have breached competition law. Secondly, the court must consider that the person's conduct as a director makes him or her unfit to be concerned with the management of a company.[174] The responsibility for assessing the appropriateness of a CDO lies with the CMA, which must follow five steps in so doing.[175]

First, it must ensure that the breach of competition law was committed by the undertaking[176] and that the nature of the infringement is serious enough to apply for disqualification.[177] Then it must assess whether the undertaking or director is qualified to benefit from leniency,[178] as well as the degree of director's responsibility in the infringement. This is necessary to determine whether such a director is unfit to be involved in the management of a company.[179] For this purpose, the issues to be determined are whether the conduct of the director contributed to the breach in question, whether the director knew of the occurrence of the misconduct in the undertaking and took no steps against it, and even if he did not know, he ought to have known about the misconduct of the undertaking.[180] The latter is the hardest

172 Company Directors Disqualification Act 1986 (n 241), s 22(4)
173 As introduced by Section 204 of the Enterprise Act 2002, as amended by the Enterprise and Regulatory Reform Act 2013
174 Company Directors Disqualification Act 1986 (n 241), ss 9A(1)-(3)
175 Office of Fair Trading, 'Director Disqualification Orders in Competition Cases: An OFT Guidance Document' (OFT510 2010) para [4.6]
176 Office of Fair Trading, 'Director Disqualification Orders in Competition Cases: An OFT Guidance Document' (OFT510 2010) para [4.6]
177 Office of Fair Trading, 'Director Disqualification Orders in Competition Cases: An OFT Guidance Document' (OFT510 2010) para [4.11]
178 Office of Fair Trading, 'Director Disqualification Orders in Competition Cases: An OFT Guidance Document' (OFT510 2010) para [4.12]
179 Office of Fair Trading, 'Director Disqualification Orders in Competition Cases: An OFT Guidance Document' (OFT510 2010) para [4.16]
180 Company Directors Disqualification Act 1986 (n 241), s 9A(6)

to prove[181] because an extensive evaluation of different matters such as the director's role in the company, his relationship with those who are responsible for the breach, general knowledge, skill, the experience that the director holds, and the availability of specific information about the breach to the director would have to be assessed.[182] Lastly, the CMA would assess whether there are aggravating factors[183] (which would increase the likelihood of making the CDO application) or mitigating factors[184] (which would reduce the order) that can be applied.[185]

That said, CDOs are not imposed arbitrarily. The director in question must be issued with a notice[186] that contains all the relevant information regarding the proposed application. He must also be given the opportunity to defend himself.[187] On hearing the application, the court will, in turn, consider whether the conditions under 9A(2) and (3) of the CDDA86 have been satisfied. If so, it would proceed to disqualify the director for up to 15 years.[188]

From the aforementioned, we can conclude that the process for the imposition of a CDO entails the conduct of a comprehensive and lengthy investigation. Perhaps this is why, although it has been more than 10 years since it was enacted, there has not been a successful imposition of a CDO. The nearest thing to a CDO for competition breaches can be found in *R. v. Whittle and others*.[189] The issue, however, is that the disqualifications imposed in that case were under the separate provision of Section 2 of the CDDA, which disqualifies directors who engage in a criminal activity.[190] In that case, three directors, Peter Whittle, Bryan Allison, and David Brammar, who were involved in a marine hose cartel, were disqualified from acting as directors for between 5 to 7 years.[191] Similarly, in *R* v. *Burns and Others*, the OFT instituted a criminal action against British Airways (BA) and its four directors for entering into an illegal price-fixing agreement with its rival, Virgin Atlantic.[192] Under the agreement, both companies agreed to increase surcharges step by step from £6 to £30 between August 2004 and January 2006.[193] Like *R v. Whittle*, the actions instituted in that case were criminal in nature, and no CDO

181 Khan (n 70) 91
182 Office of Fair Trading, 'Director Disqualification Orders in Competition Cases: An OFT Guidance Document' (OFT510 2010) para [4.6]
183 Galloway (n 9) III-415
184 Galloway (n 9) III-416
185 Office of Fair Trading, 'Director Disqualification Orders in Competition Cases: An OFT Guidance Document' (OFT510 2010) para [4.6]
186 Company Directors Disqualification Act 1986 (n 241), s 9C(4)(a)
187 Office of Fair Trading, 'Director Disqualification Orders in Competition Cases: An OFT Guidance Document' (OFT510 2010) para [5.2]
188 Company Directors Disqualification Act 1986 (n 241), s 9A(9). Competition undertakings can also be up to 15 years under s 9(B)(5) of the Act
189 [2008] EWCA Crim 2560; [2009] UKCLR 247
190 Stephan (n 77) 532
191 Competition and Market Authority, 'Marine Hose: Criminal Cartel Investigation' (2008) <https://www.gov.uk/cma-cases/marine-hose-criminal-cartel-investigation> accessed 13 March 2024
192 [2010] EWCA Crim 1148
193 Decision of the Directors General of Fair Trading, No. CA98/01/2012 para [95]

was imposed on the four directors of BA, namely Martin George, Andrew Crawley, Alan Burnett, and Iain Burns. Following this, Iain Burns and Martin George admitted their roles in the infringement and resigned from BA in October 2006. Alan Burnett also retired in the same year. Surprisingly, the fourth director, Andrew Crowley, was promoted to the board of BA 2 weeks before defending himself in a lawsuit for involvement in illegal price fixing.[194] The curious issue with this case is that although criminal proceedings were successfully instituted against the directors, the regulator did not seek the imposition of a CDO on the directors. Consequently, even though they accepted their illegality, the defaulting directors were not disqualified from being involved in the management of companies. The overall effect is to cast serious doubt on the deterrent effect of the individual sanction of competition disqualification. Another case that has some bearing on CDO on competition breaches was related to steel tanks.[195] In one such case, three directors of the Franklin Hodge Industries Ltd pleaded guilty for involvement in bid rigging and price fixing, upon which one of them was sentenced to prison for 6 months. Curiously, again, the regulator did not seek the imposition of a CDO.

Another related case recently arose as a result of a suspicious agreement to divide customers and supply and fix prices between two companies: Stanton Bonna (UK) Ltd, FP McCann Ltd, CPM Group Ltd and Milton Pipes Ltd.[196] Following their prosecution, Barry Kenneth Cooper pleaded guilty, and the prosecution is underway, and was subsequently disqualified from directing a company.[197]

In essence, there is no proof that a CDO has been sought for competition breaches in the United Kingdom. This naturally gives rise to concerns about the deterrent effect of CDOs on directors since the rule has not been tested in practice. The OFT (currently CMA) pleaded that

> [it] has not used its CDO powers to date for a number of reasons –for example because the conduct in question pre-dated CDO power, because the relevant individuals benefited from immunity from the CDOs under the leniency regime, or because of a lack of evidence.[198]

194 Michael Peel, 'BA Sale Chief on Price-Fixing Charge to Join the Board' (2008) <http://www.ft.com/cms/s/0/7902ab56-bceb-11dd-af5a-0000779fd18c.html#axzz2nC2fQgcZ> accessed 15 April 2024

195 CE/9623/12. See Competition and Markets Authority, 'Two Men Face Charges in Ongoing Criminal Cartel Investigation' <https://www.gov.uk/government/news/two-men-face-charges-in-ongoing-criminal-cartel-investigation> accessed 22 June 2024; Competition and Markets Authority, 'Director Sentenced to 6 Months for Criminal Cartel' <https://www.gov.uk/government/news/director-sentenced-to-6-months-for-criminal-cartel> accessed 15 March 2024

196 CE/9705/12. See Competition and Markets Authority, 'Supply of Precast Concrete Drainage Products: Criminal Investigation' <https://www.gov.uk/cma-cases/criminal-investigation-into-the-supply-of-products-to-the-construction-industry> accessed 5 April 2024

197 Companies House <https://find-and-update.company-information.service.gov.uk/disqualified-officers/natural/Slbl88XHJqluWz2-Eobg9fXGyOw> accessed 27 June 2024

198 Office of Fair Trading, 'Director Disqualification Orders in Competition Cases: An OFT Guidance Document' (OFT510 2010) para [2.8]

These excuses, however, may not be convincing. It is difficult to agree with the first reason because the questionable conduct in the aforementioned cases arose after the OFT was equipped with the power to apply for CDOs. On the excuse of leniency which is granted to a company and its directors who report a competition infringement and collaborate with competition law authorities, the truth is that only the 'revealing' company that may benefit from leniency. Consequently, its directors are not entitled to leniency and should still be subject to disqualification.

The practice, however, is that immunity is granted not to the cooperating company alone but to its directors as well. To buttress this point, the OFT has stated that CDOs will not be applied 'against any current director of a company whose company benefited from leniency in respect of the activities to which the grant of leniency relates'.[199] This can be called 'parallel immunity',[200] which reduces the deterrent effect of CDOs on directors since they can benefit from immunity even after the infringement has been revealed.[201] There is no doubt that the leniency strategy has considerable benefits. For one, it accelerates the process of the investigation, saves resources for investigating other cases, and encourages the company and its directors to cooperate. Even at that, the deterrent effect of CDOs is likely to disappear if directors are aware that even if the misconduct is detected, they are immune from liability.[202] Stephan identifies this issue as one of the main reasons for not having one example of CDOs in the United Kingdom.[203]

The third reason cited by the CMA is that there is often the absence of adequate evidence. This reason is also difficult to agree with because some criminal proceedings have been successfully instituted against erring directors, a fact that requires a higher standard of proof beyond a reasonable doubt. Curiously, no CDO has been brought against any of these directors. Therefore, this reason can be the lack of a 'single principle' in the implementation of the CDOs.[204] This is because, during the application process, enforcement authorities need to determine whether a director is unfit to act as a director before they make the final decision about the disqualification.

The director's 'fitness or unfitness' is one such factor. After determining that a person is unfit to direct a company, his disqualification becomes mandatory.[205] Again, this is a comprehensive task given that the concept of fitness is 'open-ended' and not 'closely defined'.[206] Essentially

> unfitness is not just a question of fact but maybe a mixed question of fact and law: the application of the standard laid down by the courts as conduct

199 Office of Fair Trading, 'Director Disqualification Orders in Competition Cases: An OFT Guidance Document' (OFT510 2010) [4.14]. This is not the case for Cartel Offence as only the employees, whose company reveals the infringement, can benefit from leniency. See Stephan (n 77) 533
200 Galloway (n 9) III-404
201 Stephan (n 77) 535
202 Stephan (n 77) 533
203 Stephan (n 77) 535
204 Meyrick Williams, 'Directors' Disqualification' (2005) 2(3) IJDG 281
205 Company Directors Disqualification Act 1986 (n 241), s 9A
206 Williams (n 204) 281–282. For further discussion, see Galloway (n 9) III-410–III-416

appropriate to a person fit to be a director (law) and as relevant to the facts of the case (fact).[207]

Therefore, disqualification can only be applied when a breach of competition law has been proved.[208] But detecting the breach itself does not guarantee that the CDO would be imposed on a director on the ground of unfitness.

On a general note, there is still a lack of clarity regarding which type of behaviour can result in a disqualification. Williams identified 'breaches of commercial morality and recklessness and incompetence' as conducts which may result in disqualification.[209] Others may include persistent breaches of company law and fraudulent trading as stated under the CDDA86. But as Galloway remarked, 'given the lack of case law under the [CDDA86, Section 9A], it is difficult to give a definitive account of the circumstances in which the conduct of a director is likely to amount to unfitness'.[210] This uncertainty is based on the two steps that are used to determine a director's unfitness, namely the degree of the misbehaviour and the extent of his culpability. In disqualifying a director, the court would have to apply its subjective judgement by interpreting and evaluating the individual circumstances of each director on its merits.[211]

Ambiguity in respect of 'what amounts to unfitness'[212] potentially results in a lack of 'knowledge of the conduct that attracts the sanction' on the part of the director.[213] Corroborating further, Williams had argued that 'if directors do not know what "unfit" conduct is, they cannot be deterred from carrying it out'.[214]

The difficulty in implementing CDOs on directors and competition law may further discourage regulatory authorities from invoking their powers in this regard since they are not obligated to do so, even in cases where 'there are reasonable grounds for bringing an application for a disqualification order'.[215] Rather, they may find it 'more appropriate to deal with the infringement by imposing a financial penalty' under Section 36 of the CA98.[216] This absence of obligation might be the reason for there being no example of CDO imposition in UK competition law.

For the sake of argument, assuming that disqualification is effectively imposed by the competition authorities, some factors may still affect the extent to which it may deter directors from competition breaches. One of which is whether or not the

207 Williams (n 204) 28(5)
208 Galloway (n 9) III-414
209 Williams (n 204) 285
210 Galloway (n 9) III-419
211 Stephen Griffin, 'The Disqualification of Unfit Directors and the Protection of the Public Interest' (2002) 53 The Northern Ireland Legal Quarterly 207, 211
212 Kingsley Ong, 'Disqualification of Directors: A Faulty Regime?' (1998) 19(1) Comp Law 7, 9
213 Richard Williams, 'Disqualifying Directors: A Remedy Worse Than the Disease?' (2007) 7 The Journal of Corporation Law 213, 234
214 Richard Williams, 'Disqualifying Directors: A Remedy Worse Than the Disease?' (2007) 7 The Journal of Corporation Law 234
215 Galloway (n 9) III-365
216 Galloway (n 9) III-365

director is close to retirement.[217] Directors who are to retire soon are unlikely to be deterred by disqualification since they would not plan to continue their directorship. The problem is worsened when the potential time gap between the formation of the cartel and the disqualification of the director is considered.[218] This issue also illustrates the need for different incentives for individuals because, as Wils argued, 'depending on the age of the person concerned, director disqualification may simply be the occasion to move into comfortable retirement, and the company could fully compensate its former director for any financial loss'.[219] Under these considerations, being disqualified does not seem a major issue for directors, and consequently, the effect of the disqualification to incentivise them is likely to be reduced.

A second reason concerns whether the disqualified director is actually prevented from taking any role in the management of companies. According to the survey undertaken by Hicks on disqualified directors, 'a large minority [of disqualified directors] thought a disqualified director is unlikely to be caught if in breach of the order'.[220] Hence, they are unlikely to be aware of the implications of being disqualified from directorship. Hicks continued to discuss that,

> Disqualification itself was not seen as a major impediment in finding work. Most were reasonably successful in setting themselves up again, usually in some line of self-employment. Few were apparently qualified for formal executive posts with companies so did not see disqualification as much of a problem in the main.[221]

The issue is that if directors do not consider disqualification as preventing them from finding work, its effect in incentivising them to obey the rules of law would be in serious doubt. Again, because of the imposition of administrative fines for competition law infringements, coupled with the fact that CDOs are often ineffective in deterring directors from infringing competition rules, the effect is that the risks of liability and loss for the infringement would consequently remain with the company.

For the sake of argument, assume for a moment that CDOs were effectively applied and had a strong deterrent effect on directors. It should be highlighted that regardless of whether a director is culpable for an anti-competitive action and he/she is determined unfit for management, he/she can still not be disqualified unless it has been proved that the company for which he/she works has breached competition.[222] As such, the company must have been punished through administrative fining before the process of disqualification can commence. Even here, the company

217 Wouter PJ Wils, 'Is Criminalization of EU Competition Law the Answer?' (2005) 28 World Competition 117, 147
218 Stephan (n 77) 533
219 Wils (n 217) 147
220 Andrew Hicks, 'Director Disqualification: Can It Deliver?' [2001] JBL 433, 435
221 Andrew Hicks, 'Director Disqualification: Can It Deliver?' [2001] JBL 436
222 Company Directors Disqualification Act 1986 (n 241), s 9A(2)

may not be able to mitigate the risk of liability and loss due to this requirement. What we are buttressing is that irrespective of whether or not it was a rogue director, disqualification itself does not remove the risk of liability since the individual culpability of its directors would not necessarily reduce the sanction that would be imposed against it. In this regard, attitudes to disqualification have been largely positive. It has been viewed as potentially more draconian than fines or imprisonment, with the prospect of achieving greater deterrence than individual punishment without entailing the complexities and uncertainties associated with criminal enforcement.[223] In terms of deterrence, it is arguable that directors' disqualification is the 'second best' individual sanction that can be imposed on an errant individual.[224] That notwithstanding, the weak implementation of this mechanism may have whittled down its overall effect.

3.5.2 The Criminal Cartel Offence

The second individual sanction that may be imposed is the criminal cartel offence, which was introduced under Sections 188–202 of Part 6 of the EA02. Under this heading of sanction, the CMA may imprison directors for up to 5 years or impose an unlimited fine on directors who are involved in cartels.[225] The criminalisation of competition law breaches has long been in practice in the United States, and individuals have regularly been jailed for competition misconduct.[226] The US approach to criminalising competition breaches was first introduced by the Sherman Act of 1890, and it has produced positive results in the reduction of competition infringements. The US approach has been replicated in the United Kingdom and several other EU countries, which also introduced criminal penalties for competition law infringements.[227]

Competition law infringements are currently in the United Kingdom through the EA02. To our mind, this is an appropriate step which is necessary to deter competition law infringements as the civil law approach of the UK competition law, which was modelled on EU civil competition law, can be said to have been a 'mistaken endeavour'.[228] This individual sanction was introduced to address the

223 Stephan (n 77) 529

224 Wouter PJ Wils, *Efficiency and Justice in European Antitrust Enforcement* (Oxford University Press 2008) 188

225 Enterprise Act 2002, s 190(1)

226 Keith Jones and Farin Harrison, 'Criminal Sanctions: An Overview of EU and national Case Law' (National Competition Laws Bulletin) 7 <http://awa2015.concurrences.com/IMG/pdf/keith_jones.pdf> accessed 15 March 2024

227 Stephen Wilks, 'Cartel Criminalisation as Juridification: Political and Regulatory Dangers' in Caron Beaton-Wells and Ariel Ezrachi (eds), *Criminalising Cartels: Critical Studies of an International Regulatory Movement* (Hart Publishing 2011) 341, 355. The countries that currently impose criminal sanctions for competition law infringements are Austria, Cyprus, Czech Republic, Denmark, Estonia, France, Germany, Greece, Hungary, Ireland, Latvia, Malta, Norway, Poland, Romania, Slovak Republic, Slovenia, and the United Kingdom. See Jones and Harrison (n 227) 7

228 Furse (n 161) 2

limited deterrent effect of administrative fines that were imposed on individuals.[229] It has been argued that sanctioning undertakings alone was not sufficient to ensure that the individuals who operated within these undertakings complied 'with the standards imposed by competition law and that these decisions by individuals are reflected in corporate conduct'.[230]

Still, on the impact of criminal sanctions, it is commonly agreed that the risk of imprisonment sends a 'uniquely strong moral message' to individuals, and it is very likely to provide a certain incentive to them to comply with the law.[231] Corroborating further, a report published by Deloitte in 2007 noted that criminal penalties were considered as the most important sanction that could be imposed on individuals.[232] This view was further endorsed by Hammond, who noted that 'jail is the most effective deterrent for antitrust defendants'.[233] In introducing the cartel offence, it was thus expected by the authorities that they would not have to prosecute more than six to ten cartel offences in a year, with the number more likely to be close to the bottom than the top of the range.[234] This assumption, however, has failed to materialise. One reason for this appears to be that there is weakness in the enforcement mechanisms, with only four cases having been instituted since the offence was introduced.[235]

First, there was the 2007 case of *R v. Whittle and Others*.[236] In that case, the OFT successfully prosecuted three businessmen who were accused of price fixing, following which they were sentenced to imprisonment for two and half to three years. After that, criminal proceedings were instituted against four directors of BA by the OFT in *R v. Burns and Others*.[237] The case was not followed through to completion, however, as it was withdrawn in May 2010, and the individuals involved were acquitted. Furse noted that this case would very likely be the 'last to have been brought within the framework originally established in 2002'.[238]

In January 2014, the OFT instituted another proceeding in what is known as the *Steel Tanks* case against Peter Nigel Snee, a former managing director at Franklin

229 Department of Trade and Industry, 'Productivity and Enterprise: A World Class Competition Regime' (Cm 5233 July 2001) paras [7.13]–[7.15]

230 Furse (n 161) 52–53

231 Wouter PJ Wils (n 163)

232 Office of Fair Trading, 'The Deterrence Effect of Competition Enforcement' (OFT962 November 2007) table [5.11]

233 Quoted in Department of Justice, 'Three United Kingdom Nationals Plead Guilty to Participating in Bid-Rigging Conspiracy in the Marine Hose Industry' (2007) <https://www.justice.gov/archive/opa/pr/2007/December/07_at_995.html> accessed 12 April 2024

234 Office of Fair Trading, 'The Proposed Criminalisation of Cartels in the UK' (OFT365 November 2001) para [3.7]

235 See A Stephan, 'Four Key Challenges to the Successful Criminalization of Cartel Laws' (2014) 2(2) Journal of Antitrust Enforcement 333–362

236 *R v. Whittle & Others* [2008] EWCA Crim 2560; [2009] UKCLR 247.See also Section 3.5.1

237 (n 193). See also Section 3.5.1

238 Furse (n 161) 3

Hodge Industries in Herefordshire.[239] In the case, which was instituted exactly 3 months before the enactment of the ERRA13, Mr. Snee pleaded guilty to a criminal charge of engaging in a price-fixing agreement for galvanised steel tanks which were used for water storage. In June 2014, the CMA took over the investigation, which was followed through by the prosecution of the remaining two directors, Clive Geoffrey Dean and Nicholas Simon Stringer, for the same infringement.[240] On 24 June 2015, Clive Geoffrey Dean and Nicholas Simon Stringer were acquitted under Section 188 of the EA02,[241] while Mr. Snee was sentenced to 6 months of imprisonment on 14 September 2015.[242]

The last example of a cartel offence, which is still underway, arose from a business relationship between Stanton Bonna (UK) Ltd, FP McCann Ltd, CPM Group Ltd, and Milton Pipes Ltd.[243] In this case, Barry Kenneth Cooper pleaded guilty to dishonestly agreeing with others to divide customers, divide supplies, and fix prices for the supply of precast concrete drainage products in the United Kingdom. The infringements occurred between 2006 and 2013. On 21 March 2016, he was charged at the Southwark Crown Court where he pleaded guilty and was subsequently convicted, following which he was disqualified from directorship via a disqualification order.[244]

As can be seen, although the cartel offence has been in place for more than 10 years, only two cases have been successfully prosecuted by the CMA (formerly OFT). They are the case relating to marine hoses[245] and that relating to steel tanks by the CMA (formerly OFT). This raises concern on whether the criminalisation of cartel actions actually deter cartel offences. In highlighting this concern, the UK government stated that

> the deterrence effect of the cartel offence is weaker than it was intended because there have been so few completed cases to date; only two cases have so far reached trial stage, and only one of them resulted in convictions.[246]

What this means is that it would appear that the introduction of the cartel offence and its harsh sanctions on individuals should unquestionably deter individuals

239 Competition and Markets Authority (n 196)

240 Competition and Markets Authority (n 196)

241 Competition and Markets Authority, 'CMA Statement Following Completion of Criminal Cartel Prosecution' <https://www.gov.uk/government/news/cma-statement-following-completion-of-criminal-cartel-prosecution> accessed 15 March 2024

242 Competition and Markets Authority, 'Director Sentenced to 6 Months for Criminal Cartel' <https://www.gov.uk/government/news/director-sentenced-to-6-months-for-criminal-cartel> accessed 15 March 2024

243 (n 197); see Competition and Markets Authority (n 197)

244 Companies House <https://find-and-update.company-information.service.gov.uk/disqualified-officers/natural/Slbl88XHJqluWz2-Eobg9fXGyOw> accessed 27 June 2024

245 Based on the fact that the investigation was initiated by the US authorities, this case was defined as 'essentially a US case' by Stephan. See Stephan (n 77) 531

246 Department for Business, Innovation, & Skills, 'A Competition Regime for Growth: A Consultation on Options for Reform' (March 2011) para [6.5]

from engaging in cartels. But the actual results tell a different story as enforcement has been a major problem, with Stephan arguing that 'credible threat of enforcement . . . is the biggest challenge for cartel criminalisation',[247] a fact that has been confirmed by two reports of the OFT.[248]

Several factors may have contributed to the weak implementation of the cartel offence. The first reason is in respect of the conflicting relationship between the cartel offence and the civil basis of UK competition law.[249] Gorecki and McFadden demonstrated that 'cartels are typically treated as civil breaches . . . criminal activity should be dealt with by the police, not by lawyers and economists that typically populate a competition agency'.[250] UK competition law authorities are faced with the challenge of enforcing the civil and criminal aspects of competition law—the first against undertakings and the second against individuals.

In effect, the United Kingdom has a dual regime.[251] But this has been a problem, which, interestingly, the Antitrust Division of the US Department of Justice did not have to face. Arguing on this issue, Furse notes that arising from 'the attempt to run a system of individual criminal prosecution alongside the civil enforcement system: in effect, operating different trains, on different tracks, with the same engine driver'.[252] In essence, while the UK government employs civil and criminal enforcement tools in order to achieve greater compliance with the regulatory competition law regime, the implementation of this 'mixed approach' has not been very effective.[253] Another effect of the dual method is that there has been a lack of attention to the matter that 'civil and criminal offences in the UK frequently overlap'.[254] Furse described this as a 'fundamental flaw' and suggested that the 'substance of the offence would be too limiting' since it may give rise to conflict between the primarily essentially civil law nature of UK competition law regime and the cartel offence as embodied in Sections 188–202 of Part 6 of the EA02.[255]

Secondly, there may be questions on how to properly identify the appropriate individual to prosecute as well as whether prosecution would be appropriate or

247 Andreas Stephan, 'Why Morality Should Be Excluded From the Cartel Criminalisation Debate' (2012) 3 New Journal of European Criminal Law 127, 128

248 Office of Fair Trading, 'The Deterrence Effect of Competition Enforcement' (OFT962 November 2007) table [5.11]; Office of Fair Trading, 'Drivers of Compliance and Non-Compliance with Competition Law' (OFT 1227 May 2010) para [1.10]

249 Furse (n 161) 108

250 Paul K Gorecki and David McFadden, 'Criminal Cartels in Ireland: The Heating Oil Case' (2006) 27(11) ECLR 631

251 Furse (n 161) 122

252 Furse (n 161) 120–121

253 See Alison Jones and Rebecca Williams, 'Deterring Cartels: Is Criminalisation the Solution? Lessons From the UK' (Presentation) <https://www.law.ox.ac.uk/sites/files/oxlaw/jones_and_williams.pdf> accessed 13 April 2024; see also Alison Jones and Rebecca Williams, 'The UK Response to the Global Effort Against Cartels: Is Criminalization Really the Solution?' [2014] JAE 1, 9

254 Alison Jones and Rebecca Williams, 'The UK Response to the Global Effort Against Cartels: Is Criminalization Really the Solution?' [2014] JAE 9

255 Furse (n 161) 108

would satisfy the public interest test in relation to every instance where there is non-compliance. This may be an issue to take into account not only for countries that are considering adopting such enforcement mechanisms but also for those that have already adopted the cartel offence approach. This uncertainty decreases the likelihood of the implementation of these sanctions, its roots in statute notwithstanding.[256] The underlying issue is that there is a lack of public support for the labelling individuals who form these cartels as 'criminals'.[257] According to a survey undertaken by Stephan in 2007, only 11% of those surveyed were in support of incarceration for cartel offences, this is despite the fact that 63% regarded price-fixing as dishonest.[258] The basis of this problem is that 'the drive for criminalization in the UK resulted not from a public sense of "moral outrage" and a bottom-up (or backward-looking) process, but from a top-down (forward-looking) one, driven by the international initiatives'.[259] At the time of the introduction of the sanction, the government and the OFT were keen to introduce different enforcement mechanisms to achieve greater deterrence of cartel activities, and potential limitations that may arise from public support were neglected. They did not, however, obtain the buy-in of the public before proceeding with the legislation.

In order to eliminate or reduce this tension, the authorities have to ensure that the sanction is imposed on the actual individuals who are implicated in a violation. This is more so as imprisonment is more severe than a fine or disqualification since it would have severe and far-reaching implications for the private life of the defaulting individual. In this respect, two issues may arise. The first has to do with rightfully ascertaining the defaulting individual within the company and then proceeding to determine the right amount of punishment. For this purpose, several factors have to be considered. They include fairness, individual autonomy, human rights, proportionality, and responsibility. This is because 'the creation of criminal offences that fail to identify the grounds for its condemnation risks trivialising criminal sanctions and ultimately their deterrent effect'.[260] The enforcement authorities thus need to find a balance between the purpose of deterrence and retribution since 'society is often founded on a plurality of values and principles; the pursuit of deterrence through the criminal law should be conditioned accordingly'.[261]

The aforementioned considerations require that a comprehensive investigation must be completed by the competition law authorities in order to determine the

256 Andreas P Reindl, 'How Strong is the Case for Criminal Sanctions in Cartel Cases' in Katalin J Cseres, Maarteen P Schinkel, and Floris OW Vogelaar (eds), *Criminalisation of Competition Law Enforcement: Economic and Legal Implications for the EU Member States* (Edward Elgar 2006) 110–132

257 Khan (n 70) 87

258 Andreas Stephan, 'Survey of Public Attitudes to Price-Fixing and Cartel Enforcement in Britain' (2008) Comp Law Review 123, 133 and 135

259 Jones and Williams (n 252) 9

260 Eléonore M Michels, 'The Real Shortcoming of the UK Cartel Offence: A Lack of Public and Political Support' [2014] Global Antitrust Review 53, 60

261 Whelan (n 156) 19

punishment to be imposed and on whom. The criminal enforcement system consists of 'more complex procedures' and requires a higher standard of proof than the administrative enforcement system.[262] The nature of these investigations gives rise to the issues of cost and time consumption.[263] Finding the particular individual within the company and determining the amount of punishment costs more and takes more time than administrative enforcement. Adopting a mixed approach that combines civil law with criminal enforcement mechanisms exacerbates the cost of an investigation and prosecution, as resources would have to be split between different types of investigations. In the same vein, a considerable amount of resources would be required for the construction and operation of prisons.[264]

Despite the fact that the resources provided to the CMA have been considerably increased, the process of enforcing the cartel offence is still not without drawbacks, as 'the inherent nature of criminal cartel work will continue to make identification, investigation and successful prosecution extremely challenging'.[265] The existence of the cartel offence notwithstanding, establishing the guilt of individuals tends to be challenging. As such, courts tend to settle with sanctioning companies since the standard of establishing corporate liability for the lesser offence is more relaxed.[266] Assuming that they apply to the same sort of evidence, judges may still not be satisfied with the level of evidence when considering whether to imprison individuals. The complex procedure and the possibility that they may not succeed in securing a conviction may potentially result in a reluctance on the part of the authorities to initiate an investigation against directors since they may assume that the deterrent effect of imprisonment can be equally achieved through the imposition of fines. They may thus settle for the administrative fining strategy, which is a much easier and less costly option.[267] Buttressing this point, Evenette *et al* have also argued that imprisonment is likely to be 'less desirable' compared to administrative fining.[268]

The third factor that may diminish the deterrent effect of the cartel offence is the fact that the statute itself was poorly drafted.[269] In order for directors to be effectively deterred by the sanction imposed for cartel offences, it is crucial that the offence be clearly defined so as to make it easy for businesses and the courts to appreciate its meaning and implications.[270] However, it has been argued that one contributing factor to the ineffectiveness of criminal cartel offences is the fact that

262 Reindl (n 255) 121

263 Stephan (n 77) 531

264 Simon J Evenett, Margaret C Levenstein, and Valerie Y Suslow, 'International Cartel Enforcement: Lessons From the 1990s' (2001) 24 World Economy 1221, 1236

265 Competition and Markets Authority, 'Competition and Markets Authority Annual Plan 2015/16' (CMA34 March 2015) para [1.9], [3.8], and [7.1]

266 Reindl (n 255) 130

267 See William Breit and Kenneth G Elzinga, *Antitrust Penalty Reform: An Economic Analysis* (American Enterprise Institute for Public Research 1986) 61

268 Evenett, Levenstein, and Suslow (n 263) 1236

269 See Julian M Joshua, 'The UK's New Cartel Offence and Its Implications for EC Competition Law: A Tangled Web' (2003) 28(5) European Law Review 620, 627

270 Department of Trade and Industry (n 232) para [7.33]

there is a lack of clarity in its definition. In this respect, Joshua views the legislation as an 'over complicated factual catalogue'.[271] The language of the legislation appears to be superficial and bogus, a fact that prompted Wilks to comment that 'the criminal cartel offence was pre-programmed to become a regulatory failure'.[272]

First, the fact that the element of 'dishonesty' on the part of directors must be established before a sanction can be imposed [273] has been blamed for impairing the enforcement of the cartel offence for a long time.[274] It was thus proposed that the 'dishonesty' element be expunged since it made the offence difficult to prosecute. Consequently, the element was removed by Section 47(2) of the ERRA13. It is hoped that the removal of the 'dishonesty' element would result in an increase in the number of cartel prosecutions, which will, in turn, deter directors from involvement in cartel offences. But whether removing the element of dishonesty completely addresses all concerns and limitations that have hindered the effect of the offence is yet to be seen. The fact that only one cartel offence prosecution has been instituted since the Act was enacted in April 2014 illustrates that competition law authorities are still reluctant to employ their powers of prosecution with the aim of imprisonment.[275]

In addition to the removal of the dishonesty element, new sections (188A, 188B, and 190A) have been introduced by Section 47 of the ERRA13. These sections are to the effect that the cartel offence would not be applicable if

> (i) the public and consumers are informed about the agreement between companies, (ii) the directors prove that they have taken reasonable steps through obtaining legal advice before the agreement is implemented, (iii) the parties of agreement publish a document regarding the agreement, and (iv) it is proved that there is no intention to conceal the agreement from customers and CMA.

That said, the question is whether directors would be allowed to plead any of these defences in order to dismiss the claims brought against them. Indeed, they can surely do so, for instance, if they have obtained legal advice before implementing the agreement in question. At this point, we should ask what would happen if directors do not follow the advice they received from their legal adviser.[276] This

271 Joshua (n 268) 627
272 Wilks (n 228) 355
273 Enterprise Act 2002, s 188(1). See also Department for Business, Innovation, & Skills (n 245) 88–92
274 See generally Andreas Stephan, 'How Dishonesty Killed the Cartel Offence' [2011] Criminal Law Review 446. See also Department for Business, Innovation, & Skills (n 245)
275 Barry Kenneth Cooper's pleading guilty for the cartel agreement between *Stanton Bonna (UK) Ltd, FP McCann Ltd, CPM Group Ltd and Milton Pipes Ltd.* See Competition and Markets Authority (n 709)
276 Richard Sallybanks and Gavin Costelloe, 'Removing the Requirement to Establish Dishonesty in the Criminal Cartel Offence – Will More Prosecutions Follow?' (2013) <https://www.lexology.com/library/detail.aspx?g=81c942a1-0388-4f6f-bb82-986b3ff24467> accessed 16 June 2024

question was addressed by Stephen Blake,[277] who affirmed that, in terms of 'legal advice defence and publication of prosecutorial guidance, all that is required is that advice is sought, no matter whether it is received or acted upon'.[278] With all due respect, this attitude may be considered superficial because what directors are required to do is prove that they made efforts to seek advice, but whether they implemented it in practice is left without consideration.

Consequently, it is difficult to state whether the existence of the offence and the possibility that it would be enforced can effectively deter directors from cartel offences. The fact that there have been so few prosecutions is clear proof of the reluctance of competition law authorities to implement the enforcement mechanism. For this reason, as Joshua described, it as 'a dead man walking',[279] and Furse argues that 'the UK's cartel offence has been the dog that did not bark'.[280] Noting further that 'the threat of effective prosecutions being brought forward under the Cartel Offence is practically close to zero'.[281]

We must reiterate, at the expense of verbosity, that whether the cartel offence can actually deter directors from cartel offences would depend on the extent of its enforcement in practice.[282] The fact that so few prosecutions have been instituted so far casts serious doubt on the assumption that it would strongly discourage directors from infringing the rules of competition law. It is, consequently, difficult to expect companies to be able to mitigate the risk of liability and loss that they may suffer if their directors commit cartel offences.

For the sake of argument, even if we assume that the cartel offence is being enforced at a desired level and effectively deters directors, it will still not remove the risk of liability and loss on the company, which is already placed by the administrative fining enforcement strategy. As shown earlier, under that strategy, parallel investigations may be undertaken against companies under Chapters 1 and 2 of the CA98 and individuals under Part 6 of the EA02. A fact that ensures that the

277 (Senior Director of the OFT Cartels & Criminal Enforcement Group) at the Competition Section Annual Conference, organised by the Law Society on 16 May 2013.

278 Quoted in Sallybanks and Costelloe (n 276)

279 Julian Joshua, 'Shooting the Messenger: Does the UK Criminal Cartel Offense Have a Future?' (2010) 10 <http://www.americanbar.org/content/dam/aba/publishing/antitrust_source/Aug10_Joshua8_2f.authcheckdam.pdf> accessed 16 April 2024

280 Furse (n 161) 2

281 Furse (n 161) 53

282 See Stephen Wilks, 'Cartel Criminalisation as Juridification: Political and Regulatory Dangers' in Caron Beaton-Wells and Ariel Ezrachi (eds), *Criminalising Cartels: Critical Studies of an International Regulatory Movement* (Hart Publishing 2011) 341, 355; The US cartel offence is always considered as having greater deterrent effect on individuals based on the number of proceedings brought every year. For example, 'in the fiscal year that ended September 30, 2006, the Division brought thirty-three cases involving violations of the Sherman Act and related federal statutes, and obtained total fines of more than $473 million, restitution of more than $2 million, and criminal sentences for nineteen individual defendants totalling 5,383 days of jail time'. See Gerald F Masoudi, 'Cartel Enforcement in the United States (and Beyond)' (Speech delivered at The Cartel Conference, Budapest, February 2007) <https://www.justice.gov/atr/speech/cartel-enforcement-united-states-and-beyond> accessed 13 April 2024

company's risk of liability and loss for infringement would not be eliminated by the introduction of the cartel offence.

3.5.3 Individual Fines

Besides the possibility of disqualification and imprisonment, directors may also be subjected to fines for competition breaches. A considerable fine may potentially deter them from such breaches because they may have severe financial consequences in their personal lives. The fines that may be imposed for cartel infractions are provided for under Section 190 of the EA02. Under that section, a person who is guilty of an offence under Section 188 (cartel offence) is liable

(i) on conviction on indictment, to imprisonment for a term not exceeding 5 years or to a fine, or to both
(ii) on summary conviction, to imprisonment for a term not exceeding 6 months or to a fine not exceeding the statutory maximum, or to both.

Additionally, an individual fine may be imposed on a disqualified director who becomes involved in forming, marketing, or running a company registered in the United Kingdom or which has a connection with the United Kingdom.[283] This strategy may potentially increase the deterrent effect of disqualification on directors even if disqualification alone fails to prevent them from taking a role in the management of a company. The issue with this enforcement strategy, however, is that its implementation is dependent on the implementation of both the disqualification and cartel offence. But considering the limited use of individual sanctions in practice,[284] its implementation and deterrence on directors is also limited. In order to conclude this section, we reiterate that the individual sanctions that are provided for under UK competition law were designed to deter directors from infringing the rules of competition law. Infringements expose the company to the risk of liability and loss. Even at that, their deterrent effect is limited because they are rarely implemented. The result is that the company remains exposed to the risk of directors' undesirable behaviours. Again, even if these individual sanctions were effectively applied to directors, the company would still bear primary responsibility for their infractions.

3.6 Conclusion

This chapter analysed the extent to which companies are impacted when they become subjected to sanctions and penalties when their directors breach competition law. It analysed UK competition policies and the administration enforcement

283 United Kingdom Government, 'Company Director Disqualification' (2024) <https://www.gov.uk/company-director-disqualification> accessed 15 April 2024
284 See Sections 3.5.1 and 3.5.2

strategies for the enforcement of competition law, as well as the theories that underlie these mechanisms. It also examined the exposure of the company to the risk of liability and loss where its directors breach competition law, noting in that vein that sanctions upon erring directors are hardly effective. It was shown that the regulatory enforcement strategies of competition law are implemented to protect its policy objectives, which are primarily aimed at promoting consumer welfare, and that for that purpose, companies, as undertakings, which breach competition law, are primarily targeted through administrative fines. This fact that gives rise to a tension between what competition law seeks to achieve and the need to safeguard companies from the undesirable behaviour of their directors. It was shown that competition law is not connected to or concerned about the company's exposure to the risk of liability and loss that may be caused by their directors' undesirable behaviours and that it rather misunderstands or oversimplifies the particular relationship between the actors of company law. It also disregards the matter that the stakeholders and the consumers whose welfare they seek to protect eventually suffer loss, and their long-term interests will be impaired as a result of administrative fining.

The chapter has shown that the foundation that underlies this enforcement strategy is based on compliance and deterrence theories. And while compliance theory considers the company to be an internal controller of its employees and is in a position to establish a compliance programme within its corporate structure, the deterrence theory primarily targets the company for infringements, a fact that is a consequence of the company's failure to establish a strong compliance programme to persuade its employees to obey the rules of law. It was shown that UK competition law has adopted a mixed approach of these theories, and even if the company establishes a very effective internal programme, it is doubtful if its directors would comply with it, which means that the company's risk of liability and loss will still not be removed.[285] Lastly, it was shown that this approach disregards the role of directors and their accountability for the law infringement in question.

The chapter also examined the imposition of sanctions on erring individuals as being a supplementary enforcement mechanism designed to address the inadequateness of the administrative fining strategy. It was shown that this strategy is inadequate for deterring directors from breaching competition law. Although it has been more than 10 years since they were introduced, the instances where they have been enforced are extremely rare. As such, the company is unlikely to mitigate the risk of liability and loss arising from directors' undesirable behaviours by the availability of these individual sanctions. Even if we assume that these mechanisms effectively deter directors from infringing the rules of competition law, the company would still not be able to mitigate the risk as it would have already been subjected to an administrative fine before proceedings against its directors would have

285 The United Kingdom provides a 10% fine reduction for a functioning strong compliance programme, but such allowance does not diminish the company's liability significantly as it is still held liable for the infringement

been completed. But despite these deficiencies, recent efforts by the authorities in terms of introducing them and seeking to address some challenges associated with them illustrate that the UK competition law authorities recognise their importance in ensuring adequate accountability for competition law infringements. However, when the preventative and deterrent approach as embodied in CA98, which solely targets companies, is considered, these are still significant developments. Even at that, there is much room for their implementations to be much improved.

To sum up, competition law does not aim to correctly ascertain the actual wrongdoer when breaches occur. Rather it has only sought to deter breaches by expanding the sanction scope through the introduction of a multi-enforcement framework. That said, the enforcement of these strategies leaves much to be desired—a situation that is unlikely to deter directors from engaging in undesirable behaviour which may expose the company to risk of liability and loss.

Flowing from this chapter, the next chapter will examine whether the company can effectively attribute and ascribe the risk of liability and loss that it suffers as a result of the undesirable behaviour of its directors by taking advantage of available legal mechanisms.

Bibliography

* This chapter was originally published in Samet Caliskan, 'Company Liability and Competition Law: Exposure of Company to Risk of Undesirable Behaviour of Directors' (2019) 40(1) Liverpool Law Review 1–29 and Samet Caliskan, 'Individual Behaviour, Regulatory Liability, and a Company's Exposure to Risk: The Deterrent Effect of Individual Sanctions in UK Competition Law' (2019) 10(6) Journal of European Competition Law & Practice 386–393.

Aaronson R, *The Future of UK Competition Policy* (Commission on Public Policy and British Business 1996)

Andreas Stephan, 'Survey of Public Attitudes to Price-Fixing and Cartel Enforcement in Britain' (2008) Comp Law Review 123, 133, 135

Arlen J, 'The Potentially Perverse Effects of Corporate Criminal Liability' (1994) 23 Journal of Legal Studies 833

Arlen J and Kraakman R, 'Controlling Corporate Misconduct: An Analysis of Corporate Liability Regimes' (1997) 72(4) New York University Law Review 687

Braithwaite J, *Restorative Justice & Responsive Regulation* (Oxford University Press 2002)

Braithwaite J and Ayres I, *Responsive Regulation: Transcending the Deregulation Debate* (Oxford University Press 1992). See also Braithwaite J, *To Punish or Persuade-Enforcement of Coal Mine Safety* (State University of New York 1985)

Breit W and Elzinga KG, *Antitrust Penalty Reform: An Economic Analysis* (American Enterprise Institute for Public Research 1986) 61

Brief AP, Dukerich JM, Brown PR, and Brett JF, 'What's Wrong With the Treadway Commission Report? Experimental Analyses of the Effects of Personal Values and Codes of Conduct on Fraudulent Financial Reporting' (1996) 15 Journal of Business Ethics 183

Calkins S, 'Corporate Compliance and the Antitrust Agencies' Bi-Modal Penalties' (1997) 60 LCP 127

Chisholm A, 'Achieving a Culture of Compliance' (Law Society Competition Section Annual Conference London 16 May 2014).

Clarkson C, 'Kicking Corporate Bodies and Damning Their Souls' (1996) 59(4) MLR 557

Combe E and Monnier C, 'Fines Against Hard Core Cartels in Europe: The Myth of Over Enforcement' (2011) 56 Antitrust Bulletin 235

Cowan D and Nazerali JS, 'Importing the E.U. Model into U.K. Competition Law: A Blueprint for Reform or a Step into "Euroblivion"?' (1999) 20(2) ECLR 55

Dabbah MM, 'Measuring the Success of a System of Competition Law: A Preliminary View' (2000) 21(8) ECLR

Evenett SJ, Levenstein MC, and Suslow VY, 'International Cartel Enforcement: Lessons From the 1990s' (2001) 24 World Economy 1221, 1236

Frazer T, 'Monopoly, Prohibition and Deterrence' (1995) 58(6) MLR 846

Furse M, *The Criminal Law of Competition in the UK and in the US: Failure and Success* (1st edn, Cheltenham 2012)

Galloway J, 'Chapter 2A: Competition Disqualification Orders' in His Honour Judge Abbas Mithani (ed.), *Mithani: Directors' Disqualification* (Butterworths 2009) III–351

Ginsburg D and Wright J, 'Antitrust Sanctions' (2010) 6(2) Competition Policy International

Gorecki PK and McFadden D, 'Criminal Cartels in Ireland: The Heating Oil Case' (2006) 27(11) ECLR 631

Graham C, 'The Reform of UK Competition Policy' (2012) ECJ 539, 556

Graham C, *EU and UK Competition Law* (2nd edn, Pearson 2013) 19

Gray J, 'Company Directors and Ignorance of the Law' (1996) 17(10) Comp Law 296, 299–300

Gürkaynak G, Olgu Kama Ç, and Ergün B, 'How to Establish and Operate an Anti-Corruption Compliance Program in Emerging Markets: The Turkish Example' (2015) 1(2) Turkish Commercial Law Review 145

Hammond SD, 'Cornerstones of an Effective Leniency Program' (November 2004) <http://www.justice.gov/atr/public/speeches/206611.htm> accessed 23 June 2024

Hart O, 'Corporate Governance: Some Theory and Implications' (1995) 105 The Economic Journal 678, 679

Hawkins K, 'Bargain and Bluff: Compliance Strategy and Deterrence in the Enforcement of Regulation' (1983) 5(1) Law and Policy Quarterly 35

Hicks A, 'Director Disqualification: Can It Deliver?' [2001] JBL 433, 435

Hüschelrath K, 'Public Enforcement of Anti-Cartel Laws – Theory and Empirical Evidence' in Kai Hüschelrath and Heike Schweitzer (eds), *Public and Private Enforcement of Competition Law in Europe Legal and Economic Perspectives* (Springer 2014) 9

Hutchings MB, 'The Need for Reform of UK Competition Policy' (1995) 16(4) ECLR

Jones A and Williams R, 'Deterring Cartels: Is Criminalisation the Solution? Lessons From the UK' (Presentation) <https://www.law.ox.ac.uk/sites/files/oxlaw/jones_and_williams.pdf> accessed 13 April 2024

Jones A and Williams R, 'The UK Response to the Global Effort Against Cartels: Is Criminalization Really the Solution?' [2014] JAE 1, 9

Jones K and Harrison F, *Criminal Sanctions: An Overview of EU and National Case Law* (National Competition Laws Bulletin) 7

Joshua J, 'Shooting the Messenger: Does the UK Criminal Cartel Offense Have a Future?' (2010)

Joshua JM, 'The UK's New Cartel Offence and Its Implications for EC Competition Law: A Tangled Web' (2003) 28(5) European Law Review 620

Khan A, 'Rethinking Sanctions for Breaching EU Competition Law: Is Director Disqualification the Answer?' (2012) 35 World Competition 77

Kitson A, 'Taking the Pulse: Ethics and the British Cooperative Bank' (1996) 15 Journal of Business Ethics 1021

Krawiec KD, 'Cosmetic Compliance and the Failure of Negotiated Governance' (2003) 81 Washington University Law Quarterly 487

Krawiec KD, 'Organizational Misconduct: Beyond the Principal-Agent Model' (2005) 32 Florida State University Law Review 571

Kriesberg SM, 'Decision-Making Models and the Control of Corporate Crime' (1976) 85 Yale Law Journal 1091

Kroes N, 'European Competition Policy- Delivering Better Markets and Better Choices' (*SPEECH/05/512* 15 September 2005) 2 <europa.eu/rapid/press-release_SPEECH-05-512_en.pdf> accessed 15 April 2024
Lowe P, 'The Design of Competition Policy Institutions for the 21st Century: The Experience of the European Commission and DG Competition' (2008) 3 Competition Policy Newsletter
Maitland-Walker J, 'The New U.K. Competition Law Regime' (1999) 20(2) ECLR 51
Masoudi GF, 'Cartel Enforcement in the United States (and Beyond)' (Speech Delivered at the Cartel Conference, Budapest, February 2007)
McKendall M, DeMarr B, and Jones-Rikkers C, 'Ethical Compliance Programs and Corporate Illegality: Testing the Assumptions of the Corporate Sentencing Guidelines' (2002) 37 Journal of Business Ethics 367
McKenzie B, 'Legal Risk and Compliance: Special Report' (2008)
Michels EM, 'The Real Shortcoming of the UK Cartel Offence: A Lack of Public and Political Support' [2014] Global Antitrust Review 53, 60
Motta M, *Competition Policy: Theory and Practice* (2nd edn, Cambridge University Press 2004)
Oded S, 'Enforcement Strategies, Compliance Programs, and the Intermediary Gatekeepers' (2010) 22–23.
Odudu O, 'The Wider Concerns of Competition Law' (2010) 30(3) OJLS 599
Ong K, 'Disqualification of Directors: A Faulty Regime?' (1998) 19(1) Comp Law 7, 9
Onwudiwe I, *et al*, 'Deterrence Theory' in Mary Bosworth (ed.), *Encyclopedia of Prisons & Correctional Facilities* (Sage 2005) 234
Parker D, 'The Competition Act 1998: Change and Continuity in U.K. Competition Policy' [2000] JBL 283
Parret L, 'Shouldn't We Know What We Are Protecting? Yes We Should! A Plea for a Solid and Comprehensive Debate About the Objectives of EU Competition Law and Policy' (2010) 6(2) ECJ 339
Pilsbury S and Jenkins H, 'The Evolution of Effects-Based Analysis Under the Competition Act 1998' [2010] Comp Law 216
Polinsky MA and Shavell S, 'Should Employees Be Subject to Fines and Imprisonment Given the Existence of Corporate Liability?' (1993) 13 International Review of Law & Economics
Reindl AP, 'How Strong is the Case for Criminal Sanctions in Cartel Cases' in KJ Cseres, MP Schinkel, and FOW Vogelaar (eds), *Criminalisation of Competition Law Enforcement: Economic and Legal Implications for the EU Member States* (Edward Elgar 2006) 110–132
Reiss AJ, 'Consequences of Compliance and Deterrence Models of Law Enforcement for the Exercise of Police Discretion' (1984) 47(4) LCP 83
Rodger BJ, 'Competition Policy, Liberalism and Globalization: A European Perspective' (2000) 6 The Columbia Journal of European Law
Rodger BJ, 'The Competition Act and The Enterprise Act Reforms: Sanctions and Deterrence in UK Competition Law' in Gerhard Dannecker and Oswald Jansen (eds), *Competition Law Sanctioning in the European Union: The EU-Law Influence on the National Law System of Sanctions in the European Area* (Kluwer 2004) 101
Rodger BJ, 'A Study of Compliance Post-OFT Infringement Action' [2009] ECJ 65
Rodger BJ and MacCulloch A, *Competition Law and Policy in the EC and UK* (5th edn, Routledge 2015)
Sallybanks R and Costelloe G, 'Removing the Requirement to Establish Dishonesty in the Criminal Cartel Offence – Will More Prosecutions Follow?' (2013)
Scholz JT, 'Cooperation, Deterrence, and the Ecology of Regulatory Enforcement' (1984) 18 Law and Society Review 179

Scholz JT, 'Enforcement Policy and Corporate Misconduct: The Changing Perspective of Deterrence Theory' 60(3) LCP 253
Scholz JT, 'Voluntary Compliance and Regulatory Enforcement' (1984) 6(4) Law & Policy 385
Schwarcz SL, 'Excessive Corporate Risk-Taking and the Decline of Personal Blame' (2015) 65 Emory Law Journal 533
Schwartz M, 'The Nature of the Relationship Between Corporate Codes of Ethics and Behaviour' (2001) 32 Journal of Business Ethics 247
Scott A, *The Evolution of Competition Law and Policy in the United Kingdom* (LSE Working Papers 2009)
Singleton S, *Competition Law Compliance 2008* (Thorogood 2008) 2. UK competition law also imposes individual sanctions.
Stephan A, 'Disqualification Orders for Directors Involved in Cartels' (2011) 2(6) Journal of European Competition Law 529
Stephan A, 'Four Key Challenges to the Successful Criminalization of Cartel Laws' (2014) 2(2) Journal of Antitrust Enforcement 333–362
Stephan A, 'See No Evil: Cartels and the Limits of Antitrust Compliance Programs' (2010) 31(8) Comp Law 231
Stephan A, 'Why Morality Should Be Excluded From the Cartel Criminalisation Debate' (2012) 3 New Journal of European Criminal Law 127, 128
Thepot F, 'Antitrust v. Anti-Corruption Policy Approaches to Compliance: Why Such a Gap?' (2015) 2 CPI Antitrust Chronicle 1
Thepot F, 'Corporate Compliance with Competition Law' (Ascola Annual Conference, Meiji University 2015)
Thepot F, *The Interaction Between Competition Law and Corporate Governance: Opening the 'Black Box'* (PhD Thesis, University College London 2014)
Turner JDC, 'The U.K. Competition Act 1998 and Private Rights' 1999 20(2) ECLR 62; Peretz G, 'Detection and Deterrence of Secret Cartels under the UK Competition Bill' (1998) 19(3) ECLR
Tyran J-R and Feld LP, 'Achieving Compliance When Legal Sanctions are Non-Deterrent' (2006) 108(1) The Scandinavian Journal of Economics 135
Weatherill S, 'Country Analysis-United Kingdom' in Gerhard Dannecker and Oswald Jansen (eds), *Competition Law Sanctioning in the European Union: The EU-Law Influence on the National Law System of Sanctions in the European Area* (Kluwer 2004) 859
Weitbrecht A, 'From Freiburg to Chicago and Beyond: The First 50 Years of European Competition Law' (2008) 29(2) ECLR 81
Whelan P, 'A Principled Argument for Personal Criminal Sanctions as Punishment Under EC Cartel Law' (2007) 4(1) Comp Law Review 7
Wilks S, 'Cartel Criminalisation as Juridification: Political and Regulatory Dangers' in Caron Beaton-Wells and Ariel Ezrachi (eds), *Criminalising Cartels: Critical Studies of an International Regulatory Movement* (Hart Publishing 2011) 341
Williams M, 'Directors' Disqualification' (2005) 2(3) IJDG 281
Williams R, 'Disqualifying Directors: A Remedy Worse Than the Disease?' (2007) 7 Journal of Corporate Law Studies 213, 234
Willimsky SM, 'The Concept(s) of Competition' (1997) 18(1) ECLR 54
Wils WPJ, 'The Undertaking as Subject of E.C. Competition Law and the Imputation of Infringements to Natural or Legal Persons' (2000) 25(2) European Law Review 99, 100
Wils WPJ, *The Optimal Enforcement of EC Antitrust Law, Essays in Law & Economics* (Kluwer 2002)
Wils WPJ, 'Optimal Antitrust Fines: Theory and Practice' (2006) 29(2) World Competition 183
Wils WPJ, *Efficiency and Justice in European Antitrust Enforcement* (Hart 2008) 188
Wils WPJ, 'Antitrust Compliance Programmes & Optimal Antitrust Enforcement' (2013) 1(1) JAE 52

4 Legal Attribution and Ascription of Risk

Preventing the Company From Passing on Liability and Loss

4.1 Introduction

Thus far, this book has examined the issues that may arise when directors engage in conduct that may expose companies to significant risks, given their limited ability to control their actions. Some of these risks, as shown earlier, include the possibility of being subjected to sanctions particularly where directors involve the company in anti-competitive conduct. Building on that foundation, this analyses the extent to which the law enables companies to transfer their risks to erring directors whose conduct exposed them to such risks in the first place. To achieve this objective, the chapter will examine the legal mechanisms that enable companies to pass their liabilities and losses to erring directors. Some of these mechanisms include the doctrine of corporate attribution and the illegality defence known by the Latin maxim *ex turpi causa* ('the maxim'). The chapter will, however, ask whether these mechanisms are adequate in the circumstances.

Our focus in this chapter is to critically examine the operation of the attribution doctrine and the maxim in the distribution of risks that may arise from the undesirable behaviour of directors. We aim to determine whether these mechanisms truly protect companies or potentially expose them to further risks. The potential risks to companies are a paramount concern in our analysis.

Firstly, we will delve into the principle of corporate attribution, which determines the extent to which the acts of directors on behalf of a company can be attributed to it. This principle holds the company liable for the acts of its directors, whether contractually, criminally, tortuously, or statutorily. We will then explore the concept of the maxim, a doctrine that prevents a claimant from pursuing a legal remedy for a loss that arises from his illegal or immoral acts. We will examine whether the maxim prevents individuals from relying on their wrongdoing and what implications this has for the company, which acts through individuals. We will also consider whether the company can recover losses arising from the undesirable behaviour of its directors on its behalf. This chapter will also focus on how the maxim is applied to companies and whether its joint application with corporate attribution can enable the company to pass on the risks of liability and loss that arise from the undesirable behaviour of its directors to the latter. These two distinct but related issues will be addressed since the maxim is connected to corporate

DOI: 10.4324/9781003461562-4

attribution in the company's relationship with its directors. In essence, where a company is found liable for the acts of its directors by virtue of the doctrine of corporate attribution, the maxim acts to debar it from ascribing the liability or loss to those directors. Consequently, its effect is to prevent appropriate individual accountability on the part of those directors.[1] The application of corporate attribution and the maxim in the relationship of company/directors is usually *ex post*. As such, companies can only rely on them when the liability or loss has arisen from the conduct of their directors, following which they may institute claims against them with a view to passing on their liabilities or losses. Thus, they determine the party to bear liability for losses suffered by a company, and as should be expected, their application would raise tension between the company and its directors.

In order to achieve its objectives, the chapter is divided into three sections. Section 4.2 examines different approaches to corporate attribution, how they operate to distribute the liability and loss between the company and directors, and whether they expose the company to a heightened risk of liability and loss as a result of the undesirable behaviour of their directors. The section also investigates the relationship between attribution and the directors' fiduciary duties when used by the company as a shield against attribution. Following this, Section 4.3 explores the operation of the maxim, its public policy foundation, and considerations of public policy. It will, in that vein, demonstrate what the maxim protects, promotes, and deters. It will also consider the impact of its application in enabling the company to recover losses it suffers by reason of the directors' undesirable behaviours. Section 4.4 concludes the chapter by demonstrating that the availability of these measures notwithstanding, the company is often unable to attribute and ascribe its risks to its directors as a result of the joint operation of the doctrine of corporate attribution and the maxim.

4.2 The Principle of Corporate Attribution and the Direct Liability of the Company

It is trite law that the company is an abstraction with a distinct personality from its directors. It acts solely through its organs, directors, agents, and officers. Flowing from this is the fact that the company can be held liable for the acts and intentions of its directors. The doctrine of attribution directly imputes the knowledge or acts of directors to the company and makes it liable for their acts. In such cases, the company cannot deny liability for the acts of its directors, as they are considered its own.[2]

4.2.1 The Doctrine of Corporate Attribution

To appreciate the doctrine of corporate attribution, it is imperative that we appreciate how corporate culpability is determined. This is more so when we consider

1 It should be noted here that there are several approaches to the illegality defence in tort, and the maxim is the one which is widely used in this context. Paul Davies, 'The Illegality Defence and Public Policy' (2009) 125 LQR 556

2 Eilis Ferran, 'Corporate Attribution and the Directing Mind and Will' (2011) 127 LQR 239

that a company's exposure can have potentially negative consequences on its performance and reputation in cases where it is found liable for breaching the law, for example, by violating competition law through the formation of cartels or abusing its dominant position.[3] Several rules for corporate attribution have been established under company law to determine 'whose actions and whose knowledge can be said to represent' the company.[4] They can be classified as principles of special attribution and the identification doctrine.

4.2.1.1 Special Rules of Attribution

The first approach of attribution is to utilise 'special rules of attribution'.[5] This doctrine was formulated by Lord Hoffmann in *Meridian Global Funds Management Asia Ltd v. Securities Commission*.[6] The learned justice opined that,

> A company exists because there is a rule (usually in a statute) which says that a *persona ficta* shall be deemed to exist and to have certain of the powers, rights and duties of a natural person. But there would be little sense in deeming such a *persona ficta* to exist unless there were also rules to tell one what acts were to count as acts of the company. It is, therefore, a necessary part of corporate personality that there should be rules by which acts are attributed to the company.[7]

In that case, Meridian, an investment company based in Hong Kong, and its two senior investment managers used their powers and authority to inappropriately buy shares for the purpose of obtaining control of a New Zealand company. The company did not disclose this fact to the New Zealand Securities Commission because the same fact was hidden from it by its managers. Consequently, the New Zealand Securities Commission imposed fines on Meridian and two of its managers. But Meridian argued that it should not have been held liable, having not been aware of the existence of the transaction. Even then, it was held liable because, on the basis of the doctrine of corporate attribution, the knowledge of its managers was directly attributed to it.

Despite the fact that the basis of the special rules of attribution spring from *Meridian*, which was a criminal case, the principle has also been applied to civil cases by the courts.[8] In applying the rule, the courts will treat each case on its mer-

3 Celia Wells, 'Corporate Liability for Crime-*Tesco v. Nattrass* on the Danger List?' (1996) 3(1) Architecture News 5, 7

4 Celia Wells, 'Corporate Liability for Crime-*Tesco v. Nattrass* on the Danger List?' (1996) 3(1) Architecture News 7

5 See Stephen Griffin, 'The One-Man Type Company and the Removal of Corporate Personality in the Context of the Attribution Rules' (2011) 22(5) ICCLR 158, 159

6 [1995] 2 AC 500 PC

7 [1995] 2 AC 500 PC 506

8 Jennifer Payne, 'Corporate Attribution and the Lessons of *Meridian*' in Paul Davies and Justine Pila (eds), *The Jurisprudence of Lord Hoffmann* (Hart Publishing 2015) 364

its as its facts determine. In so doing, they would interpret and analyse common law rules, the language of the rule of a particular piece of legislation, as well as its content and policy.[9] In that regard, a rule may be couched 'in language primarily applicable to a natural person and require some act or state of mind on the part of that person "himself," as opposed to his servants or agents'.[10] In such a case, the courts will form special rules of attribution to determine whose intention, act, and knowledge could be considered as that of the company for this purpose.[11] The answer to this question can be found 'by applying the usual canons of interpretation, taking into account the language of the rule (if it is a statute) and its content and policy'.[12] The approach can thus be considered flexible in the issue of attribution. In addition, the principle is rooted in the agency theory, which regards people as working for the company and not as the company themselves. The separation between the members and the company is protected in this approach[13] because it relies on 'the operational autonomy of employees instead of the company's internal hierarchy,'[14] which is based on the organic theory.

Initially, the doctrine was limited to recognising different circumstances. This was because the rule has to be applied dynamically since different circumstances cannot be forced into the same formula.[15] In this sense, the doctrine introduces 'a nuanced form of contextualised attribution'.[16] It asks the question of how liability should be attributed to the company when there is no directing mind and there is the absence of authorisation.[17] Considerations of 'specific language and interpretation of statutory rule, [the] effect of which justifies the imposition of liability' were considered.[18] Therefore, this approach is usually regarded as a doctrine that had set up 'contextualisation, rather than [an] anthropomorphic inquiry into corporate personality'.[19] This illustrates a non-mechanical or non-automatic approach adopted by the doctrine of attribution.[20] On this characteristic, the doctrine has been well received. For example, Sealy expressed that it brings 'a welcome degree of flexibility into a difficult area of the law'.[21] Grantham pointed out that it has a

9 *Meridian Global* (n 6) [507]
10 *Meridian Global* (n 6) 507
11 *Meridian Global* (n 6) 507
12 Saleem Sheikh, 'The Corporation-Villain or Victim?' (2008) 19(11) ICCLR 248, 351
13 Jennifer Payne, 'The Attribution of Tortious Liability Between Director and Company' [1998] JBL 153, 159
14 Vrinda Bhandari, 'Meridian to Iridium: An Analysis of Attribution' (2012) 23(8) ICCLR 253, 254
15 See also *Meridian Global Funds Management Asia Ltd v. Securities Commission* [1995] 2 AC 500 PC (n 14) [511]
16 Kunal Ambasta, 'A Leap of Reasoning, But for Special Cases: An Analysis of the "Expiry" of the Directing Mind and Will Test in Attribution of Corporate Liability' (2012) 33(8) Comp Law 227, 229
17 Ernest Lim, 'A Critique of Corporate Attribution: "Directing Mind and Will" and Corporate Objectives' [2013] JBL 333
18 Griffin (n 5) 159
19 Ferran (n 2) 239
20 Leonard S Sealy, 'The Corporate Ego and Agency Untwined' (1995) 54(3) CLJ 507, 508
21 Sealy (n 20) 509

'sound intellectual footing', and Anchayli opines that the attribution test was clarified by 're-establish[ing] the dynamics of the theory of corporate attribution in the context-specific, rule-oriented manner'.[22]

4.2.1.2 The Doctrine of Directing Mind and Will and Its Exception

The second approach to corporate attribution is the identification doctrine, which is also known as the alter ego principle. This doctrine determines attribution by ascertaining the directing mind and will of the company.[23] The doctrine is a 'general rule' that courts apply to justify the imposition of liability on companies and their directors.[24] Essentially, it enables the determination of a company's identity.[25] It is to the effect that liability arising from the acts of the directing mind can be attributed to the company, which is consequently personally liable. The primary focus is the position held by the director within the company, and whether they can be regarded as an agent or a mind of the latter is ascertained.

The identification doctrine is rooted in German law, and it was first postulated by Viscount Haldane LC[26] in *Lennard's Carrying Co Ltd v. Asiatic Petroleum Co Ltd*.[27] Since then, it has been widely used in cases involving liability distribution between the company and directors. In that case, Asiatic Petroleum suffered a loss due to the negligence of Lennard's director, Mr. Lennard, and instituted a claim against Lennard. The House of Lords held that Mr. Lennard was the directing mind of Lennard; as such, his negligence could be attributed to it. Viscount Haldane L.C. stated,

> [A] corporation is an abstraction. It has no mind of its own any more than it has a body of its own; its active and directing will must consequently be sought in the person of somebody who for some purposes may be called an agent but who is really the directing mind and will of the corporation, the very ego and centre of the personality of the corporation.[28]

This approach was also adopted by Lord Reid in *Tesco Supermarkets Ltd v. Nattrass*,[29] who opined that if the culpable man is identifiable with the company,

22 Anjali Anchayli, 'The "Directing Mind and Will" Test in Corporate Attribution: Iridium and Meridian – A Comparison' (2012) 33(8) Comp Law 252, 254

23 *Lennard's Carrying Co Ltd v. Asiastic Petroleum Co Ltd* [1915] A.C. 705 HL; *Tesco Supermarkets Ltd v. Nattrass* [1972] A.C. 153; *El-Ajou v. Dollar Land Holdings Plc* [1994] 2 All E.R. 685 CA (Civ Div); *Attorney General's Reference (No.2 of 1999)* [2000] Q.B. 796

24 CA Ong and RJ Wickins, 'Confusion Worse Confounded: The End of the Directing Mind Theory?' [1997] JBL 524

25 Yedidia Z Stern, 'Corporate Criminal Personal Liability: Who is the Corporation' (1987) 13 The Journal of Corporation Law 125

26 Andrew Hicks and SH Goo, *Cases and Materials on Company Law* (6th edn, Oxford University Press 2008) 129

27 *Lennard* (n 23)

28 *Lennard* (n 23) [713]

29 *Tesco Supermarkets Ltd v. Nattrass* (n 23)

his act would be that of the company, regardless of whether his offence was serious or venial.[30] He went on to state that,

> A living person has a mind that can have knowledge or intention or be negligent and has hands to carry out his intentions. A corporation has none of these: it must act through living persons, though not always one or the same person. Then, the person who acts is not speaking or acting for the company. He is acting as the company and his mind which directs his acts is the mind of the company. There is no question of the company being vicariously liable. He is not acting as a servant, representative, agent or delegate. He is an embodiment of the company or, one could say, he hears and speaks through the persona of the company, within his appropriate sphere, and his mind is the mind of the company. If it is a guilty mind then that guilt is the guilt of the company.[31]

The crux of this approach is that if a company is identified with a particular individual, it cannot escape the liability that may come from that person's acts or intentions. The identification doctrine is based on the organic theory that distinguishes mere agents, who are not to be regarded as the company's directing mind, and the organs whose acts are regarded as those of the company.[32] This distinction was demonstrated by Lord Denning in *H L Bolton (Engineering) Co Ltd v. TJ Graham and Sons Ltd*[33] as follows:

> A company may in many ways be likened to a human body. It has a brain and nerve centre which controls what it does. It also has hands which hold the tools and act in accordance with directions from the centre. Some of the people in the company are mere servants and agents who are nothing more than hands to do the work and cannot be said to represent the mind or will. Others are directors and managers who represent the directing mind and will of the company and control what it does. The state of mind of these managers is the state of mind of the company and is treated by the law as such. So you will find that in cases where the law requires personal fault as a condition of liability in tort, the fault of the manager will be the personal fault of the company.[34]

Thus, with the identification doctrine, the question of who is an organ requires an answer to determine whether the company is directly or vicariously liable.[35] Different suggestions have been put forward for defining an 'organ' of a company. In *Lennard*, it was defined as 'the directing mind and will' and 'the very ego and

30 (n 23) [173]
31 (n 23) [170]
32 Stern (n 25) 129
33 [1957] 1 Q.B. 159
34 [1957] 1 Q.B. 159 [172]
35 Stern (n 25) 129–130

centre'.[36] In addition, the Court of Appeal in *Bolton* defined it as 'a brain and nerve centre'.[37] In order to pin down who is the organ, the very ego, or brain of the company, the corporate veil needs to be pierced to investigate the structure of the company's management.[38] This investigation helps to determine whether a person has substantial authority and the power to act on behalf of a company. For example, a person who is associated with the actual authority to bind the company on specific matters by the board of directors can be regarded as a directing mind.[39] In addition, as seen in *El Ajou v. Dollar Land Holdings Plc*,[40] a person who acts with ostensible authority can also be perceived as a directing mind.[41] In that case, a company's fiduciary who was delegated with power to obtain funds for a particular project was regarded as its directing mind even though he had no responsibility for the whole project or for the general business affairs of the company. Based on the outcome of this case, it can be stated that 'those who have only de facto management of a company or aspects of its operations, such as shadow directors and managers, can often constitute the directing mind'.[42] Also, in *Bolton*[43] it was held that a wrongdoing in which three directors were involved, without obtaining the approval of the board of directors, could be attributed to the company on the basis that the board meetings at which approvals could have been obtained for the act, were held infrequently (once a year) The directors were consequently considered as constituting the directing mind of Bolton.[44]

A similar issue was also discussed in *The Lady Gwendolen, Arthur Guinness, Son & Co. (Dublin) Ltd v. MV Freshfield*.[45] In that case, one of the three assistant managing directors who controlled the shipping department of a company was held to be its directing mind. What this means is that in addition to directors, employees may also be regarded as the company's directing mind if they are conferred with powers by the general management of the company to perform certain managerial responsibilities. Accordingly, determining whether the intention of a particular person can be attributed to a company 'depends on the nature of the matter under consideration, the relative position of the officer or agent and other relevant factors and the circumstances of the case'.[46]

36 *Lennard* (n 23) [713] per Viscount Haldane

37 (n 33) [172] per Denning L.J.

38 See Chapter 1, Section 1.2. Finding the organ of the company is much easier in one-man type companies. In this regard, Lord Phillips argued that 'where those managing the company are using it as a vehicle for fraud, or where there is only one person who is managing all aspects of the company's activities, there is no difficulty in identifying the fraud as the fraud of the company'. See *Stone & Rolls Ltd v. Moore Stephens* [2009] UKHL 39, [2009] 1 A.C. 1391

39 Griffin (n 5) 159

40 [1994] BCC 143 CA (Civ Div)

41 See Griffin (n 5) 159

42 Wickins and Ong (n 24) 544

43 *Bolton* (n 33)

44 *Bolton* (n 33)

45 [1965] 2 All E.R. 283

46 *Bolton* (n 33) [173]

Based on this approach, it can be suggested that the conduct of a person who holds a directorship position within a company can be easily attributed to it. Even at that, cases such as the *In Re Hampshire Land Co (No. 2)*, have demonstrated that this doctrine is not without exceptions.[47] In that case, a principal was regarded as the victim of a fraud perpetrated by its agent, who was precluded from attributing the liability to the former. The exception can be defined as positing that 'the knowledge of the agent should not be attributed to the principal when the agent commits a fraud or breach of duty'.[48] This principle, which is known as the 'Hampshire Land doctrine', has been commonly invoked by companies as a counter argument to claims brought by its directors and as a means of attributing liability to the latter.[49] This was described by Mummery LJ in *Bank of India v. Morris*[50] as follows:

> Clearly there are some circumstances in which an individual's knowledge of fraud cannot and should not be attributed to a company. The classic case is where the company is itself the target of an agent's or employee's dishonesty. In general, it would not be sensible or realistic to attribute knowledge to the company concerned, if attribution had the effect of defeating the right of the company to recover from a dishonest agent or employee or from a third party.[51]

This exception was applied by the Supreme Court in the case of *Jetivia SA and Another v. Bilta (UK) Ltd (in liquidation) and Others*.[52] In that case, Bilta, an English company, had two directors: Mr. Nazir and Mr. Chopra. The latter was also the sole shareholder of the company. Both men were involved in a conspiracy between April 2009 and July 2009, which resulted in Bilta engaging in a number of transactions regarding carbon credits under the European Emissions Trading Scheme Allowances (EUAs) with numerous third parties, including Jetivia. Bilta purchased the EUAs from Jetivia free of value added tax (VAT), but it incurred significant liabilities relating to VAT when it sold them to UK traders and was consequently unable to meet its VAT obligations, which amounted to £38 million.

Through its liquidators, Bilta sought recovery against its two directors, Jetivia and its chief executive officer, Mr. Brunschweiler, alleging that they breached their fiduciary duties with the assistance of the latter. The defendants applied to strike Bilta's claim, but the High Court refused the defendant's application and held that the facts in *Bilta* differed from that of *Stone* (discussed next) for two reasons.[53] The

47 [1896] 2 Ch. 743

48 Ernest Lim, 'Attribution in Company Law' (2014) 77(5) MLR 794, 796

49 See *Stone & Rolls Ltd v. Moore Stephens* (n 2); *Safeway Stores Ltd v. Twigger* [2010] EWCA Civ 1472 (n 2) [28]–[29] and [59]; *Jetivia SA and Another v. Bilta (UK) Ltd (in liquidation) and Others* [2015] UKSC 23

50 [2005] EWCA Civ 693, [2005] BCC 739

51 [2005] EWCA Civ 693, [2005] BCC 739 [114]

52 (n 49)

53 [2012] EWHC 2163 (Ch), [2013] 2 WLR 825 [25]

first was that the company in *Bilta* was a victim. In contrast, the company in *Stone* was the actual wrongdoer since, as a result of the wrongdoing of the directors of Bilta, the company failed to fulfil its VAT obligations by transferring the proceeds to the defendants. The second reason was that, while the directors in *Bilta* owed a duty to the company, they also had to consider creditors' interests regulated under Section 172(3) of the CA06. The auditors in *Stone* did not have, as such a duty. Sir Andrew Morritt C stated,

> in my judgment, the ratio decidendi of Stone . . . is not applicable to cases in which the claim is based on a breach of duty, the scope of which encompasses persons or interests other than the fraudsters in corporate form.[54]

The defendants appealed the decision and argued that Bilta was not a victim but a villain. The Court of Appeal relied on the decision in *Belmont Finance Corp Ltd v. Williams Furniture Ltd.* and held that Bilta was a victim because it was not a party to the conspiracy.[55] The defendants also argued that the liabilities of the directors should be attributed to the company based on *Stone*'s reasoning since Bilta was a one-man company and there was no innocent constituency within it. However, Patten LJ asserted that the exception of the directing mind was inapplicable in that case since it

> would directly contradict the protection given to creditors under [sections 172 and 239 of the CA06], which applies regardless of whether the company is what Lord Walker described as a one-man company or one in which there are innocent directors and shareholders.[56]

He opined that the court did not have to apply the sole actor exception of *Stone* because there was 'a significant difference between the liability of an auditor for failing to notify the company about what was taking place and a conspiracy against the company by its directors and others to deprive it of its assets'.[57] The defendants' appeal was unanimously dismissed by the Supreme Court, which held that Bilta could not be barred from recovery as the act of its directors, who had breached their fiduciary duties, could not be attributed to it.[58]

Based on the outcome of this case, it can be concluded that the directing mind and will doctrine does not always attribute the conduct of a director to the company and that there are some circumstances where directors may be prevented from

54 [2012] EWHC 2163 (Ch), [2013] 2 WLR 825 [36]

55 [2013] EWCA Civ 968, [2014] Ch 52 [81]. It should be noted here that the court also considered the reasoning of dissenting judges in *Stone & Rolls* (n 49). Lord Mance and Lord Scott, who discussed that the identification doctrine should not be the answer to the claim of the company against its wrongdoing directors for breach of duty, held that sole actor exception was not applicable

56 [2013] EWCA Civ 968, [2014] Ch 52 [79]

57 [2013] EWCA Civ 968, [2014] Ch 52 [81]

58 [2013] EWCA Civ 968, [2014] Ch 52 [92]

passing on the liability of their conduct to the company. The following section will examine how the doctrine of corporate attribution and the exception to the identification doctrine operate when directors are involved in undesirable behaviour.

4.2.2 The Doctrines of Corporate Attribution and the Attribution of a Company's risks to its Directors

As we have seen, two doctrines are employed in determining the attribution of the conduct of directors to the company. The operation of these doctrines is crucial in general but also with respect to the attribution of risks of liability and loss arising from undesirable behaviour by directors in their relationship to the company. In this respect, while the identification doctrine has been widely applied in the corporate context, it has been suggested that it is problematic in its distribution of the risk of liability and loss between the company and its directors,[59] and viewing the company as an 'abstract entity' that can be held criminally and civilly liable on the basis of the 'intention or state of mind' of its managers is narrow and somewhat problematic.[60] The approach adopted by the court in *Lennard* underlies this issue. As previously shown, the House of Lords held in that case that Mr. Lennard should have been aware of the existence of the defect in the ship, and this proved his negligence in the loss that the other party suffered. That notwithstanding, the liability for the third-party damages was still attributed to the company which served as director.

Lim identified at least three issues with the approach adopted by the identification doctrine.[61] For him, automatically attributing the wrongdoing of a company's single member to it, will unfairly prejudice it, while large companies may be allowed to escape liability given that it is more difficult to determine the directing mind and will in the latter. The second problem with the doctrine arises when neither the wrongdoing was authorised by the board or shareholders' meeting and the company's directing mind and will of the company cannot be identified. In such cases, it could be said that the law was intended to be applied to companies while excluding liability on vicarious or agency grounds.[62] Thirdly for him is the fact that the doctrine automatically attributes the acts of the directing mind and will of the one-man company to the latter without asking 'why it should be attributed . . . ., for what purposes and to what ends'.[63]

There are two instances where the courts have considered the application of the identification doctrine in dealing with the distribution of liability for losses arising when directors engage in undesirable behaviour. The first case was in *Stone & Rolls Ltd v. Moore Stephens*.[64] In that case, Mr. Stojevic, who was the sole director and shareholder of a company, had defrauded several third-party banks, as a result

59 Ernest Lim, A Critique of Corporate Attribution (n 17) 333
60 Anchayli (n 22) 252
61 Lim, A Critique of Corporate Attribution (n 17) 333–334
62 Lim, A Critique of Corporate Attribution (n 17) 333
63 Lim, A Critique of Corporate Attribution (n 17) 340
64 [2009] UKHL 39, [2009] 1 A.C. 1391

of which the company suffered significant losses from claims instituted against it in that regard. The company, in turn, claimed against its auditors for failing to detect the fraud. But the claim was rejected on the grounds of the identification doctrine and the maxim, as the company was regarded as a 'participant in the fraud' and was thus held personally liable.[65] In view of the need to protect the long-term interests of the company's stakeholders who suffered losses as a result of Mr. Stojevic's fraud, the company was viewed as a 'victim of the fraud' and as a vehicle to perpetrate fraud, which resulted in its insolvency. Hence, the first and the third problems identified by Lim played out in that case. A different outcome, however, would have been contrary to common sense.[66] This is because the director in *Stone* was the sole shareholder and director of the company, who also acted as its 'board of directors'. Accordingly, his act could be reasonably attributed to the company based on 'the role of the board [being] the mechanism by which the company incurs primary liability'.[67] This suggests that although the outcome is correct, the reasoning is not ideal[68] because

> [T]he basis on which that finding was made set a dangerous precedent. Rather than using the rules of attribution to conclude that the company was primarily liable through the knowledge of its board, Stojevic, the majority concluded that Stojevic was the directing mind of the company and that the company was, therefore, primarily liable.[69]

The reasoning of the court on the basis of the identification doctrine caused some consternation, although it did not lead to different outcomes in *Stone*. Even at that, the Court of Appeal's reliance on that reasoning in *Safeway Stores Ltd v. Twigger* resulted in a wrong outcome, which defied logic.[70] In that case, a company claimed against its former directors and employees for losses that it suffered as a result of a fine imposed on it by the OFT for its involvement in a price-fixing agreement with its rivals. The defendants argued that the company should be precluded from attributing its liability as it was personally liable for the losses it suffered based on the doctrine of corporate attribution. The High Court held that it could not decide which of the defendants was the directing mind and will of the claimant company. This fact had a real prospect of defeating any defence that may be raised on the basis of the maxim.[71] The crucial point in the judgement was that the miscon-

65 Griffin (n 5) 164

66 Susan Watson, 'Conceptual Confusion: Organs, Agents and Identity in the English Courts' (2011) 23 SAcLJ 762, 789

67 Susan Watson, 'Conceptual Confusion: Organs, Agents and Identity in the English Courts' (2011) 23 SAcLJ 789

68 QC Peter Watts, 'Corrupt Company Controllers, Their Companies, and Their Companies' Creditors – Dealing with Pleas of Ex Turpi Causa' [2014] JBL 161, 165

69 Watson (n 67) 789–790

70 Watson (n 67) 790

71 *Safeway* (n 2) [2010] EWHC 11 (Comm); [2010] Bus. L.R. 974 [974]

duct of the directors would have been attributed to the company if it had been established that the directors were its directing mind and will.[72] But the Court of Appeal reversed the judgement of the trial court and held that the application of the maxim in that case should prevent the company from recovering the loss it suffered as a result of the conduct of its directors. The court held that there was no need to determine whether the directors were the directing mind because it was obvious that the claimant company had intentionally breached the rules of competition law.

This approach, however, raises the concern regarding 'how an artificial entity like the claimant company could have infringed the Act without the aid of anyone'.[73] It can be assumed that the illegality was conducted by individuals who were to be considered as the directing mind and will of the company, and the Court of Appeal applied the identification doctrine without indicating so explicitly when it 'concluded that it necessarily followed that the wrongdoers as the mind of the company could not be personally liable'.[74] Consequently, it held that despite the fact that the company must have benefitted from the price fixing, it also suffered a significant amount of loss as a result of the undesirable behaviour of its directors.

This outcome of the case illustrates that the identification doctrine is heavily concerned with the position of directors when it concerns the attribution of liability and loss. This is because, where the subject of a case is the liability arising from the conduct of an ordinary employee who does not hold a position in management, the courts tend to investigate whether the employee was appointed by the shareholders or by the board of directors to undertake a particular task on behalf of the company. However, when they deal with the acts or the intentions of directors, they tend to attribute liability automatically to the company without considering whether the directors were acting as part of the board. This is based on the presumption that the directors are the controlling minds of the company. In such a case, 'the company's guilt is demonstrated rather than attributed to it'.[75] This could then be another issue with the doctrine which was not identified by Lim. Relying heavily on the position of directors to determine attribution without considering the nature of their particular conduct may potentially expose the company to the risk of liability and loss.

In respect of directors' undesirable behaviours, there are three possible situations[76] in which the identification doctrine may prevent a company from attributing the risk of liability and loss to its directors for losses caused by their wrongdoing. The first situation arises when the company institutes a claim against its directors for breach of duties and breach of contract. In such cases, the acts of the directors can be attributed to the company without considering whether they were acting as part of the board and whether they breached their fiduciary duties and contracts.[77] It is

72 Lim, A Critique of Corporate Attribution (n 17) 343
73 Lim, A Critique of Corporate Attribution (n 17) 343
74 Watson (n 67) 790
75 GR Sullivan, 'The Attribution of Culpability to Limited Companies' (1996) 55(3) CLJ 515, 518
76 Lim, A Critique of Corporate Attribution (n 17) 799–780
77 *Safeway* (n 2), for further reading, see B Choudhury and M Petrin, *Corporate Duties to the Public* (Cambridge University Press 2019) 142

an established company law principle that directors who act as part of the board can be considered as the company's directing mind, and their intention or liability will be attributed to it.[78] In this situation, it would be logical to attribute the acts of directors to the company, as in the outcome of *Stone*. In contrast, directors are normally considered as agents when they are not acting as part of the board, and the liability arising from their particular acts should not be directly attributed to the company.[79] In *Safeway*, for instance, despite the fact that the directors were not acting as part of the board, liability for their actions was attributed to the company, which was thus deprived of the remedies for the loss it suffered by the breach of their fiduciary duties. Accordingly, it can arguably be stated that a 'claimant [company] would have no resources whatsoever against the directors who breached their fiduciary duties or employees who breached their contract. This is an unsatisfactory result'.[80]

The second situation arises when a third party sues a company for breach of contract or tort or when a regulatory fine has been imposed on it for breach of a statutory provision as a result of its directors' undesirable behaviours. In such cases, the act or intention of the directors will be automatically attributed to the company, and it will have to compensate a wronged third party[81] or pay a fine for regulatory wrongdoing.[82] This is notwithstanding that the misconduct was undertaken by directors who did not act as part of its board of directors.[83] The third situation arises when the company sues third parties. In this regard, the operation of the doctrine would bar the company from claiming against third parties who breach any duties owed to it. This 'would mean that third parties can breach their duties to the company with impunity and yet be given immunity under the law from lawsuits from the company'.[84] This can lead to a 'startling result' because, in this sense, the company can never sue any third party.[85] In these situations, the directors' acts are likely to be attributed to the company. This can be considered a primary barrier to the company in attributing the risk of liability and loss that may arise from the undesirable behaviour of its directors because the company may not only be deprived of remedies but may also suffer loss as a result of a claim for damages that is brought by third parties or through the imposition of regulatory fines.

Based on this mechanical approach, the exception to the identification doctrine, which was introduced in *Hampshire Land Co (No. 2)*, can be regarded as a tool that provides little protection to the company; however, this protection is only valid when directors perpetrate fraud on their own company. This was the case in *Bilta*, where the defendant directors failed to attribute liability to the company because the latter was held to be a victim of the former's wrongdoing. The logic behind this

78 Watson (n 67) 791
79 Watson (n 67) 791
80 Lim, A Critique of Corporate Attribution (n 17) 344
81 *Stone & Rolls* (n 49)
82 *Safeway* (n 2)
83 Lim, A Critique of Corporate Attribution (n 17) 336
84 Ernest Lim, 'Attribution in Company Law' (2014) 77(5) M.L.R. 804
85 Lim, 'Attribution in Company Law' (n 84) 804

approach is that if the directing mind perpetrates fraud on the company, he should not be deemed to be acting in the capacity of its directing mind.[86] In this sense, such an exception might be regarded as a principle that provides a small opportunity for the company to mitigate the risk of liability and loss that may be caused by its directors' undesirable behaviours. Even at that, the exception is not without drawbacks, which limit its application.

The main issue is that the exception precludes directors from attributing liability or loss to the company where they defraud it for their personal gain. It is, thus, called the 'fraud exception'.[87] The logic behind this exception is that the company should be able to sue its directors when it suffers damages as a result of their breach of duty. In this respect, this exception is unlikely to be reliable for every such case in which the company suffers losses as a result of the conduct of its directors. This means that the fact that a company is not targeted by its errant directors does not mean that it would not be exposed to the risk of liability and loss. The involvement of directors in undesirable behaviour still exposes the company to risks even if they did not directly target the company. For example, the company in *Safeway* was not directly targeted by the erring directors, but it still suffered significant losses due to their behaviour. In addition, in *Stone*, it was obvious that the sole director used the company as a vehicle to perpetrate fraud on third parties as a result of which the company suffered losses. However, it was forced to bear personal liability because the fraud was not perpetrated on it by the director. Hence, the director's fraud was automatically perceived as a fraud of the company on the basis of the identification doctrine. This was because, as Lord Walker, Lord Brown, and Lord Phillips observed in *Stone*, it is impossible to regard the one-man type of company as a victim. Corroborating further, Rimer LJ also stated that,

> The essence of the case is that it is one in which the sole directing mind and will of the company procured it to enter into fraudulent transactions with banks. It was the company that dealt with the banks . . . as between the company and the banks, the principles of attribution require the dishonesty of the company's sole human agent to be imputed to the company.[88]

It was determined that the company could not allege that it was a victim because it was engaged in fraud by extracting money dishonestly from third parties for goods which did not exist. In respect of the particular undesirable behaviour of directors, it was overlooked that the fraud was actually conducted by its sole director and that the company was consequently exposed to a significant risk of liability and loss due to the damages claim of third parties and bankruptcy.

86 Mihir Naniwadekar, 'Directing Minds and Agents: An Essay on Fraud and Attribution' [2010] JBL 271, 279

87 Mihir Naniwadekar, 'Directing Minds and Agents: An Essay on Fraud and Attribution' [2010] JBL 272

88 *Stone & Rolls* (n 49) [73]

In this sense, the problematic issue is the determination of whether the company is a victim or a villain, based on the person to whom the fraud was directed.[89] If the company is targeted by directors, then the victim exception is applied, but if it is not, then the negative consequences of the directors' misconduct on the company will not be taken under consideration. Hence, the key point which is typically considered by the courts is 'the effects of the fraud themselves, not their consequential effect on the company'.[90] In this respect, the wording of 'victim' on which this exception relies is 'unhelpful and distracting'.[91] In order to broaden the exception, Lord Neuberger, Lord Sumption, Lord Toulson, and Lord Hodge agreed that the expression 'the fraud exception' should be abandoned since it is not restricted to fraud,[92] with Lord Sumption calling it the 'breach of duty exception'.[93]

At face value, this exception can be considered a tool that would protect the company from any liability or loss arising from directors' breach of fiduciary duties for either their own benefit or the benefit of the company. However, it can be respectably discussed that a breach of duty to the company may not be the sole trigger of this exception. Lim discussed that,

> [T]he fraud exception applies *only* to a 'redress' situation whereby a company sues its directors, employees or their accomplices for wrongdoing committed against it but not to a 'liability' situation under which a company is liable to a third party for the dishonest conduct of a director or employee.[94]

In the first situation, the company is a victim whose interests need to be protected, whereas, in the second situation, the victim is the third party 'whose interests take precedence over the company's loss'.[95] This difference can be seen in the outcome of *Safeway* because, in that case, although the directors breached their fiduciary duties to the company, their acts and liabilities were attributed to it, and the exception was not applied.

A breach of duty exception can be invoked in cases that involve insolvent companies because issues usually arise with respect to the interest of creditors and the duty that directors owe to them. This was the second ground on which the decision in *Bilta* was based. In that case, the fraud of a company's directors was not attributed to it on the basis of the fraud exception and the purpose of protecting the company's creditors' interest. The courts had to ask,

> whether it is contrary to public policy that the company, through the liquidators, should enforce for the benefit of its creditors the duty which the

89 Sheikh (n 12) 353
90 Sheikh (n 12) 353
91 Lim, Attribution in Company Law (n 84) 806
92 *Jetivia SA and Another v. Bilta (UK) Limited (in liquidation) and others* [2015] UKSC 23[9]
93 *Jetivia SA* (n 92) 23
94 Ernest Lim, 'Attribution and Fraud Exception' [2015] LMCLQ 14
95 Ernest Lim, 'Attribution and Fraud Exception' [2015] LMCLQ 14–15

directors owed for the protection of the creditors' interests as part of their fiduciary duty to the company.[96]

The court responded that,

> It is well established that the fiduciary duties of a director of a company which is insolvent or bordering on insolvency differ from the duties of a company which is able to meet its liabilities, because in the case of the former the director's duty towards the company requires him to have proper regard for the interest of its creditors and prospective creditors.[97]

These is no doubt that liquidators may institute a claim against a company's directors in the name of the company in order to protect the interests of the company's creditors. This issue was discussed by Lim regarding *Stone*, in that the fraud of the sole director would not have been attributed to the company had the liquidators of the company issued a misfeasance summons against the director under the IA86.[98] According to Lim, this was also a concern in *Royal Brunei Airlines Sdn Bhd v. Tan*.[99] The issue in that case was whether the company was guilty of misusing money that it held in trust for the claimant airline. The company became insolvent, and the claimant company sued its sole director on the basis that he had intentionally provided assistance to the company in order to misuse the money in question. The dishonesty of the director was consequently attributed to the company. Lim argued that if the company's liquidator had issued misfeasance proceedings against the director for breaching his duty or involving it in such dishonesty under the IA86, his dishonesty would not have been attributed to the company in the proceedings instituted by the liquidator.[100]

This exception can thus be considered the protection for stakeholders, whose interests should be taken into account by directors when making decisions on company business;[101] however, it can only protect the creditors since the interests of other stakeholders are not likely to be considered. The involvement of creditors' interest and the duty that the director owed to them reversed the outcome of the case in question, and it can be said that while protecting the interests of creditors is the primary purpose in the second scenario, the interests of the company in the first scenario were very much disregarded. This is based on the principle that 'once a company is insolvent, the interests of the company become those of its creditors';[102] however, when the company is solvent, the interests of the company as a whole are not considered as adequately, as the interests of creditors are only seriously taken

96 [2015] UKSC 23 (n 92) [166]
97 [2015] UKSC 23 (n 92) [123]
98 Ernest Lim, 'Formalism and Companies' (2013) 13(2) JCLS 477, 486
99 [1995] 2 AC 378, [1995] 3 WLR 64
100 Ernest Lim, 'Formalism and Companies' (n 98)
101 See Chapter 2, Section 2.2
102 *Berg, Sons & Co Ltd v. Mervyn Hampton Adams (1992)* [2002] Lloyd's Rep PN 41 [55]

into account when it is insolvent. For this reason, the exception can still be called the 'breach of duty exception', but it is a duty to creditors rather than the duty to the company as a whole. The logic behind having these two very different scenarios on a similar issue is that while creditors are regarded as innocent parties to the case, the company is regarded as the villain which is actually involved in the wrongdoing.

Consequently, the exception does not apply to cases which do not involve fraud perpetrated by directors on the company and the interests of creditors. However, as previously stated, this exception disregards the fact that not having been targeted by directors does not mean that a company would not be exposed to the risk of liability and loss that are caused by directors' undesirable behaviours. For example, in *Safeway*, despite the fact that the company might have benefitted from the illegality in the short term, it suffered a significant loss in the long term, and no remedy was provided. Therefore, the narrow approach of this exception still exposes the company to the risk of liability and loss caused by directors' undesirable behaviours with respect to its inability to protect the interests of the stakeholders.

Despite the limitations with the fraud exception of the identification doctrine and the narrow approach of *Bilta* in disregarding the issue of the company's protection against the consequences of undesirable behaviour by directors, *Bilta* can still be considered a positive development. This is because the underlying reasoning of the outcome of *Bilta* was the directors' breach of fiduciary duties and contracts by the perpetuation of fraud and the loss that the company consequently suffered. This exception to the attribution could lead courts to recognise the negative consequences of allowing directors to attribute the loss and liability arising from their undesirable behaviour to the company based on the interests of the stakeholders. Despite the present law not adequately recognising the particular policy objective of the protection of stakeholders, *Bilta* may be the underlying basis of the general direction in which the law should progress. Therefore, the approach adopted in *Bilta* can shape the foundation of the matters that could be taken into account to determine the attribution of the risk of loss and liability arising from directors' behaviours.

Regarding the doctrine of special attribution, despite the positive reception of the *Meridian* principle, the approach has also been criticised in terms of the uncertainty it has brought to the principle of attribution.[103] A more flexible approach has been established by Lord Hoffmann when compared to the identification doctrine. However, the courts are still vexed by the question of when the knowledge or acts of an individual should be attributed to the company. This point was discussed by Payne, who stated that not giving a specific answer to this question is one of the disadvantages of the principle.[104] Cartwright also discussed how the approach has brought flexibility, 'but this flexibility, inevitably, has come at the expense

103 Peter Cartwright, *Consumer Protection and the Criminal Law: Law, Theory, and Policy in the UK* (2nd edn, Cambridge University Press 2001) 104

104 Payne (n 13) 363

of certainty'.[105] For this reason, Wells regarded *Meridian* as 'a step of uncertain dimensions'.[106]

This lack of clarity has cast some doubt on whether the principle has brought a fundamentally different approach to the corporate attribution as 'a break from the past or an extension of the identification approach'.[107] Bhandari asserted that although the principle of *Meridian* has introduced a new approach to attribution, it still tends to rely on the inflexible approach of the identification doctrine and it can thus be perceived as 'having added another layer' to this doctrine.[108] Ferran also argued that the *Meridian* principle is not a departure from the identification doctrine, and the former rather reaffirms the latter, as has been judicially illustrated.[109]

This approach has thus had less impact than the initial commentary would suggest.[110] As Watson discussed, 'despite commentary being generally favourable towards *Meridian*, and the predicted demise of the directing mind and will test, the courts have continued to apply that test, either instead of, or in conjunction with, the rules of attribution'.[111] This was supported by Wells, who noted that although the identification doctrine was not considered an appropriate approach in *Meridian*, it was not rejected altogether by Lord Hoffmann.[112] This may be because

> [R]esort to the principle of statutory construction requires well-thought-out guidance. How is one to determine, in relation to any particular offence, whether it is appropriate to look merely at the board of directors or further? It is difficult to imagine that the answer will come from looking at the statutory provision.[113]

In a nutshell, under the *Meridian* principle, complexities and difficulties with respect to measuring the culpability of the company and determining whose acts, intentions, and knowledge can be considered as its representation[114] may underlie the tendency to apply the identification doctrine to determine the issue of who bears the liability or loss between the company and its directors.

For example, the judgement delivered by the Supreme Court in *Bilta* requires further analysis. Since the fiduciary duties of directors and the nature of the

105 Cartwright (n 103) 104

106 Celia Wells, 'The Law Commission Report on Involuntary Manslaughter: The Corporate Manslaughter Proposals: Pragmatism, Paradox and Peninsularity' [1996] Criminal Law Review 545, 548

107 Bhandari (n 14) 254

108 Bhandari (n 14) 254–255

109 Ferran (n 19) 245

110 See John C. Coffee, '"No Soul to Damn: No Body to Kick": An Unscandalized Inquiry into the Problem of Corporate Punishment' (1981) 79 Mich. L. Rev. 386. See also Eilis Ferran, 'Corporate Attribution and the Directing Mind and Will' (2011) 127 L.Q.R. 239, 239

111 Watson (n 67) 782

112 Wells (n 106) 7. See also Bhandari (n 14) 258

113 Wells (n 106) 7

114 Wells (n 106) 7

directors' misconduct were considered by the court, the reasoning adopted in that case may be perceived as based on the *Meridian* principle; however, with respect to the first ground of the decision, the fraud of the directors was not attributed to the company based on the reasoning of the directors' breach of their fiduciary duties to the company. It was rather the fraud exception to the identification doctrine, which was initially taken into consideration to determine whether the fraudulent behaviour of the directors could be attributed to the company. The court stated that,

> [W]here a company has been the victim of wrongdoing by its directors, or of which its directors had notice, then the wrongdoing, or knowledge, of the directors cannot be attributed to the company as a defence to a claim brought against the directors by the company's liquidator, in the name of the company and/or on behalf of its creditors, for the loss suffered by the company as a result of the wrongdoing, even where the directors were the only directors and shareholders of the company, and even though the wrongdoing or knowledge of the directors may be attributed to the company in many other types of proceedings.[115]

This approach is based on the fraud exception of the identification doctrine, which prevents errant directors from attributing the liability and loss arising from their fraud on the company. Therefore, although the importance of the *Meridian* principle was highlighted by explaining the key considerations of context and the purpose of attribution,[116] the approach adopted by the Supreme Court to deal with attribution issues illustrates the employment of the identification doctrine regarding the determination of the attribution of liability and loss.[117]

With respect to the second reasoning on which the decision was based, the court considered the extra-territorial effect of Section 213 of the IA86 to determine whether the defendants sought to defraud the creditors. Taking into account specific statutory provisions which promote the duties of directors to creditors, and seeking to protect creditors' interests, the adoption of special rules of attribution to determine the attribution of the liability of directors to the company can be illustrated. This is because, in contrast to the identification doctrine which relies on the position of directors, the impact of particular acts by directors on the creditors' interests, and the consequences of not allowing the creditors to pursue wrongdoing directors in the public interest, were both considered based on Section 216 of the IA86. However, the court arguably relied on the fraud exception of the identification doctrine because allowing directors to attribute the liability to the company would damage the interest of creditors. This is because the exception protects the solvent company's interests when its directors perpetrate fraud on it. If the company is insolvent, this exception is typically triggered to protect the interests of

115 (n 92) [7]
116 (n 92) [20] *per* Lord Neuberger and [41] per Lord Mance
117 (n 92) [180]–[181]

its creditors. Accordingly, it can be stated that this approach still relies on 'metaphors that can appear to make corporate liabilities and rights turn on whether natural persons, who can be described as the "embodiment" of a company'.[118]

There is no doubt that the approach of *Meridian* potentially leads to more sensible outcomes than the identification doctrine since it seeks to find out whether the acts of a person shall be deemed to be the acts of a company rather than regarding a particular director as the company; however, its application in practice is problematic. This is due to the courts' tendency to rely on the identification doctrine. For this reason, 'Lord Hoffmann's context-sensitive rule-based approach has limited usefulness'.[119]

Based on this problem regarding the nature of the principle, it is difficult to expect that the principle gives adequate attention to the nature of the particular undesirable behaviour of directors and its negative consequences on the company. To attribute the act of directors to the company, its tendency to focus on the position of directors within the company casts serious doubts on whether it considers when and why the act of directors should be attributed to the company. Consequently, as with the identification doctrine, applying this principle will likely prevent the company from attributing to directors the risk of liability and loss caused by undesirable behaviour.

To conclude Section 4.2.2, the types of undesirable behaviours of directors identified in competition law, such as cartel conduct and abusing dominant position, are detrimental to the interests of the company in terms of protecting the interests of its stakeholders (except for creditors in the application of the fraud exception), and it can harm the company financially; however, the identification doctrine still debars the company from attributing the risks of loss and liability arising from such behaviour. The rule has an exception that prevents fraudulent directors from attributing liability or loss, and the approach adopted by *Bilta* based on this exception can be taken as an initial point for developing the law further. However, the present law does not adequately recognise how harmful directors' undesirable behaviours can be to a company's stakeholders. In such a case, the company 'feels hurt, used, dejected – incensed by the very directors it trusted to control and manage its affairs',[120] even if the fraud was directed to some other party on its behalf. For this reason, Watts opined that 'the notion that companies are to be identified with their senior management under the directing mind and will notion has insinuated itself into the English case law which bound the judge. This case law needs to be stripped out'.[121]

4.2.3 Corporate Attribution and the Fiduciary Duties of Directors

A company's inability to pass on the risk of loss and liability as a result of the inadequate application of the corporate attribution rule raises the question of whether

118 Ferran (n 2) 240
119 Lim, A Critique of Corporate Attribution (n 17) 353
120 Sheikh (n 12) 348
121 Watts (n 68) 165

it can protect itself by invoking the directors' breach of fiduciary duties. In the application of attribution rules to a case between the company and directors, the directors' fiduciary duties form the basis of the company's counterargument to the latter's attempt at attributing the liability or loss to the company. In this context, the extent to which the courts consider these duties when corporate attribution is applied will now be examined.

Typically, a company would institute a claim for breach of fiduciary duty against its directors after it has compensated an injured third party or after it has suffered losses due to the wrongdoing of its directors. The potential counterargument of directors would be to rely on the attribution doctrine to claim that the wrongdoing arose due to the company's misconduct; as such, it should not recover the loss it suffered from the acts of the directors. In this respect, the role of directors' duties becomes significant for the company because, while the directors seek to pass the liability onto the company by applying the rules of attribution, the company can potentially push the liability back towards its directors by invoking these duties. Therefore, directors' duties can be considered a shield by which the company can protect itself.

However, the question is whether this shield truly protects the company from the potential risks of directors' undesirable behaviours. This issue will now be discussed in light of the outcomes of *Stone*, *Safeway*, and *Bilta*. In *Stone*, despite the fact that the company's liquidator claimed against its auditors for failing to detect fraud of a director, this did not change the fact that the director breached his fiduciary duties to the company and escaped liability through the application of the identification doctrine. The company was exposed to the risk of liability and loss due to insolvency and damages claims instituted by third parties, and the directors' fiduciary duties did not prevent the attribution of liability to the company. In consideration of the fact that the company had a sole shareholder and director, the outcome may not be considered contrary to common sense since the director represented the company's board. That said, this did not change the fact that the company was exposed to the risks of undesirable behaviour by its director, which had adverse consequences for its long-term interests and those of its stakeholders. Also, the reasoning adopted in that case underpins the rationale behind preventing *Safeway* from protecting itself against the risk of liability and loss by invoking the directors' fiduciary duties.

In *Safeway*, a company's claim against its former directors for breach of fiduciary duties and breach of contract failed because the infringement in that case was directly attributed to the company. It was thus debarred from attributing the liability and loss to its directors by invoking their breach of fiduciary duties. Based on the outcomes of these two cases, it appears that companies cannot, in all confidence, rely on the fiduciary duties of their directors as a shield to protect themselves against the consequences of directors' undesirable behaviours. However, as Lim argued,

> [T]o impute the wrongdoing of the directors to the company in order to bar the latter from suing the former for breach of duties would amount to

equating the acts or intent of the directors with that of the company, which would in effect bypass or ignore the well-established principle of separate legal personality.[122]

When the acts of directors are attributed to the company, the latter's claim for directors' breach of fiduciary duties is not likely to succeed in passing the liability and loss to the directors. Since undesirable behaviour is just one type of directorial conduct and is usually considered the act of a company, the company is likely to fail to pass the liability and loss to the directors on the basis of the director's fiduciary duties.

This argument can be challenged by the outcome of *Bilta* because, in that case, the directors were found to be in breach of their fiduciary duties and were prevented from attributing the liability of their fraud to the company. However, there are some particular issues which prevent the case from being taken as a reference for the discussion. The first issue is that the fraud perpetrated by the directors in that case is not the type of undesirable behaviour by directors which is examined in this book. At the same time, the concept of undesirable behaviour consists of conduct that benefits the company in the short term but exposes it to significant risks in the long term (as typically regulatory wrongdoings);[123] the nature of the conduct in *Bilta* is fraud perpetrated by the directors on their company to gain personal benefit at the company's expense.

The second issue is that the company in *Bilta* protected itself from the attribution of its directors' illegality by relying on the fraud exception of the identification doctrine rather than on the directors' breach of their fiduciary duties. This exception is only triggered when directors perpetrate fraud on their company or where the court aims to protect the interest of the creditors of an insolvent company.[124] The exception was named the 'breach of duty exception' by Lord Sumption in *Bilta*; however, the outcome of *Safeway* illustrates that this is not an exception to the breach of fiduciary duties to the company and is rather an exception to the breach of duties to creditors when the company is insolvent, as demonstrated in *Bilta*.

Based on the outcomes of *Stone* and *Safeway* and the exceptional circumstance of *Bilta*, it can arguably be stated that a company is unlikely to be able to invoke fiduciary duties as a shield to prevent the attribution of liability and loss arising from directors' undesirable behaviours, and consequently the risk of liability and loss will remain with it. Not allowing the company to enforce the directors' duties would 'produce a startling result' because wrongdoing directors can cause the company to engage with serious misconduct and escape responsibility with impunity,

however egregious the damage they inflict on the company and however grave the losses that might subsequently be caused to the innocent shareholders

122 Lim, 'Attribution in Company Law' (n 84) 802
123 See Chapter 2, Sections 2.2 and 2.3
124 See Section 4.2.1.2

during solvency and innocent stakeholders (such as employees, suppliers and especially creditors) during insolvency, if the company were to plead or rely on this illegality to establish its claim.[125]

This obviously impairs the company's ability to protect the long-term interests of its stakeholders by preventing its directors from attributing liability arising from their engagement in anti-competitive behaviour to the company. The next section examines the application of the maxim to the ascription of risk of liability and loss between the company and directors when the former is found personally liable through corporate attribution.

4.3 The *Ex Turpi Causa* Maxim and the Ascription of Risk to Directors

The second element in the apportionment of risk of liability and loss between a company and its directors is the application of the *ex turpi causa* maxim ('the maxim'). The essence of the doctrine is to bar a plaintiff from obtaining a relief in law which arises from his own wrongdoing. In essence, the maxim is a defence to a claim if the defendant can establish a causal link between the illegality of the claimant and the claim itself. Widely referred to as the 'illegality defence', the *ex turpi causa* maxim can be applied where there is illegality, criminality or a morally reprehensible behaviour in areas of law, such as contract, tort, unjust enrichment, property rights, or trusts law.[126]

The Law Commission defined the maxim as a concept that 'arises when the defendant in a private law action argues that the claimant should not be entitled to their normal rights or remedies because they have been involved in illegal conduct which is linked to the claim'.[127] It seeks to determine the extent to which the courts would prevent a claimant from enforcing his normal rights where there is proof that he was involved in some form of illegality.[128] The rationale behind the maxim is that if a claimant is not barred from seeking relief when he is involved in some form of illegality relating to the claim in question, he might essentially benefit from rights that he should rightfully forfeit. For this reason, Turner has defined the maxim as a principle under which a claim is impossible if damages arise from a criminal venture in which the claimant is involved.[129]

The connection between the maxim and corporate attribution stems from its application to instances of personal wrongdoing that are particularly evident in the relationship between a company and its directors. In other words, where a company

125 Ernest Lim, 'The Illegality Defence and Company Law' (2013) 13(1) JCLS 49, 57

126 See generally James Goudkamp, 'Ex Turpi Causa and Immoral Behaviour in the Tort Context' (2011) 127 LQR 354. See also Law Commission, 'The Illegality Defence Report' (Law Com No 320 2010) para [1.3]

127 Law Commission, 'The Illegality Defence Report' (Law Com No 320 2010) para [1.2]

128 Law Commission, 'The Illegality Defence Report' (Law Com No 320 2010) para [1.1]

129 Chris Turner, *Unlocking Torts* (4th edn, Routledge 2013) 431

is deemed to be directly responsible for damages inflicted on third parties or incurs losses, the maxim will prohibit it from pursuing claims against its directors to recover those losses. Consequently, the company may be unable to argue that its directors breached their fiduciary duties. As such, it would forfeit the opportunity to seek equitable remedies against them due to the association of its claim with its own illegal or immoral actions.

The maxim has found application within the corporate realm in various cases, with notable examples being *Stone* and *Safeway*. In those instances, it served as the foundation for dismissing claims filed by companies against their auditors and directors. These outcomes raise a pivotal question: does the application of the maxim essentially enable companies to attribute the risk of liability and loss stemming from misconduct to their directors?

4.3.1 Application of the Maxim to the Illegality Defence and Its Foundation

It is uncertain how the maxim would be applied in practice since it is not bound by strict statutory rules. Instead, it is viewed as 'flexible', with its application contingent upon the specific circumstances at hand.[130] In *Gray v. Thames Trains Ltd*,[131] Lord Hoffmann observed that the maxim 'expresses not so much a principle as a policy'. Moreover, he noted that the policy is not founded on a singular justification but rather on a range of reasons that vary across different situations.[132] In applying the maxim, the courts have developed several tests to guide it. They include the public conscience test, the reliance test, the causation test, the inextricable test, and the consistency test. And although the courts are not consistent in applying these tests, the public conscience test, which aims to uphold the dignity of the law, ensure deterrence, and administer punishment, has been used more frequently.[133]

It was common for defendants to employ the public conscience test in cases where granting relief would offend the public conscience.[134] Even at that, the test has been criticised for its flexibility, subjectivity, reliance on guesswork, and the resulting uncertainty it introduces.[135] In *Tinsley v. Milligan*,[136] Ralph Gibson LJ of the Court of Appeal advocated for a more defined approach. He suggested that the maxim's deterrent effect lies in the existence of a clear rule and its consistent enforcement.[137] Subsequently, the House of Lords moved away from the public conscience

130 *Safeway* (n 2) [2010] EWHC 11 (Comm) [21]
131 [2009] UKHL 33; [2009] 1 A.C. 1339
132 *Gray* [30]
133 Niamh Connolly, 'Re-Examining Illegality in Restitution: A Reason to Deny Restitution, Or to Grant It?' (SLS Conference Edinburgh 2013) 15 <http://www.archive.legalscholars.ac.uk/edinburgh/restricted/paper.cfm?id=315> accessed 25 April 2024
134 Graham Virgo, *The Principles of the Law of Restitution* (3rd edn, Oxford University Press 2015) 710
135 See Margaret Fordham, 'The Role of Ex Turpi Causa in Tort Law' [1998] Sing JLS 238, 255. See also Connolly (n 133) 15
136 *Tinsley v. Milligan* [1992] Ch. 310; [1992] 2 WLR 508
137 *Tinsley v. Milligan* [1992] Ch. 310; [1992] 2 WLR 508 [334]

test[138] and emphasised the reliance test. According to Lord Browne-Wilkinson, this test applies when a claimant is entitled to recover without being compelled to plead or rely on illegality, even if it is revealed that the claimant's title was obtained through an illegal transaction.[139] Following the rejection of the public conscience test by the House of Lords in *Tinsley*, it was thought that the test is 'no longer accepted in England';[140] however, the House of Lords in *Gray* regarded the reliance test as formalistic and technical and restrained the approach adopted in *Tinsley* to cases involving property rights.[141] Rather, the court 'suggested a new two-part rationale [causation test and consistency test], which is not dissimilar from the affront to the public conscience approach'.[142]

4.3.1.1 The Aim of Protecting Public Policy

Despite the fact that several tests are being applied by the courts to justify the application of the maxim, 'whatever "test" is eventually used by a court, the truth is that courts tend to consider a variety of factors relevant in deciding whether a defence based on public policy should succeed'.[143] Since a defendant can invoke the maxim defence, it could be perceived that the maxim is a protection for the defendant rather than for public policy.[144] If a defendant and a claimant were to change sides, the latter would benefit from the defence of the maxim because he would have had the opportunity to rely on it.[145] This was explained by Goudkamp, who said that 'the defence of illegality should be engaged only if considerations of public policy call for it to be engaged'.[146] This public policy foundation of the maxim was established in *Holman* v. *Johnson*.[147] Lord Mansfield stated in that case that

> The objection that a contract is immoral or illegal as between plaintiff and defendant sounds very ill in the defendant's mouth at all times. It is not for his sake, however, that the objection is ever allowed; it is founded in general principles of policy, which the defendant has the advantage of, contrary to

138 *Tinsley v. Milligan* [1992] Ch. 310; [1992] 2 WLR 508
139 *Tinsley v. Milligan* [1992] Ch. 310; [1992] 2 WLR 508 [376]
140 Connolly (n 133) 14. See also Michael A Jones, Anthony M Dugdale, and Mark Simpson, *Clerk & Lindsell on Torts* (21th edn, Sweet & Maxwell 2014) para [3.06]
141 Michael A Jones, Anthony M Dugdale, and Mark Simpson, *Clerk & Lindsell on Torts* (21th edn, Sweet & Maxwell 2014) para [3.10]. The reliance test was also criticised in the recent judgment of the Supreme Court in *Patel (Respondent) v. Mirza (Appellant)* [2024] UKSC 42. It was agreed that the test should no longer be followed. See [2024] UKSC 42 [110]
142 Jones, Dugdale, and Simpson (n 142) para [3.06] (emphasis added)
143 Law Commission, 'The Illegality Defence' (Law Com No 189, 2009) para [3.123]
144 Jenny Steele, *Tort Law: Text, Cases, and Materials* (3rd edn, Oxford University Press 2014) 285
145 *Holman v. Johnson* (1775) 1 Cowp. 341 [343]
146 James Goudkamp, 'The Defence of Illegality: *Gray v. Thames Trains Ltd*' (2009) 17 TLJ 205, 213
147 *Holman* (n 144) [343]

> the real justice, as between him and the plaintiff, by accident, if I may so say. The principle of public policy is this: *ex dolo malo non oritur actio*.[148]

The principle of public policy can be defined as it being 'readily comprehensible—namely, that those engaged in criminal activity should not be permitted to use the legal process to recover damages for losses incurred whilst acting outside the law'.[149] To achieve this purpose, the issue of whether a claimant's wrongdoing is illegal or immoral and whether allowing him to pursue a claim is against public policy requires investigation. This was stated by Kerr LJ in *Euro-Diam Ltd v. Bathurst*,[150]

> The *ex turpi causa* defence ultimately rests on a principle of public policy that the courts will not assist a plaintiff who has been guilty of illegal (or immoral) conduct of which the courts should take notice. It applies if, in all circumstances, it would be an affront to the public conscience to grant the plaintiff the relief which he seeks because the court would thereby appear to assist or encourage the plaintiff in his illegal conduct or to encourage others in similar acts.[151]

This gives rise to questions as to how the public policy foundation is referred to in the application of the maxim with respect to the distribution of the risk of liability and loss between a company and its directors and whether the maxim has a distinctive application for companies and their directors when compared to cases involving individuals. It is crucial to examine this issue because if the maxim is to apply to companies without particular considerations of company law and corporate governance, and issues such as the need to protect the long-term interests of corporate stakeholders, it may possibly leave a heightened risk of liability and loss to which the company may be exposed when its directors are involved in undesirable behaviour.

4.3.1.2 The Public Policy Rationale

The main objective that underpins the maxim is the protection of public policy, and there are some rationales that justify this foundation. Virgo identifies them as including consistency, deterrence, punishment, and the dignity of the court.[152] Based on the way in which these rationales are referred to in case law, this chapter will categorise them as deterring wrongdoers through punishment, maintaining the integrity of the legal system by not allowing wrongdoers to benefit from his/her

148 *Holman* (n 145) [343]
149 Jones, Dugdale, and Simpson (n 142) para [3.06]
150 [1990] 1 Q.B. 1
151 [1990] 1 Q.B. 1 [35]
152 Virgo (n 134) 715

own illegality,[153] and protecting the internal consistency of the criminal and civil laws.[154]

The public policy rationale promotes deterrence by punishing wrongdoers. Its proponents argue that if wrongdoers are not punished, they and others will be encouraged to engage in similar wrongdoings. This rationale thus protects public policy by deterring actual wrongdoers and others by imposing punishment. The rationale of deterrence is the justification that the illegality defence has traditionally relied on,[155] and it is usually regarded as the deterrence of immoral, criminal, and quasi-criminal behaviour.[156] The main logic behind this objective is to discourage actual wrongdoers from engaging in the same wrongdoing again because, as Johnston and Zimmermann illustrated, 'in any lawsuit, whoever wins will feel encouraged, and whoever loses will feel discouraged'.[157] Thus, the deterrence objective seeks to 'warn any sensible person to keep well away from the trap of illegality'.[158]

This rationale has been commonly referred to in case law. For example, Justice Coulson in *K/S Lincoln v. CB Richard Ellis Hotels Ltd*[159] stated that 'it seems clear that the underlying principle or policy is one of deterrence; that the courts will not encourage illegal acts by allowing claims based upon them'.[160] It was similarly stated in *Tinsley v. Milligan*[161] that 'as a matter of public policy, the court should be particularly vigilant in deterring frauds upon the public purse'.[162]

The second rationale of public policy frequently cited by the courts in applying the maxim is the principle of not allowing wrongdoers to benefit from their own illegal actions through the court system. This principle is commonly known as the 'no-benefit rule'.[163] Lord Mansfield articulated this rationale in *Holman v. Johnson*,[164] stating

> No court will lend its aid to a man who founds his cause of action upon an immoral or an illegal act. If, from the plaintiff's own stating or otherwise, the cause of action appears to arise *ex turpi causa*, or the transgression of a positive law of this country, there the court says he has no right to be assisted.[165]

153 *Beresford v. Royal Insurance Company Limited* [1938] AC 586; *Stone & Rolls* (n 49) [20]

154 Law Commission, 'The Illegality Defence in Tort' (Law Com No 160, 2001) para [4.100]. See also Ernest Lim, 'Attribution and Fraud Exception' [2015] L.M.C.L.Q. 52–54; *Gray* (n 939) [2009] UKHL 33 [66]

155 Connolly (n 133) 22

156 Goudkamp, Ex Turpi Causa and Immoral Behaviour (n 126) 356

157 Gerhard Dannemann, 'Illegality as a Defence Against Unjust Enrichment Claims' in David Johnston and Reinhard Zimmermann (eds), *Unjustified Enrichment: Key Issues in Comparative Perspective* (1st edn, Cambridge University Press 2002) 310, 314

158 Connolly (n 133) 22

159 [2009] EWHC 2344

160 [2009] EWHC 2344 [22]

161 [1994] 1 AC 340

162 [1994] 1 AC 340 [347]

163 Steele (n 144) 291

164 *Holman* (n 145)

165 *Holman* (n 145) [343]

In *Beresford v. Royal Insurance Company Limited*,[166] Lord Atkin characterised this rationale as an 'absolute rule' that the courts will not recognise benefits accruing to a criminal from their own wrongdoing. [167] Similarly, the House of Lords in *Stone* succinctly stated that the maxim serves as a 'principle that prevents a claimant from using the court to obtain benefits from their own illegal conduct'. This rationale is grounded on the notion that allowing a claimant to recover would unfairly distribute public funds, essentially rewarding them for their illegal actions. In this sense, the no-benefit rule is also viewed as a principle of public policy that is aimed at safeguarding the integrity of the legal system. It is based on the premise that providing recovery to individuals deserving of punishment could undermine the dignity of the courts. This sentiment was echoed by Ungoed-Thomas J in *Selangor United Rubber Estates v. Cradock*,[168] who asserted that 'the courts are not to be instruments for aiding illegality'.[169] Additionally, the Law Commission has emphasised this consideration, noting that the 'dignity of the courts' policy justification holds merit. In cases where the disputed transaction is morally reprehensible, or the claimant's behaviour is particularly egregious, the court may be justified in refusing any assistance.[170] This is because 'the proper role of the court is not to provide an arena in which wrongdoers may fight over their spoils'.[171]

The last but not least rationale of public policy is to maintain the internal consistency between criminal and civil laws since allowing a claimant to be compensated for loss from a defendant under civil law would be inconsistent with the idea of punishing the former under criminal law. This objective is defined as a 'central policy rationale' that underlies public policy.[172] For Goudkamp, this approach '*prevents offenders from frustrating the goals of criminal law by recruiting tort law to take some of the sting out of sanctions imposed on them*'.[173] The logic behind this objective is, as McLachlin J described in *Hall v. Hebert*,[174] that,

> [T]o allow recovery . . . . would be to allow recovery for what is illegal. It would put the courts in the position of saying that the same conduct is both legal, in the sense of being capable of rectification by the court, and illegal. It would, in short, introduce an inconsistency in the law. It is particularly important in this context that we bear in mind that the law must aspire to be a unified institution, the parts of which – contract, tort, the criminal law –must be in essential harmony. For the courts to punish conduct with the one hand

166 [1938] A.C. 586
167 [1938] A.C. 586 [599]
168 *Selangor United Rubber Estates v. Cradock* [1968] 1 WLR 1555.
169 *Selangor United Rubber Estates v. Cradock* [1968] 1 WLR 1555. [1653]
170 Law Commission, 'Illegal Transactions: The Effect of Illegality on Contracts and Trusts' (Law Com No 154 1999) para [6.10]. See also Connolly (n 133) 22, para [6.6]
171 Law Commission, para [6.6]
172 Ernest Lim, 'Attribution and Fraud Exception' [2015] L.M.C.L.Q. (n 127) 52
173 James Goudkamp, 'The Defence of Illegality: *Gray v Thames Trains Ltd*' (2009) 17 TLJ 205, 208
174 *Hall v. Hebert* [1993] 2 SCR 159

> while rewarding it with the other would be to create an intolerable fissure in the law's conceptually seamless web. . . . We thus see that the concern, put at its most fundamental, is with the integrity of the legal system.[175]

The Supreme Court in *Gray* has comprehensively considered this rationale. Lord Rodger cited the Law Commission's statement, which was to the effect that imprisoning a person on the basis that he/she was found liable for an offence and then allowing him/her to be compensated for the imprisonment would cause inconsistency in law.[176] The learned lord also opined that,

> [Y]ou cannot recover for damage which flows from loss of liberty, a fine or other punishment lawfully imposed upon you in consequence of your own unlawful act. In such a case it is the law which, as a matter of penal policy, causes the damage and it would be inconsistent for the law to require you to be compensated for that damage.[177]

This rationale was also the basis for striking out the claimant's claim in *Safeway*, where the court opined that allowing the claimant company to recover the loss suffered because of its directors' unlawful acts would cause inconsistency between the civil and criminal laws. Longmore LJ argued that,

> The rationale of the maxim is the need for the criminal courts and the civil courts to speak with a consistent voice. It would be inconsistent for a claimant to be criminally and personally liable . . . but for the same claimant to say to a civil court that he is not personally answerable for that conduct.[178]

As can be seen, these three rationales of public policy have commonly referred to cases that involve the maxim. The question that arises concerns the impact of the maxim in cases involving the ascription of risk of liability and losses that are caused by undesirable behaviour between a company and its directors. To respond to this, the next section will examine the way in which the public policy foundation of the maxim and its three rationales are interpreted by the courts in cases that involve individuals or companies.

4.3.1.3 Public Policy Foundation and Case Law

The initial case for review is *Gray v. Thames Trains Ltd*. In that case, the plaintiff, Mr. Gray (G), sustained injuries in a train collision, resulting in significant

175 *Hall v. Hebert* [1993] 2 SCR 159 [165]

176 *Gray* (n 939) [2009] UKHL 33 [66]. See Law Commission, 'The Illegality Defence Report' (Law Com No 160, 2001) para [4.100]

177 [2009] 1 AC 1339 [29]

178 *Safeway* (n 2) [2010] EWCA Civ 1472 [16]

mental and psychiatric harm. Before the incident, G enjoyed robust physical and mental well-being. He also had a successful employment track record that was devoid of any history of violence or absenteeism. Following the incident, he developed post-traumatic stress disorder and began to consume alcohol excessively. He also started absenting himself from work without obtaining the permission of his employers. Two years later, while driving, he became embroiled in a confrontation with an inebriated pedestrian, resulting in the latter's fatal stabbing. Although he admitted to diminished responsibility for manslaughter, he contended that he should still be entitled to compensation for the damages that he incurred while he was incarcerated since his injury arose from the defendant's negligence. *Gray v. Thames* was the first time the House of Lords was called upon to deliberate on the defence of illegality and its relation to tort liability.[179] Resolving the case turned on the extent of the loss for which G could be compensated before and after the manslaughter.[180] At the trial court it was held that as a matter of public policy under the rule of *ex turpi causa*, a person could not recover general damages that arise from their own criminal act. The Court of Appeal, however, followed a narrow approach in holding that while Gray could not recover general damages, he was entitled to recover special damage for his loss of earnings. In arriving at this position, the court was of the view that the public policy rule did not apply to the claim for his loss of earnings since the defendant's negligence had actually damaged Gray's ability to work even before the manslaughter. As such, public policy was not inextricably linked with his conduct.[181] On appeal, the House of Lords overturned the decision of the Court of Appeal, in holding that

> A rule of law that was based on public policy and which was an aspect of the principle of *ex turpi causa* precluded a person from recovering compensation either for losses suffered in consequence of his own criminal act or for damage that was the consequence of a sentence imposed on him for a criminal act.[182]

Although the court considered the causation test, it chose to apply the maxim on the basis that allowing the claimant to obtain compensation would be contrary to

179 Goudkamp, *Gray v. Thames Trains* (n 173) 205

180 The Trial Court held that none of these damages that the claimant pursued were recoverable based on the maxim, which precludes recovery for any damages arising from the claimant's own illegal act. However, the Court of Appeal overturned the decision that loss of earnings was recoverable but any other claims for damages should be precluded. The House of Lords reversed the decision of the Appeal Court, and restored the decision of the Trial Court that the Court of Appeal rightly precluded the claimant from recovering the general damages, but they failed to allow the claimant to recover his loss of earnings after the manslaughter since the general damages and loss of earnings following the manslaughter fall foul of the maxim

181 [2008] EWCA Civ 713

182 *Gray* [2009] UKHL 33

public policy.[183] In that case, Lord Hoffmann identified two forms of the maxim. First, there is the narrow version, under which a person is prevented from recovering damages that arise as a result of a sentence imposed on him for a criminal act.[184] Then there is the broader version, under which such a person would be prevented from recovering damages which arise due to his/her own criminal act.[185] The narrow version is justified on the basis of the public policy rationale of maintaining consistency between criminal and civil laws. This version aims to prevent a claimant from undermining the goals of criminal law. While making sense *prima facie*, it was criticised by Goudkamp, who questioned why the version chooses to sacrifice the purposes of tort law instead in order to achieve the so-called 'consistency'.[186] Goudkamp further argued that while the narrow version may have some merits, the 'consistency' reasoning adopted by the House of Lords in *Gray* 'fell short of making out a complete case in support of it'.[187] Accordingly, he asserted that the assumption that 'inconsistency in the law should never be tolerated . . . should be scrutinised'.[188] Goudkamp has also criticised the broader version, which seeks justification on the basis of fair distribution of resources, which can be considered as the no-benefit rationale of public policy, as 'indefensible'.[189] He further argued that,

> It is not an effective instrument of punishment since it has the potential to hand out punishment that is disproportionate to the gravity of the claimant's wrongdoing. This is because the punishment that it dispenses depends on the extent of the claimant's loss rather than on his or her culpability.[190]

This weakness of the broader version was manifested in *Gray*. In that case, it was uncontested that the claimant was guilty of manslaughter and deserved to be punished. However, it was overlooked that he escaped being liable to the claimant and would have had to reimburse him for the loss of his earnings if the manslaughter had not occurred. This was because the claimant's earning capacity was already impaired as a result of the defendant's negligence. We, therefore, submit respectfully that the House of Lords erred by considering the broader version of the illegality defence in that case because, although it sought to prevent the claimant from benefitting from his wrongdoing, it provided a windfall to the negligent defendant by neglecting to consider that the negligent defendant relied on the manslaughter of the claimant to escape liability for reimbursing the claimant's loss of earnings. In addition to this, the broader version could be justified on the basis of the

183 Joel Townsend, '*Gray v. Thames Trains*: Another Causation Dilemma' (2009) 16(3) Psychiatry, Psychology and Law 333, 338
184 *Gray* [2009] UKHL 33 [32]
185 *Gray* [2009] UKHL 33 [32]
186 Goudkamp, *Gray v. Thames Trains* (n 173) 208
187 Goudkamp, *Gray v. Thames Trains* (n 173) 211
188 Goudkamp, *Gray v. Thames Trains* (n 173) 211
189 Goudkamp, *Gray v. Thames Trains* (n 173) 212
190 Goudkamp, *Gray v. Thames Trains* (n 173) 212

no-benefit rule. However, Goudkamp argued that maintaining the fair distribution of resources is not a consideration of tort law.[191] His assessment was that,

> This argument does not make any sense not least because it assumes that tort law is concerned with achieving just distributions in material wealth. This is not necessarily part of tort law's agenda. On the contrary, it is well known that tort law is liable to perpetuate or aggravate distributive injustices on account of its regressive nature.[192]

The rationale behind the broader version may hinge on the need to safeguard the integrity of the court since assisting a claimant who has committed wrongdoing could be construed as undermining the court's integrity. However, this approach can be censured as it 'does not preserve the dignity of the court, since in all illegality cases the court assists a wrongdoer no matter how it rules'.[193] This is because, as the example in *Gray* shows, while the claimant was prevented from recovering the loss of earnings based on the no-benefit rule and the notion of protecting the integrity of the courts, the defendant was still allowed to escape liability against the claimant. This discussion was taken further by Goudkamp, who argued that,

> [It] is afflicted by serious . . . confusion because it cannot explain why morally bankrupt individuals are entitled relief in respect of torts committed against them provided that their base conduct is unrelated to their damage. If relief is granted to the claimants, courts will be seen to lend their assistance to the claimant. If a remedy is denied, the courts will be ruling in favour of a tortfeasor. Significantly, the tortfeasor may have been implicated in precisely the same immoral conduct as the claimant. Very often, his or her behaviour will be more egregious than the claimant's. . . . It may be criminal.[194]

For this reason, the suggestion that wrongdoers should not be assisted by law may be too broad.[195] In *Gray*, the House of Lords 'paid insufficient attention to the justifications for the defence and consequently gave it a far broader scope than is appropriate'.[196] This led the negligent defendant to escape being liable to the claimant, who was prevented from recovering the loss of earnings suffered due to the defendant's negligence.

Based on the prevailing stance of public policy and the court's approach in the *Gray* case, it seems that while the maxim primarily aims to prevent claimants from

191 James Goudkamp, 'The Defence of Illegality in Tort Law: Wither the Rule in *Pitts v. Hunt*?' (2012) 71(3) CLJ 481, 484

192 James Goudkamp, 'The Defence of Illegality in Tort Law: Wither the Rule in *Pitts v. Hunt*?' (2012) 71(3) CLJ 484

193 Goudkamp, *Gray v Thames Trains* (n 173) 213

194 Goudkamp, Ex Turpi Causa and Immoral Behaviour (126) 356–357

195 Connolly (n 133) 12

196 Goudkamp, *Gray v. Thames Trains Ltd* (n 173) 205

securing relief by citing public policy rationales, it may overlook other crucial policy considerations, such as safeguarding victims who have suffered due to someone else's negligence. Moreover, it is arguable that in applying the maxim, courts tend to lean towards leaving losses unaddressed. This raises significant concerns about the adequacy of the maxim in gauging whether it is appropriate to deny relief based solely on the nature of the claimant's wrongdoing.

Recognising the limitations of solely relying on public policy considerations to deny reliefs to claimants, there has been a growing acknowledgement of the need to consider the underlying policy considerations specific to the area of law at hand when apportioning illegality between the defendant and claimant. This trend reflects a shift towards a more nuanced approach in the application of the maxim in case law. The first case in which such an approach was adopted was *Hounga (Appellant) v. Allen and Another (Respondents)*.[197] In that case, Miss Hounga (H), a Nigerian, had come to the United Kingdom on the invitation of Mrs. and Mr. Allen (A). Although her visa was for 6 months, she remained in the United Kingdom for 18 months and lived in the defendants' house. Mrs. Allen employed H to take care of her children without any wage, and H sustained serious physical abuse inflicted by A. H brought a claim against A, who counter-argued that the illegality defence should bar the claim.[198]

The Supreme Court departed from *Gray* and relied on the inextricable link test. Based on this test, the court considered whether there was an inextricable link between H's claim and her illegality.[199] The court adopted 'a more flexible approach which balanced the public policy underlying racial discrimination law against the public policy underlying immigration law'.[200] H's appeal was allowed on the grounds that there was an insufficiently close link between the immigration offence of the claimant and her claim for the statutory tort of discrimination in the course of employment.[201] The underlying policy reason behind this outcome was that, 'to hold otherwise would encourage employers to enter into illegal contracts of employment, as that would let them discriminate without legal consequences'.[202] Hence, the court ruled in favour of protecting the policy considerations that underlie the prohibition of racial discrimination.[203]

197 [2014] UKSC 47

198 In the Employment Tribunal (ET), the issue considered was regarding race discrimination and unlawful dismissal from employment. The ET held in favour of Miss Hounga. Mrs. Allen appealed to the Employment Appeal Tribunal (EAT), but the appeal and the cross-appeal were dismissed. Mrs. Allen brought further cross-appeal to the Court of Appeal by asserting that the illegality defence should bar the claim. The appeal was allowed based on the reasoning that Miss Hounga's illegality was inextricably bound up with her claim and allowing the claimant to proceed would condone her illegality

199 *Hounga* (n 197), [31]–[41]

200 TT Arvind, *Contract Law* (OUP 2017) Chapter 14

201 *Hounga* (n 197) [67]

202 Arvind (n 200) Chapter 14

203 Arvind (n 200) Chapter 14

The approach of the case, a clear departure from the previous mechanical presumption, is a positive development. The court's introduction of a new rationale, 'considering the policy underlying law', in the application of the maxim, is a significant shift in the legal landscape.

Although the approach put forward by the court is a promising development, the outcome of the case can still be criticised in different aspects. For example, although H remained in the United Kingdom illegally with no permission to work, her claim for compensation from her employer was allowed on the ground that she was discriminated against in the course of her employment. A was punished for discrimination, whereas the illegality of H for being involved in the conspiracy to arrive, remain, and work in the United Kingdom without a valid visa and on an illegal employment contract was not taken into account as seriously as race discrimination, despite these issues arising for consideration. As such, compensation was awarded to H based on the illegal employment contract. Fisher argued that this may have been because several factors might legitimately be incorporated into the court's deliberation and would 'cohere with the principle's goal of maintaining legal integrity, but the gravity of the illegality is not among them'.[204]

Rimer LJ raised this particular issue in the Court of Appeal, whereby if the claimant were allowed to make the case and rely on her illegality, the court would have forgiven her illegal actions.[205] Contrarily, Lord Sumption in *Bilta* stated that, to make that a good cause of action, H did not rely and did not have to rely on 'the circumstances in which she had entered into the United Kingdom, either by way of pleading or by way of evidence. They were, in reality, no more than background facts'.[206] Strauss QC criticised this argument on the basis that,

> [T]his misses the point. The circumstances of the claimant's entry into the UK may have been background, but the illegal contract of employment clearly was not. It was central to a claim for the statutory tort of racially discriminatory dismissal, as it was to an unfair dismissal claim.[207]

Interestingly, the case of the defaulting defendant was dismissed, while the claimant, whose claim was also connected with her illegality, was awarded compensation. In our view, this is an inherent deficiency of the maxim because when the illegality is raised as a defence, upholding the defence will often leave one of the parties to the illegal activity holding a windfall.[208] Despite the current limitation, the precedent set by *Hounga* introduces a non-automatic policy approach that courts can utilise to reason and balance the wrongdoings of both claimant and defendant. This approach is grounded in the specific policy considerations of the

204 James C Fisher, 'The Ex Turpi Causa Principle in *Hounga* and *Servier*' (2015) 78(5) MLR 854, 863
205 [2012] EWCA Civ 609 [61]
206 [2015] 2 All E.R. 1083 [102]
207 QC Nicholas Strauss, 'Ex Turpi Causa Oritur Actio?' (2024) 132 LQR 236, 252
208 Arvind (n 200) Chapter 14

relevant law rather than offering an automatic response of denying relief to the claimant. The court considered the importance of the negative consequences of allowing the defendant to succeed with the illegality defence and favoured the need to deter future unlawful employment discrimination practices.

The third case in which the maxim was applied is *Les Laboratoires Servier and Another (Appellants) v. Apotex Inc and Others (Respondents)*.[209] In this case, the defendant companies, which are collectively referred to as Servier, had several patents for perindopril erbumine.[210] By June 2003, the patent protection for a compound form in Europe had expired, while the patent to protect a crystalline form in the United Kingdom was still valid, with Servier's UK subsidiary having an exclusive licence. Similarly, the Canadian patent protection remained valid until 2018. The claimant companies, which were collectively named Apotex, specialised in producing and selling generic pharmaceutical products. In July 2006, Apotex started importing and selling generic perindopril erbumine tablets in the United Kingdom, and Servier brought and obtained an interim injunction against them to prevent them from doing business in the United Kingdom. In order to obtain the injunction, Servier made a cross-undertaking as to damages for losses that Apotex should suffer if it was later determined that the injunction should not have been granted in the first place.

The Patents Court held that Servier's UK patent was not valid, following which Apotex claimed compensation on the basis of the cross-undertaking. Servier relied on the maxim and argued that it would be against public policy to allow Apotex to recover the loss. Its defence was grounded on the argument that its products were manufactured in Canada, and, as a result, the Canadian patent, which was still valid, would have been infringed.[211]

The Supreme Court held that the maxim was not applicable on the grounds that the context of turpitude included criminal and quasi-criminal conduct. It held that civil wrongs, such as patent infringements, are private rights and do not fall within

209 [2014] UKSC 55

210 A drug used for hypertension and cardiac insufficiency treatment

211 In the Patents Court, judgement was delivered by Arnold J in favour of Servier and held that the maxim applied to Apotex's claim on the grounds that it was unlawful to manufacture in Canada, and the claim failed as it is contrary to public policy. The reasoning was that illegality was sufficiently serious because it was knowingly and deliberately conducted by Apotex [2011] RPC 574. This decision was reversed by the Court of Appeal that the maxim defence did not bar the claim based on the concession made by Apotex to reduce the damages awarded for the amount that is equal to what the court in Canada would have ordered to pay [2013] Bus LR 80. Etherton LJ determined that the infringement conducted by Apotex through violating the Servier's Canadian patent was not a relevant illegality for the purposes of the defence. The logic behind this approach is that, in the application of illegality defence, the court is to 'take into account a broad range of considerations in order to ensure that the defence only applies where it is a just and proportionate response to the illegality involved in the light of the policy considerations underlying it', and Etherton LJ did not consider the aforementioned reasoning as a satisfactory test because Apotex honestly and reasonably believed that the Canadian patent was not valid [2013] Bus LR 80 [73], [81]. Thus, the infringement of the Canadian patent was not considered an issue to be relevant to the illegality because there is a close link between the patent infringement and the loss suffered by Apotex. Servier appealed to the Supreme Court

the ambit of the maxim.[212] The reasoning behind this exception stemmed from the idea that safeguarding private rights was not a priority in the context of protecting public interests and as such did not trigger the maxim defence. The court stressed the necessity of protecting public policy when it stated that the illegality defence is 'based on public policy, and not on the perceived balance of merits between the parties to any particular dispute'.[213] As such it disregarded the private rights of parties because 'the illegality defence, where it arises, arises in the public interest, irrespective of the interests or rights of the parties'.[214]

In this case, the court applied the maxim in a more conservative way than in *Hounga*.[215] While it did not consider *Hounga*, it brought a distinctive approach in considering the maxim, having been heard nearly 6 weeks before the judgement in *Hounga* was delivered.[216] The truth is that, even if the *Servier* appeal was heard after the judgement of *Hounga*, there is no guarantee that the case would have extended the development put forward by *Hounga*. This was because the core issue was whether civil wrongs should be covered by the illegality defence. Consequently, the approach taken by *Servier* remained limited by the considerations of public policy.

Of recent, the most influential case in which the maxim was mentioned is *Patel v. Mirza*.[217] In that case, Mr. Mirza (M), a foreign exchange broker, permitted Mr. Patel (P) to use his account to bet on the share price movements of the Royal Bank of Scotland. Consequently, P transferred £620,000 to M's account. But M did not carry out the agreement, and P did not receive the money back from him. Subsequently, P brought a claim against M based on unjust enrichment, and M set out the facts of the illegal agreement. Two issues were thus considered by the court: (i) whether the claim would fail for illegality based on the fact that there was insider dealing, which is criminalised under the Criminal Justice Act 1993; (ii) if so, whether there was any remedy for P under the principles of equity and trust?[218] Upholding M's illegality defence, the court dismissed P's claim. His appeal to the Court of Appeal was allowed on the basis that,

> [A] party who had withdrawn from an illegal agreement because it could no longer be performed was not prevented by public policy from relying on that agreement, provided that no part of it had been carried into effect; and that, accordingly, since no part of the illegal insider dealing agreement had been

212 Servier (n 209) [23]–[28]. As long as they do not involve dishonesty or corruption. See Servier (n 209) [25]

213 Servier (n 209) [13]

214 Servier (n 209) [23]

215 Fisher (n 204) 854

216 Fisher (n 204) 867

217 *Patel* (n 141) 42. Since then, the UK courts have applied the ruling in *Patel* in several cases such as *Stoffel & Co v. Grondona* [2020] UKSC 42; *Henderson v. Dorset Healthcare University NHS Foundation Trust* [2020] UKSC 43; *Singularis Holdings Limited v. Daiwa Capital Markets Europe Ltd* [2019] UKSC 50; *Bank St Petersburg PJSC v. Arkhangelsky* [2020] EWCA Civ 408 etc.

218 [2013] EWHC 1892

> carried into effect, the claimant was not barred from relying on it and his claim would be allowed.[219]

Aggrieved, M appealed to the Supreme Court, which considered whether P was entitled to recover the money transferred to M for the illegal purpose from which P had withdrawn when the agreement had not been performed. The Supreme Court dismissed M's appeal and held that P was entitled to restitution for the amount he had paid to M. On this basis, it was suggested that the reliance test should no longer be followed,[220] and two rationales of public policy were emphasised. They were, first, that nobody should be allowed to benefit from his/her own illegality and, second, the law should be consistent and 'not self-defeating, condoning illegality by giving with the left hand what it takes with the right hand'.[221]

Normally, if the general approach of the maxim had been applied against the claimant as was done in *Gray*, it should have barred P from recovering the money from M on the basis that allowing him to do so would be contrary to public policy. However, the court significantly departed from that automatic approach, considering rather a 'range of factors', termed by Lord Toulson as a 'trio of considerations'.[222] This was stated as,

> In assessing whether the public interest would be harmed in that way, it is necessary (a) to consider the underlying purpose of the prohibition which has been transgressed and whether that purpose will be enhanced by denial of the claim, (b) to consider any other relevant public policy on which the denial of the claim may have an impact and (c) to consider whether denial of the claim would be a proportionate response to the illegality, bearing in mind that punishment is a matter for the criminal courts.[223]

This approach marks a departure from the presumption that a party to a contract tainted by illegality would not be eligible for relief. The case has solidified the court's stance established in *Hounga* and further advanced the law. In doing so, the court considered the underlying policies for denying relief, as well as additional policy considerations, to balance the illegal actions of both parties. These considerations include 'the . . . seriousness of the conduct, its centrality to the contract, whether it was intentional and whether there was marked disparity in the parties' respective culpability'.[224] Consequently, based on the policy of deterring unjust enrichment, the defendant was barred from invoking the illegality defence. This is because denying the claimant recovery would result in unjust enrichment for the defendant.

219 [2014] EWCA Civ 1047
220 *Patel* (n 141) [2024] UKSC 42 [110]
221 *Patel* (n 141) [2024] UKSC 42 [99]
222 *Patel* (n 141) [2024] UKSC 42 [101]
223 *Patel* (n 141) [2024] UKSC 42 [120] per Lord Toulson
224 *Patel* (n 141) [2024] UKSC 42 [107]

4.3.1.4 Certainty, Consistency, and Proportionality in the Concept of the Maxim

As previously demonstrated, in determining the application of the maxim in law, we can decipher two periods: case law pre-*Patel* and case law post-*Patel*. In pre-*Patel* case law, the maxim was criticised for lacking certainty and consistency and for its proportionality. On the issue of certainty and consistency, the first concern was whether there was a practical way to distinguish the different facts of a case so that a decision on whether the doctrine should be applied could be made. It appeared there was no adequate mechanism to determine this question. This fact was emphasised by Fordham when he noted that[225]

> When one adds to this scenario the fact that the role of [the maxim] in tort law is ill-defined, that there is little consensus about how or when it should be applied, and that it frequently involves policy judgments of the most subjective kind, then one is left with a concept which is far from satisfactory.[226]

This issue was also highlighted in *Patel* by Gloster LJ, who stated, 'it is almost impossible to ascertain or articulate principled rules from the authorities relating to the recovery of money or other assets paid or transferred under illegal contracts'.[227] The absence of an adequate method of rationalising the defence typically provoked the thought that 'the ritual incantation of the maxim . . . is more likely to confuse than to illuminate',[228] with 'each case typically raising more questions about the nature of the defence than it answers'.[229] The effect was that the maxim came to be defined as 'an unhappy mix of rigid rules and value judgments, and its application has unpredictable and haphazard consequences'.[230]

Despite the fact that the maxim was invoked for a considerable time in contract, tort, unjust enrichment, and trust cases and that there was some attempt to clarify its underlying public policy considerations, determining its exact scope remained blurred.[231] Keen to illuminate its exact scope, the Law Commission published a number of reports on the illegality defence.[232] The Commission stated that,

> The present law is unnecessarily complex, uncertain, arbitrary and lacks transparency. This largely results from the fact that the illegality rules have to cover

225 Bruce MacDougall, '*Ex Turpi Causa:* Should a Defence arise From a Base Cause?' (1991) 55 Saskatchewan Law Review 1, 21
226 Fordham (n 135) 258
227 [2014] EWCA Civ 1047 [47]
228 *Pitts v. Hunt* [1991] 1 Q.B. 24 [49] per Balcombe LJ
229 MacDougall (n 225) 1
230 Jonathan Mance, 'Ex Turpi Causa – When Latin Avoids Liability' (2014) 18(2) Edinburgh Law Review 175, 185
231 Francis Kean, 'Safeway Versus Twigger: The Door is Still Open' (2012) <http://blog.willis.com/2012/10/safeway-versus-twigger-the-door-is-still-open/> accessed 20 May 2024
232 Law Commission (n 961); Law Commission (n 987); Law Commission (n 951); Law Commission (n 934)

> a huge variety of cases. The unlawful conduct in question may range from the heinous to the trivial, and its connection to the claim may be inextricably close or merely incidental. To expect one set of detailed and ostensibly rigid rules to cater for all circumstances that may be encountered is overly ambitious.[233]

And despite acknowledging the issues of uncertainty and inconsistency in the application of the maxim, the Commission interestingly considered them as normal in view of the fact that the defence covers several cases. As such, the courts were encouraged to employ a 'discretionary approach'[234] in determining cases on the basis of the public policy rationale. This approach may have been founded on the assumption that the courts are in the best position to develop the law. That said, the exercise of discretion on the basis of public policy considerations in cases involving the maxim resulted in further uncertainty in determining the actual basis for the application of the maxim and muddied the waters of this concept further.

Besides the issue of uncertainty, perhaps the more important concern about the application of the maxim was that the principle might result in the courts neglecting to maintain proportionality between the parties. In effect, while the courts consider the public policy rationale as underlying the reasoning of several cases, the concern was that the fundamental facts of particular cases were in danger of being ignored. In this regard, Davies observed that, 'the illegality defence is not a principle of justice but of policy, designed to be uniformly applied rather than tailored to the particular facts of a case'.[235] As a result it was criticised as a 'blunt instrument' that was 'unforgiving and uncompromising'.[236]

The nature of the maxim casts serious doubt on whether it can maintain justice between claimants and defendants. Millett LJ in *Tribe v. Tribe*[237] observed that it 'often leads to a denial of justice'.[238] While Etherton LJ in *Servier* opined that 'it is clear . . . that the illegality defence is not aimed at achieving a just result between the parties'.[239] The common justification for this issue is that the maxim is not a principle of justice but of policy.[240] In other words, the balance that public policy seeks to achieve is not a balance between parties.[241]

According to the Commission, the problem which led to the rise of these issues was that the policy reasoning underlying the judgement of the cases was inadequately articulated by the courts.[242] Despite the issues of lack of certainty, consistency, and justice, the Commission still insisted on the idea that court decisions

233 Law Commission, 'The Illegality Defence Report' (Law Com No 189, 2009) (n 951) para [3.52]

234 Law Commission (n 987) paras [A.20], [A.43]. See also Paul S Davies, 'The Illegality Defence – Two Steps Forward, One Step Back?' [2009] Conversation 182, 185

235 Davies 188

236 *Stone & Rolls* (n 49) [185]

237 [1996] Ch. 107

238 *Tribe* (n 237) [133]

239 [2012] EWCA Civ 593 [73]

240 *Tribe* (n 237) [133]

241 *Steele* (n 144) 285

242 Law Commission (n 934) para [3.9]

should be based on the policies underlying the maxim and that the particular reasoning should be submitted accordingly.[243] This approach was based on the notion that protecting the public interest would ensure justice between the parties.[244] The concept of proportionality was used in reference to the relationship between turpitude and claims rather than the particular guiltiness and blameworthiness on the part of defendants and claimants.[245] Hence, whereas the maxim sought to prevent one party from benefitting from their own illegality, it may have condoned the illegality of the other party, and this illustrated how inadequate it was at recognising the gravity of the illegality. Consequently, Goudkamp and MacDougall suggested that this doctrine ought to be 'abolished' and 'jettisoned'.[246]

Accordingly, there was a tendency to consider the defence as 'occasionally proclaimed dead'.[247] Nevertheless, the approach adopted by the Supreme Court in *Patel* has brought a new perspective that might potentially clarify the concept. Based on the suggestion of the court to consider the 'trio of considerations', the issues with the maxim regarding lack of clarity, certainty, and proportionality have arguably begun to be addressed. This is because this approach requires the court to consider 'the policy underlying the prohibition which gives rise to the potential illegality' and 'whether a denial of relief will be proportionate to the nature and degree of the illegality involved', as well as taking into account the considerations of public policy, which may be impaired by the denial of the relief.[248] This had actually been suggested before the judgement of *Patel* was delivered by Mance, who stated

> The law does better to analyse the relevant factors in different situations separately, rather than grasp at a loose maxim like *ex turpi causa* which suggests that there is some blanket answer covering all situations, and has been explained, to the extent that it has been at all, in terms of inflexible sub-rules.[249]

Moving away from the idea of solely relying on the considerations of public policy is the notion that the judicial tool of public policy consists of different but limited rationales, which only consider punishing the perceived wrongdoer and preventing them from benefitting from their own illegality so that the desired deterrence and consistency in law are maintained. This was stated by Lord Sumption in *Patel* as follows:

> I regret that I cannot agree with the conclusion of Lord Toulson JSC . . . that the application of the illegality principle should depend on 'the policy factors

243 Law Commission (n 934) para [3.9]
244 *Parking Eye Ltd v. Somerfield Stores* [2013] Q.B. 840 [45] per Toulson L.J
245 *Hounga* (n 199), [58] *per* Lord Hughes; *Servier* (n 211), [16] per Lord Sumption
246 MacDougall (n 225) 37; Goudkamp, The Defence of Illegality: *Gray v. Thames Trains Ltd*' (n 173) 214
247 MacDougall (n 225) 1
248 Arvind (n 200) Chapter 14
249 Mance (n 230) 190

> involved and . . . the nature and circumstances of the illegal conduct, in determining whether the public interest in preserving the integrity of the justice system should result in the denial of the relief claimed'.[250]

For this reason, he suggested that,

> In my opinion, this is far too vague and potentially far too wide to serve as the basis on which a person may be denied his legal rights. It converts a legal principle into an exercise of judicial discretion, in the process exhibiting all the vices of 'complexity, uncertainty, arbitrariness and lack of transparency' which Lord Toulson JSC attributes to the present law. I would not deny that in the past the law of illegality has been a mess. The proper response of this court is not to leave the problem to case by case evaluation by the lower courts by reference to a potentially unlimited range of factors, but to address the problem by supplying a framework of principle which accommodates legitimate concerns about the present law. We would be doing no service to the coherent development of the law if we simply substituted a new mess for the old one.

The aforementioned dictum of Lord Sumption illustrates a significant development in law. Besides being a potential solution to the issue of proportionality, the approach can potentially increase the certainty and consistency in case law because it will make it much easier to enforce an illegal contract. This creates the possibility of developing the law in a better direction, and in order to resolve the problems, the opportunity provided by *Patel* should be harnessed.

The next section examines how the maxim operates in the relationship between the company and directors and the extent to which it allows the company to ascribe the risk of liability and loss caused by directors' undesirable behaviours. Thereafter, it will consider the possible impact of *Patel* on the application of the maxim in corporate cases when directors' undesirable acts expose companies to heightened risks which may harm the long-term interests of stakeholders.

4.3.2 The Illegality Defence and the Ascription of Risks to Directors Through Loss Recovery

As we embark on our exploration, it's crucial to grasp the historical significance of the illegality defence. In pre-*Patel* case law, public policy often took centre stage, overshadowing the twin issues of the gravity of the illegality by both parties and the need to maintain justice between them. This historical context piques our curiosity about how the maxim is applied in corporate cases. If it is applied to a company in the same way as it is to individuals, it may potentially be an inadequate tool

250 *Patel (Respondent) v. Mirza (Appellant)* [2024] UKSC, 265

in the ascription of the heightened risk of undesirable behaviour to the company's directors in recovering losses from them. This raises intriguing questions about the maxim's ability to provide sufficient individual accountability.

Despite the uncertainties surrounding the maxim, its application and outcomes in the corporate context are relatively more certain and clearer than in other areas of law. This clarity is not due to different considerations but rather because of its joint operation with the doctrine of corporate attribution. The maxim, which typically prevents a person who is liable for his wrongdoing from invoking his normal rights, also relies on the doctrine of corporate attribution to determine the liability of the company and its directors. In cases where the company is found liable for the undesirable actions of its directors, it is almost certain that the maxim would prevent it from ascribing the risk of the liability and loss that it suffers as a result.

In the context of ascribing liability, the application of the maxim and the consideration of public policy have come to the fore in three cases. The first case, *Stone*, is a prime example. Here, the company's claim against negligent auditors was dismissed by the maxim. The reason was that the 'directing' mind had used the company as a vehicle for fraud. To allow the company to recover the loss would have been contrary to the deterrence, no benefit, and consistency rationales of public policy since the director's act was the company's liability.

In this scenario, the problem with applying the maxim is that it would automatically prevent a company that is liable for its director's behaviour from recovering the losses it suffered, regardless of whether its claim is against negligent auditors or fraudulent directors. This outcome was justified by the public policy rationale. Even at that, the main limitation of this approach is the lack of attention given to directors' fiduciary duties and the protection of the long-term interests of stakeholders whose interests are to be taken into account by directors. The application of the maxim arguably did not result in a different outcome in that case, but its reasoning led to a wrong outcome in *Safeway*.

In *Safeway*, the company was held liable for its directors' and employees' illegal behaviours through corporate attribution. However, the application of the maxim prevented it from recovering the losses it had suffered because it was viewed as a wrongdoer who sought to benefit from its illegality. It was thought that preventing it from recovering the loss would fulfil the deterrence objective of public policy.[251] Consequently, the maxim barred the company from making a recovery for the losses it suffered.

The issue with this case with respect to the application of the maxim is that it automatically impeded the company, which was found liable, without considering the long-established principles of company law. Despite the fact that a certain number of directors and employees who were not acting as part of the board had entered into an illegal price-fixing agreement, the company was held liable for their actions

251 *Safeway* (n 2) [2010] EWCA Civ 1472 [44]–[45]

and was thus prevented from ascribing the liability for the loss to the directors. In this regard, Lim argued that,

> *Safeway* is another example of why it is so problematic to attribute the wrongdoing of the directing mind and will for the purpose of the maxim defence without critically examining whether or not such attribution is justified in the context in which it is used and the implications of such use.[252]

The company was regarded as the primary wrongdoer, with the court holding that 'it would be inconsistent with [the] liability for the claimants to be able to recover the amount of the penalty in the civil courts from the defendants'.[253] The narrow version of the maxim was explicitly articulated to strike the company's claim for recovery based on the consideration that allowing it to recover the loss would have been inconsistent with the idea of deterring wrongdoing through the imposition of punishment. However, the application of the maxim to companies on the basis of the consistency objective should not be the same when it is applied to individuals. This is because there are various considerations that the court should take into account in terms of the relationship between a company and its directors.[254] This was explicitly demonstrated by Lim, who noted that

> [C]ourts should carefully bear in mind the distinctive considerations pertaining to company law whenever defendants invoke the illegality defence to defeat the claims brought by companies seeking to enforce duties owed to them. Failure to do so will lead to a distorted application of the consistency rationale underlying the illegality defence.[255]

In essence, the effect of the maxim in *Safeway* was to debar the company from accessing the civil remedies available to it for its directors' breach of their duties.[256] The result was that the purposes and considerations of company law were arguably sacrificed to promote the consistent rationale of public policy.

Safeway is an excellent example of how companies are sometimes subjected to the risks of liability and loss that arise when their directors engage in undesirable behaviour. This is because directors may involve companies in illegal agreements, which may benefit them in the short term but also expose them to significant risks in the long term. In this sense, the company becomes a victim of the wrongdoing of its directors who breached their fiduciary duties, a factor which the maxim did not adequately consider. Accordingly, the court in *Safeway* failed to 'take into account

252 Lim, 'A Critique of Corporate Attribution' (n 17) 344
253 *Safeway* (n 2)
254 Lim, The Illegality Defence and Company Law (n 125)
255 Lim, The Illegality Defence and Company Law (n 125) 61
256 Lim, The Illegality Defence and Company Law (n 125) 59–60

the special doctrinal and policy features in company law when [it] examined the policy rationales underlying the illegality defence'.[257]

The outcome of the *Safeway* case brings back the concern of whether or not the maxim adequately justifies the quantum of punishment in the corporate context. This is a potential issue in the relationship between the company and its directors because 'the gravity of the sanction imposed by rejecting the claimant's action depends on the magnitude of . . . loss rather than . . . culpability'.[258] The severity of punishment is determined based on the company's loss rather than 'on the moral obloquy of [its] behaviour in question'.[259] On the basis of the company's liability for the undesirable behaviour of its directors,[260] the maxim leaves the liability and loss caused by such behaviour where it falls, which again illustrates that the maxim has 'nothing to do with justice and fairness, but with public policy'.[261] This nature of the maxim is problematic in cases that involve two individuals. That said, it has severe consequences for the company when its directors are involved in undesirable behaviour because

> in the absence of some countervailing policy reason, it is not just for someone who falls foul of a statute by reason of the acts of its employees or other agents to add to its burdens and disabilities by depriving it of any recourse against those employees or other agents.[262]

Such an approach can cause companies to suffer severe harm since they will be left with 'no recourse . . . against their very own agents or representatives, however egregious the breaches of duties committed against the companies by these . . . agents, and however severe the losses they cause to the companies'.[263] This issue was also emphasised by Watts, 'on the reasoning adopted [in *Safeway* that] it would seem that a principal could not even dismiss the miscreant servants'.[264]

In terms of corporate objectives, *Safeway*, following *Stone*, once again illustrated that the maxim disregards the enlightened shareholder theory and stakeholder theory of corporate objectives when it dismisses the company's claim. This is problematic since the company typically initiates recovery claims to safeguard the interests of both shareholders and other stakeholders. Preventing it from doing so will result in these corporate stakeholders bearing the adverse consequences of directors' misconduct, putting their interests at risk.[265]

257 Lim, The Illegality Defence and Company Law (n 125) 50
258 Goudkamp, Ex Turpi Causa and Immoral Behaviour (126) 357
259 Goudkamp, Ex Turpi Causa and Immoral Behaviour (126) 356
260 See Section 4.2
261 *Safeway* (n 2) [2010] EWHC 11 (Comm) [106]
262 Peter Watts, 'Illegality and Agency Law: Authorising Illegal Action' [2011] JBL 213, 220
263 Lim, A Critique of Corporate Attribution (n 17) 353
264 Peter Watts (n 262) 219
265 Lim, The Illegality Defence and Company Law (n 125) 58 and 59

An influential corporate case in which the maxim was applied is *Bilta*.[266] In that case, a company was allowed to recover losses that it suffered as a result of a fraud that its director perpetrated with the assistance of other companies. However, this outcome has cast some doubt on the judgements delivered in *Stone* and *Safeway* since the recovery was allowed even though the doctrine of corporate attribution and the maxim illegality defence were considered in the case. That said, the court also recognised the differences between the facts of these groups of cases. This is because the companies in *Stone* and *Safeway* were regarded as culpable, but as the victim in *Bilta*. In addition, although the company was protected from the fraudulent behaviour of its directors in that case, the court's rationale was not founded on the illegality defence. And despite the assertion of Lord Sumption that 'the illegality defence is available against a company only where it was directly, as opposed to vicariously, responsible for it',[267] this view was not explicitly endorsed by the majority of the court, which held that 'the defence of [the maxim] was not available to the defendant directors against the company's claim because the defendants' wrongful activities could not be attributed to the company in the proceedings brought by the liquidators'.[268] Hence, the illegality defence did not operate on the basis that the company was held to have been vicariously liable for its directors' fraud. Interestingly, if the directors' fraud had been committed on a third party, as in *Stone*, the company would have arguably been found personally liable and prevented from recovering the loss from its directors.

For the sake of argument, assuming that the maxim operated in that case and protected the company from the consequences of its directors' fraud, it is still arguable that the maxim still exposes the company to the risk of undesirable behaviour by the directors. Hence this case cannot be taken as a reference to assert that the maxim allows the company to ascribe the risks of undesirable behaviour to its directors.

The issue that underlies the company's inability to ascribe the risk of undesirable behaviour is that the application of the maxim to companies is considered similar to its application to individuals. For this reason, 'while it seems to have been assumed that this principle applies, and in the same way as it applies to individuals, its application to a corporate entity is problematic both conceptually and in terms of the authorities'.[269] The foundation of this approach may be that 'the law's disfavour extends only to those who were parties to the illegality'.[270]

> When directors act for a company in an illegal transaction with a stranger, the company is itself a party to that transaction and therefore to the illegality.

266 (n 49). Since then, the UK Supreme Court has also applied the doctrine in *Singularis Holdings Limited (in liquidation) v. Daiwa Capital Markets Europe Limited* [2019] UKSC 50

267 (n 49) [80]

268 (n 49)

269 Ross Grantham, 'Illegal Transactions and the Powers of Company Directors' (1999) 115 LQR 296

270 Grantham (n 269) 298

The company, therefore, could not rely on that transaction as the source of civil rights.[271]

In principle, directors are authorised to act generally. They are expected to act within the confines of the law but may choose to act illegally. In such cases, the company is not entitled to avoid liability by distinguishing the actions of its directors in the exercise of such authority. This is also the position of modern company law.[272]

All these issues with the application of the maxim in the corporate context illustrate that the maxim disregards the long-standing considerations underlying company law, and the approach of *Patel* does not currently protect the company against the consequences of directors' undesirable behaviours. However, *Patel* can also still be considered a promising development in respect of the application of the maxim in the corporate context. Despite the present law potentially not being adequate to recognise the particular policy objective of the stakeholders' protection, *Patel* may be a positive step in the future direction of the law. This is because the way in which the court interpreted the facts of the case and based the foundation of the reasoning on Patel could be replicated in corporate cases. In this case, the court should have prevented the claimant from recovery based on the approach adopted by pre-*Patel* case law. However, it departed from solely relying on public policy considerations and suggested the consideration of two other factors, namely the policy underlying the prohibition and the proportionality of remedy denial. In the end the appeal failed because the court held that allowing the defendant to invoke the defence would result in his unjust enrichment.

In order to solve the issues arising from the maxim in corporate cases, it is posited that there should be a clear departure from the old case law and the adoption of a new approach, which recognises the individual accountability and negative consequences of preventing the company from passing on the liability and loss arising from undesirable behaviour to directors upon the long-term interests of stakeholders. In this way, the approach of the maxim will be more flexible in evaluating the specific facts of each case, and the purpose of balancing the proportionality between the company and directors, depending on the amount of illegality on their parts, is much easier to assess.

To conclude this section, we have attempted to show that the maxim operates on the basis of public policy and has been widely referred to in tort, equity, contract, and corporate cases. Its application has caused a lack of certainty, justice, and fairness in a general sense. However, for the purposes of this work, it, more importantly, does not allow the company to ascribe the risk of liability and loss to which it is exposed due to directors' undesirable behaviours by abolishing its ability to enforce the directors' duties and invoking the remedies provided to it under common law and statute, as allowing it to do so is typically considered an affront

271 *Selangor United Rubber Estates Ltd v. Cradock* [1968] 1 WLR 1555 [1655]
272 Watts (n 262) 217

to public policy. There is, however, a tendency to consider other policy considerations besides that of public policy, and this may shape the future case law, but the current approach of the maxim impairs the long-term interests of stakeholders who are affected by directors' decisions.

4.4 Conclusion

This chapter has analysed the ability of the company to attribute and ascribe the risks of liability and loss arising from undesirable behaviour onto directors through legal mechanisms. In terms of apportioning the risk between the company and its directors, there is a very strong tension between the rules of corporate attribution, the fiduciary duties of directors, and the illegality defence. Through corporate attribution, the company can be made to bear liability for its directors' undesirable behaviours. As such, its ability to invoke the fiduciary duties of directors as a shield to protect itself from the consequences of such behaviour is restricted. When the company is found liable based on the attribution doctrine, the maxim prevents it from relying on its illegality to recover the loss in spite of the fact that the directors have breached their duties to it.

The first doctrine examined was corporate attribution, which consists of two principles: the special rules of corporate attribution and the identification doctrine. Despite the fact that the principle of the special rules of attribution has brought a nuanced approach to attribution, this principle is limited in terms of the recognition of the long-established principles of company law, and there is a great tendency to rely on the position of the directors within the company. On the contrary, while the identification doctrine has traditionally been prominent in company law, there is a growing recognition that it fails to fully encompass modern corporate practices. Based on this doctrine, even a sole director can involve the company in a binding transaction, which may result in the latter bearing liability and suffering losses. The company is, in that case, unable to attribute its liability and losses to the director as his/her act is perceived as the act of the company. However, based on the principle of separate legal personality, even if only one individual controls the affairs of the company and has various roles in the corporate structure, no member can ordinarily be considered as 'the company'.[273] Equating the act of the directors to that of the company is, therefore, the major drawback of the identification doctrine. The doctrine places 'an undue emphasis on the descriptive fact',[274] exposing the company to significant risk of liability and loss. The fraud exception provides some help to companies. Still, it is limited to the cases that involve fraud perpetrated by directors on the company. Thus, the company cannot protect itself against the risk of liability and loss when its directors are involved in undesirable behaviour.

The overall effect of these doctrines is to hold the company liable for its directors' undesirable behaviours, and in such cases, the directors' fiduciary duties

273 Griffin (n 5) 158
274 Ferran (n 2) 251

have limited usefulness as a shield with which the company can protect itself. This outcome shouldn't come as a surprise, as a Google search reveals that no book specifically focused on 'the law of attribution' has been published.[275] This fact underscores the limited attention given to this crucial mechanism, which significantly influences the relationship between a company and its directors.

The second consideration examined was the illegality defence, which seeks to protect public policy by considering its rationales: deterrence, the no-benefit rule, and maintaining consistency in the law. It was shown that the limitation in the general application of the doctrine stems from the fact that it is primarily concerned with the potential negative impact of the particular behaviour on public policy, while disregarding the issues of the gravity of the illegality by two parties in the case and the subsequent need to ascertain justice between them. This has cast serious doubts on the adequacy of the doctrine in apportioning liability and loss between two parties.

This is also a valid issue in the corporate context because the doctrine prevents a company that is found liable through corporate attribution from ascribing the risk of liability and loss to its directors without sufficiently considering the exclusive policy considerations involved in the relationship between the company and directors. The defence overly disregards how public policy rationales, usually referred to in cases involving individuals, 'cannot be so easily transposed to cases involving the company as a claimant without careful attention' in distinguishing considerations regarding company law.[276] This failure has led to incorrect outcomes in cases involving the company's claim to ascribe the risk of liability and loss to its directors since the company is usually regarded as the one that seeks to recover the loss it has suffered due to its liability that it suffers as a result of their default. For this reason, the involvement of the maxim in the corporate context is problematic[277] and not completely appropriate.[278]

Consequently, despite the fact that the types of directors' undesirable behaviours identified in regulatory competition law benefit the company in the short term, neither the doctrine of corporate attribution nor the maxim considers the fact that the company is exposed to the risk of liability and loss in the long term, to the detriment of the interests of stakeholders. The approaches adopted in *Bilta* and *Patel* can be considered positive developments in terms of widening the policy considerations of the doctrine of corporate attribution and the maxim illegality defence, but these policy objectives should go further to consider the protection of stakeholders when the company is exposed to heightened risk arising from undesirable behaviour by directors. The next chapter will examine whether the company can mitigate the risk of loss caused by the undesirable behaviour of directors through liability insurance.

275 Nicholas Davidson, 'A Sideways Look at Stone & Rolls' (2010) 26(2) PN 66, 69
276 Lim, The Illegality Defence and Company Law (n 125) 49
277 Grantham (n 269) 296
278 Mance (n 230) 187

Bibliography

Ambasta K, 'A Leap of Reasoning, but for Special Cases: An Analysis of the "Expiry" of the Directing Mind and Will Test in Attribution of Corporate Liability' (2012) 33(8) Comp Law 227

Anchayli A, 'The "Directing Mind and Will" Test in Corporate Attribution: Iridium and Meridian – A Comparison' (2012) 33(8) Comp Law 252

Arvind TT, *Contract Law* (Oxford University Press 2017) Chapter 14

Bhandari V, 'Meridian to Iridium: An Analysis of Attribution' (2012) 23(8) ICCLR 253, 254

Cartwright P, *Consumer Protection and the Criminal Law: Law, Theory, and Policy in the UK* (2nd edn, Cambridge University Press 2001) 104

Connolly N, 'Re-Examining Illegality in Restitution: A Reason to Deny Restitution, or to Grant It?' (SLS Conference Edinburgh 2013)

Dannemann G, 'Illegality as a Defence Against Unjust Enrichment Claims' in David Johnston and Reinhard Zimmermann (eds), *Unjustified Enrichment: Key Issues in Comparative Perspective* (1st edn, Cambridge University Press 2002) 310

Ferran E, 'Corporate Attribution and the Directing Mind and Will' (2011) 127 LQR 239

Fisher JC, 'The Ex Turpi Causa Principle in *Hounga* and *Servier*' (2015) 78(5) MLR 854, 863

Fordham M, 'The Role of Ex Turpi Causa in Tort Law' [1998] The Singapore Journal of Legal Studies 238

Goudkamp J, 'The Defence of Illegality: *Gray v Thames Trains Ltd*' (2009) 17 TLJ 205, 208

Goudkamp J, 'Ex Turpi Causa and Immoral Behaviour in the Tort Context' (2011) 127 LQR 354

Goudkamp J, 'The Defence of Illegality in Tort Law: Wither the Rule in *Pitts v. Hunt*?' (2012) 71(3) CLJ 481

Griffin S, 'The One-Man Type Company and the Removal of Corporate Personality in the Context of the Attribution Rules' (2011) 22(5) ICCLR 158

Hicks A and Goo SH, *Cases and Materials on Company Law* (6th edn, Oxford University Press 2008) 129

Kean F, 'Safeway Versus Twigger: The Door is Still Open' (2012) <http://blog.willis.com/2012/10/safeway-versus-twigger-the-door-is-still-open/> accessed 20 May 2024

Lim E, 'A Critique of Corporate Attribution: "Directing Mind and Will" and Corporate Objectives' [2013a] JBL 333

Lim E, 'Formalism and Companies' (2013b) 13(2) JCLS 477

Lim E, 'The Illegality Defence and Company Law' (2013c) 13(1) JCLS 49

Lim E, 'Attribution in Company Law' (2014) 77(5) MLR 794

Lim E, 'Attribution and Fraud Exception' [2015] LMCLQ 14

MacDougall B, '*Ex Turpi Causa:* Should a Defence Arise From a Base Cause?' (1991) 55 Saskatchewan Law Review 1

Mance J, 'Ex Turpi Causa – When Latin Avoids Liability' (2014) 18(2) Edinburgh Law Review 175

Naniwadekar M, 'Directing Minds and Agents: An Essay on Fraud and Attribution' [2010] JBL 271

Ong CA and Wickins RJ, 'Confusion Worse Confounded: The End of the Directing Mind Theory?' [1997] JBL 524

Payne J, 'The Attribution of Tortious Liability Between Director and Company' [1998] JBL 153

Payne J, 'Corporate Attribution and the Lessons of *Meridian*' in Paul Davies and Justine Pila (eds), *The Jurisprudence of Lord Hoffmann* (Hart Publishing 2015) 364

Sealy LS, 'The Corporate Ego and Agency Untwined' (1995) 54(3) CLJ 507

Sheikh S, 'The Corporation-Villain or Victim?' (2008) 19(11) ICCLR 248

Steele J, *Tort Law: Text, Cases, and Materials* (3rd edn, Oxford University Press 2014) 285

Stern YZ, 'Corporate Criminal Personal Liability: Who is the Corporation' (1987) 13 Journal of Corporate Law 125

Strauss N, 'Ex Turpi Causa Oritur Actio?' (2016) 132 LQR 236
Sullivan GR, 'The Attribution of Culpability to Limited Companies' (1996) 55(3) CLJ 515
Townsend J, '*Gray v. Thames Trains*: Another Causation Dilemma' (2009) 16(3) Psychiatry, Psychology and Law 333
Virgo G, *The Principles of the Law of Restitution* (3rd edn, Oxford University Press 2015) 710
Watts P, 'Corrupt Company Controllers, Their Companies, and Their Companies' Creditors – Dealing With Pleas of Ex Turpi Causa' [2014] JBL 161
Wells C, 'Corporate Liability for Crime-*Tesco v. Nattrass* on the Danger List?' (1996a) 3(1) Architectural News 5
Wells C, 'The Law Commission Report on Involuntary Manslaughter: The Corporate Manslaughter Proposals: Pragmatism, Paradox and Peninsularity' [1996b] Criminal Law Review 545

5 Managing Risk

Neutering Insurance in the Face of Individuals' Undesirable Behaviours*

5.1 Introduction

Thus far, this book has raised concerns about the roots and consequences of companies' exposure to the risk of undesirable behaviour by their directors. It has also noted the inability of companies to attribute and ascribe the risk of liability and loss to their directors. Going further, this chapter examines the extent to which companies may mitigate the risks of directors' undesirable behaviours through standard commercial risk management tools, one of which is insurance. In view of the fact that such behaviours expose companies to significant corporate risks which cannot be shifted elsewhere by the operation of the legal mechanisms and rules examined in previous chapters, companies have had to manage and minimise their risk exposure by employing other mechanisms.

Insurance, as a formal and potentially powerful tool, offers a unique advantage among the available risk management mechanisms. It allows for the transfer or shifting of risk from an individual to a group, thereby providing a potential remedy for companies seeking to mitigate the risk of loss from directors' undesirable behaviours. This, in turn, plays a crucial role in safeguarding the long-term interests of stakeholders. The central question this chapter aims to address is whether insurance can truly be an effective risk mitigation strategy, and if there are any potential obstacles that may hinder its effectiveness.

The ability to mitigate corporate risks by transferring losses to an insurer is a significant advantage of corporate insurance policies. One such policy coverage, typically provided to companies, is Directors and Officers Liability Insurance (D&O insurance). Introduced by Lloyds of London in the late 1930s, D&O insurance aims to protect the company and its directors from losses suffered by themselves or by third parties. This means that a company can seek recovery under the insurance policy for various types of loss due to the operational deficiencies of its business and the behavioural shortcomings of its directors.

The question at this stage concerns the extent to which insurance provides coverage and recovery to the company. To determine this issue, different jurisdictions have adopted certain insurance categories. In civil law jurisdictions, this aim is achieved through commercial or particular insurance codes which set out insurance coverage rules for a particular action. On the other hand, in common law

DOI: 10.4324/9781003461562-5

jurisdictions, public policy considerations are taken into account to specify the extent of insurance protection.[1] In the latter jurisdictions, the insurer may raise the defence of public policy to prevent the insured from seeking indemnification for losses suffered as a result of the illegality of the insured.[2] The extent of the insurance coverage is more likely to be determined by case law, which illustrates how public policy considerations are applied in insurance.

The application of public policy is made through a range of doctrines, including the *ex turpi causa* or the illegality defence (hereafter maxim).[3] As shown earlier, the maxim aims to protect public policy by taking its rationales into account. In so doing, it sets limits in relation to the risks that cannot be managed through insurance.[4] Therefore, the approach of the maxim is important in determining whether an insured will be able to mitigate his/her risk exposure through insurance. The issue is that while the maxim does not always automatically render the policy void, it will serve to debar an insured from recovering losses arising from particular acts on the basis of public policy considerations.[5]

In this regard, it is crucial to analyse how the maxim operates in insurance law in order to determine the extent to which insurance can be used to mitigate the risk exposure of an insured company. In a literal sense, the company is unlikely to be 'personally' liable since it cannot be physically involved in any action. If that were the case, it is unlikely that the maxim would prevent it from making any recovery. However, the insurance law interacts with the doctrine of corporate attribution, which attributes the acts of directors and their liability to the company. Hence, a company can be found liable for the acts of its directors, and its claim for recovery under an insurance policy may still be prevented through the joint operation of the doctrine of attribution and the maxim.

This chapter investigates how this triangular relationship between liability insurance, the maxim, and the doctrine of corporate attribution operates in the context of D&O insurance and the impact of the approach adopted by these principles on the ability of companies to mitigate their risk exposure through insurance. In this regard, it considers how risk distribution can be achieved between the three actors of the D&O insurance, namely, the company, the directors, and the insurer. If the liability arising from directors' behaviours is determined as that of the company through the principle of corporate attribution, the question that arises is whether an insurance contract it enters is itself tainted with illegality and, therefore, unenforceable.

Accordingly, from the company's perspective, determining its ability to protect itself against risks through insurance is based on how the maxim and doctrine

1 Chris Parsons, 'Managerial Liability, Risk and Insurance: An International View' (2001) 3(1) ICCLJ 1, 8
2 Malcolm A Clarke, *The Law of Liability Insurance* (1st edn, Informa 2014) 15
3 See Chapter 4, Section 4.3
4 Digby C Jess, *The Insurance of Commercial Risks: Law and Practice* (3rd edn, Sweet Maxwell 2001) 466–472
5 Digby C Jess, *The Insurance of Commercial Risks: Law and Practice* (3rd edn, Sweet Maxwell 2001) 467

of attribution operate. Particularly, this chapter will analyse the specific risks that arise from the undesirable behaviour of directors, for which the company is responsible, and the tension between the risk management role of insurance and such risks. In addition, it will also evaluate how the maxim captures particular corporate risks and whether such risks should be caught by illegality or should be part of the broader set of risks that the companies shall or can be allowed to manage through insurance.

Section 5.2 will dissect the risk management role of insurance law, particularly in liability insurance, and the extent to which D&O insurance can mitigate the risks stemming from directors' undesirable behaviours. Section 5.3 then turns its attention to the role of the maxim, considerations of public policy, and rules of attribution in determining the availability of recovery for the losses that companies typically endure. Section 5.4 concludes the chapter by underscoring the limitations of insurance law while also recognising the crucial importance of allowing companies to recover losses caused by directors' undesirable behaviours for the protection of stakeholders' long-term interests.

5.2 Operation of Liability Insurance as a Risk Management Method

Although insurance is a general risk management strategy, its role in risk management can differ depending on the insurance type. In this regard, types of insurance can be divided into two primary categories, namely life insurance or non-indemnity insurance, and non-life insurance or indemnity insurance. Indemnity insurance is also subcategorised into liability and property insurance. To determine whether insurance can be used to reduce corporate risks, this chapter focuses primarily on liability insurance with specific focus on D&O insurance.

Compared to other types of insurance, liability insurance is a 'recent phenomenon'.[6] It came into existence in the 1880s.[7] And even at that, its introduction was widely condemned because the idea of 'protecting' a wrongdoer was seen as aberrant and antisocial.[8] However, it gained traction in the 19th century and has had a significant impact on the law, especially in the area of tort liability for injuries caused by personal fault.[9] Liability insurance is different from other types of insurance as its subject is 'less obvious'.[10] As Waller LJ noted in *Feasey v. Sun Life Assurance Co of Canada*,[11]

> there is no hard and fast rule that because the nature of an insurable interest relates to a liability to compensate for loss, that insurable interest could only

6 Peter Cane, *Responsibility in Law and Morality* (1st edn, Hart Publishing 2002) 242

7 Tom Baker, 'Liability Insurance at Tort-Crime Boundary' in David M Engel and Michael McCann (eds), *Fault Lines – Tort Law as a Cultural Practice* (Stanford University Press 2009) 66, 67

8 Mary C McNeely, 'Illegality as a Factor in Liability Insurance' (1941) 41 Columbia Law Review 26

9 Tom Baker (n 7) 67–68

10 Malcolm A Clarke, *The Law of Liability Insurance* (1st edn, Informa 2014) 15

11 [2003] EWCA Civ 885

be covered by a liability policy rather than a policy insuring properties or lives.[12]

Under liability insurance, several forms of coverage are provided. They include employers' liability insurance, public liability insurance, product liability insurance, directors' and officers' liability insurance, warranty and indemnity insurance, and commercial vehicle insurance.[13] Although liability insurance policies usually extend to cover 'liability at law',[14] there are certain restrictions on the coverage to restrict the policy from being available to the insured for those losses arising from certain types of liabilities. These restrictions may arise in a number of situations:[15] (i) where the policy in its formation is illegal, (ii) where the insurance covers an action that is prohibited by law, (iii) where the object of the insurance is tainted by illegality, (iv) where the conduct of the insured may negatively affect public policy, (v) where the loss arises by virtue of the deliberate and wilful act of the insured, and (vi) where the insured caused his/her loss by acting negligently.[16] It is in this vein that insurance will avoid providing policy coverages for punitive damages.[17] Similarly, compensatory damages may not be provided if the same would contravene public policy. This is notwithstanding that a valid policy coverage has been provided for such claims. That said, while an insured would be barred from recovering the loss from the insurer in all these situations, the essential difference between situations (i), (ii), (iv) and (iii), (v), (vi) is that while the entire insurance policy is itself illegal and void in the former, the insured is not allowed to recover the loss in the latter as his/her particular conduct is tainted by illegality. This is despite the fact that the illegal conduct may not automatically render the policy entirely void.[18]

Although these restrictions may seem strict, they can be flexible depending on whose interest is protected by liability insurance. This is because, while these restrictions may be firmly applied against an insured person who commits a wrong to debar him/her from benefitting from his/her illegality, their application may be different when the interest of a third party victim is involved. For example, in motor liability insurance, a third-party victim may still be entitled to recovery even though the insured driver intentionally sets out to cause harm to him/her.[19] The same consideration is valid when the third party, who has been victimised due to

12 [97]

13 See Jess (n 4) 135–288

14 Robert Merkin, *Colinvaux's Law of Insurance* (8th edn, Sweet & Maxwell 2006) 687. See also Robert Merkin, 'Motor and Other Liability Insurance' in Robert Merkin (ed.), *Insurance Law: An Introduction* (1st edn, Informa 2007) 275

15 Merkin, *Colinvaux's Law of Insurance* (n 14) 119

16 Merkin, *Colinvaux's Law of Insurance* (n 14) 119

17 With an exception. See Section 5.2.2.3.2

18 Merkin (n 14) *Colinvaux's Law of Insurance* 119–120

19 *Charlton v. Fisher* [2002] QB 578. See also Rob Merkin and Jenny Steele, *Insurance and the Law of Obligations* (1st edn, Oxford University Press 2013) 350

the fraudulent act of an insured, seeks to bring a claim against the insured's insurer to recover the loss he/she suffered. In such a case, the victim of the fraudulent act may be indemnified even in cases where the insured's claim is dismissed.[20]

This again raises the question as to whether liability insurance protects third-party victims or the insured himself.[21] The answer to this question has significant implications for D&O insurance because it helps in determining whether such insurance aims to protect the insured, who in the case of the company, may include the company itself or its directors on the one hand, or to the third party, who may have been victimised by the company's business practices. The next section will aim to develop this question further.

5.2.1 Liability Insurance Protection for Whom?

Liability insurance seeks to protect an insured person against losses that may arise as a result of third-party claims.[22] But in its application, the public policy foundation of insurance is applied strictly so as to prevent a wrongdoer from recovery. In this regard, Merkin has noted that the courts have narrowed the principle of public policy so as to ensure that the real beneficiary of the insurance policy is not the erring insured person, but rather the third-party victim who has been harmed by his/her wrong and may not be able to recover the loss he/she suffered from the insured in another way.[23] In noting that there is a common tendency among lawyers and politicians to consider liability insurance as a protection vehicle for victims, Wagner however argues that, 'victim compensation should not be counted among the purposes of liability insurance',[24] noting that such objective of liability insurance has been rejected by a majority of the economic literature.[25] Corroborating Wagner, Baker argues that 'liability insurance is a victim compensation fund, but it is not only that – and not even primarily that'.[26] In contrast, McNeely observes that liability insurance is gradually becoming a tool which provides a fund for the injured party, while moving away from being a tool for the protection of the insured.[27] She defines this as a 'substantial shift'.[28] Fleming supported this argument by stating that 'liability insurance is now generally recognised as in essence a contract for the benefit of third parties'.[29]

20 *Total Graphics Ltd v. AGF Insurance Ltd* [1997] 1 Lloyd's Rep 599
21 Clarke (n 2) 2
22 Merkin (n 14), 'Motor and Other Liability Insurance' 275
23 Merkin (n 14) *Colinvaux's Law of Insurance* 725
24 Gerhard Wagner, 'Tort Law and Liability Insurance' in Michael Faure (ed.), *Tort Law and Economics* (2nd edn, Cheltenham 2009) 377, 384
25 Gerhard Wagner, 'Tort Law and Liability Insurance' in Michael Faure (ed.), *Tort Law and Economics* (2nd edn, Cheltenham 2009) 384
26 Baker (n 7) 69
27 McNeely (n 8) 60
28 McNeely (n 8) 60
29 John G Fleming, 'Insurance for the Criminal' (1971) 34 MLR 176, 177

Liability insurance as a third-party protection fund was demonstrated in the Third Parties (Rights Against Insurers) Act 1930 (TPA30),[30] which transferred the rights of the insured under his/her policy to the victim who has suffered a loss as a result of his/her default. It was initially designed to indemnify victims of speed[31] and drunken[32] driving, where it was thought as being contrary to public policy to allow an insured driver to recover the loss through insurance when he/she has acted wilfully and culpably. But regardless of how wilful the insured was, a third party that was harmed by him/her may still claim against his/her insurance policy.[33] Although this may not provide direct indemnification to the defaulting insured, his/her liability to the third party would automatically be transferred to the insurer because the insurance policy would not be rendered void. This is because the one who has suffered the actual loss in such a case is the innocent victim. In a nutshell, illegality on the part of the insured, for which it will normally be contrary to public policy to award indemnification, may not be a reason to prevent the third-party victim from being indemnified for the loss suffered due to the default of the insured party. The justification for this lies in the fact that the recovery would be awarded to the third-party victim rather than the defaulting insured. Such situations arise especially when a third party is deprived of indemnity where the insured does not have sufficient funds.[34]

The Act was applied in *Total Graphics Ltd v. AGF Insurance Ltd*,[35] where, despite the fact that a claim under an insurance policy was rejected because of the fraudulent conduct of the insured, the third party who was injured by his/her act was allowed to recover the loss from the insurer. A similar approach was adopted by the Court of Appeal in *Charlton v. Fisher*,[36] where the defendant driver drove his car deliberately towards the stationary car of the claimant in a hotel car park and rammed it. The damage to the third-party victim by the insured driver was regarded as 'accidental'. This approach was adopted to protect the interests of third-party victims, even though the defaulting insured intentionally caused the loss. As can be seen in both cases, protecting third-party victims is a major consideration of liability insurance, as it disregards the 'wilfulness' in the insured's act which led to the loss itself. From this perspective, it is obvious that insurance is a protection fund for the victim.

In respect of the second approach, insurance is regarded as protection for the insured against any possible loss suffered. This is the primary objective why

30 This Act was repealed by the Third Parties (Rights against Insurers) Act 2010, which came into force on 1 August 2024; however, the Act 2010 has introduced a more extended version of providing protection to victim third parties. See CMS, 'Third Parties (Rights Against Insurers) Act 2010 – Commencement Date' (2024) <http://www.cms-lawnow.com/ealerts/2024/05/third-parties-rights-against-insurers-act-2010-commencement-date> accessed 22 August 2024

31 *Tinline v. White Cross Insurance Association Ltd* [1921] 3 KB 327

32 *James v. British General Insurance Co* [1927] 2 KB 311

33 Ray Hodgin, *Insurance Law: Text and Materials* (2nd edn, Covendish 2002) 131–132

34 Jess (n 4) 427

35 *Total Graphics* (n 20) 599

36 *Charlton* (1111) [2002] QB 578

individuals and companies have increasingly sought to acquire insurance as they seek ways of mitigating their risks of liability and loss. Those who are insured would not pay such considerable premiums to purchase policy coverage for the sake of protecting any potential third-party victim; rather, they seek to recover the loss suffered due to any liability they may bear.

In this approach, the possibility of providing recovery by insurance is not as high as in the first approach. This is because, in the second approach, the nature of the illegal act of the defaulting insured is an important factor in determining whether providing recovery is against public policy. However, this consideration is not such an issue when protecting a third-party victim is the primary purpose of insurance. The rationales of public policy would be heavily referred to in cases involving a recovery claim of wrongdoing by an insured person, as the maxim seeks to prevent recovery by any wrongdoing insured who has acted deliberately, wilfully, or intentionally.

It can be seen that this discussion is more about which purpose of insurance is given more weight because when the vulnerability of the victim is considered, the indemnification aim of insurance attains priority. The basis of this approach is mainly distributive and compensatory justice.[37] This is also identified as 'ethical compensation' by Williams.[38] In the other situation, if the deterrence aim of insurance is prioritised, the gravity of the act of the insured will be subject to determination, as the question of how the insured, and others involved in such wrongdoing, should be deterred is to be answered. The foundation of this approach is the promotion of corrective and retributive justice, which is an important objective of tort law.[39]

Although this is a confusing matter to determine in liability insurance, the confusion arises when the issue is viewed from different perspectives. From the perspective of the third-party victim, it is surely regarded as a protection fund; however, it may also relieve the erring insured from liability.[40] Although discussions are still in place as to whether liability insurance seeks to maintain distributive justice or corrective justice, all these determinations differ depending on the context in which it is dealt with. The reason that underlies this difference is the nature of the particular type of liability insurance. This is because there are some compulsory types of liability insurance which primarily aim to protect the third party who has been victimised by the insured. This is the main reason why insurance is compulsory in some instances, because such types aim to avoid the victim being left without any aid should his/her claim not be satisfied by the wrongdoer. Motor insurance is one such form of insurance. On the other hand, there are other types of liability insurance which are optional purchases for individuals and companies. The aim of these

37 Gary T Schwartz, 'The Ethics and the Economics of Tort Liability Insurance' (1989) 75 Cornell Law Review 312, 328. See also Malcolm A Clarke (n 37), *The Law of Insurance Contracts* (5th edn, Informa 2006) 578

38 Glanville Williams, 'The Aims of the Law of Tort' (1951) 4(1) Current Leg. Probs. 137, 141

39 See Clarke (n 37) 578. See also Schwartz (n 1129) 326

40 Clarke (n 37) (n 2) 2

is primarily to provide recovery to the insured for loss, rather than providing a fund to the victim's third party. In the next section, the relation between this determination and D&O insurance will be examined.

5.2.2 The Operation of D&O Insurance in Mitigating Corporate Risk

As can be seen, the answer to the question as to whether liability insurance is a protection fund for third-party victims or an insured person may differ depending on whether the insurance is compulsory or optional. We will now examine whether D&O insurance is compulsory or optional for the company to purchase and whether it aims to protect the third party or the insured.

5.2.2.1 Coverage of D&O Insurance

Understanding the operation of D&O insurance requires some basic knowledge of the types of coverage this insurance provides. Although the extent of D&O insurance coverage varies depending on the requirements of a particular company and directors, it usually applies to the 'judgement, settlements, defence and legal costs incurred by directors as a result of claims against them for wrongful acts'.[41] This can be interpreted in different ways, but it typically covers the loss arising from 'actual or alleged neglect, error, misstatement, misleading statements, omission or other breach of duty'.[42]

The coverage provided by D&O insurance is categorised into three different clauses. These are termed as sides A, B, and C. Sides A and B are a type of uniform coverage provided by the insurer as they are usually purchased simultaneously.[43] They are Personal Coverage (Side A) and Corporate Reimbursement Cover (Side B).[44] While Side A provides coverage to directors for their liability to third parties due to a breach of contract or to the company for breaching fiduciary duties, Side B provides coverage for reimbursing the company when it has indemnified its directors and officers.[45] These are not only the main areas of coverage provided by D&O insurance but also two main ways through which the company indemnifies its directors. This is because, under Side A, the directors are directly indemnified by the insurance policy purchased by the company, and the company is reimbursed by the insurance for the amount that it has indemnified its directors under Side B.

41 Noel O'Sullivan, 'The Demand for Directors' and Officers' Insurance by Large UK Companies' (2000) 20(5) European Management Journal 574, 575

42 Noel O'Sullivan, 'The Demand for Directors' and Officers' Insurance by Large UK Companies' (2000) 20(5) European Management Journal 575

43 Noel O'Sullivan, 'The Demand for Directors' and Officers' Insurance by Large UK Companies' (2000) 20(5) European Management Journal 575

44 Noel O'Sullivan, 'The Demand for Directors' and Officers' Insurance by Large UK Companies' (2000) 20(5) European Management Journal 575

45 For this reason, Side B is considered as 'balance sheet protection'. See Arthur J Gallagher International, 'Directors' & Officers' Liability Insurance (D&O)' (2012) 3 <http://www.ajginternational.com/media/95298/airmic-do-guide-dec-2012.pdf> accessed 15 June 2024

In addition, despite the fact that Sides A and B have become part of the common language of D&O insurance coverage, additional protection is also offered by some policies to the company under Side C for claims brought against it.[46] Such coverage is needed by the company when it is a named defendant in a D&O claim, and it has become a common practice, especially in US-based securities claims and employment disputes where the company and its directors are targeted by the litigants.[47] That is why it is called 'entity' or 'corporate' cover.[48]

5.2.2.2 D&O Insurance as a Protection for Whom

D&O insurance is an optional form of liability insurance for the company to purchase to protect its directors and itself against the risk of loss. As D&O insurance is not mandatory, some underlying reasons must incentivise the company to pay a considerable premium for the coverage. Based on the types of coverage provided by D&O insurance,[49] these reasons can mainly be classified into two categories, namely the demand of individual directors and the company's desire to protect itself against potential corporate risk.

The first reason is the directors' high demands, as they tend to protect themselves against any type of potential personal liability to which they may be subjected as a result of being the director of a company. This is because, as Kirman stated,

> [A]n effective D&O insurance program, in combination with well drafted indemnification and exculpation provisions in corporate charters and by-laws, is a critical component of protection for directors and officers at a time of increased scrutiny by shareholders, courts, and regulators.[50]

The level of directorial demand can differ depending on the litigation risk that they may encounter, as they are risk-averse individuals and insurance can be considered part of the director's compensation package, in addition to their remuneration. In this way, directors are also encouraged to take higher risks to increase the value of the company because directors with D&O insurance can be 'less risk-averse and consequently are less likely to reject attractive new, risky projects'.[51]

In addition, future directors may request policy coverage before they are appointed. Directors typically consider D&O insurance as an 'indispensable

46 Gregory Boop, 'Directors and Officers Insurance' (2024) <http://businessinsure.about.com/od/liabilityinsurance/a/Directors-And-Officers-Insurance.htm> accessed 31 March 2024

47 Arthur J Gallagher International (n 1137) 3. See also Chris Parsons, 'Directors' and Officers' Liability Insurance: A Target of a Shield' (2000) 21(3) Comp Law 77, 80

48 Adolfo Paolini and Deepak Nambisan, *Directors' and Officer's Liability Insurance* (1st edn, Informa 2008) 60

49 See Section 5.2.2.1

50 Igor Kirman, 'Directors' and Officers' Insurance' (2009) <https://corpgov.law.harvard.edu/2009/08/07/directors-and-officers-insurance/> accessed 15 May 2024

51 O'Sullivan (n 51) 576

prerequisite' for the company[52] because they tend to ensure that the risk of personal liability for the conduct in which they are involved on behalf of the company is as low as possible. As Hon. T.F. Bathurst observed,

> The rationale for providing such insurance is clear. In its absence, capable and talented individuals may be unwilling to join boards of directors . . . or may become excessively risk averse on boards, to the detriment of the individual company and the broader commercial community.[53]

Neither of the scenarios in this statement are palatable for the company, and thus it provides insurance coverage to its directors.[54]

The second reason that underlies the corporate demand for insurance is the company's desire to mitigate the potential risks that may arise from its day-to-day business. Although directors' motivation to possess insurance is an important factor in terms of protecting their interests, insurance is also a significant tool by which the company can run its business efficiently, as it may be subjected to several risks whose occurrence may even jeopardise its existence in the market. Therefore, it purchases insurance as part of its corporate insurance programme to reduce the risk as low as possible.[55]

O'Sullivan points out three types of large companies which are more likely to purchase D&O insurance.[56] These are companies with a higher probability of distress, companies with greater growth opportunities, and companies with significant managerial ownership. Core agrees with O'Sullivan in respect of the first type while noting that companies with higher litigation risks are more likely to purchase D&O insurance.[57] Mayers and Smith also argued that 'firms whose managers have greater discretion over the choice of hazard-reducing projects will be more likely to purchase insurance'.[58] In addition, MacMinn analysed that the purpose of eliminating and reducing bankruptcy/or agency costs incentivises the company to purchase insurance.[59] Moreover, Baker and Griffith note that companies purchase entity cover to address agency costs.[60] Agency costs are common risks to which companies are

52 Kevin LaCroix, 'Executive Protection: Private Company D&O Insurance' (2010) <http://www.dandodiary.com/2010/09/articles/d-o-insurance/executive-protection-private-company-do-insurance/> accessed 20 June 2024

53 Hon TF Bathurst, 'Insurance Law – A View From the Bench' (2013) 3–4 <http://www.austlii.edu.au/au/journals/NSWJSchol/2013/35.html> accessed 15 May 2024

54 Tom Baker and Sean J Griffith, *Ensuring Corporate Misconduct: How Liability Insurance Undermines Shareholder Litigation* (1st edn, The University of Chicago Press 2010) 57

55 O'Sullivan (n 51) 574

56 O'Sullivan (n 51) 575

57 John E Core, 'On the Corporate Demand for Directors' and Officer's Insurance' (1997) 64(1) The Journal of Risk and Insurance 84

58 David Mayers and Clifford W Smith, 'On the Corporate Demand for Insurance' (1982) 55(2) The Journal of Business 281, 286

59 Richard D MacMinn, 'Insurance and Corporate Risk Management' (1987) 54(4) Insurance and Corporate Risk Management 658, 658

60 Baker and Griffith (n 54) 72

routinely subjected. They stem largely from factors such as managerial ownership, growth opportunities, and managerial discretion over hazard-reducing projects. Other factors that may inform the purchase of entity insurance include bankruptcy and litigation costs.

The two reasons identified earlier for the acquisition of D&O insurance can be considered beneficial to both the company and its directors. It should be noted, however, that premiums and deductibles of D&O insurance are paid by the company,[61] and, for that reason, it may be regarded as 'corporate owned'.[62] To determine who the insured is under D&O policies, 'it is immaterial that . . . the company solely pays the premiums, since such payment may be viewed as consideration for the insurer's promise to indemnify both the directors and the company'.[63] Even though the company may obtain the policy in its name while stating its directors as beneficiaries, they can be still identified as contracting parties who can rely on the contract in their own right. Accordingly, they can be considered as the insured who may claim under the policy.[64]

A misunderstanding may arise from the fact that there are several types of policy coverages with D&O insurance that solely aim to protect directors or the company. For example, whereas directors are insured under Side A, as their liability is the subject of the cover, the company can be considered as the insured under Sides B and C[65] since it can be reimbursed for the loss suffered due to indemnifying directors and claims brought against it by third parties. However, it may be a misconception to label each of these types of coverage as exclusively protecting directors or the company because the company and directors can be recognised as direct and indirect beneficiaries under Sides A and B. For example, even though the company is insured under Side B, directors still benefit from this coverage indirectly.[66] A similar case is valid regarding Side A under which directors are insured, but the company indirectly benefits from the policy when it brings a recovery claim against its directors for the loss it has suffered due to their behaviour. Accordingly, although the demand by and request of current and future directors may seem to be the primary underlying reason for purchasing Side A coverage of D&O insurance, the company also considers protecting itself from risk by recovering the loss from directors' insurance. Therefore, it can be suggested that the company purchases insurance to protect its directors as long as they do not go beyond a certain point at which their acts start to harm it. Such harmful conduct can be defined 'undesirable behaviour',[67] in which the company does not wish its directors to become involved on its behalf, as it is a form of illegal behaviour. In this situation, the company

61 Vanessa Finch, 'Company Directors: Who Cares About Skill and Care?' (1992) 55 MLR (n 118) 912
62 Core (n 57) 63
63 Paolini and Nambisan (n 48) 60–61
64 This is valid as long as the Contracts (Rights of Third Parties) Act 1999 is not excluded by the particular policy contract. See, Paolini and Nambisan (n 48) 61. See also Merkin (n 14) *Colinvaux's Law of Insurance* (n 14) 721
65 See Paolini and Nambisan (n 48) 60–63
66 Baker and Griffith (n 54) 48
67 See Chapter 2, Section 2.2

does not tend to protect directors who expose it to a number of corporate risks, namely regulatory risk, litigation risk, reputational risk, and insolvency risk,[68] but rather considers how it can mitigate these risks through insurance. The next section examines the ability of the company to mitigate these risks through recovering the loss it has suffered from insurance.

5.2.2.3 *Availability of Recovery for Loss Caused by Directors' Undesirable Behaviours*

There are four types of losses that a company may suffer when its directors engage in undesirable behaviour. They include losses that arise as a result of regulatory sanctions, third-party litigation losses, reputational losses, and those arising as a result of corporate insolvency. The losses arising from the third and fourth situations are borne by the company independent of external sanction or action, while the first and second arise by third-party actions, either through the imposition of fines by regulatory authorities or as a result of claims brought by third parties against it for compensation. Together, these losses form the basis of the potential recovery claims that the company may make to mitigate the risks of directors' undesirable behaviour. The availability of recovery for such losses is an important issue for the company in terms of decreasing its risk levels while protecting the long-term interests of its stakeholders. To assess the ability of the company in this respect, the availability of policy coverage for such losses will be examined separately.

5.2.2.3.1 REGULATORY LOSS

Regulatory risk means that the company is perpetually exposed to the possibility that it may be subjected to fines by regulatory authorities if it breaches regulatory standards. [69] The issue of whether such losses can be recuperated from insurers is a 'hot topic in the insurance market'.[70] To mitigate the constant threat of regulatory sanctions, companies transfer their risks directly by filing claims against insurers or indirectly by pursuing claims against culpable directors. The issue is that breaches of statutory laws resulting in fines or penalties are typically excluded from coverage under directors and officers (D&O) insurance policies.[71]

And even where there is nonavailability of market coverage, a company may still claim against its directors to obtain a claim from their insurance; that said, such claims are hardly countenanced. A case at hand is *Safeway*, where the company was prevented from recovering the losses it suffered as a result of a regulatory fine which arose from the illegal actions of its directors. Although the court considered

68 See Chapter 2, Section 2.3
69 See Goldring (n 121)
70 Goldring (n 121)
71 Merkin (n 14), *Colinvaux's Law of Insurance*, 723; Edie and Nober (n 1163) 16. See also Barham and Sapte Volume I 323; Ian Youngman, *Directors' and Officers' Liability Insurance: A Guide to International Practice* (2nd edn, Woodhead 1999) 35, 39

several factors in reaching its conclusion, the most prominent reason for disallowing the company from 'pursuing' the insurer was because it was aware of the fact that the ultimate aim of the company was to recover the loss through directors' insurance.[72] Pill LJ stated that,

> The policy of the [CA98] is to protect the public and to do so by imposing obligations on the undertaking specifically. The policy of the statute would be undermined if undertakings were able to pass on the liability to their employees or the employees' insurers.[73]

For this reason, the claim of the company was rejected to prevent it from claiming a recovery under the D&O insurance policy. It was also emphasised by Morfey and Patton that,

> The reference to the employees' directors and officers (D&O) insurers is significant. It was common ground that Safeway would not have been able to insure itself against the risk of being subject to an OFT fine. However, unless its claim was barred by the *ex turpi causa* doctrine, Safeway would in principle have been able to recover the fine from its former directors and employees, who were all beneficiaries of D&O insurance policies. The claim thus potentially offered a means of accessing insurance cover indirectly, in circumstances where Safeway could never have obtained cover in its own right for the penalties.[74]

Hence, the rule of disallowing companies from recovering losses suffered due to regulatory penalties underlies the reasoning which led to the outcome in favour of the directors. This statement of the court was, however, challenged by Watts, who stated that,

> It is hard to see that this is so. One might not want business owners insuring themselves against the penalties, civil and criminal, that flow from illegal action by their servants, but it is quite another thing to eviscerate the contractual and other rights that they have against their servants who have failed in their duties. Business owners in such circumstances are not 'passing on the liability to their employees', but suing those employees who were the very cause of the liability in the first place.[75]

The court disregarded this point and emphasised the issues around the attribution of the directors' acts, as well as the maxim whose applications caused the company

72 Morfey and Patton (n 33) 63
73 *Safeway* [2010] EWHC 11 (Comm), [2010] EWCA Civ 1472
74 Morfey and Patton (n 33) 63
75 Peter Watts, 'Illegality and Agency Law: Authorising Illegal Action' [2011] JBL 213, 220

to suffer regulatory loss as a result of directors' undesirable behaviours. Consequently, a company can neither obtain an insurance policy itself for the risk of regulatory losses nor can it claim against its directors to recover the regulatory loss from the directors' insurance.

There is a need to analyse the Supreme Court's judgement in *Bilta* as this will enable us to appreciate the different approaches adopted by the courts in responding to the issue of recoverability of regulatory losses through insurance. Recall that in that case, the company was allowed to recover the losses it suffered from its directors, an outcome that may automatically open the door to a company that seeks to recover losses from directors' insurance. The question that, however, arises at this point is whether the difference between the purposes of the directors that were involved in misconduct in both cases matter in respect of the company's ability to recover the loss of regulatory penalties.

In *Bilta*, the directors' express aim was to perpetrate fraud, which caused the company to suffer loss, and to gain personal benefit, whereas in *Safeway* they sought to increase the value of the company by increasing prices. The difference between the purposes of the directors in both cases has a direct bearing on the availability of recovery; as such, while the company in *Safeway* was precluded, it was allowed in *Bilta*. The difference was founded on the fact that the company in *Bilta* was regarded as a victim of its directors who sought to benefit at its expense, while the company in *Safeway* was viewed as a villain which sought to profit by breaching the law. However, it was overlooked that the breach of the statutory rule by the directors in *Safeway* was undesirable to the company in terms of protecting its long-term interests even if it increased its short-term benefit. And while the company was not directly targeted, the truth remained that it was victimised by the actions of its directors, which exposed it to regulatory sanctions in the long term. It is our position that whether directors perpetrate fraud on the company for their personal benefit or are involved in illegal conduct to make the company more profitable should not normally make a difference because, in both cases, the company was exposed to heightened risk due to the directors' conduct, and the long-term interest of the stakeholders was harmed.

5.2.2.3.2 THIRD PARTY LITIGATION LOSS

The second category of loss typically arises from the potential liability of the company for harm suffered by a third party due to the misconduct of its directors. In such instances, the third party can file a claim against the company to seek compensation for the damages incurred, prompting the company to seek recourse from its insurer. The potential threat of such claims underscores the company's need for policy coverage.[76] And in this regard, its ability to recover losses incurred from indemnifying third parties is a crucial concern. This is because such liabilities can impact the company's financial stability, potentially jeopardising its future in the market.

76 See Section 5.2.2.1

Third parties can bring two types of claims against a company: compensatory damages and exemplary (punitive) damages. Compensatory damages refer to the actual harm suffered by a third-party victim due to the actions of another party. These damages are designed at restoring the third party to the position they would have been in if the incident had never occurred. In cases where a third party has been harmed by the actions of directors, they are likely to bring a claim against the company, which in turn seeks to recoup the amounts it has paid to indemnify the third party from its insurance.

An example of such an issue arose in the case of *Stone*. Here, the director's fraud was attributed to the company, and attempting to recover from auditors the loss incurred due to its own fraud was deemed contrary to public policy. Lord Walker referenced Langley J.'s statement in the High Court that 'Stone & Rolls lost nothing to which it was ever entitled', as the company itself perpetrated the fraud on the banks.[77] In this perspective, the company's loss was seen as a deserved consequence, given that the fraud was its own fault according to the principles of corporate attribution. Although it did not seek recovery for the loss from directors' insurance in this case, potential claims against the insurer would be barred by the maxim on the basis of public policy considerations. This is because the insurer's liability is typically excluded from providing recovery to individuals or companies that are engaged in dishonest or fraudulent acts. [78] Consequently, the company would be unable to utilise directors' insurance to mitigate the risk of loss arising from compensatory damages suffered by third parties due to the misconduct of directors.

The second category pertains to exemplary damages. The question of whether liability insurance provides coverage for losses resulting from exemplary damages has long been debated by the courts, the insurance market, and the general public. [79] Insurers have typically taken two approaches to this issue. The first approach contends that a claim for exemplary damages falls 'customary language of liability policies [which] restricts coverage to "damages because of" bodily injury or destruction of property'.[80] Insurers argue that such policies should not extend to cover punitive damages resulting from civil law penalties.[81] The second approach is based on the argument that liability insurance may cover punitive damages under certain conditions: (i) if they stem from unintentional actions, (ii) if the insurance policy does not expressly exclude coverage for such damages, and (iii) if awarding such damages is not deemed against public policy.[82]

To assess whether insurance coverage is available for punitive damages, it is essential to understand the nature of the loss incurred. Unlike compensatory damages, which aim to compensate victims for actual losses suffered, punitive damages

77 (n 12) [198]
78 Nicholas Davidson, 'A Sideways Look at Stone & Rolls' (2010) 26(2) PN 66, 69
79 John D Long, 'Punitive Damages: An Unsettled Doctrine' (1975) 25 Drake Law Review 870
80 John D Long, 'Punitive Damages: An Unsettled Doctrine' (1975) 25 Drake Law Review 871
81 John D Long, 'Punitive Damages: An Unsettled Doctrine' (1975) 25 Drake Law Review 871
82 John D Long, 'Punitive Damages: An Unsettled Doctrine' (1975) 25 Drake Law Review 870

serve a different purpose in that they aim to 'punish flagrant wrongdoers and to deter them and others from engaging in flagrant conduct in the future', by imposing sanctions on the wrongdoer rather than merely compensating the victim.[83] In *Huckle v. Money*,[84] which was the first instance where punitive damages were recognised in English law, the court acknowledged that such awards not only compensate the claimant but also serve to punish the defendant for their misconduct. Additionally, Lord Devlin in *Rookes v. Barnard*[85] emphasised that exemplary damages can be awarded to demonstrate that tortious actions do not go unpunished.[86] Stoll further argued that this principle embodies the punitive aspect of private law, indicating that exemplary damages serve the legitimate purpose of deterring calculated wrongdoing.[87] Consequently, indemnifying the victim can be viewed as a consequence of deterring and punishing the wrongdoer, which aligns with the primary objective of punitive damages. Therefore, the availability of insurance recovery for losses incurred due to indemnifying third parties for punitive damages hinges on the wrongdoing of the defendant rather than the injury suffered by the claimant.[88]

Indeed, providing coverage for exemplary damages directly conflicts with the fundamental nature and primary purpose of punitive awards, which are designed to punish and deter wrongdoing rather than solely indemnifying third-party victims. Allowing wrongdoers to shift the burden of indemnifying third parties for exemplary damages onto insurance could undermine the efficacy of punitive measures in law, as it would run counter to their punitive and deterrent elements. This preventative measure is rooted in public policy, which serves as a significant barrier to insurance coverage. Deterrence is a crucial consideration within public policy, and allowing insured individuals to transfer the consequences of punitive damages—designed to deter their own misconduct—onto insurance would be contrary to this principle.[89] This may explain why courts in England rarely award recovery for the loss arising from punitive damages.[90]

In the corporate context, claims for punitive damages may be instituted against companies by third parties who have suffered losses as a result of the defaults of its directors. Following which the company may be required to indemnify the third

83 John D Long, 'Punitive Damages: An Unsettled Doctrine' (1975) 25 Drake Law Review 876. See also Joseph W Cotchett and Mark C Molumphy, 'Punitive Damages: How Much is Enough?' (1998) 20(1) Civil Litigation Reporter <http://www.cpmlegal.com/pp/publication-17.pdf> accessed 17 April 2024; Columbia Law Review Association, 'Public Policy Prohibits Insurance Indemnification Against Awards of Punitive Damages' (1963) 63(5) Columbia Law Review 944, 945

84 (KB 1763) 95 Eng Rep 768

85 [1964] A.C. 1129

86 [1964] A.C. 1129 [1227]

87 Hans Stoll, 'Penal Purposes in the Law of Tort' (1970) 18(1) The American Journal of Comparative Law 3, 5

88 Bruce D Hall, 'The Validity of Insurance Coverage for Punitive Damages: An Unresolved Question? (1973) 4 New Mexico Law Review 65

89 Bruce D Hall, 'The Validity of Insurance Coverage for Punitive Damages: An Unresolved Question? (1973) 4 New Mexico Law Review 65

90 Merkin (n 14) 'Motor and Other Liability Insurance' 282

party for and may itself, subsequently, seek recourse against the culpable directors' insurance to recover the losses. The issue is that policies typically exclude insurance coverage for punitive damages.[91] This is premised on the assumption that permitting claimant companies, which should ideally be punished and deterred by punitive damages to recover such losses through insurance would, contravene public policy. This approach informed the limited consideration of the issue of policy coverage for punitive damages by English courts until the case of *Lancashire County Council v. Municipal Mutual Insurance Co*.[92] The outcome of this case prompted insurers to reassess their stance on the idea of allowing recovery for punitive damages, leading to a shift in their approach.[93]

In that case, Lancashire County Council (the Council) sued Municipal Mutual Insurance Ltd (the insurer) to recover the loss arising from the imposition of punitive damages to a third party, who suffered losses as a result of the acts of its police officers. The Council argued that the insurer had agreed to indemnify 'in respect of all sums which the insured shall become legally liable to pay as compensation'.[94] The insurer, however, refused to provide recovery for these punitive damages based on the reasoning that the concept of compensation excludes the recovery of punitive damages. It also pleaded that awarding such damages to the insured would be contrary to the deterrent objective of both punitive damages and public policy, as the wrongdoer would thus benefit from its own wrongdoing.

Based on these assertions, the court grappled with two key questions. Firstly, it scrutinised whether the Council's insurance policy covered punitive damages. And if such coverage existed, whether providing it would violate public policy. Addressing the first issue, the court acknowledged that the terms of compensation could be construed as excluding punitive damages. However, since the policy explicitly included punitive damages, the insurer was obligated to adhere to the stipulations outlined in the insurance contract.

On the second question, the court recognised the principle that individuals should not be indemnified against liabilities that arise from their unlawful actions since the same would be contrary to public policy. Nevertheless, it asserted that public policy could not serve as a ground for an insurer to reject recovery since the Council's liability stemmed from vicarious, rather than personal, responsibility for the deliberate actions of its agents.[95] Moreover, the court contended that allowing

91 Youngman (n 1164) 35 and 39

92 [1996] 3 All E.R. 545, [1997] QB 897; see also Lyanne Loucas, 'Exemplary Damages: Policy Terms' (1996) 4(7) International Labour Review 131

93 Clarke (n 37) (n 1129) 757. See also Merkin (n 14) *Colinvaux's Law of Insurance*, 723

94 The sums that arise 'out of (a) accidental bodily injury or illness (fatal or otherwise) to any person . . .; (b) accidental loss or accidental damage caused to property; (c) wrongful arrest, malicious prosecution and false imprisonment by a constable, when such injury illness loss or damage occurs during the currency of the policy and arises out of the exercise of the functions of a local authority'. See [1997] Q.B. 897 [903]

95 Ozlem Gurses, 'Extra-Contractual Liability: An Insurance Overhead or a Reinsurance Recovery?' (2011) 8 JBL 763, 776

such recovery would not contravene public policy; rather, it would safeguard it. If punitive damages were not recovered from the insurer by the Council, the public would ultimately shoulder the burden through increased taxes.[96] Additionally, the court noted that the deterrent effect, aimed at dissuading the insured from seeking reimbursement for losses, could still be achieved by the Council through deductibles and elevated future liability insurance premiums.

Accordingly, the court allowed the Council's punitive damages claim. From the foregoing, it appears that the word 'compensation' has been extended to accommodate punitive damages. The outcome of the Lancashire case can be considered to have removed the barriers to recovering the loss of punitive damages from insurance; however, similar conclusions may not have been reached in corporate cases that involve directors' undesirable behaviours.

The first reason is based on the requirement of finding the entity vicariously liable for its agents' conduct in order to recover the punitive damages from the insurer. In the context of the company–directors relationship, the sole exception to the company's personal liability arises when directors commit fraud against the company, and the interests of creditors are taken into account in cases of insolvency.[97] Since the misconduct of directors does not constitute the type of wrongdoing perpetrated against the company itself, the maxim dictates that the company should bear personal liability for its directors' actions, thus hindering its potential claim to recoup losses incurred due to punitive damages. Consequently, the exception of vicarious liability cannot be extended to a company that has incurred punitive damages owing to the misconduct of its directors. In the *Lancashire* case, the Court of Appeal found no public policy rationale to bar the insured Council from seeking recompense for losses incurred due to punitive damages, as it was vicariously liable for the acts of its agents. Had the liability of the Council been grounded in the attribution of the act itself, the insurer would not have been compelled to provide assistance, as the Council would bear personal liability, and public policy would have prevented it from benefitting from its own transgressions.[98]

Another significant factor is that, in the *Lancashire* case, the Council's insurance policy explicitly stipulated that coverage extended to punitive damages as part of the losses covered by the policy. Providing such coverage to the insured is ordinarily considered contrary to public policy; however, punitive damages arising from the arbitrary conduct of the government or public officials are one of the very few exceptions for which recovery can be provided by an insurer.[99] The foundation that underpins this approach is that losses that public and governmental organisations suffer would usually fall on the public since they are financed through taxes. In such cases, allowing recovery for the loss of punitive damages would protect the public, which is the purpose of public policy. Consequently, even though the loss

96 For discussion on similar consequences of not awarding punitive damages, See Long (n 1172) 872

97 See Chapter 4, Section 4.2

98 Merkin and Steele (n 19) 319

99 Merkin (n 14) *Colinvaux's Law of Insurance* 689

arising from punitive damages was awarded to the insured Council in *Lancashire*, this does not assure that the same conclusion can be reached for the corporate cases as the considerations of public policy and corporate attribution would be the main obstacles preventing a company from not only obtaining a policy coverage for itself but also from recovering the loss from directors' insurance. The company suffers loss as a result of indemnifying the third party, and insurance leaves the loss where it falls.[100]

In summation, the company is unlikely to mitigate the risk of third-party litigation loss arising from compensatory and punitive damages caused by directors' undesirable behaviours through insurance, and this illustrates the lack of attention that D&O insurance gives to the negative consequences of preventing the company from recovery upon the long-term interests of stakeholders.

5.2.2.3.3 REPUTATIONAL LOSS

The third category of losses that a company may attempt to recover through insurance is reputational loss. This loss arises from the occurrence of the reputational risk and will be considered alongside other regulatory, litigation, and bankruptcy risks. Mitigating such risk is an important consideration for the company, as it potentially has short-term and, more importantly, long term, implications for the company. For this reason, companies not only 'need to mitigate against the effect of loss of reputation, but they also need to be looking for the upside opportunities to enhance their reputations'.[101]

Reputational risks can be avoided and managed to a certain extent by the company before it occurs, but after it has occurred, it is very challenging to transfer and mitigate this risk. This is because reputational risk has distinctive characteristics that differentiate it from the other risks to which the company is subjected. These are that (i) reputational risk is an exclusive risk to which only the company as an entity can be subjected, and (ii) the reputational damage of the company cannot be expressed financially.

First it should be noted that the company, and not the persons who associate with it such as directors and members, are the victims of reputational risks where it occurs. And the reputational losses that it suffers cannot be measured when the risk occurs. According to a report published by the Chartered Institute of Management Accountants (CIMA), reputational damage 'cost can only be really known five to ten years after an event, and even that might be too soon'.[102] In the short term, it is more about losing the public trust rather than monetary loss, which can only

100 Merkin and Steele (n 19) 319

101 Chartered Institute of Management Accountants, 'Corporate Reputation: Perspectives of Measuring and Managing a Principle Risk' (2010) 1 <http://www.cimaglobal.com/Documents/Thought_leadership_docs/cid_exrep_corporate_reputation_june07.pdf> accessed 16 June 2024

102 Chartered Institute of Management Accountants, 'Corporate Reputation: Perspectives of Measuring and Managing a Principle Risk' (2010) 24 <http://www.cimaglobal.com/Documents/Thought_leadership_docs/cid_exrep_corporate_reputation_june07.pdf> accessed 16 June 2024

roughly be known in the long term. This is because of the public perception that the company has engaged in misconduct.[103] The company may seek to transfer such risk by recovering the reputational loss through insurance. Even at that, this is a risk for which insurance cannot be purchased. This may be because there are also several considerations to be taken into account by an insurer providing such an insurance policy. These considerations are defined by Honey as 'barriers to cover'.[104]

Six main barriers will now be considered, and the first of these is capacity. This is an important issue which dissuades the insurer from providing cover for reputational loss. Both uncertain amounts of insurance coverage and uncertain limits on claims are subjects for serious consideration by the insurer because possible reputational loss is difficult to estimate.[105] Although this uncertainty is in the nature of reputational loss, it is likely to discourage the insurer from providing such cover. The second barrier is hazards. This consideration is based on the possibility that the company may deliberately influence the claim value to accidentally increase the damages payable. As a result, the insurer may have to indemnify the company for an undeserved inflated loss. The third barrier concerns a lack of required information about the company and its directors business in the market. And while insurers can obtain such information from the public domain, the company may not provide confidential information to the insurer as it may be uncomfortable with sharing such information in case it becomes public knowledge. In these cases, an insurer cannot be sure that all the required information is obtained from the company, and this discourages it from providing coverage to the company because of the high risk.

The fourth barrier is the risk that there is no single claim which can trigger reputational loss because the company may claim under its policy for the recovery of loss arising from any incident that the company has faced, based on the reasoning that the loss arose from reputational damage. Thus, there can be a wide range of losses for which the company can bring a recovery claim, and this leads to a high degree of uncertainty from the perspective of the insurer. The fifth barrier concerns outage, which is an issue about the uncertainty of how damage to the reputation is measured, and indeed there is no clear way to measure what a company typically suffers from loss of public trust. This is because the loss is non-monetary in the short term but becomes monetary over time. With such a high level of uncertainty, the insurer is therefore dissuaded from providing coverage. The final barrier is notice, where again there is the issue of uncertainty as reputation cannot be 'identified as an asset on the balance sheet'.[106] Thus, reputational loss is typically intangible as goodwill, and as present or future opportunities, so proof of the exact loss cannot be provided by the company. In sum, then, a company can almost certainly not be given insurance coverage for reputational risk because of these limitations.

103 See generally Robert G Eccles, Scott C Newquist, and Roland Schatz, 'Reputation and Its Risks' (2007) 85(2) Harvard Business Review 104d

104 Garry Honey, *What is Reputation Worth?: How to Protect and Enhance Value* (1st edn, Gower 2013)

105 Garry Honey, *What is Reputation Worth?: How to Protect and Enhance Value* (1st edn, Gower 2013)

106 Chartered Institute of Management Accountants (n 1197) 6

Even if it is assumed for the sake of the argument that policy coverage and recovery for reputational loss were available to the company, its risk would not be completely mitigated or transferred, as the existence of the risk is based on what Honey identified as 'trust erosion'.[107] In this sense, recovering the loss from the insurer would be a temporary solution as the 'goodwill restoration' or 'trust recovery' is unlikely to be achieved in this way.[108] Accordingly, the negative consequences of reputational loss upon the stakeholders could potentially be much harsher than regulatory and third-party litigation losses, as even conjectural insurance policy cover is unlikely to mitigate the risk for the company.

5.2.2.3.4 INSOLVENCY LOSS

The last type of loss to consider is the potential for the company to suffer insolvency arising from directors' undesirable behaviours. The risk of suffering such a loss is always upon the entity of the company, as the directors run its business, and their considerations and desires are important in its present and future life. As a consequence of the undesirable behaviour of directors, a company can suffer regulatory, litigation, and reputational losses, all of which can cause it to be unable to fulfil its financial obligations and lead to liquidation. From this view, an insolvency loss can be considered a further consequence of the company's inability to transfer or mitigate these losses through corporate tools. However, insolvency is one type of loss for which the market does not provide insurance coverage. Therefore, insurance is unlikely to be a way for stakeholders, particularly shareholders and creditors, to protect their interests.

Even if there were market coverage for insolvency loss, there would be still serious issues that limit the ability of the company to protect the interests of its stakeholders against directors' undesirable behaviours. The first issue would be the unavailability of recovery for the loss arising from directors' undesirable behaviours. An example of such a loss was witnessed in *Stone*.[109] In this case, the company went into liquidation as a result of the director's fraud which was perpetrated on the banks. Creditors on behalf of the company brought a claim against the auditors to recover the loss, but the claim was rejected on the basis that the company was personally liable. No claim was brought against insurance to recover insolvency loss, but even if there had been the personal liability of the company would automatically prevent shareholders from bringing a recovery claim against insurance.

In another scenario, assuming that the company were to obtain an insurance policy for the insolvency loss and could recover the loss from insurance, the company would still not be able to mitigate the insolvency risk of the directors' undesirable behaviours to protect the long-term interests of its stakeholders. This is because, although the recovery was for the shareholders for the loss suffered, the interests

107 Honey (n 1200)
108 Honey (n 1200)
109 (n 12)

of other stakeholders such as employees, suppliers, and consumers would be still impaired, as they would have lost their jobs, a continuing business relationship, and the opportunity to have a wider choice with fair prices in the market. Consequently, despite the negative consequences of insolvency loss being much harsher than that of other types of loss caused by directors' undesirable behaviours, insurance provides no protection remedy for the long-term interests of stakeholders.

To conclude Section 5.2.2.3, there is a wide range of risks with the undesirable behaviour of directors, and their occurrence can cause the company to suffer significant losses which it cannot recover through insurance. In the next section, the principles that set barriers to the company will be analysed.

5.3 Setting Limits to Risk Management

It has been shown that D&O insurance is limited in the extent to which it can satisfy market coverage demand and recovery claims of companies because it does not extend to mitigating risks that may arise from the undesirable behaviour of directors. It was also shown that companies typically purchase insurance for their protection when the behaviour of their directors harms their interests. However, several restrictions limit the ability of the company to recover losses that may arise from directorial undesirable behaviour. Consequently, although insurance is the last remedy for the company to mitigate the risks of undesirable behaviour, it is also inadequate to protect the interests of the company's stakeholders.

At this stage, it is pertinent that we identify the underlying factors that prevent companies from obtaining policy coverage and from making recovery. Several factors and considerations influence the determination of the insurability of the risk. As outlined by Berliner and Buhlmann, they include randomness, maximum potential loss, average loss amount per incident, average time interval between two-loss occurrences, insurance premiums, moral hazard, public policy, and legal restrictions.[110] Among these limitations, public policy and moral hazards are also the general foundations that the courts commonly consider in determining the availability of market and insurance policies for particular losses. This section will examine these considerations in order to determine the availability of recovery for insured persons, along with the principles guiding their application in insurance cases. Furthermore, within the corporate sphere, we will analyse the attribution doctrine, which assigns the actions and liabilities of directors to the company.

5.3.1 The Maxim Illegality Principle and Liability Insurance

Having policy coverage does not guarantee that all types of risks to which the insured is subjected can be covered by insurance because there are certain limitations. And although an insured person may be aware of this, he may still claim to

110 Baruch Berliner and Niklaus Buhlmann, 'Subjective Determination of Limits of Insurability on the Grounds of Strategic Planning' (1986) 11 The Geneva Papers on Risk and Insurance 94, 95

recover any loss he suffers under his/her policy. In that case, the insurer may rely on the maxim to prevent the insured from recovering the loss. And in accordance with public policy considerations, the maxim imposes certain limitations on the scope of insurance coverage that may be available in the market. Consequently, there are specific types of risks and losses for which individuals or companies may be unable to secure coverage. Before liability insurance was introduced to the insurance market, there were serious concerns about the morality of providing policy coverage for the personal liability of wrongdoers. Tunc described this as follows:

> [A]t the beginning of the nineteenth century, liability insurance would have been unthinkable. It would have been considered as immoral to take out an insurance against the consequences of civil liability as to take out one against the consequences of criminal liability.[111]

The foundation that underpins this concern was that such a policy would cause a moral hazard since 'freeing' him from liability for wrongdoing might motivate the insured to become involved in further wrongdoing. Although this approach has softened significantly, and there are liability insurance limitations that have been placed on it through the maxim and public policy, such concerns about liability insurance are minimised.

In the context of insurance, the application of the maxim arises

> where the insured has deliberately infringed the law to procure or keep the insured goods [and] public policy will prevent his recovery for their loss or damage under the policy, for otherwise the court would be assisting the insured to derive a profit from his illegal acts. When applied, the maxim operates to 'set limits to the distribution of risks and losses'.[112]

This explains how close the relationship between liability insurance and the maxim is since it has a significant role in determining the recoverability of loss in the context of insurance.

The crucial question here concerns when the maxim is triggered to prevent the insured from relying on insurance. The application of the maxim differs depending on the nature of the act with which the insured is engaged and the involvement of third-party interests in the case. In some cases, recovery can still be provided by insurance if there is a third party involved in the case, even though the insured is personally liable or if allowing him/her to recover would be contrary to public policy.[113] In this situation, the court may not consider the rationales of public policy as restrictions for the sake of protecting the interests of third parties.

111 Andre Tunc, 'An Historical and Geographical Survey of the Law of Tort' in Viktor Knapp (ed.), *International Encyclopedia of Comparative Law* (International Association of Legal Science Volume 11 1983) 50

112 Merkin and Steele (n 19) 331

113 See Section 5.2.1

In *Safeway*, the Court of Appeal highlighted the application of the maxim in a case that involved the recovery of a loss in the corporate context. In that case, although the company did not institute a direct claim against the insurer to recover the loss, it instituted an indirect claim against its defaulting directors to proceed against the directors' insurance. However the operation of the maxim served to prevent the company from passing on its personal liability to directors, which automatically prevented the recovery of the loss from insurance.[114] In the next section, the public policy basis of the maxim in general liability insurance and particular D&O insurance will be examined.

5.3.1.1 Restrictions of Public Policy

Since liability insurance became available as a mechanism for the spreading of risk liability and the mitigation of losses, the issue of moral hazards that may arise when wrongdoers are indemnified has remained a significant concern. To mitigate this potential negative outcome that may arise from the application of the maxim, public policy has often been invoked to assess whether an insured's liability can ethically be absolved through insurance. The role of public policy in the realm of liability insurance mirrors its broader function, [115] which is primarily aimed at preventing wrongdoers from making recovery for losses that arise by virtue of their misconduct. This serves to foster sufficient deterrence within society, a sentiment that was underscored by Mance J in *Total Graphics Ltd v. AGF Insurance Ltd Hence*,[116] where the court held that 'public policy creates a personal disability to recover'.[117] While the exact foundation of public policy may lack clarity, the objectives of deterrence through punishment and denying wrongdoers the benefits of their misconduct are commonly cited as fundamental principles.[118]

Nevertheless, the importance of the role of public policy on the subject of insurance has not been truly assessed, as 'most of the decisions of the courts contain little or no discussion of the effect of public policy upon insurance arrangements'.[119] However, its implications for insurance arrangements are 'profound'[120] for claims that may be instituted against insured persons by third parties or claims that insured persons may institute in order to recover losses under insurance policies. This is because 'the public policy rules for tort claims and for insurance indemnity claims are derived from the same sources'.[121]

114 See Section 5.2.2.3.1
115 See Chapter 4, Section 4.3.1
116 *Total Graphics* (n 20) 599
117 *Total Graphics* (n 20) 606
118 Merkin (n 14), *Colinvaux's Law of Insurance*, 126
119 Merkin and Steele (n 19) 333
120 Merkin and Steele (n 19) 333
121 Merkin and Steele (n 19) 335

The courts adopt three steps in determining whether public policy would be violated should a claimant be allowed to recover.[122] Firstly, they assess the gravity of the illegal conduct to see whether the claimant's wrongdoing was done intentionally or negligently. Secondly, they ask whether allowing the enforcement of the insurance contract would spur other persons to engage in illegal conduct. Lastly, the courts consider the negative effect of not awarding a recovery, not only on victims but also on society. These three steps demonstrate that the determination is based on the need to balance the twin protections of the rationales of public policy and the interests of third-party victims.[123]

When an insured party claims for recovery under an insurance policy, the court will be initially inclined to enforce the terms of the insurance contract. But when it considers other issues, such as the need to protect public policy by preventing an insured person from benefitting from his/her illegality, and the need to cater to the interests of other innocent parties, the court may retreat from this approach. This consequently gives rise to a requirement that risks covered by insurance should be consistent with the rationale of public policy. The logic behind this approach is that insurance should not offend the public conscience.[124]

We have now established that the maxim is routinely applied to prevent the enforcement of illegal transactions. The crucial question to ask is, 'where does that leave the parties?'[125] There are two approaches to this issue. The first seeks to place the parties in the position that they would have been in if the transaction had not occurred by seeking to reverse the consequences of the transaction. This is the approach adopted in France.[126] The second approach seeks to disable the right-holder from seeking a remedy and usually 'leaves the loss to lie where it falls', which is to say that 'the past consequences of the transaction are left undisturbed'.[127] This is the approach adopted in England. The logic of this approach is based on the fact that historically, English law frowned at providing aid to wrongdoers and views it as being inconsistent with the dignity of the courts.[128]

In England, this rigid rule has gradually evolved to become more flexible over the years. For instance, initially, insuring a person for their legal liability for causing harm to others and insuring against the risk of business profit loss due to fire were deemed immoral and improper; these two forms of insurance have since become integral sectors within the insurance industry.[129] The rationale behind this flexibility lies in the recognition that determinations regarding which risks are covered and which are not can vary based on the type of insurance in question and the specific circumstances of each case. Emphasising this point, Lord Mustill noted

122 Hodgin (n 33) 144
123 See Section 5.2.1
124 DS Hansell, *Introduction to Insurance* (2nd edn, Lloyd's of London Press 1999) 15
125 Lord Sumption, 'Reflections on the Law of Illegality' (2012) 20 Restitution Law Review 1, 3
126 Lord Sumption, 'Reflections on the Law of Illegality' (2012) 20 Restitution Law Review 3
127 Lord Sumption, 'Reflections on the Law of Illegality' (2012) 20 Restitution Law Review 3–4
128 Lord Sumption, 'Reflections on the Law of Illegality' (2012) 20 Restitution Law Review 3–4
129 Hansell (n 124) 15

that although the 'general principles of insurance law should be the same wherever they are applied, the overlay of public policy entails that the actual decisions may well differ from time to time and place to place'.[130] Similarly, in *James v. British General Ins Co Ltd*,[131] Roche J echoed the same thoughts when he noted that 'the principles of public policy, which I suppose are only a branch of the principles of ethics, are themselves unchanging, but their applications may be infinitely various from time to time and from place to place'.[132]

In essence, there are still certain risks for which recovery may not be provided by insurance as doing so would be contrary to public policy.[133] Having different implications of public policy in insurance law is usually based on one question of whether insurance protects third-party victims or insured persons. This is because if the protection of the victim's third party is considered, the court will be less concerned about the preventative measures of public policy for the sake of protecting such victims. In the contrary scenario, if allowing an insured person to recover his/her loss is subject to a case, the considerations of public policy are strictly applied to prevent the wrongdoing insured from recovery.[134]

Such consideration is also valid in the context of D&O insurance. This insurance is a type of optional liability insurance that aims to protect the insured directors and company,[135] and considerations of public policy are strictly involved in D&O insurance cases, bringing rigid exclusions to policy coverage. In general terms, 'the primary insuring words will refer to claims for actual or alleged breach of contract, misstatement, breach of trust, breach of duty, act, neglect, error, omission, breach of warranty of authority or wrongful trading';[136] however, certain exclusions are still specified under D&O insurance.

According to Merkin, these exclusions can be separated into two categories.[137] The first category pertains to insurance policy exclusions, which typically encompass legal liabilities stemming from deliberate, wilful, or wrongful acts, as well as fraud, dishonesty, criminal activity, wrongful trading, and intentional insider dealing.[138] In the second category, regardless of whether there are other exclusions expressly stated along these lines, public policy may confine the types of wrongful acts for which recovery is possible. Deliberate criminal acts and intentional acts causing a loss to the third party can be examples of such exclusions.

Although these exceptions should be assessed under the two different categories, the basis that underlies them is arguably the same, which is the protection of

130 M Mustill, 'Fault and Marine Losses' [1988] LMCLQ 310, 320
131 *James* (n 32) 311
132 *James* (n 32) 322
133 Hansell (n 124) 15
134 See Section 5.2.1
135 See Sections 5.2.2.1 and 5.2.2.2
136 Jess (n 4) 228
137 Merkin (n 14) *Colinvaux's Law of Insurance*, 724
138 In spite of these preclusions of D&O insurance, defence cost is still available for directors to recover from insurance. See Merkin (n 14) *Colinvaux's Law of Insurance*, 724

public policy. As such, the exclusion of insurance coverage in the first category relies on public policy because preventing insured directors from relying upon their illegality remains the primary rationale underlying public policy.[139] As such, allowing recovery by an insured director engaged in any acts under this category would be contrary to the objectives of public policy. Thus, public policy can be considered as the major obstacle that limits the ability of directors to seek indemnification through insurance.

Considerations of public policy may also arise when a company seeks to make a recovery by claiming against its directors' insurance policies for the loss it has suffered due to directors' undesirable behaviours. Regulatory, reputational, and insolvency losses are types of losses that markets will not cover. In addition, losses from punitive damages have never been provided for by the market. In essence, market coverage is available for the loss of compensatory damages, but a company is unlikely to recover such loss from directors' insurance if it is found personally liable for directors' behaviours. It is typically prevented from attributing the risk of loss to directors or their insurance based on the objectives of public policy.[140]

To justify the application of public policy in the area of insurance law, two main rationales are often referred to in case law. They include achieving deterrence through punishment and maintaining the integrity of the courts by preventing wrongdoers from benefitting from their wrongs (the no-benefit rule).[141]

5.3.1.1.1 MAINTAINING DETERRENCE

The first rationale of achieving deterrence is aimed at preventing an insured person who has been convicted of illegal conduct from relying on his/her illegality to recover the loss he/she suffered from the insurer. By relying on punishment, it aims to discourage not only the wrongdoer but also potential wrongdoers from becoming involved in similar illegality in future. This rationale of public policy is very important in determining the availability of recovery to the insured because, as Clarke stated, 'non-enforcement of insurance is said to help to deter crime'.[142] This point was also emphasised by Bugra and Merkin, who stated that the 'loss of the entirety of an insurance claim where part of it is fraudulent is simply one means to achieve the aim of deterrence'.[143]

The case of *Gray v. Barr*[144] is a well-known example where this rule was applied to insurance. In that case, Barr (B) suspected that his wife was having an affair with Gray (G), and he went to G's home with a loaded shotgun, which fired accidentally, and G was killed. G's widow brought a damages claim against B for his manslaughter, and it was awarded. B claimed a recovery under his insurance

139 See Merkin (n 14) 'Motor and Other Liability Insurance' 282
140 See Section 5.2.2.3
141 See Clarke (n 37) 759–763
142 Clarke (n 37) 759
143 Aysegul Bugra and Rob Merkin, '"Fraud" and Fraudulent Claims' (2012) 125 The Journal of the British Insurance Law Association 3, 9
144 [1971] 2 QB 554

policy for the loss he suffered resulting from his liability to the widow. The court held that he could not recover such a loss from the insurer as his insurance policy only covered the accidents, and the manslaughter was not regarded as an accident. Salmon LJ indicated that,

> Crimes of violence, particularly when committed with loaded guns, are amongst the worst curses of this age. It is very much in the public interest that they should be deterred . . . no one who threatens unlawful violence with a loaded gun should be allowed to enforce a claim for indemnity against any liability he may incur as a result of having so acted. I do not intend to lay down any wider proposition.[145]

Although the defendant had only intended to frighten the victim, he was still found guilty of manslaughter as he had carried a gun to the victim's house, making his act deliberate and wilful. The outcome of that case served to send a deterrence message to insured persons that they would have no recourse to recovery from insurance where they deliberately indulge in wrongdoing.[146] Therefore, based on the deterrence objective of public policy, the court considered 'the necessity of deterring him and others from doing the same thing again, to reform him and, in cases such as this, to make him and others more careful in their dealings'.[147] The logic behind this approach is that providing recovery for such a criminal or tortious act 'would be productive of great evil if the courts were to encourage such an engagement as this and thereby hold out an inducement to the propagation of illegal and unfounded charges'.[148]

The deterrence objective of public policy is also a major consideration in D&O insurance. It can be a significant barrier that can limit a company's ability to recover the loss from undesirable behaviour from insurance if it is found liable for the acts of its directors. In this case, the court typically considers that allowing a company to recover the loss would undermine the deterrence objective of public policy, and it should rather be punished by depriving it of recovery. This objective was one of the underlying reasons that the Court of Appeal referred to in the judgement of *Safeway*. Since the company was found liable and the court was aware of the fact that it was seeking to recover the loss from the insurer, its claim against its directors was rejected. Pill LJ argued that,

> Only if the undertaking itself bears the responsibilities and meets the consequences of their non-observance are the public protected. A deterrent effect is contemplated and the obligation to provide effective preventive measures is upon the undertaking itself.[149]

145 [1971] 2 QB 554 [581]
146 Merkin and Steele (n 19) 357
147 *Askey v. Golden Wine Co Ltd* (1948) 64 TLR 379 [380]
148 *Shackell v. Rosier* (1836) 2 Bing NC 634 [648] per Park J
149 *Safeway* (n 73) 1472

It was considered that if the company should be allowed to recover the loss from insurance, it and other companies would be encouraged to become involved in further illegal behaviour to increase their value.

5.3.1.1.2 THE RULE OF NO BENEFIT

The rule of no benefit is the second objective of public policy which aims to prevent an insured person from profiting from his illegality.[150] This rationale is also the second basis that underlies the non-enforcement of some insurance policies. Two considerations underpin the public policy. The first is that compensating a claimant for his illegality would damage 'public notions of the fair distribution of resources'.[151] The second is that 'preserv[ing] the dignity of the courts and the reputations of the legal system' by not 'enforc[ing] any right in law under the insurance'.[152]

Reference to this rule can be seen in several insurance cases. For example, on the basis of this rationale, a person seeking professional indemnity cannot recover the losses that he suffers as a result of his/her fraud or illegality. In addition, in product liability insurance, a claim instituted by a seller who supplies defective or dangerous goods will also be precluded from recovery. This objective of public policy was aptly captured by Lord Macmillan in *Beresford v. Royal Insurance Co. Ltd*,[153] who stated that as a matter of public polity,' no court ought to assist a criminal to derive benefit from his crime'.[154] In addition, Pearson L.J. in *Hardy v. Motor Insurers Bureau*[155] opined that,

> There is a principle of public policy that an insured person cannot recover an indemnity from his insurers in respect of the consequences of the insured person's own intentional criminal act. If he were allowed to do so, he would be reaping the fruits of his own crime and profiting by his own wrong, and that is contrary to public policy.[156]

This objective was also demonstrated in the court's reasoning in *Geismar v. Sun Alliance and London Insurance Ltd.*[157] In that case, the claimant imported items of jewellery without paying the required excise duty. The items of jewellery were stolen from his house, and he sought to recover the loss from the insurer. The claim was rejected, and Talbot J stated that,

> where there is a deliberate breach of the law I do not think that the court ought to assist the plaintiff to derive a profit from it, even though it is sought indirectly through an indemnity under an insurance policy.[158]

150 For general application of this rationale, See Chapter 4, Section 4.3.1.2
151 [2009] UKHL 33; [2009] 1 A.C. 1339
152 Merkin and Steele (n 19) 760
153 [1938] A.C. 586
154 (n 154) [603]
155 [1964] 2 Q.B. 745, CA
156 [1964] 2 Q.B. 745, CA [762]
157 [1977] Q.B. 383
158 [1977] Q.B. 383 [395]

The rule has also been applied in D&O insurance cases. In *Safeway*, for instance, a defaulting company which sought to benefit from its illegality was prevented from proceeding against its directors and their insurance since that would have been contrary to the benefit notion of public policy if the company had been so allowed. Although there was no direct reference to this rationale, the court indirectly considered it while the deterrence objective was emphasised because the court was aware that allowing the company to recover the loss would allow it to benefit from its illegality, thus undermining the integrity of the court.

In sum, to determine the availability of market and policy coverages, the maxim relies largely on public policy and its two rationales of deterrence, as well as the no-benefit rule, which is routinely used to bar insured persons from making recovery for losses that arise as a result of their wrongs. These policy objectives also form the basis for barring companies from making recovery for losses that arise from the undesirable behaviour of directors where they are found liable for the wrong of their directors as a result of corporate attribution. And it is the role of the latter in insurance which will be examined in the next section.

5.3.2 The Doctrine of Corporate Attribution

Besides the application of the maxim and public policy to the company's recovery claim, there is also the doctrine of corporate attribution, which also impacts the company's ability to recover losses through insurance. The doctrine attributes the acts or intentions of directors on companies as a result; the latter are made to bear liability for their actions. However it allows companies to claim recovery from defaulting directors or from their insurance as long as the company itself is not held personally liable for the wrong.[159] In support of this, Merkin and Steele stated that

> An organisation which faces liability for the acts of an employee or agent may seek indemnification from tortfeasor or insurers unless the employee/agent is the alter ego of the organisation, or the organisation has condoned or participated in the conduct of the employee/agent.[160]

The underlying foundation of this approach is deterrence and the no-benefit rationales of public policy, which seek to prevent any wrongdoer who is personally liable for his/her own act from making a recovery. Such prevention may make sense on its face, but it may cause harsh consequences in terms of the ability of the company to protect the long-term interests of its stakeholders by recovering the loss caused by the directors' undesirable behaviours.

The main issue is that in directing companies, directors are conferred with extensive powers. And for this reason, they are usually seen as the 'managing agents' of companies.[161] With very limited exception, they are usually considered the mind of

159 See Chapter 4, Section 4.2
160 Merkin and Steele (n 19) 334–335
161 *Re Faure Electric Accumulator Co.* (1888) 40 Ch. D. 141 [151]

the company, and their liability is likely to be attributed to it even though they do not act as part of the board.[162]

This issue was witnessed in *Safeway*.[163] Although there were a number of considerations regarding how UK competition law viewed the company as the primary wrongdoer in this case, the reasoning of the identification doctrine, which was the main focus of the court in *Stone*, also influenced the court's approach in that case, and the company was consequently precluded from recovery based on its perceived personal liability.[164]

In this respect, the doctrine of corporate attribution is the first step in analysing the ability of companies to recover losses through insurance because when a company is found liable for the acts of its directors, it will still be barred from making recovery on the basis of public policy. In this respect, Bugra and Merkin argued that

> if the controller of a company deliberately sets fire to the company's property, the doctrine of attribution will treat the acts of the controller as if they were the acts of the company, thereby depriving other shareholders of the benefits of the policy.[165]

This is because the company is considered to be directly liable for the acts of its directors, and the deterrence and no-benefit rule of public policy would be undermined if it were allowed to recover losses.

But when we consider the judgement of the Supreme Court in *Bilta*, we may come to a different position. Recall that in that case, the court found the company vicariously liable despite the fact that the directors, who were involved in fraud, were its directing mind and will. The company was thus allowed to recover losses from its directors and other defendants. This decision may be considered as opening the door to companies to recover losses from insurance. But this outcome is based on the fraud exception, which is not applicable to a case that involves directors' undesirable behaviours. The behaviours usually involve fraud perpetrated on a third party or regulatory infringements, which are usually attributed to companies. Therefore, the outcome of the case may not be considered as a reference to a company's ability to recover through insurance the losses it suffers by virtue of its directors' undesirable behaviours.

Taking a contrary position, Davidson opines that the application of attribution for liability purposes and the application of attribution for insurance purposes may differ. This is because although dishonesty, fraud, or an omission of a single director would be attributed to the company for liability purposes, the situation will

162 See Chapter 4, Section 4.2
163 (n 2)
164 See Chapter 4, Section 4.2.2.2
165 Bugra and Merkin (n 143) 10

not validate the attribution of his liability to the company for insurance purposes, unless all the directors of the company were collectively involved.[166] He asserted that there will be a number of cases in which directors' conduct may be attributed to a company for liability purposes, whereas the same conduct may not be attributed to it for insurance purposes.[167] This argument, however, is not without serious drawbacks in terms of the company's ability to mitigate the risks of undesirable behaviour.

Firstly, such an application of attribution may be valid when the company makes a direct claim against an insurer to recover the loss. However, the company may obtain policy coverage for regulatory loss, loss of punitive damages, insolvency loss, and reputational loss caused by directors' undesirable behaviour. When the loss caused when compensatory damages is imposed, the company will not be able to make an indirect claim against directors' insurance for a recovery because, when the rules of attribution are applied to it, it would be personally liable for a claim instituted by a third party against it and its directors for the loss he suffers as a result of the directors' undesirable behaviours. This is because, following the third party claim, the personal liability on the parts of the company and directors must be initially determined before the recovery claim can be brought against insurance. Based on the nature of the directors' undesirable behaviours, the company is likely to be regarded as being involved in the conduct personally, and it would be prevented from recovery by the maxim based on public policy.

Secondly, even assuming that the fraud perpetrated by the directors on the third party was not to be attributed to the company for insurance purposes, this would not mean that the company can recover the loss it has suffered from directors' insurance, as the basis of the claim would be directors' fraud, and this is commonly excluded in D&O insurance. The insurer would refuse to provide recovery on the basis of public policy. Thirdly, again even assuming that recovery is available, the company would still not be able to mitigate through insurance all types of risk and recover all types of loss caused by directors' undesirable behaviours as the extent of this conduct is limited to fraud perpetrated on third parties. Even in this scenario, regulatory loss, reputational loss, and insolvency loss would still remain with the company.

To summarise, the personal liability of the company which arises as a result of the doctrine of corporate attribution underlies the application of the maxim for the prevention of recovery claims that may be instituted by a company against its directors with the intention of pursuing their insurance. Consequently, neither the maxim nor the doctrine of corporate attribution covers the consideration of the protection of the long-term interests of stakeholders, as their joint operation impairs the ability of the company to mitigate the risk of losses caused by directors' undesirable behaviours.

166 Davidson (n 78) 69–70
167 Davidson (n 78) 69–70

5.4 Suggestions for Further Development

Relying exclusively on the maxim in order to determine the availability of market and policy coverage may result in the disregard of other policy considerations which underlie a particular subject of law. In respect of a company's recovery claims, the doctrine of attribution also does not have a distinctive application for insurance purposes other than for liability. This gives rise to the question of whether these principles should have different applications in the context of D&O insurance.

When directors engage in undesirable behaviour, the companies they manage may suffer severe losses. For example, they may not have access to market coverage or loss recovery. Furthermore, while market coverage may be available for third-party litigation loss, recovery is not, and the market does not provide policy coverage for regulatory, insolvency, or reputational losses. This illustrates the inadequacy of insurance law in recognising the serious negative consequences of directors' undesirable behaviours on the long-term interests of stakeholders. The issue that then arises is whether D&O insurance should have policy considerations for stakeholder protection to take into account situations when a company seeks to obtain policy coverage or institute a recovery claim for losses that were caused by directors' undesirable behaviour. This is based on the fact that different types of insurance have different considerations to determine the availability of the market and policy coverage for particular loss, and therefore D&O insurance should be developed in such a way as to widen the considerations regarding the relationship between the company and directors.

In order to develop the law in a much more nuanced way, the cases of *Bilta*, *Patel*, and *Lancashire County Council* can be taken as references. In respect of the application of corporate attribution in D&O insurance, the approach adopted by the court in *Bilta* may underlie the foundation of the distinctive approach which should be adopted when a company brings a recovery claim for the loss caused by directors' undesirable behaviours. This is because the outcome of the case illustrates the court's recognition of how harmful the directors' behaviours were for the company, and consequently the claim was allowed. A similar approach which recognises individual accountability and allows the company to recover loss could be introduced in D&O insurance by establishing a policy consideration for stakeholder protection against the adverse consequences of directorial actions.

In addition, the unavailability of market and policy coverage to companies is usually determined by the maxim, which relies purely on the rationales of public policy. The question that arises is whether there should be a different application of the maxim to the concept of D&O insurance, rather than providing an automatic response to the company's demand to have policy coverage and its recovery claims for losses. The maxim works differently with different concepts, for example in marine insurance and liability insurance, and it can also have different applications in D&O insurance by taking into account specific policy considerations, such as the protection of the long-term interests of stakeholders against directorial actions.

With respect to the suggested application of the maxim in D&O insurance, *Patel* could be taken as a reference for the development of a different approach to the application of the maxim to a company's recovery claim.[168] In this case, in departing from previous case law, the court went further from *Hounga*, which solely relied on public policy considerations, by widening the scope of the maxim to other policy considerations that underlie the unjust enrichment law. This more nuanced approach can therefore serve as the foundation for applying the maxim in D&O insurance regarding company recovery claims for losses stemming from directors' undesirable behaviours, with a focus on protecting stakeholders.

This widened policy consideration was also seen in *Lancashire County Council*. Although there was no market coverage provided for the loss of punitive damages, the Council obtained a policy which explicitly covered the losses that arose from punitive damages. In addition, as a response to the recovery claim for punitive damages by the Council, the court considered the negative consequences of preventing the Council from recovering upon the public and allowed the Council to recover. The case is therefore a significant development as the Council was not only allowed to have policy coverage for punitive damages, but it was also able to recover the loss caused by such damages. The court took into account other policy considerations, such as the possible higher taxes that the public would have to pay, rather than giving an automatic response that the recovery for punitive damages is never available based on the maxim. When it is considered that the recovery for loss of punitive damages is not available to companies, and they may not even arguably obtain policy coverage for such a loss, *Lancashire County Council* could be the foundation of a new approach that takes into account other policy considerations such as stakeholder protection when the company demands market coverage or brings a recovery claim for punitive damages. In short, despite the current regime failing to take into account the policy consideration of stakeholder protection, the awareness and understanding that these cases have brought should shape the way in which these developments are taken further.

5.5 Concluding Remarks

This chapter has examined the insurance sector's response to the company's insurance policy demand and recovery claims for losses arising from directors' undesirable behaviours. The question which was addressed was whether the company could mitigate the risks of undesirable behaviour through liability insurance—the risks by directors for the purpose of protecting the long-term interests of stakeholders. The chapter outlined the foundations of liability insurance as they determine the availability of market and policy coverage in general liability insurance, and one of its types, which is D&O insurance. It analysed how liability insurance and D&O insurance operate in practice and the considerations that are usually taken into account when the company demands policy coverage or brings a claim to directors' insurance to recover the loss it has suffered due to undesirable behaviour. The conclusion reached in the chapter is that neither market coverage nor policy

168 For further discussions, see Chapter 4, Sections 4.3.1.3 and 4.3.1.4

coverage is available to the company for the losses it may suffer due to undesirable behaviour by directors, and it is not consequently able to mitigate the risks of undesirable behaviour through insurance.

In order to reach this conclusion, the chapter initially examined how liability insurance operates in practice by considering the question of whether the aim is to protect a third-party victim or the insured. The same question was also analysed in the concept of D&O insurance, and it was determined that the company and directors are protected by insurance. This finding gave rise to the concern that insurance actually protects the company by allowing it to mitigate the risks of undesirable behaviour.

Based on the four types of risks of undesirable behaviour identified in Chapter 2,[169] four types of losses were identified, and it was ascertained whether market coverage for these losses is available. Where available, the chapter considered whether the policy coverage obtained by a company could provide recovery for them. Although a company can arguably bring a claim against directors' insurance for third-party litigation loss, recovery is not available for such loss caused by directors' undesirable behaviours. On the other hand, market coverage for regulatory, reputational, and insolvency losses is also not available for the company to purchase. Accordingly, insurance leaves the loss where it falls.

Public policy is the major underlying foundation of liability insurance regarding the determination of the availability of market and policy coverage, and the maxim is involved in insurance claim cases to protect the objectives of public policy. These objectives may be put aside by the courts when the interest of a victim third party rather than that of a wrongdoing insured is to be protected; however, these objectives are strictly applied when an insured brings a recovery claim to prevent him/her from benefitting from his/her wrongdoing for the sake of maintaining the desired deterrence in society.

The company, as the insured under a D&O policy, potentially encounters such obstacles when it demands market coverage or brings a recovery claim against directors' insurance for the loss arising from undesirable behaviour by directors. This is because the company is usually considered personally liable for the acts of its directors through the doctrine of corporate attribution. Moreover, the maxim and public policy prevent it from recovering, as otherwise, the company would benefit from its wrongdoing.

The application of the maxim in corporate cases does not differ from its application in cases that involve individuals. It prevents the company from obtaining policy coverage for itself and recovery from directors' insurance without considering policy considerations regarding its particular relationship with directors, such as the impairment of the long-term interests of stakeholders by directorial actions. This may be because of the 'imprecise' nature of the maxim.[170] The application of this principle is to protect public policy, but it prevents the company from mitigating

169 See Chapter 2, Section 2.3
170 Merkin and Steele (n 19) 329

the risks of directors' undesirable behaviours through insurance. It can, therefore, be argued that 'denials of insurance coverage based on broad principles and exhortations to public policy gradually but surely fail'.[171] Despite this deficiency of law, there have been some developments to recognise other policy considerations underlying the law in the cases of *Bilta*, *Patel*, and *Lancashire County Council*, and for a more nuanced application of the maxim, public policy, and corporate attribution, approaches adopted by the courts in these cases should be followed to develop the law further.

Bibliography

* This chapter was originally published in Samet Caliskan, 'Managing the Risk of Directors' Wrongful Conduct Through D&O Insurance' (2019) The Journal of British Insurance Law Association 43 and Samet Caliskan, 'Mitigating Risk Through D&O Insurance: Assessing the Role of Illegality Defence and Corporate Attribution' (2019) The Journal of British Insurance Law Association 67

Baker T, 'Liability Insurance at Tort-Crime Boundary' in David M Engel and Michael McCann (eds), *Fault Lines – Tort Law as a Cultural Practice* (Stanford University Press 2009) 66

Baker T and Griffith SJ, *Ensuring Corporate Misconduct: How Liability Insurance Undermines Shareholder Litigation* (1st edn, The University of Chicago Press 2010)

Bathurst TF, 'Insurance Law – A View From the Bench' (2013) 3

Berliner B and Buhlmann N, 'Subjective Determination of Limits of Insurability on the Grounds of Strategic Planning' (1986) 11 The Geneva Papers on Risk and Insurance 94

Boop G, 'Directors and Officers Insurance' (2016)

Bugra A and Merkin R, '"Fraud" and Fraudulent Claims' (2012) 125 The Journal of the British Insurance Law Association 3

Cane P, *Responsibility in Law and Morality* (1st edn, Hart Publishing 2002) 242

Clarke MA, *The Law of Insurance Contracts* (5th edn, Informa 2006) 578

Clarke MA, *The Law of Liability Insurance* (1st edn, Informa 2014) 15

Core JE, 'On the Corporate Demand for Directors' and Officer's Insurance' (1997) 64(1) The Journal of Risk and Insurance 84

Cotchett JW and Molumphy MC, 'Punitive Damages: How Much Is Enough?' (1998) 20(1) Civil Litigation Reporter

Fleming JG, 'Insurance for the Criminal' (1971) 34 MLR 176

Hall BD, 'The Validity of Insurance Coverage for Punitive Damages: An Unresolved Question? (1973) 4 New Mexico Law Review 65

Hansell DS, *Introduction to Insurance* (2nd edn, Lloyd's of London Press 1999)

Honey G, *What is Reputation Worth?: How to Protect and Enhance Value* (1st edn, Gower 2013)

Jess DC, *The Insurance of Commercial Risks: Law and Practice* (3rd edn, Sweet Maxwell 2001) 466

Kirman I, 'Directors' and Officers' Insurance' (2009)

LaCroix K, 'Executive Protection: Private Company D&O Insurance' (2010)

Long JD, 'Punitive Damages: An Unsettled Doctrine' (1975) 25 Drake Law Review 870

MacMinn RD, 'Insurance and Corporate Risk Management' (1987) 54(4) Insurance and Corporate Risk Management 658

Mayers D and Smith CW, 'On the Corporate Demand for Insurance' (1982) 55(2) The Journal of Business 281

171 Baker (n 7) 68

McNeely MC, 'Illegality as a Factor in Liability Insurance' (1941) 41 Columbia Law Review 26
Merkin R, *Colinvaux's Law of Insurance* (8th edn, Sweet & Maxwell 2006) 687
Merkin R, 'Motor and Other Liability Insurance' in Robert Merkin (ed.), *Insurance Law: An Introduction* (1st edn, Informa 2007) 275
Mustill M, 'Fault and Marine Losses' [1988] LMCLQ 310
O'Sullivan N, 'The Demand for Directors' and Officers' Insurance by Large UK Companies' (2000) 20(5) European Management Journal 574
Paolini A and Nambisan D, *Directors' and Officer's Liability Insurance* (1st edn, Informa 2008) 60
Parsons C, 'Directors' and Officers' Liability Insurance: A Target of a Shield' (2000) 21(3) Comp Law 77
Parsons C, 'Managerial Liability, Risk and Insurance: An International View' (2001) 3(1) ICCLJ 1
Schwartz GT, 'The Ethics and the Economics of Tort Liability Insurance' (1989) 75 Cornell Law Review 312
Stoll H, 'Penal Purposes in the Law of Tort' (1970) 18(1) The American Journal of Comparative Law 3
Tunc A, 'An Historical and Geographical Survey of the Law of Tort' in Viktor Knapp (ed.), *International Encyclopedia of Comparative Law* (International Association of Legal Science Volume 11 1983) 50
Wagner G, 'Tort Law and Liability Insurance' in Michael Faure (ed.), *Tort Law and Economics* (2nd edn, Cheltenham 2009) 377
Williams G, 'The Aims of the Law of Tort' (1951) 4(1) Current Legal Problems 137
Youngman I, *Directors' and Officers' Liability Insurance: A Guide to International Practice* (2nd edn, Woodhead 1999)

6 Conclusion

6.1 Introduction

This book has undertaken a comprehensive examination of the cumulative impact of various legal frameworks on the relationship between a company and its directors, particularly in the context of the company's exposure to liability and loss due to directors' undesirable behaviours. It has illuminated a broad spectrum of risks that the company is exposed to and the adverse implications of these risks for safeguarding the long-term interests of stakeholders. This concluding chapter not only summarises the research findings and developments but also highlights the comprehensive nature of the book and its overall contribution to the literature.

6.2 Summary of Findings and Developments

The main focus of the book was to ascertain the nature of the cumulative impact of different aspects of the law on the relationship between the company and directors and the ability of the former to protect the long-term interests of stakeholders against the risks of undesirable behaviour by directors. In order to answer this question, the following research questions were raised:

- To what extent can a company control its directors by the employment of internal and external legal mechanisms?
- To what extent can a company hold its directors to account for regulatory infringements and sanctions that it may face when its directors engage in anti-competitive behaviour?
- To what extent can a company transfer the risks that may arise when directors engage in undesirable behaviour?
- Can the company mitigate the risks of undesirable behaviour by directors through standard commercial risk management tools, such as insurance?

We conclude by noting that the cumulative operation of corporate governance, company law, competition law, tort law, and insurance law not only exposes companies to the risk of liability and loss that may arise when directors engage in undesirable behaviour but also debars them from attributing and ascribing such risks to

DOI: 10.4324/9781003461562-6

directors through legal mechanisms. In addition, it debars them from mitigating risks by relying on risk management tools.

Each of the aforementioned mechanisms do not adequately recognise the importance of individual accountability for the sake of maintaining good corporate practices. The result is that the risk of liability and loss largely remains with the company, whose risk exposure continues to have long-term consequences for stakeholders. Despite the significant and positive developments that illustrate a departure from the usual approach, the law still does not adequately recognise the harmful consequences of directors' undesirable behaviours on the long-term interests of stakeholders. Thus, it is imperative that reforms be introduced in this regard.

For example, the introduction of individual sanctions for competition law infringements is a significant development when it is considered that the approach of solely targeting the company through administrative fines has remained inadequate. However, these sanctions are not effective, as they have been very rarely implemented, nor do they remove the primary risk of liability and loss from the company. Also, the approach of the court in *Bilta* illustrates that the doctrine of attribution has certain considerations that recognise how harmful the fraudulent behaviour of directors can be for the company, in a departure from its usual application. In addition, *Patel* is also a promising development because it demonstrates that the maxim illegality defence can have a more nuanced approach by taking into account other policy considerations that underlie the law alongside considerations of public policy. Lastly, *Lancashire County Council* establishes that, depending on the circumstances, market and policy coverages for the loss of punitive damages can be available. All these developments demonstrate that the law has started recognising the different considerations that may have different implications in different areas rather than applying a mechanical approach that provides the same response to cases with distinctive facts. However, the law still does not consider the particular policy objectives of protecting the long-term interests of stakeholders when directors are involved in a transaction that benefits the company in the short term but exposes it to the risk of liability and loss in the long term. The notion of the company protecting its stakeholders against the consequences of directorial misbehaviour is an important theme, but this is not expressly recognised by the law. However, if the law expressly recognises this notion, all these smaller positive developments could be united and placed in the context of the broader policy theme.

6.3 Review of the Book

The absence of personal liability on the part of directors cannot potentially constrain them from entering into illegal transactions which are beneficial to the company in the short term, but which expose it to the risk of liability and loss in the long term. The mechanisms a company can employ to control its directors have significant limitations, making it unlikely that they will effectively deter directors from engaging in undesirable behaviour. As such, the company remains exposed to the risk of regulatory sanctions where its directors engage in anti-competitive behaviour on its behalf. Where this occurs, the company, not the directors, bears liability and suffers losses, although it may eventually seek to attribute and ascribe the same to its directors. The issue is that in such cases, the company is often held to be directly liable for the losses of its directors' actions and is thus prevented from passing these on. The last remedy that the company can invoke is to seek recovery of its losses through insurance, but its ability to do so is again limited due to the barriers placed on its path by the maxim, public policy, and the doctrine of corporate attribution. Accordingly, the general conclusion that the research has reached is that the risk of liability and loss arising from directors' undesirable behaviours remains with the company, and this substantially threatens the long-term interests of stakeholders, even though these are supposed to be taken into account by directors when running the company's business.

The book started by exploring the company's separate personality and the veil-piercing exception.[1] It was shown that while the company has a separate personality through which it can be held directly liable for the acts of its directors, the latter can still be held accountable for acts carried out on its behalf if the courts determine that it is appropriate to pierce the corporate veil. Directorial accountability is an important mechanism for the maintenance of compliance with the rules of law. For one, the possibility of bearing liability for their actions deters them from infringing the law. Even at that, the courts rarely pierce the corporate veil because, to do so, certain factors have to be established. Consequently, there are few situations in which directors are held personally liable for their actions on behalf of the company. This lack of accountability increases the likelihood of directors engaging in undesirable behaviour.

This finding raises a concern about whose interests directors actually consider. Their undesirable behaviour may seemingly benefit the shareholders in the short run by increasing the company's value, but such behaviour would be detrimental to the long-term interests of its other stakeholders by exposing the company to liability and loss over time. For this purpose, Chapter 2 emphasised the need to protect the long-term interests of the company's stakeholders. It categorised two types of decisions that the directors may take in the course of advancing the company's commercial interests. They are directors' personal enrichment and excessive risk-taking. Excessive risk-taking was further subcategorised as directors' commercial judgements and directorial behaviour that put the company at risk of regulatory action, resulting in liability and losses. The last type of behaviour was introduced as an inherently illegal 'undesirable behaviour that increases the value of the company in the short term but exposes it to a number of risks, such as regulatory risk, third-party litigation risk, reputational risk, and insolvency risk in the long term'.[2]

Directors' self-enrichment is commonly recognised as a primarily harmful behaviour designed to enrich the directors at the expense of the company and its

1 See Chapter 1, Section 1.2
2 See Chapter 2, Section 2.3

constituents. However, it is our position that academic research has not focused on the type of undesirable behaviour identified in this research in the same way that self-enrichment has. Even at that, the same can be as harmful (or arguably even more) in the consideration of how detrimental it is to the long-term interests of stakeholders.[3]

The potential significant loss that arises from the occurrence of these four types of risk gave rise to the question of how the company disciplines its directors so as to deter them from engaging in such behaviour. In that regard we identified a number of control mechanisms that can be exercised by a company's internal and external constituents. They include the authority of directors, directors' duties and remedies, NEDs, auditors, market control, disclosure requirements, Corporate Governance Codes, and shareholders.[4]

The research has shown that these mechanisms have serious drawbacks which decrease their deterrent effectiveness on directors in terms of involvement in undesirable behaviour, whereas there are fewer limitations on controlling and monitoring the directors when the issue is the director's bad performance or self-enrichment. This is because two major groups of stakeholders, the shareholders and investors, usually employ their controlling power when directors use the company for personal benefit or the company is not financially performing well. This distinctive nature of undesirable behaviour, which may satisfy the short-term interests of shareholders and investors, harms the long-term interests of stakeholders.

In respect of directors' authority to bind the company, individual directors or employees delegated by the director can enter into a binding transaction on behalf of the company and, in case of conflict, the statute tends to protect the interests of the third party rather than the company. To avoid being bound by the transaction, the company can assert that the third party is not in good faith; however, the statute assumes good faith on the part of the third party and the burden to prove the contrary is upon the company. This causes a lack of personal accountability on the part of directors, whereas it exposes the company to the risk of liability and loss. The second limitation is regarding remedies, which are not either as effective as they are supposed to be, or available to be imposed on directors. This potentially decreases the deterrent effect of duties as the negative consequences of a breach of these duties may not be taken seriously by directors. Regarding NEDs and auditors as external control mechanisms, their involvement in the management of the company may impair their independence, which hinders their ability to deliver impartial and unbiased judgement on the way in which directors manage the company. Another externally exercised mechanism is market control through takeover. The limitation of this mechanism is that its process can be interrupted by directors by employing resistance tactics against the potential bidder. Even assuming that these tactics were not available to directors to employ, this mechanism would still not have the desired deterrent effect on directors as it primarily takes the interest

3 See Chapter 2, Section 2.2
4 See Chapter 2, Section 2.4

of shareholders into account, and not the protection of the long-term interests of stakeholders. In terms of the requirements and guidance put forward by the government for the purpose of achieving better corporate governance, the issue of flexibility limits the deterrent effectiveness of these reforms. Disclosure requirements are principle-based rather than rule-based, and this gives free rein to directors to review their own performance and determine the way in which they report required information about the company's business. This is also a valid issue for the Corporate Governance Codes, which provide far-reaching flexibility to directors to determine whether to comply or opt out of the provisions. In terms of shareholders' power to control directors, despite being empowered with certain tools such as approving or disapproving directors' decisions, removing or disapproving of the re-election of directors, and bringing a derivative action against directors, there are serious issues that discourage or prevent them from employing these tools to discipline directors.

The company's limited control of directors gave rise to concerns regarding their possible involvement in undesirable behaviour and exposure of the company to the risk of liability and loss. The book chose competition law as the regulatory law to examine based on the tension between competition law, which concerns the impact of the company's behaviour in the market, and corporate governance, which focuses more on the behaviour of individuals within the corporate structure.[5] The company' inability to control its directors may cause the director to involve the company in competition law infringements, and public enforcement strategies initially target companies perceived as primarily liable for these infringements. The foundation that underlies this approach is the aim of protecting the objective of consumer welfare and the idea of achieving this aim primarily by punishing the company.[6] Based on the mixed approach of deterrence and compliance theories, the company is regarded as a principal that persuades its directors to comply with the law and, if any infringement arises, it is the one who should be punished to prevent future infringements.[7] The company is consequently exposed to the risk of liability and loss caused by directors' undesirable behaviours. Based on the lack of deterrent effectiveness of this administrative enforcement strategy on directors, individual sanctions have been introduced in UK competition law; however, these sanctions are likely to be inadequate not only because they are limited at deterring directors from being involved in infringements as there have been only couple of example cases so far, but because they also do not assist the company to remove the liability and loss caused by undesirable behaviour as the company is, in any case, initially punished.[8] Consequently, the company is exposed to the risk of liability and loss caused by directors' infringement of rules of competition law.

5 See Chapter 3
6 See Chapter 3, Section 3.3.3
7 See Chapter 3, Section 3.4
8 See Chapter 3, Section 3.5

The company's exposure to the risk of liability and loss engenders the question of whether it can attribute and ascribe the risk to directors. The book identified two principles commonly applied in cases involving attribution and ascription between the company and directors. These are, namely, the doctrine of corporate attribution and the illegality defence principle of the maxim *ex turpi causa*.[9] They engage with a case that involves risk, liability, and loss distribution between the company and directors. It was illustrated that whereas the doctrine of corporate attribution typically attributes directors' undesirable behaviours to the company that is consequently held personally liable,[10] the maxim prevents it from passing on the risk of liability and loss to its directors, based on the purpose of protecting public policy.[11] The research has illustrated that the implication of these principles can be different when directors gain self-benefit through using the company as a vehicle since they are usually found personally liable for such behaviour, but this is not a valid case when directors are involved in undesirable behaviour for which the company is often found personally liable. Therefore, these principles do not adequately recognise the matter that undesirable behaviour is as harmful as directors' self-enrichment in respect of the long-term interests of the company.

In order to determine the personal liability on the part of the company, the book identified two doctrines. These are the doctrine of the special rules of attribution and the doctrine of directing mind and will, which consider the position held by directors to determine the attribution of risk. This approach is likely to find the company personally liability for directors' undesirable behaviours. The company also has limited use of the directors' fiduciary duties as a shield to place the risk back onto directors.[12] At this point, the maxim involves the case and prevents the company from ascribing the risk to directors based on the objectives of public policy. These are maintaining deterrence on the wrongdoer, not allowing the wrongdoer to benefit from illegality, and maintaining the internal consistency between criminal and civil law.[13]

The book thus far explored the lack of accountability of directors, the deficiency of control mechanisms on directors, the company's exposure to the risk of undesirable behaviour, and the inability of the company to attribute and ascribe the risk of liability and loss to directors. Based on these findings, the research has shown that the company is exposed to the risk of undesirable behaviour and cannot pass it on to its directors. In order to widen the scope of discussion, the book examined insurance as a risk management mechanism that the company usually employs to manage the risk.[14] The book initially discussed how the company purchases an insurance policy not only for its directors' protection but also for itself, with the intention of protecting the directors as long as they do not harm the interests of

9 See Chapter 4
10 See Chapter 4, Section 4.2
11 See Chapter 4, Section 4.3
12 See Chapter 4, Section 4.2.3
13 See Chapter 4, Section 4.3.1.2
14 See Chapter 5

the company. When the acts of directors start harming the company, the company considers its own protection through mitigating the risks arising from directors' undesirable behaviours. However, it was argued that the company is likely to be prevented from mitigating the risks caused by undesirable behaviour through recovering the loss it suffers. Based on these risks, losses were identified as regulatory loss, third party litigation loss, reputational loss, and insolvency loss.[15] The foundation underpinning this prevention is recognised as the considerations of the maxim illegality defence, which aims to protect public policy, and the doctrine of corporate attribution.[16] The rationales of public policy, which are maintaining deterrence and the no-benefit rule, are put aside for the sake of protecting the victim third party through providing indemnification; however, they are strictly and commonly applied by the courts to prevent recovery when the company demands policy coverage or brings a claim against directors' insurance for the loss caused by undesirable behaviour. The chapter discussed how market coverage is not available for regulatory loss, reputational loss, and insolvency loss, and recovery is unavailable for a third party litigation loss event, but market coverage is arguably available for such loss. As seen in the discussions in Chapter 4, the company is usually found personally liable through corporate attribution when it brings a claim, and it is prevented from recovery on the grounds of the maxim and public policy. Accordingly, the risk remains with the company due to the operational deficiencies of insurance law.

Based on these analyses, the general conclusion the book reached is that the operations of company law, corporate governance, competition law, tort law, and insurance law have a serious negative cumulative impact on the distribution of the risk of liability and loss between the company and directors; moreover, the company is consequently not able to protect the long-term interests of its stakeholders due to directors' undesirable behaviours. Despite some positive developments, these have still not identified the issue of the protection of the long-term interests of stakeholders in the way that this book has revealed.

6.4 Contribution to Knowledge

This book has contributed widely to the literature, but the main contribution is that it has identified how the cumulative impact of several areas of law has serious and undesirable consequences for the way in which the company is managed by directors. It has drawn on in-depth research from several areas of the law to examine the relationship between the company and its directors from a number of perspectives. This approach required the examination of particular law subjects, initially by assessing how these areas individually operate before analysing the type of impact they have on the distribution of the risk of liability and loss between the company and directors.

15 See Chapter 5, Section 5.2.2.3

16 See Chapter 5, Section 5.3

The book has introduced to the literature the concept of undesirable behaviour of directors, which can result in the company committing regulatory infringements, and analysed how the cumulative impact of several areas of law means that a blind eye is turned to the company's exposure to the risk of liability and loss arising from such behaviour. It has raised the concern that, due to this cumulative impact, the company is unlikely to protect the long-term interests of its stakeholders. Although self-enrichment behaviour by directors is well-known and commonly considered undesirable by any constituents of a company, the book has put forward a new consideration that can be potentially more undesirable than self-enrichment in terms of the company's long-term sustainability. Undesirable behaviour can be perceived as an innocent and ordinary practice to maintain the short term financial stability of the company since it increases the short-term value, but the study has illustrated how harmful such behaviour could potentially be to stakeholders, whose interests should be considered by directors when running the company. The identified nature of undesirable behaviour and its serious negative consequences for the company will change the attitudes of individuals, public authorities, and the company's constituents towards the way in which directors manage the company's business. It has also put forward an idea of how the operational deficiencies of a number of subjects of law have a cumulative impact on the company's exposure to the risk of liability and loss and its inability to attribute, ascribe, and mitigate this risk.

Besides this wider contribution, the book has made a particular contribution to each individual subject of law analysed in the book. An examination of particular subjects of law was presented in order in accordance with the issues of directors' personal liability, the company's ability to control directors, its exposure to risk of loss, attribution, ascription, and the mitigation of risk.

It initially contributed to company law literature by raising a concern regarding the small possibility of holding directors accountable for their acts on the company's behalf as the corporate veil is very rarely pierced, whereas the separate personality of the company has been heavily emphasised to hold the company personally liable. In such a case, it is difficult to expect the threat of personal liability to have the desired deterrent effect on directors.

The second chapter has contributed to the company law and corporate governance literature by introducing the concept of the undesirable behaviour of directors to these literatures and raising a concern about how this behaviour threatens the long-term interests of stakeholders. This chapter emphasised the serious impact of a number of corporate risks to which the company is subjected due to directors' undesirable behaviours. It also combined a number of mechanisms which were not originally established to control directors directly, but which may have an indirect disciplinary effect. It also discussed how these mechanisms have serious limitations that are likely to decrease their constraining effectiveness on directors. This does not mean that these mechanisms inadequately control directors in respect of all types of behaviour, but the chapter highlights how they have limitations for protecting the company when directors are involved in undesirable behaviour.

In addition, Chapter 3 contributes to the literature on the impact of interaction between competition law and corporate governance on the company's exposure to the risk of liability and loss due to directorial actions that involve the company in competition law infringements. The chapter mainly argues how competition law, as a regulatory law, exposes the company to the risks of undesirable behaviour, whereas it seeks to maximise consumer welfare. Besides looking at the approach of competition law from the company's perspective, the adequateness of the enforcement strategies adopted by UK competition law to prevent law infringements was also criticised. It was demonstrated that the mixed approach of compliance and deterrence theories underlies the foundation of UK competition law for the purpose of preventing infringement of the rules of this law; however, this approach does not fit the purpose because the administrative fines imposed on companies usually punish the wrong people, who are typically shareholders and consumers. In addition to this, individual sanctions introduced to UK competition law at a later stage were also found inadequate to achieve the desired deterrent effect on directors.

The contribution of the fourth chapter is mainly to company law, as it explores the joint operation of the doctrine of corporate attribution and the principle of the maxim *ex turpi causa* on the attribution and ascription of risk of liability and loss between the company and directors; it also illustrated that fiduciary duties, which underlie the company's claim to push the risk back towards its directors, are only a limited shield. The doctrine of corporate attribution was criticised in respect of its inadequate approach and reliance on directors' position to determine the attribution. This approach may still protect the company against the self-enrichment behaviour of directors, but it is limited in recognising how harmful the directors' undesirable behaviours are to the long-term interests of stakeholders. The chapter also contributes to tort law literature by criticising the public policy foundation of the maxim of the illegality defence and the operational deficiencies inherent in cases involving negligent, immoral, or illegal acts on the part of both parties. In respect of the ascription of the risk of liability and loss between the company and directors, this approach was found superficial as it automatically prevents a company found personally liable through corporate attribution from recovering the loss, without considering the nature of directors' behaviours.

The contribution of the fifth chapter is mainly to insurance law in respect of the inability of the company to mitigate the risks of directors' undesirable behaviours. In addition, this chapter contributes to the literature of insurance law as it explored how liability insurance works and considerations that the courts take into account when the insured or the victim third party claims a recovery. Besides the purpose of protecting directors from personal liability, the company aims to purchase insurance to protect itself when directions' actions are harmful. However, the company is likely to be prevented from mitigating the risk of loss caused by directors' undesirable behaviours as either market coverage is unavailable or policy coverage is not available to provide a recovery. Based on the four types of risks of undesirable behaviour, the chapter introduced four types of loss to which the company is subjected due to the occurrence of these risks, and examined the foundation of the maxim, public policy, and corporate attribution, as underlying aspects of the reasoning adopted by insurance law to prevent the company from recovery. The finding of this chapter illustrates that the last remedy for the company to invoke to mitigate the risks of undesirable behaviour is not available.

Despite the fact that the current regime fails to consider stakeholder protection, the distinctive approach put forward by the courts in *Bilta*, *Patel*, and *Lancashire County Council* should shape the way in which these developments progress.

Index

FSC
www.fsc.org
MIX
Papier | Fördert
gute Waldnutzung
FSC® C083411

Kolibri 360 GmbH
Ferdinand-Jühlke-Straße 7
99095 Erfurt, Deutschland
produktsicherheit@kolibri360.de